1987

A Handbook of

Christian Theology

A HANDBOOK OF

CHRISTIAN THEOLOGY

Definition Essays on Concepts
and Movements of Thought
in Contemporary Protestantism

Abingdon Press
Nashville

A HANDBOOK OF CHRISTIAN THEOLOGY

ISBN 0-687-16567-9

PREVIOUSLY PUBLISHED AS ISBN 0-529-02087-4
BY THE WORLD PUBLISHING COMPANY.

Library of Congress catalog card number: 57-10852

MANUFACTURED BY THE PARTHENON PRESS AT
NASHVILLE, TENNESSEE, UNITED STATES OF AMERICA

EDITORS' PREFACE

The Christian message, although basically a simple one, contains within it potential complexity of thought and variety of statement. For Christianity is not a religion based on immutable truths but a religion in which man's confrontation with God takes place in terms of man's situation. The decisive elements of the Reformation mind—its discontent with the architectonic order and fixities of medieval thought and its insistence upon recovery of the biblical foundations of Christian faith—made fresh statements of the Christian faith and explication of its relevance for the whole of man's life inevitable.

A fundamental of Protestantism, that the Church itself must be subject to continuing reformation according to the Word of God, has had enormous consequences for theology. One must be aware that tradition continued to exercise influence, the sacraments were recovered as signs and seals of the faith, and to succeeding generations of Protestant theologians the writings of the Reformers provided structure and substance. But the tension between the rediscovered nature of the biblical revelation and the world afforded the basis of encounter and defined the area of activity for Protestant theologians interpreting the faith.

In addressing the Pilgrims as they left Holland for the New World, Pastor John Robinson reminded them that "God hath yet more light to break forth from His Holy Word." Although it has sometimes been forgotten, this conviction is basic to Protestant thought and the fresh statements of the Christian faith which each generation has been impelled to make.

This is particularly true of the remarkable renewal of Protestant thought in the United States which has taken place in the last decades. After a long period of attempting to accommodate the Christian message to a world-view based upon contrary assumptions, Protestant theologians rediscovered the insights of the Reformers, the dialectical richness of the religious thought of the New England mind, and the abiding pertinence of the Bible.

As a result, the world, man and his society, have been treated with new seriousness as the biblical source of Christian understanding has been reopened during this century.

It is appropriate midway in the twentieth century, therefore, to summarize and examine the consequences of this
renewed tension between an historical and conditioning
faith and a modernity which contests the faith and challenges its assumption. *A Handbook of Christian Theology*
presents such a summary and evaluation. The *Handbook*
consists of one hundred and one essays written especially
for the volume. Quite obviously, the concepts, terms, and
movements discussed do not exhaust the conceptual range
of Protestant thinking. Yet the limitations of a single volume, while preventing completeness, enable one to perceive more sharply the emergent emphases and new directions in Protestant thought. Thus, *A Handbook of Christian
Theology* is not only a source-book to the understanding
of Protestant thinking, but an original document of our
times and a record of the theological situation of the
twentieth century.

Marvin Halverson
Arthur A. Cohen

CONTENTS

ADAM AND SECOND ADAM

Adam was the first man created by God, and all men are descended from him. The name Adam is, in the first instance, a common noun (*'adam*) and is used collectively in the sense of mankind, as in Gen. 1:27. While the early Yahwist source traces its origin to the Hebrew word *'adamah,* meaning "ground," it is more probably to be derived from the Hebrew *'adam,* which means "red" or "to be red" (cf. the *Ugaritid'dm,* with the same meaning) or from the Accadian *'adamu,* "make" or "produce" (cf. Accad. *'admu,* "child"). The sources are by no means consistent in their understanding of the word. In the Yahwist it is generally given as *the man* (*ha-'adam*), although in our present text the proper name is to be found in Gen. 3:17, 21 (cf. also 4:1, 25), probably a later alteration. In the Priestly history the meaning *mankind* is present in Gen. 1:27, but in Gen. 5:1-5 the proper noun appears. Elsewhere in the Old Testament the name is found only in I Chron. 1:1, with which Sirach 46:16 should be compared ("the glory of Adam"). The proper rendering in Job 31:33 is *man,* not Adam.

In the early source (Gen. 2:4-3:24) Yahweh forms man from the dust of the ground, breathes into his nostrils the breath of life, and he becomes a living being (*nephesh hayyah*). Gen. 2:7 is the central statement of biblical anthropology: man is an animated body, body and spirit. The *man* is placed in the primeval garden of Eden and is commanded to cultivate it and keep watch over it. He is commanded not to eat of the tree of knowledge of good and evil; "in the day that you eat of it you will surely die." The woman yields to the serpent's tempting and the man eats of the forbidden fruit with her. Dire punishment follows. A curse is pronounced upon each of them, and they are driven from the garden of primal felicity. In the Priestly history man is created on the sixth day, the culminating creative act of God; he is created in the image of God, and as male and female. His creation is accompanied with a blessing, and the blessing is followed by a command (Gen. 1:27-28). Ezekiel 28 is familiar with a different form of the tradition, probably of Phoe-

11

nician provenance, though the name Adam does not appear.

Only twice in the New Testament is Adam mentioned in a "historical" way: Jude 14 (Enoch, the seventh from Adam) and Luke 3:27, the close of the genealogy of Jesus (Adam, the son of God). Elsewhere he is the antitype of Christ, notably in Mark 1:13; Romans 5:12-21; and I Corinthians 15:21-22, 45-49. In all of these passages the contrast between Adam and Christ is sharply drawn. Adam is the type of the one who was to come (Romans 5:14). Adam yielded to temptation, but Christ overcame it (Mark 1:13). Adam ushers in the old age, Christ the new age. Through the sin of one man death entered the world; through the one man, Jesus Christ, those who are willing to receive "the abundance of grace and the free gift of righteousness" reign in life (Romans 5:12-21). The trespass of the one brought judgment and condemnation; Christ's free gift of grace brought justification. "As by one man's disobedience many were made sinners, so by one man's obedience many will be made righteous" (Romans 5:19). It is possible that Gnostic influences are at work in Paul's dualistic world view here (see Rudolf Bultmann, *Theology of the New Testament,* Vol. I, p. 204).

In I Corinthians 15 we meet the same sharp contrasts as in Romans. In Adam all men die; in Christ all shall be made alive (I Cor. 15:22). The first Adam became a living being, the last Adam a life-giving spirit. Here, strangely, the apostle speaks of the psyche (Hebrew *nephesh*) in a somewhat derogatory fashion. He contrasts the physical body with the spiritual body in a manner quite alien to the original of the passage which he quotes from Genesis. The first man was from the earth, a man of dust; the second is from heaven (15:47). In their earthy flesh Christians are like the first Adam; "as was the man of dust, so are those who are of dust"; but in the resurrection from the dead they are like the second Adam, "the man of heaven."

In extra-biblical literature Adam plays a significant role. A number of pseudepigraphical works bear his name; some of them, however, are lost. In the Testament of Levi (18:10 ff.) a messianic hymn describes how the messiah will open the gates of paradise and remove the threatening sword against Adam. In IV Ezra the evil impulse was sown in the heart of Adam (cf. the later *yecer ha-ra'* of the rabbis), and transmitted to his descendants (3:2-21). "For a grain of seed was sown in the heart of Adam from the beginning, and how much fruit of ungodliness has it produced until this time" (4:30. Cf. also 4:11). The moving passage in 7:118 is also to be noted: "O thou Adam, what hast thou done? For though it was thou that sinned, the fall was not thine alone, but ours also who are thy descendants." II Baruch reflects in a similar vein: "Adam is therefore not the cause, save only of his own soul, but each of us has been the Adam of his own soul."

JAMES MUILENBURG

Bibliography

Rudolf Bultmann, *Theology of the New Testament.*
Joachim Jeremias, "Adam," *Theologisches Wörterbuch zum Neuen Testament.*

ANTICHRIST

Biblical teaching. The term "Antichrist" occurs for the first time in I John. In 2:22 the writer states that the Antichrist denies that Jesus is the Messiah, and in 4:3 the "spirit of the Antichrist" is characterized as "dissolving" Jesus, i.e., attempting by means of supernatural power to break the sway of Jesus. Both in 2:18 and 4:3 the "coming" of Antichrist is considered as the fulfillment of a former prophecy. In 2:18 the writer sees its fulfillment in the false views of the many dissenters who have split off from the Church. Each one of them is an Antichrist. They attempt to lead the Church astray (2:26; 3:7). The prophecy referred to is probably Jesus' word recorded in Mark 13:14 and Matthew 24:15, where Jesus is quoted as saying: "When you see the desolating sacrilege standing where it ought not to be (Matthew: in the holy place;

. . ." The reference is to a human being claiming divine worship. In the same eschatological speech, Jesus is also reported as saying that "many false Christs and false prophets will arise . . . to lead astray even the elect, if possible" (Mark 13:22; Matthew 24:24). In the Gospels, these events are mentioned as signs of the impending return of the Messiah in glory, and accordingly John points out that the appearance of the many Antichrists assures us that "this is the last hour" (I John 3:18).

Without using the term "Antichrist," Paul refers (2 Thess. 2:1-12) obviously to the same prophecy. To counteract rumors that the Lord had already returned, he reminds his readers that the "Man of Lawlessness (or: Sin), the Son of Perdition, the Adversary" (v. 3-4), must first come and, setting himself in the Temple, will pretend that he is divine. But forces are at work, which at present restrain him from manifesting himself (v. 6-7). When he finally appears, his whole wickedness will be made manifest, and then the returning Christ will annihilate him "with the breath of his mouth" (v. 8).

Whereas in the passages discussed thus far Antichrist's main wickedness lies in his claim to be divine, or the returning Messiah, the Revelation of John adds a political note. The Beast that arises from the Abyss (Rev. 11:7; 13:1) symbolizes the powers by which the Church is persecuted (13:7). In its second appearance the Beast is pictured with features of the Antichrist. It looks like a lamb, i.e., Christ (13:11), yet speaks like a dragon, i.e., a ruler (13:15). The second Beast is accompanied by the false prophet (16:13; 19:20; 20:10), and through him, i.e., under a false religious pretext, organizes the nations of the earth for the final battle against God at Armageddon (16:16). The Beast and the false prophet are characterized as deceiving people (13:14; 19:20). For the Seer, the Beast is identical with Rome (cf. 17:9) and more generally with all the governments of the earth who follow its instigation. In the literature of the sub-apostolic age we have only one direct reference to Antichrist (Did. 16:4). The name is not used; rather, he is called the "Deceiver of the World" (*kosmoplanes*).

Summing up, it can be said that the early Church believed that the redemptive work of Christ and His Church were bitterly fought by Satan. His enmity would reach its climax when by his power he would enable a person, or persons, to appear like Christ pretending to bring ultimate redemption, when in fact he intended to destroy Christ's work. So great would be the cunning of Antichrist that a portion of the Christians would abandon the true faith. This would be the last act of history, and it would be followed by Christ's return for judgment.

Roots. Bousset and other scholars have attempted to trace the idea of Antichrist back to the Old Testament and beyond it to Babylonian and Iranian mythology. In common with those religions, the religion of the Israelites held that God's rule was opposed by supranatural forces of wickedness, yet that God Himself would vanquish and destroy them. But in none of them is the idea of an anti-Messiah or of a deceiver of the believers found. The reason is that according to Jewish belief the Messiah was not divine. Only on the foundation of the New Testament concept that the Messiah was the Son of God was the idea of an anti-Messiah, who claimed divine worship, conceivable. Similarly, the notion of the great deceiver presupposes Jesus' insight that religion itself can become an occasion for unbelief. The Jews took it for granted that having the true religion and keeping it they would be saved. The Book of Revelation shows, however, that the early Church eventually transferred certain features of the older notion of God's opponent to their idea of Antichrist, especially those of his political power, and of the final combat. It is true that in the Jewish portion of Sibyllines Book V, Nero *redivivus* is the anti-God, whom the Messiah will destroy. However, in view of the late date of that section (A.D. 120), Christian influence will best explain this novel feature of the Jewish view of the Messiah.

History of the idea. With varying degrees of intensity the idea of Antichrist has preoccupied the minds of

Christians throughout the centuries. In the light of the New Testament references to Antichrist, some were frightened by the thought that even the believers could be misled to a worship of the adversary of Christ. Others thought that in contemporary events they could discern the work of Antichrist and that the end of all things had come. For many the idea was a convenient way of taunting their theological or political opponents by proclaiming them to be Antichrist.

Conflicts with the Jews and the part they had played in the persecution of the Christians in the first three centuries was probably responsible for the belief that Antichrist would be a Jew. From the Fathers of the ancient Church to the dawn of the modern age this view was widely held. However, throughout the ancient Church Antichrist is purely an eschatological figure. Some of the Fathers taught that he would not be able to appear as long as the Roman Empire was in existence. When Islam ravaged the Christian churches in the Near East and North Africa and many Christians embraced the new religion, the idea was gradually given credence that Mohammed, or Islam, was Antichrist. In the Middle Ages people were haunted by fear of the impending Final Judgment, and the "Play of Antichrist" was performed in many churches. Significantly, Antichrist is portrayed therein as destroying the German Empire.

With the spiritualizing of the Christian faith, particularly in the sects, Antichrist is identified with the hierarchy or the pope (e.g., by Joachim da Fiore, Wyclif). The Waldensians applied the designation to all the opponents of their teaching. A similar view was responsible for the brutal and reckless treatment of the clergy by the Hussites. Luther and his Church followed a related line of reasoning. They held that the Papacy is Antichrist, because it refused to give the believers the comfort of the Gospel.

Together with the general abandonment of eschatology the idea of Antichrist disappears from the modern world except for small apocalyptic groups, who in succession nave discovered Antichrist in Napoleon, Bismarck, the Czar, and other politicians with whom they happened to disagree. According to Selma Lagerlöf, socialism is the Antichrist. Ecclesiastical splinter groups like to denounce the larger denominations or central ecclesiastical organizations (e.g., the World Council of Churches) as the Antichrist. The only instance of a genuine understanding of the New Testament idea that is found in modern times is Nietzsche's use of the term as a self-designation. He posed as the only radical opponent of Christ, and acted in the eschatological assurance that he would usher in the new and final age of mankind. He admitted that the change required was so complete that he had to deceive even his own followers concerning his goal.

OTTO A. PIPER

Bibliography

Wm. Bousset, *The Antichrist Legend.*
J. C. Lambert, "Antichrist" in *Dict. Ap.,* Ch. Vol. I, 67-69.
Friedrich Wm. Nietzsche, *Antichrist.*
F. Sieffert, "Antichrist" in *New Schaff-Herzog,* Vol. I, p. 194-196.

ATHEISM

The Bible does not really countenance the possibility of atheism. It is only the fool who can say in his heart that there is no God (Ps. 10:4; 14:1; 53:2).

Atheism, although having no parallel in biblical terminology, is implicit in biblical theology, the literature of the primitive Church, and Rabbinic tradition. In Judaism and Christianity atheism is defined and proscribed by three manifestations: the holding of false conceptions of God (paganism and idolatry), judged equal to believing in no God at all (Ps. 115:7); the denial that expectations assured by scripture and vouchsafed by revelation shall come to pass—that God neither saves nor redeems, that He is unconcerned with human pain and suffering; and, lastly, the denial of principles of dogma which testify to the existence of God and the efficacy of His attributes of wisdom and power. Atheism is therefore construed as false belief, the perversity of the heart, the judgment of folly, and the unwillingness to accept the power and activity of God.

The biblical conception of atheism prevailed until the disappearance in the West of a religiously structured culture. Atheism in Christian culture, *epikursut* (the Hebrew euphemism for "Epicurean" free-thinking) and *cephirat ha-ēkar* (denial of the divine principle) in Judaism passed from the language of theological accusation and debate. In the modern world atheism has entered upon a new moment which recalls, nevertheless, the accents of the biblical conception.

In *The Gay Science* (1882) Nietzsche submits the parable of the madman announcing the death of God in the marketplace and entering the churches of the realm to sing a *requiem aeternam deo* in recollection of the God who once was, but is now slain. It is clear that Nietzsche construes the death of God as the work of man.

The course of the West since the sixteenth century has been to render God useless and without efficacy—to shut God out of the life of nature and man with the optimism and simplification which often attends the truths of science, psychology, and sociology. As in the biblical tradition, it is once again the fool who says in his heart that there is no God. The categories of biblical estimation retain their validity. It is not that man denies God, but rather that he seeks to interpose between himself and God the work of his own imagination. If the efficiency of the divine is the measure of its life, then indeed the progressive withdrawal of areas of human life and understanding, previously conceived within God's provenance, has the effect of rendering God without role or significance. In this sense is God slain—or rather, the "blood" of the divine life is drawn away by man's self-arrogation of the power and wisdom of God.

Sartre is uncompromising in affirming that *"Dieu n'existe pas."* He proclaims: "He (God) is dead, He spoke to us and now is silent. . . ." The center of concern is the phrase: ". . . He spoke to us and now is silent. . . ." It is this profound observation which binds the atheism of our day to the atheism to which the Prophets and

Psalter testify. In apposition to the fool, to the idol "who has ears but hears not," to the paganism against which biblical religion gave protest, is the word of God which once broke forth and was heard.

The Bible conceived the heart to be the seat of understanding. The fool was one who presumably lacked the heart of understanding, who lacked the sensibility to trust the evidence of concretion—the disclosure of God in the order of nature and the address of revelation. Religions of revelation are essentially religions of the ear. Characteristic of our age is the unwillingness to hear. Sartre acknowledges that though the transcendent is presently silent, man continues to anguish for divine disclosure. He does not countenance the possibility that an empirical description of the divine silence cannot pass, with such evident haste and ease, to the pronouncement of non-existence. Nietzsche does not deny that God once lived. Sartre does, evidently considering Nietzsche's formulation but an elliptical metaphor for non-existence.

It must be allowed, however, that if man would wish God "revived" it is from man that God will receive "life." God speaks, but is not heard. He lives again, if man hears.

ARTHUR A. COHEN

Bibliography

Martin Buber, *The Eclipse of God.*
Jean Paul Sartre, "Existentialism and Humanism," *Existentialism from Dostoevsky to Sartre,* ed. by Walter Kaufmann.

ATONEMENT

In most general terms, atonement is the restoration of man to a right relationship with God through the obedience and death of Jesus Christ. Beyond this, the doctrine of the atonement is as many-sided as man's alienation from God and the aspects of "the work of Christ" which correspond to it. As sin against God has been thought of in terms of disobedience to the Law, a criminal act, a corruption, an alienation, a bondage; so, correspondingly, the atonement has been thought of in terms of the satisfaction of God's justice (Anselm), the expiation of crimes by punishment (Calvin), a cleansing or purification especially by the self-sacrifice of Christ, a reconciliation, and a victory over the devil and deliverance from the thralldom of evil powers such as sin, the law, death, wrath, the world (Luther). Since evidence for such conceptions of the atonement is readily available in Scripture (e.g., Is. 53; John 1:35-36; Mark, 10:45; Rom. 3:24-25; 5:18 f; I Cor. 2:8; II Cor. 5:19-20; Gal. 3:13-14; Heb. 2:14-15; I John 2:2; 4:10), in different ages the theologians of the Church have emphasized one or another conception according to their understanding of the nature of sin and salvation.

In our own age, the orthodox "satisfaction theories" have failed to grip the mind of Christians, perhaps because they are not convinced of man's sin against God and His Law. Modern Christians, like modern religious men in general, cannot take seriously the assumption that sin is an infinitely heinous crime against God. Self-pity in the modern world works against such a view of man's situation. Hence, the doctrine that sin had to be expiated, or that the wrath of God had to be appeased by the sufferings and death of the Son of God, does not find ready response. Therefore modern theologians like McLeod Campbell, Horace Bushnell, James Denney, have emphasized "the moral influence" of the "sacrificial love" displayed in the life and death of Jesus Christ. Lately, perhaps due to changes in "the condition of man," there has been a new and rather profound appreciation of the death of Christ as victory over the devil, sin, law, death, wrath, and the world (Aulen). And under the impact of present-day concern with man's alienation from himself, his neighbor, his world, there has been a revival of the doctrine of reconciliation with God which orthodox theology was unable to take seriously (Tillich and Barth).

Enmity and bondage are peculiar manifestations of sin in our time; it is proper, therefore, that the biblical doctrines of reconciliation and deliverance, of course in new and appropriate versions, have received new attention from theology. Therefore, the atonement as reconciliation and the restoration of the right relationship between the creature and the Creator, and therewith between creature and creature, through the faithfulness of Jesus Christ to God and men as revealed in His life and death, is perhaps most fitting and meaningful in man's private and public situation today. And, in this age of power and power conflict, the atonement as deliverance from the power of sin, death, the world, the devil, also seems to have a special relevance. When the man of today becomes reconciled to himself and his world, when he tastes of the freedom which is his as a human being, perhaps he will be more receptive both to the historic "satisfaction" doctrines and to the "moral influence" of Jesus.

Since God has reconciled the world to Himself by the all-too-human death of His "son," the question arises why He has chosen to do so. There must be a congruity between man's alienation from the Creator, and the way God has reconciled the creature to Himself; that is, by the obedient death of a man. Human alienation itself must be related to death, in the sense that man's rebellion against death, his anticipation and dread before it, must be at the very source of alienation. Man as the "rational animal" or "intelligent creation" is called upon by his very reason or intelligence to enjoy his life in all its circumscription as a creature's life; and this is what man has been (witness his religions and cultures) unwilling and in effect unable to do. The prospect of the loss of life fills the spirit of the creature with a dismay which is inevitably rebellious and itself destructive. So it is that man hates his life, his neighbor, and his God. Thus arises the lovelessness, the injustice, the cruelty, the inhumanity, which pervade human life.

The whole "history of redemption," from Abraham to our own day, could well be understood as God's effort to reconcile man to himself, to God, and to his neighbor. To this end was the exodus and the covenant, the Law and the prophets, and the whole controversy of God with His people, culminating in Him who lived and died in freedom from man's universal subjection to the power of death, sin, the devil, and the world. Jesus Christ thus became the possibility created by "the living God" for a restoration of man to sanity and wholeness as "intelligent creation," and the possibility of freedom from the dominion of death. Thus God's justice, which is the law of man's existence as creature, was satisfied, man's sin covered, man's spirit purified, and the condition of man's love for man as creature, without which there can be no human fruition, fulfilled. And this is what we might today understand by the atonement.

JOSEPH HAROUTUNIAN

Bibliography

Frederick William Dillistone, *The Significance of the Cross.*
George Barker Stevens, *The Christian Doctrine of Salvation.*
Vincent Taylor, *The Atonement in New Testament Teaching.*

AUGUSTINIANISM

Augustinianism denotes the interpretation of Christian faith, especially with regard to the doctrine of sin and redemption, which has its origin in the teaching of Augustine (354-430), Bishop of Hippo in North Africa.

To understand the position of Augustine, it is necessary to know something of his life. Born to a Christian mother and a pagan father, Augustine sought desperately, throughout his youth and early manhood, for a faith which would be meaningful philosophically and effectual in delivering him from his own sense of sin and guilt. It was, he believed, through no effort of his own but through the sheer grace of God that he was finally converted. This conviction so governed his later thought that, when a monk from the British Isles, Pelagius, began to teach that man's effort was instrumental in salvation, Augustine reacted by articulating his own position of man's helplessness and God's free and unmerited grace.

While the Catholic Church never accepted Augustine's views as a whole—and, indeed, rejected the more pessimistic side of them at the Council of Orange—they were vigorously revived at the time of the Reformation and in one way or another have influenced the thought of all the Protestant Churches.

In essence, Augustinianism affirms strongly the fact of original sin—that is, the state in which man finds himself because of the Fall of Adam. In Adam, as the father of the race in whom men are a unity, the manhood which we all share is thought to have lost its relationship of communion and fellowship with God. The resultant alienation is passed on to all his descendants, whose situation is thus one of deprivation of the grace of God and, in consequence, one of chaotic disordering of the will. To be alienated from God results in the human tendency toward self-assertion in contradiction to the will and plan of God. Man is therefore helpless to "save" himself, since his will is perverted at its very root.

In Christ, seen as the embodiment of Divine Charity, God acts to give His "fallen" creatures a new beginning. This is accomplished by Christ as the new and perfect Man in whom God establishes the principle of grace. To this we can only respond in faith, by surrender of our wills to His. And yet this surrender is itself made possible only because God elects those who shall respond and Himself creates both the conditions for that response and the possibility of the response itself.

Once man has thus been caught up into this new relationship his will is freed. No longer possessed by original sin, he is in the state of grace. The drive to evil which yet abides in him is conquered only by God's active love, which is both irresistible and indefectible and will accomplish that which God purposes. Thus, as Augustine puts it, God both gives what He commands and commands what He wills.

As noted above, Augustine links this teaching with the view that only those who are "elected" shall be "saved." He derives this, as all of his views, from his reading of the Epistle to the Romans. Whether Paul himself, in that epistle, intended to teach what Augustine understood him to teach is a much-debated question. Probably most contemporary theologians would say that he does not intend to teach "reprobation" of those who are not "of the elect," but only to give assurance to Christians that, despite their failures, God will conquer the evil in them and bring them to Himself.

In most Augustinian teaching in the Reformed churches, insufficient emphasis has been placed on Augustine's other doctrines, especially those having to do with life in the community of grace (the Church) and the power imparted through sacramental participation. However this may be, it is a fact that the recovery of the Augustinian emphasis in the sixteenth century by Luther and Calvin, and again in the twentieth century by such thinkers as Karl Barth and Reinhold Niebuhr, has given a new depth to the understanding of man's actual situation. Modern Augustinianism would stress man's sinful state, resulting from his estrangement from God, as an existential fact; the necessity for divine grace to restore (or, in some theologians, to provide as a new status) the right relationship to God; the abiding fact of sinful tendencies even in those who are "redeemed"; and the assurance of forgiveness and the hope of final "liberty" to will perfectly what God purposes for us—but this, not in the present world (*in via*) but in the eschatological Kingdom (*in patria*).

W. NORMAN PITTENGER

Bibliography

R. W. Battenhouse (editor), *Companion to the Study of St. Augustine.*
D'Arcy, Dawson etc., *St. Augustine.*

AUTHORITY

Man is essentially a being who rebels. This is not because he is perverse. It is because he is made in the image of God. Ultimately he is responsible only to God. Therefore, he must rebel against anything that compromises this ultimate responsibility.

Theology, however, works within conditions which seem to require the rebel spirit to be tamed. For theology holds that the God who has created man for responsibility to Himself has also revealed Himself decisively in Jesus Christ. The Councils of Nicaea and Chalcedon in the fourth and fifth centuries made it clear that the revelation of God in Christ is not simply a surrogate for God. According to these ecumenical decisions, the revelation of God in Christ is God revealing Himself. Loyalty to that revelation is considered synonymous with loyalty to God. Human rebellion can be authentically suspended at that point only.

Jesus Christ, however, was an historical figure. The paramount question for theology is posed by the historical gap which exists between God's advent in the world two thousand years ago and the sources of religious authenticity today. Here the major communions of Christianity divide more fundamentally than at almost any other point.

Catholic bodies principally fill the gap between Jesus Christ and the modern Christian by the authority of the Church and what it calls its *magisterium*. The *magisterium* is the official teaching body of the Church whose spokesman is the Pope. This position is based on the supposition that Jesus Christ transferred His authority to the apostles and their ecclesiastically certified successors, the Bishops. Eastern orthodoxy slightly alters that base of authority, accenting the liturgical authority more than the teaching authority. Through the ministry of the Church—priesthood and laity together—the reality of Christ is believed continually present in the sacraments.

Protestantism in a sense concedes that Christ conferred authority upon the apostles. It believes, however, that the apostles were unique. Their authority cannot be handed on to others. What, then, is the basis for the continuity of Christians today with the authoritative Christ? The answer is that the written words of the Bible are the authority, conserving quite concretely the apostolic authority. The words of the Bible are the recorded testimony of the apostles to what they alone "have seen and heard."

Are the lifeless words of the scriptures, then, meant to play the part of divine authority in the life of the Christian? Does Protestantism have, indeed, a paper pope? Have we really anything in sacred scriptures but the burnt-out clinker marking the fiery miracle where God once spoke? Implicit in the scriptural testimony is the promise that when the apostles, through their written record, remind the Church of God's presence in Jesus Christ, God by the spirit of Christ will be really present. As the Reformers observed, the exterior spirit of the biblical clinker is re-ignited by the Holy Spirit to make it glow again interiorly.

The authority of God never requires a person to be what Kierkegaard disapprovingly called "a disciple at second hand." Jesus Christ lives again in the spirit of man through the equilibrium of the apostolic word and the Holy Spirit. In that process, what becomes of the rebel in every man? It does not submit, as if to a way of life alien to its nature. It rather discovers the rationale of its rebellion, the true ground and goal of the strivings which up to the moment of that revelation were present, though nebulous, chaotic, and ill-directed. By virtue of this, the claims of Christian authority need never be antagonistic to human reason, insofar as the reason represents the intention of the Creator that man's image reflect God's reality.

The rebel spirit, although domesticated by the authenticity of faith, must be kept alive. This is what theology primarily means by dialectic. Every claim to Christian truth, whether in the Church or outside the Church, must be held under judgment. Only the ultimate is ultimately true. Hence, all claims to truth must be kept in dialogue with the ultimate truth. Protestants do not believe in private judgment, however. Others "in authority" must help the individual to *locate* the ultimate truth. But the Christian must hear it for himself. It is the task of a theology to purge dialectically all surrogate claims of truth to the point where Christians may enjoy free access to a dialogue with God.

How seriously should theology's inquisitorial task be taken? It is here that real delicacy is demanded. From the beginning, the purists have tempted the Church to become self-righteous. Tertullian once called the Church a brothel because it "keeps" those who adulterate the truth. Jesus counseled wisely, however, when He ordered the Church to let the tares and the wheat grow up together until the *final* judgment. In the field of the Church, it is precarious to judge. Tares and wheat look too much alike.

But then if God has deposited the truth with the Church, ought not the Church have hierarchical superiority over all other agencies in society? Even though its spiritual truth pertains to the total life of man and the world, the authority of the Church cannot be totalitarian. It is only the steward of the truth which, as the Westminster Confession says, "is necessary for salvation." It, therefore, has authority to stand in judgment upon the agencies of society when they obstruct or usurp the Church's redemptive mission.

Authority for the Christian is therefore not so much a privilege as it is a responsibility. When it is vested in the Church, it becomes not a mark of superiority but the source of a mission. Christians do not claim to have the truth. They are claimed by it, and communicate the truth in the expectation that it will claim others as they are claimed.

Every man holds the truth in two ways. He holds it as sinner, whose claims to truth are always precarious and destructible. He also holds it as the image of God, responsible for bearing the truth and for reflecting the light of truth as God grants it. As sinner he is unable to speak the truth. As image of God he is obliged to do so.

Relations between God and man are always relations between two spiritual freedoms. In this case one is not dealing with the type of regularities controllable in the laboratory or customarily associated with the manipulable phenomena we have learned to call "nature." Christian realities are spiritual, personal, historical realities. The certainties that exist therein are certainties of personal trust. Truths of faith are always possibilities, never necessities. This is not to denigrate them; quite the opposite. Any form of compulsion is a contradiction of faith. The highest truths are the truths which are spiritually discerned, and spiritual discernment, as the Bible says, always takes place in freedom. Christian authority is always consistent with assurance, never with certainty. A quest for certainty in the Christian life is an expression of bad faith. It is the antimony of trust. The corollary of this is that the truth of the Christian faith does not inhere in propositions. Its propositions are always invocations. The proper response to an invocation is not, "I consent intellectually" or "I believe it to be true." It is a *sursum corda*, a lifting up of the heart in willing response. Faith is expressed as the promise, "I will be true." Man, the rebel, realizes himself when he makes that promise. Man is a rebel by the very fact that he is essentially a creature who makes promises. He refuses all attachments which are less than ultimate in order to pledge himself to God.

CARL MICHALSON

Bibliography

Edwin Lewis, *The Biblical Faith and Christian Freedom.*
H. Richard Niebuhr, *The Meaning of Revelation.*
Paul Tillich, *Systematic Theology,* Vol. I, introd.

BAPTIST

Baptists make up the largest group of Protestants in the United States today—about twenty million, organized into some twenty-seven bodies. While there are some Baptists who believe that a continuity of Baptist churches can be traced from early Christian times, recent Baptist historiography demonstrates that the Baptist movement arose in the early seventeenth century among English Puritans, with perhaps some indirect influence from continental Anabaptism. John Smyth, former Anglican clergyman who had turned Puritan Separatist and had taken refuge in Holland, became convinced that only adult believers should be baptized. In 1609 he led a group of followers to adopt the practice of believers' baptism, beginning by baptizing himself and then administering the ordinance to his supporters. These first English Baptists tended toward Arminianism in theology, declaring that the atonement of Christ is for all men; hence they became known as General Baptists. Though Smyth soon left the church he had founded, others adhered to the position, some returning to England. About thirty years later a second stream of Baptist life arose; this group was made up of stricter Calvinists who asserted that the atonement is limited to those predestined to be saved, and hence were known as Particular Baptists. A few years after their founding, the Particular Baptists came to the conviction that immersion is the only scriptural form of baptism, and this mode soon came to be adopted generally by all Baptists. The Particular Baptists became the more conspicuous group in England; the two streams finally merged in 1891 as the Baptist Union of Great Britain and Ireland.

In America, organized Baptist work developed first in New England beginning in the late 1630's, with the General Baptist trend strong. It was in the middle colonies, however, that Baptists flourished especially in the first hundred years of their new world history; there the Particular Baptist tradition dominated. There, too, the first association of Baptist churches in America, the Philadelphia Baptist Association, was organized in 1707. Baptists found revivalism quite congenial, and during the Great Awakenings of the eighteenth century they grew rapidly, though revivalism led to the softening of the strict Calvinism of many Baptists. In the struggle for religious liberty, the Baptist churches and associations found a common cause. The first Baptist organizations to win general national support were the General Missionary Convention of the Baptist Denomination in the United States (1814), the American Baptist Publication Society (1824), and the American Baptist Home Mission Society (1832). In 1845, the nation's Baptists lost the unity they had found in missionary effort over the slavery issue, as the southerners withdrew to form the Southern Baptist Convention. Northern Baptists continued the existing organizations, reorganizing them in 1907 as the Northern (now American) Baptist Convention. Many American Negroes are Baptists, grouped chiefly in the two National Baptist Conventions.

There is a wide range of belief and practice among Baptists; their distinctive character and witness arise out of a few cardinal points of emphasis. First, Baptists strive to follow the New Testament as the sufficient guide in matters of faith and life. They claim that their major emphases arise out of the teachings of the Bible. Some Baptists hold a theory of the plenary inspiration of scripture, while others take a critical-historical approach to the Bible, but all stress the centrality of the scriptures in matters of doctrine and polity.

Second, Baptists practice the baptism of believers only; it was from this principle that their name was derived. They believe in salvation by personal faith in Jesus Christ alone; only the person mature enough to recognize and confess his sins, experience forgiveness and salvation through Christ, and testify to his faith should, they believe, be baptized. Baptist emphasis falls on *believers'* baptism more than on baptism by immersion, though that mode has become the accepted one, defended on the basis of the New Testament.

Third, Baptists believe in the gathered church; they are congregational in polity. They believe that Christ is the head and center of each congregation. They affirm that the local fellowship of baptized believers, convenanted into a worshipping congregation, bears the marks of a true church. Though they therefore emphasize the autonomy of the local congregation, equally important to them is the acceptance of the associational principle, by which Baptist churches unite in local associations and in state and national conventions for mutual support and co-operative efforts. Baptists are committed to democratic processes of church government at congregational, associational, and convention levels; they strive to protect the freedom of the local congregation without losing the benefits of the larger structures. Baptists have endeavored to take seriously the doctrine of "the priesthood of all believers." Though they have generally agreed that certain individuals are called and ordained as ministers of the Word, they have not regarded them as forming a priestly caste or order. Baptists have stressed the responsibility of all church members and have sought to give wide opportunity for the leadership talents of laymen and laywomen. They ordain women as ministers.

Finally, Baptists have always believed strongly in religious liberty and the separation of church and state. With their emphasis on "the free congregation of the free Word of God," they have demanded that churches be free from governmental control, free to follow the leading of God in Christ. In the struggle for religious freedom in many lands, Baptists have taken a leading role, at times suffering for their stand.

In the United States, Baptists of the North and the South hold these basic principles in common, though the Southerners are more insistent upon close communion and localism in church polity. They also do not belong to the National or World Councils of Churches, while the American and National Conventions do. In general, Baptists have been conspicuous in the modern missionary movement, which owes much to the pioneering efforts of English Baptist William Carey. Hence, Baptists are today found in many countries of the world. In 1905, the Baptists World Alliance was founded as an advisory body for Baptists of all lands and traditions. It meets every five years, for considering themes and problems of mutual concern, and for safeguarding the principle of religious liberty.

ROBERT T. HANDY

Bibliography

Ernest A. Payne, *The Fellowship of Believers: Baptist Thought and Practice Yesterday and Today.*
Robert G. Torbet, *A History of the Baptists.*

BEING

Being is the subject-matter of philosophy, or more specifically of that aspect of philosophy which is commonly called ontology or metaphysics. Conversely, metaphysics or ontology may be defined as the enterprise of thinking about being. The term "being" is admittedly abstract and far removed from the concrete images and ideas of everyday life. Nevertheless, theologians and philosophers have insisted that it has an importance for the common man and the common life.

Being is the present participle of the verb "to be." Thus all that *is* has *being*. If this sounds remote from concrete experience, the reader is invited to perform an operation which may suggest its relevance. Take all objects to which the verb "to be" may be attached. The class of all such objects is the class, being. To be sure, being is not the sum of all these many objects, but rather the defining trait of the class thus assembled.

Another operation may also suggest the meaning of the term "being." Begin with a single object to which the verb "to be" may be attached, and strip away from it, one by one, all the traits or properties which make the object specific or particular. At the end of this process of divestment lies the idea of being. Again, if the term sounds abstract, it is precisely this ladder of abstraction which the human mind climbs in the activity of metaphysical thinking.

Historically speaking, this type of thinking has arisen in cultural situations in which men have sought to think rigorously, critically and comprehensively about religion. Notable instances have taken place in ancient China and India, and in the West in ancient Greece and medieval Europe. In the West, thinking about being-as-such, or metaphysics, began effectively in Greece during the fifth and sixth centuries B.C. The West has had a continuous tradition of such metaphysical or ontological thinking in varying degrees of creativity, since that time.

The words "ontology" and "metaphysics" are Greek in origin. *On, ontos,* is the present participle of the verb "to be" in Greek, while *logos* is an almost untranslatable Greek term freely rendered as "inquiry" or "study." Ontology is thus the study of being-as-such. In the case of metaphysics, Aristotle had written a treatise on physics but had left over some very general topics such as the nature of a first cause. These topics he dealt with in a treatise called *meta ta physika* or "after the physics." The word, thus accidentally coined, has long been established as the name for the study of being-as-such, or reality-as-a-whole.

The methods of study by which philosophers have pursued metaphysics or ontology have varied widely during the centuries. Some philosophers, of a mystical turn of mind, have held that man knows being only by immediate mystical intuition. Others, often called rationalists, have believed that man may inspect the contents of his intellect and attain a knowledge of being, apparently on the assumption that there is a harmonious correspondence between mind and reality. Some philosophers have held that by extending the scientific method of knowing beyond the domain of any particular science, a knowledge of total being may be obtained.

In the recent past and present, many philosophers have assumed an anti-metaphysical attitude. Thus they have argued that the human mind is incapable of the very general form of knowledge which ontology claims to possess, that it is limited to the specific and concrete domains of common sense and science. Such philosophers are often called positivists or empiricists.

It is not hard to show that the category "being" is difficult or even impossible for man to evade or avoid. In criticizing metaphysics or established metaphysical systems, positivistic philosophers have done a great service in exposing loose thinking. But unwittingly they have appealed to some view of being in their critical enterprise. Being, shut out the front door, forces an entrance through the back door! The back door in this case may be understood as the set of assumptions or presuppositions, often unconscious, but nevertheless present, which guides the philosopher's critical activity. Thus a presuppositional method for metaphysics or ontology is indicated. Being is given not so much in the conclusions of our philosophic thinking as in its premises.

What is the relation of the term "being" and the attendant activity of philosophizing to religion and religious faith? To be sure, the religious believer is frequently untroubled by philosophic thought about being. Yet it is a historic fact that in many or most of the world's great religious traditions such thinking has emerged in a notable way. What then is the connection?

In the Book of Exodus Moses asks the Lord for his name, and the Lord replies "I Am Who I Am." (Exodus 3:14.) Many philosophers have held that philosophic thinking about being begins at this point, with what has been termed the "metaphysics of Exodus." Thus God is equated with being; the Lord of the Bible is "He Who Is." However, modern biblical scholarship tends to be critical of this reading of the Exodus text.

In any case, the union of Greek philosophy and Judaeo-Christian or biblical religion in the first three or four centuries A.D. marked a fusion of the Lord God of the Bible and the Ultimate Reality or Supreme Being of Greek philosophic thinking. This union created the great tradition of metaphysical thinking of the West.

The attitude which has motivated this tradition may be described as a desire to be intellectually responsible in the field of religion. The religious attitude may be described as "ultimate concern" or "ultimate valuation." The term "ultimate" here refers both to the highest concern or value and to a concern or value which is deployed in all of human existence. As men reflect upon the religious attitude, so conceived, they are led to relate it to all of reality, to the whole of being. Since the interest or value is thus held to be ultimate or absolute, it must bear some relation to all things. At precisely this point, the conception of being, with the attendant activity of metaphysical or ontological thinking, emerges.

From this viewpoint, religion and philosophy may be seen as intimately correlated. All philosophies have religious premises (whether they are conscious of this fact or not); and all religions have philosophic implications (whether they are conscious of these implications or not).

Recurrently in Western history and frequently in the recent past, many religious adherents and theologians have denied this relation between religion and philosophy, between faith and being. Often they have done so in critical reaction against philosophic views and systems which have twisted important aspects of faith. It may be doubted that this divorce either can or ought to be permanently maintained. Philosophic thinking about being is essential to the task of responsibly conceiving, communicating and criticizing religious faith.

JOHN A. HUTCHISON

Bibliography

Aristotle, *Metaphysics.*
Paul Tillich, *Systematic Theology,* Vol. I.

THE BIBLE

That the Bible is fundamental for Christian worship and theology is a conviction shared in common by the various Protestant denominations and confessions, even when there is disagreement as to why this is so. Protestants, of course, are not alone in their estimation of the supreme significance of the Bible. The two other major branches of Christendom—Eastern Orthodox and Roman Catholic—also affirm that the Bible is sacred scripture and that, in some sense, it is indispensable for the Christian witness. The difference is one of emphasis: Protestantism vigorously insists that the Bible is the authoritative basis for our knowledge of God who is revealed in Jesus Christ. It is the norm by which the Church must test its faithfulness to the mission it has been given to proclaim the gospel. Read and interpreted within the Church, it is, so to speak, the rendezvous which God has chosen for meeting and speaking with man, the "holy ground" on which God confronts man with his humbling and forgiving Word. To this source Christians return for understanding their vocation and destiny within the perspective of God's historical purpose. And as the Church thinks out the meanings of its faith, its theology must be basically biblical.

Scripture and tradition. Sometimes Protestants have stated the case for the primacy of scripture in a one-sided fashion: *sola scriptura,* "scripture alone." The primacy of scripture corresponds to the primacy of faith (*sola fide*), for, as Protestants see it, the Bible testifies that a man is justified solely by God's grace through faith. "Scripture alone" has been an effective slogan for counteracting the equally one-sided claims on behalf of the Pope, of ecclesiastical tradition, or of reason. But when Protestants reflect upon the authority of the Bible in a non-polemical mood, they recognize that it does not stand by itself. Its sacred meaning is not self-evident to anyone who happens to turn to its pages. Inevitably the Christian reads the Bible in a context of interpretation, which is to say, with the aid of a tradition. Increasingly it is acknowledged that the Bible cannot be separated from the Church, broadly conceived as the people of God who are gathered together in Christ. Within this community of faith scripture was produced, and within this community it has been preserved, treasured, and interpreted through the ages to the present day.

Granting that the interpreter must stand within the Christian community, understanding the Bible in the light of the worship, theology, and traditions of the historical Church, Protestants characteristically insist upon a return to the original witness of scripture, in so far as it can be recovered. When Luther advocated starting with the literal meaning of scripture, rather than the allegorical or doctrinal interpretations superimposed on the text, he was stating in his own way a truth with which Protestants today would agree, even when they deplore and reject the literalism which has often afflicted Protestantism. The primary task is to understand the meaning originally intended by biblical writers in their time, and this demands the most careful critical procedure. It is not accidental that biblical criticism has flourished most vigorously in Protestant circles. Admittedly, the critical approach to scripture also had its source in the Renaissance and received great impetus from the modern scientific movement. Moreover, it cannot be denied that in past decades the tide of biblical criticism has swept many Protestant interpreters into secular views, with the result that the biblical message has been toned down or reconstructed to fit modern categories. But far from being destructive of faith, biblical criticism can aid in the accomplishment of the task which Protestants regard as vitally important: the opening of the Bible so that it may speak its original, authentic message. In the

Protestant view, a teaching that contradicts the clear intention of scripture cannot be regarded as Christian, regardless
of how much support it may derive from ecclesiastical
tradition or any other court of appeal.

Christ and scripture. To speak of having "faith in the
Bible" is a violation of the Protestant principle, according·
to which all historical forms stand under the judgment of
God. Admittedly, Protestant biblicism has sometimes
lapsed into bibliolatry—the veneration of the Bible as a
perfect, infallible, divine book. To the discerning Protestant, however, this idolatry defies the prophetic message of
the Bible itself, just as much as the absolutizing of the
Church, the State, or Reason. The Bible is holy because it
bears witness to Jesus Christ, who alone is Lord. He is the
center and goal of scripture, and He alone gives to the
whole Bible its fundamental spiritual unity. Broadly speaking, the Old Testament points toward the Christ who is to
come; the New Testament proclaims that the Christ has
come—Jesus of Nazareth. This messianic or christocentric
unity of scripture does not mean that the full gospel of the
New Testament should be read back into the Old Testament, as though the two Testaments were virtually identical. Rather, Jesus Christ is the fulfillment of the Old Testament—the fulfillment which completes God's revelation in
Israel's history and at the same time revolutionizes the
understanding of the Old Testament.

Since Protestantism is Christ-centered, rather than Bible-
centered, it can advocate freedom from the bondage of
scripture. For instance, while the canon of scripture is
closed, just because God's act in Christ is decisive and
final, it is conceivable that some parts of the Bible—say,
the book of Esther—have only a marginal significance for
Christian faith, or that literature not included in the
Protestant canon, like the Apocrypha, can enrich Christian
understanding of God's revelation in Christ. Moreover, it
is no embarrassment to the Protestant to realize that the
Bible is a very human book, whose writers reflect the cultural views of their day or the gifts and limitations of
human temperament. The rich diversity of scripture is a

concomitant of God's revelation in human history under the conditions of concrete times, places, and circumstances. Protestant theology ascribes perfection (that is, sinlessness) only to Christ—not to the scriptures that bear witness to Him. Of the "good news" contained in the Bible the Protestant can say, as Paul said in another connection, "we have this treasure in frail earthen vessels."

The Bible as sacred history. Under the influence of Hegelian and evolutionary philosophies of the modern period, it was once fashionable to speak of "progressive revelation," by which was meant an evolutionary ascent from the most primitive levels of Old Testament religion to the "ethical monotheism" of the prophets and the lofty New Testament teaching about the Fatherhood of God and the brotherhood of man. According to this view, the biblical development is part of a historical process which is not essentially different from cultural evolution in any of its manifestations.

It is now increasingly recognized that this reconstruction neither does justice to the biblical evidence nor to the central tenets of biblical faith. The biblical message does not focus primarily upon man's ideas, ideals, or values, but upon the gracious and redemptive activity of God, who cannot be imprisoned within men's system of ideas, and who judges human ideals and values. Biblical faith is radically historical in character, not just in the sense that it deals with happenings in ancient Palestine, but in the deeper sense that God makes Himself known historically—that is, through events that are prophetically interpreted as His deeds. To Israel, the Exodus is the crucial event through which God displayed His initiative and saving power, and thereby called a people to serve Him. To the Church, the story of Christ's life, death, and resurrection is the sign of God's action to deliver men from all forms of bondage and to introduce His Kingdom. According to the Bible, history is the narration of God's deeds and of the progress of events toward the fulfillment of His purpose. Therefore, in both Testaments the biblical message finds characteristic expression in a *kerygma:* the proclamation of what God has done, is doing, and will do, accompanied by an appeal to men to serve Him with the full gratitude and devotion of the heart.

Thus the Old and New Testaments are inseparably related, not like the child to the mature man, but like the acts of a drama which press forward toward the denouement and finale. The Bible is essentially *Heilsgeschichte*— the history of divine revelation which reaches its crowning climax and fulfillment in Jesus Christ. In recent years this dimension of the Bible has been taken with great seriousness by Protestant interpreters, although it must be added that, with appropriate modifications, the view is shared by Jewish, Roman Catholic, and Eastern Orthodox theologians.

The contemporary word. More distinctive of Protestantism is the conviction that the Bible may be, through the activity of the Holy Spirit, the medium through which God speaks to men today, calling them to respond in faith and obedience. Although the Bible's anchorage in past historical experiences is vital to Christian faith, sacred history is not just history of long ago. Out of this sacred past God continues to speak in the present, summoning each person to take his part in the ongoing redemptive drama.

The contemporaneity of God's address is a corollary of the biblical view of life as a dialogue between God and man, a relation between "I and thou." Hence the significance of the covenant, the unifying motif of the whole Bible. The axis of biblical faith is not man's ideas about God, but rather God's relation to him and his relation to God within the chosen community, Israel in the Old Testament and the Church in the New. To be sure, the covenant relation is often expressed in language which reflects ancient culture. Moreover, the understanding of the covenant did not remain static. Deepened and refined during the Old Testament period by worship practice and prophetic interpretation, it finally reached a profoundly new expression in the New Testament. Still, the relationship of faith is fundamentally the same throughout the Bible. The Christian believes that he is involved in this relationship, that he participates in the drama of God's redemption. Through the witness of scripture God speaks to him *now* in judgment and mercy, and the language of the Bible becomes the believer's response to God's revelation in humility, contrition, trust, thanksgiving, praise.

In the Protestant conviction, the Bible becomes true *for me* through "the inward testimony of the Holy Spirit." The Spirit, mediated historically through the Church, makes the Word of God contemporary, binds Speaker and hearer together in covenant relation. Biblical criticism can help us to understand the original historical context of a biblical passage, and the traditions of the Church can enable us to perceive the range and depth of biblical truth. But the lifeless words of scripture become the living Word when the Spirit illumines the mind of man and convinces him in his heart that God speaks to *him,* that he acts for *him* through Jesus Christ. Then he is placed in the covenant relationship which was made with Israel and which was renewed through Christ in the Church. Then he knows that God has called him to take his part in the divine drama which moves from Creation to Consummation and which has its redemptive center in the revealing event of the crucifixion and resurrection of Christ.

BERNHARD W. ANDERSON

Bibliography

Bernhard W. Anderson, *The Unfolding Drama of the Bible.*
Karl Barth, *Church Dogmatics,* Vol. I-II, chap. 3.
Hubert Cunliffe-Jones, *The Authority of the Biblical Revelation.*
C. W. Dugmore (editor), *The Interpretation of the Bible.*

CALVINISM

Calvinism is a designation, roughly equivalent to the terms Reformed or Presbyterian Christianity, which refers to the Protestant religious ethos that developed out of the sixteenth-century Reformation in Switzerland, Alsace, the Rhineland, France, Holland, Scotland, and England (puritanism). Decisive theological aspects of the tradition were defined in Zurich (Zwingli), Strasburg (Bucer), and Basel (Oecolampad), before the Frenchman, John Calvin (1509-1564), had been converted to Protestantism. The comprehensive achievements of Calvin, however, as theologian, biblical commentator, churchman, lawyer, educator, and political, social, and economic thinker and organizer, make him, without question, the leading figure of the movement.

Calvin's apprehension of salvation by faith alone (to the exclusion of all human merit) and of Christ as the sole object of faith and the sole Lord of the Church (to the exclusion of the authority of the papal tradition) dominates Calvinism and shows its basic identity with and derivation from Luther's teaching. As well, the doctrine of election and reprobation, built on a biblical conception of covenant, is substantially identical with that of Luther. The veracity and authority of the Bible, witnessed by the testimony of the Holy Spirit, was asserted for the entire canon, minus the Apocrypha. Among numerous special features of Reformed thought in the earliest period, primarily defined by but not solely derived from Calvin, were 1) a restatement of the doctrine of the presence of Christ in the communion, 2) a positive conception of the use of law as a guide to the Christian even under grace, 3) a concern for responsible Christian mores, expressed in a stern church discipline and implemented by public education, 4) a system of representative polity, 5) a positive evaluation and critique of the state as a divinely ordained but separate regimen from the Church, 6) the adoption of progressive economic ideas, e.g., the approval of the taking of interest in business loans. Over all, the Calvinist ethos showed a tendency toward orderly thought and organized life that was a boon to all Protestantism during its chaotic first century.

Orthodox or scholastic Calvinism of the late sixteenth and the seventeenth centuries represents the absolutist and rationalist system-building spirit of the age. In addition to a form more reminiscent of medieval theology than of Calvin, this theology is chiefly characterized by the following: 1) It became a "federal" theology, i.e., the theology of *two* covenants, whereby God's conditional Covenant of Works with Adam in paradise ("deduced" from scripture) is contrasted with the demonstrably biblical Covenant of Grace as a rationale for explaining universal guilt and as a device for understanding human life under the norm of natural law in the created order. 2) Orthodoxy also was marked by disputes occasioned by a deterministic formulation of predestination. Defections occurred among those who rejected the doctrine *in toto* (Arminianism), and internal disagreement occurred over whether the "decree" of God preceded or followed man's fall (supra- and infra-lapsarianism). 3) Total depravity (meaning that all aspects of human life are affected by sin) was the touchstone of an orthodox doctrine of sin and the correlate of covenant and predestinarian theology. Further systematic elements were 4) a doctrine of irresistible grace and 5) the belief in the continuing role of the saints, which Augustine had originally seen as necessary implications of thorough-going predestinationism. Thus, also, 6) "limited" atonement was projected as a doctrine holding that Christ died for the elect rather than for all men. F. Turretin of Geneva (d. 1687) was an example of high scholastic Calvinism, while his son J. A. Turretin (d. 1737), of a broad liberalizing cast, was but shortly thereafter well on his way to Enlightenment theology. Though there was much defection from orthodoxy in the Age of Reason, there was considerable holding to older standards, and some examples of highly creative theology within the confessional church, as witness the thought of Jonathan Edwards.

The British-American character type called "puritan" is a much wider phenomenon than official Calvinism; therefore the term may be used only with great caution in a primarily theological analysis. In this regard the Weber-Tawney theses on the partnership of Calvinism and capitalism is lamentably unclear. English and New England puritanism, however, represents to a significant extent a social ethos and a theory of state developed under special historical conditions from evolving Calvinist-Reformed principles.

The nineteenth cenutry, showing both confessional hardening and competent confessional theology (Hodge, Bavinck, Warfield), also saw produced from Reformed background the towering achievement of Schleiermacher. A broadening confessional theology, in some sense embracing and in others reacting to liberalism, but with only minor changes in the official doctrinal standards of the churches, has characterized most of British-American Calvinism in the twentieth century. The yet inestimable impact of the major neo-Reformation thinkers Karl Barth and Emil Brunner, and interconfessional discussions within the ecumenical movement, appear to indicate the trends of current development in Calvinism.

EDWARD DOWEY

Bibliography

J. T. McNeill, *The History and Character of Calvinism.*
P. Schaaf, *Creeds of Christendom.*

CATHOLICISM

At least two meanings of "catholicism" stand out clearly in the historical use of the term: the first is roughly what is signified by the English word "universal"; the second suggests "wholeness" or "integrity." *Katholou* is a Greek phrase which means either "in terms of the whole" or "in terms of everything." If the former meaning is taken, "catholicism" suggests organic unity or integrity of nature; if the latter is taken, "catholicism" suggests the Church of Christ throughout the world—in other words, "all those who profess and call themselves Christians."

For Christians who are not *Roman* Catholics, the noun "catholicism" and the adjective from which it is derived do not properly designate that communion of Christians which is under the Pope or Bishop of Rome. It is true that in popular usage the adjective "Roman" is often omitted from the description of the Roman Catholic Church; hence for many who are careless in speech, or who disregard the niceties of meaning, the term "catholicism" often means simply Christianity as professed by the Roman See and its adherents. But such common use should not be considered adequate for informed and careful thinkers.

Members of the Eastern Churches, while they usually call themselves "Orthodox," are strong in their insistence that the Christianity which they profess is definitely "catholic" and that they hold to "catholicism" in its basic sense. Members of the Western Reformed communions almost all employ the word "catholic" in their credal statements or confessions of faith, and would as strongly insist that Christianity, as they know and practice it, is true "catholicism."

As the uses of the term "catholicism" have varied, so have the definitions of its essential meaning.

In the first place, catholicism suggests a view of Christianity which lays strong emphasis on the *structures* which have appeared historically in the Christian body. Thus catholicism implies a conception of the Christian religion in which there is an emphasis upon the community, the Church, as integral to the whole message, life, and purpose of the fellowship of Christian believers. This articulates itself into certain forms or structures—sacraments, creeds, ministry, etc.—which are regarded as not only highly important and valuable, but as in some way necessary to the persistence of Christianity as an identifiable reality through historical change. There may be considerable difference in the ways in which this necessity is defined; that there is some such necessity would be accepted by all who insist on a "catholic" interpretation of the Christian faith.

In the second place, such an insistence leads to and expresses itself in a very high valuation of institutional religious life as such. Thus liturgical worship, in which established forms are employed, is felt to be more desirable than 'free' worship, without such forms. The "means of grace"—Baptism, Holy Communion, and other sacramental ordinances and practices, sometimes including confession and absolution—are believed to be churchly rites, ceremonies, or actions which are "generally necessary for salvation" in some serious sense, rather than optional or occasional in nature.

Christians who maintain their catholicism as part of their total Christian profession also lay stress on the continuity which is, they insist, observable in the history of the Christian fellowship. This continuity is shown in the use of ancient creeds, such as the Apostles' and Nicene, in public worship; the maintenance of the ministry through a succession deriving from primitive Christian practice; the unfailing use of sacramental rites, finding their center and focus in the Eucharist or Holy Communion; and the disciplines—of abstinence and fasting, of observance of holy days and the church-year in general, etc.—which have their origin in the early days of the Church.

At the same time, it is clear that there is no necessary contradiction between "Protestantism," in the sense of the "protest" or witness for the gospel renewed in the sixteenth century, and "catholicism," in the sense in which it has just been defined. Indeed it is characteristic of Anglican Christianity especially, and in a degree true also of other communions which insist on "the reform" then effected, to maintain that the two terms are complementary rather than contradictory. It is their belief that genuine catholicism, in the best meaning of that word, is possible only when there is a constant appeal to the formative—and, for that reason, normative—days of Christianity. That is to say, it is by an appeal to the Holy Scriptures, especially as interpreted and understood in the patristic period, that the essential spirit or *ethos* of Christianity is rightly apprehended, and thus that a true catholicism—with its continuity, its structures, and its institutional life and disciplines—is made possible.

It remains to say that one of the significant developments of the past quarter-century, especially through the ecumenical movement and the revival of interest in classical theology and worship, has been this deeper grasp on the "catholicism" which is integral to Christianity of all kinds. What seems to be emerging is a conception of an "evangelical catholicism," grounded in scripture, strongly supported by the sense of community and institution, giving a central place in worship to the Holy Communion, and alert to the changing thought-patterns of the world in which the Church is set.

W. NORMAN PITTENGER

Bibliography

W. Adams Brown, *The Church Catholic and Protestant.*
Robert Newton Flew (editor), *The Nature of the Church.*

CHRIST (JESUS CHRIST)

Word meanings. The name "Jesus" is the Latinized form of the Hebrew word for "Joshua" and means approximately "God will save." The early Fathers liked to point out the parallelism between the Joshua of the Old Testament who led his people across the Jordan into the promised land and the Jesus of the New Covenant who by His death and resurrection led the New Israel through the waters of baptism to salvation.

The title "Christ" is from the Greek version of a Hebrew verb meaning "the anointed one," or "the Messiah." Its early use in connection with the name Jesus constituted the believing affirmation that Jesus of Nazareth was the Messiah of Jewish expectation. As the gentile mission progressed and more inclusive titles were found to describe the person of Christ, the significance of the distinctly Jewish title "Messiah" receded into the background. "Christ" became more and more a proper name. It is important to remember that in the Old Testament the Messiah refers to the human son of David whom God will in his good time raise up to restore the Davidic kingdom.

The problem of the New Testament documents. Every attempt to state the contemporary significance of Christ must use the light thrown on the gospel sources by historical scholarship and by new discoveries such as the Dead Sea scrolls. Since the Christian faith is founded upon the act of God in the person of a Nazarene carpenter, the determination of "what actually happened" is decisive for it in a way not comparable for a religion based upon mystical experience, custom, or law. The denial that the historical record is significant marks a special development that will be analyzed later. The refusal to apply historical-scientific methodology to the New Testament documents constitutes another option. This is usually called fundamentalism.

The complexity of the historical problems can be illustrated from the varying perspectives of the four Gospels on whether Jesus regarded Himself as the Messiah. In Matthew, Mark, and Luke Jesus never openly claims to be the Messiah. When He asked His disciples at Caesarea Philippi who people thought He was, He received the answers, "John the Baptist, Elijah, one of the prophets" (Mark 8:27). When Peter then gives the classic form of all subsequent Christian witness and calls Him the Messiah, Jesus charges the disciples not to tell anyone (Mark 8:29; Luke 9:20). Matthew adds that Peter is blessed for he could know this not "by flesh and blood," but only by revelation from God. Mark, the earliest Gospel, records that at His trial before Sanhedrin Jesus admits that He is the Christ (Mark 14:62), but Matthew and Luke state that He refused to give a direct answer to the question (Matt. 26:63 and Luke 22:67). He was, however, crucified as a pretended Messiah although His accusers could produce no evidence that He had made the claim for Himself. The Gospel of John, the latest of the four, presents Jesus as the recognized Messiah from the beginning of His ministry, making His own claim explicit in John 4:26 f. Here is an outright contradiction that cannot be dismissed by the old method of "harmonizing." Either Jesus said He was Messiah or He did not. Most historical scholars prefer the evidence of the earlier Gospels to the latest one.

What is of much more significance than a debate about titles of interpretation in the New Testament is the impression conveyed to the reader that the richness of Jesus exceeds the limitations of the old titles. God's act in Him is like new wine poured into old skins. The categories of "Messiah," "Servant," "Son of Man," etc., were the only

meaningful ways that His reality could be glimpsed by His
Jewish contemporaries, but these functional titles began
early to yield to the logos-incarnational one of "Son." The
"Logos" had a long history in Greek philosophy behind it.
It represented the principle of universal reason or the
divine principle of creativity. The assertion that in Christ
this universal principle had "become flesh" and its association with the title "Son" made the Christian claim both
completely universal and absolutely concrete.

Despite difference in approach and in emphasis it may
be said that all the writers of the New Testament shared
two convictions in common: 1) that the life of Jesus is
fully and completely a human life, and 2) that in a unique
and unrepeatable way that human life is one with the life
of God. This two-fold affirmation would later be expressed
in the language of the Council of Chalcedon that two full
and perfect natures, the divine and the human, were
united in one person.

*The development of the classic statement of Christ's per-
son.* It was the challenge of heresy that led the early
Church to define ever more precisely what it understood to
be the essence of the "Christ-event." The test was employed to eliminate certain views as heretical if they were
inadequate to describe the salvation accomplished by God
for man in Jesus Christ. Some heresies (docetism and
gnosticism, for example) denied the reality of Christ's
manhood. The divine would have been contaminated by
real association with matter. In a slightly different version
of a common perspective Appolinarius taught that while
Christ had a human body and a human soul His spirit
was not human, but divine. These views presented less
than a full incarnation. Under the criterion of "what is
unassumed is unhealed" they were gradually excluded in
favor of the statement that Christ possesses a human
nature in every point like ours except for sin.

The opposite tendency was to minimize the fullness of
deity in Christ. The adoptionists spoke of a good man
"adopted" into godhead at his baptism or resurrection
along the lines of pagan conceptions of apotheosis. Arius,

whose teaching precipitated the first of the ecumenical councils called to deal with heresy, described Christ as the Son of God born before the worlds, but still a creature of time. ("There was when he was not.") This view still moved within the circle of a pagan pantheon where multiple theophanies were possible. God remained essentially unknowable. In opposition to Arianism it was declared in the Nicene Creed that Christ was "begotten, not made" and "of the same substance with the Father." The Greek word for this last statement was *homo-ousious,* a purely philosophical and non-biblical word which many opposed from the conviction that non-scriptural words should not be made definitive. The general resolution of adoptionism and Arianism and the tendencies represented by them was in the direction of the statement that Christ had a fully divine nature.

The fullness of each nature now being unquestioned, the debate shifted to the manner of the combination of the two natures in the one person. Nestorius was condemned because it was believed that he separated the natures by teaching that they were conjoined in a moral but not organic union. The actual Greek word for this last phrase was hypostatic from the word for "person." Eutyches on the opposite side was condemned for "confusing" the natures by maintaining that before the union in Christ there were two natures, but after the union only one nature. The monophysite (or "one-nature") churches today are the heirs of the line of thought suggested by Eutyches, although their actual position is defined by their opposition to the decress of the Council of Chalcedon in 451. The heart of this classic pronouncement is that "We confess our Lord Jesus Christ, the same perfect in Godhead and the same perfect in manhood, truly God and the same truly man . . . to be acknowledged in two natures, without confusion, without change, without division, without separation . . ."

The technical words borrowed from Greek philosophy have been a source of controversy. Ritschl, in the nineteenth century, wished to abandon completely Greek metaphysics, which he felt obscured the biblical portrait of

Christ. His own approach was along the line that ethically Christ had the value of God for us. Recent attempts to interpret the Chalcedonian orthodoxy in more modern terms have produced in Lionell Thornton (*The Incarnate Lord*) a description of Christ by means of Whitehead's process-philosophy and Morgan's emergent evolutionism. Pittenger in *Christ and Christian Faith* tends to translate the classic terms into the act of God in the man Jesus.

Another illustration of the problem of contemporary interpretation of patristic theology is the issue posed by the term 'impersonal humanity." The fathers taught that Jesus was not *a* man, but Man in the generic sense. If there is one assured result of current studies of the New Testament it is the conviction that, whatever else He may be, Christ is definitely an individual man.

Issues in comtemporary christology. The first impact of historical studies in the nineteenth century was to produce the "Jesus of history" movement as a radical swing away from the "Christ of dogma." Renan's classic picture of Jesus as a gentle humanitarian delivering rationalist lectures on love has been discredited as a reflection of Renan's own century and of his personal predilections (cf. Cadbury, *The Peril of Modernizing Jesus*). Schweitzer's *The Quest of the Historical Jesus,* in emphasizing the element of eschatology in the Gospels, brought an end to the "liberal lives," but presented a Jesus totally foreign to our day. The critical tradition has been maintained in biographies by Goguel and Guignebert.

The permanent deposit left by the "Jesus of history" movement, according to Donald Baillie, is "the end of docetism." Specifically this means a full acceptance of the humanity of Christ in a way never before grasped by classic theologians. Whereas writers in the patristic and medieval periods would not have admitted that Jesus' knowledge was limited by human conditions, there is nearly universal acceptance of such limitation today. Likewise there is an acceptance of the fully human character of His healings and of His moral and religious life. He overcame His temptations, according to Archbishop

Temple, "exactly as every man . . . by the constancy of the will."

The rise of "form-criticism" started the pendulum swinging to the other side. Form-criticism is a method of analysis of the gospel stories that seeks to interpret concrete situations in the life of the early Christian community that explain the preservation or modification of sayings of Jesus. It quickly acquired an overtone of historical skepticism about our chances of knowing the Jesus of history and, in many of its representatives, asserted that all that was recoverable was the Christ of the community's faith. At this point some Continental theologians like Barth and Brunner, interested in recalling the Church to its historic faith in the Incarnation and Atonement, accepted in general the results of "form-criticism" and affirmed that Christianity had no essential interest in the "Jesus of history," but only in the "Christ of faith." Barth, to be sure, accepted theologically the full humanity of Jesus (even to the point of insisting against catholic tradition that Christ assumed fallen human nature), but he showed no real concern for Jesus' specific teaching in its historical setting. Paul Tillich's emphasis upon the portrait of Christ in the Gospels and his earlier lack of concern whether Jesus really lived or not was a variant of the same theme. Kierkegaard's "absolute paradox" as a category for interpreting the Incarnation contributed to this development.

Bultmann, one of the form-critics, has combined a radical historical skepticism about the possibilities of knowing the "Jesus of history" with a conviction that the Gospels must be "demythologized" for modern man. His program has excited widespread debate as to the adequacy of the method and its controls. He reduces the "Christ" of the New Testament to the achievement of authentic selfhood by a believer in terms of existentialist philosophy. When "Christ" is demythologized we have not a supernatural event in space-time but an announcement that God comes to man. Humanists have carried this method a step further and "demythologized" God into "man at his best."

Donald Baillie may be said to sum up the evolving consensus in the Christian community about the person of

Christ when he argues that the "Jesus of history" is the indispensable foundation for Christology, but that the "Christ of faith" is required to make the picture understandable. The method of bringing the two together is not simple juxtaposition, but the realization that in order to understand the "Jesus of history" we require the faith-explanation of the Christ. Thus Jesus' teaching on love is rescued from the suspicion of a rootless idealism and given confirmation by the faith that He who speaks so eloquently about love is Himself the active outreaching love of God present in the savior-teacher. Baillie makes a further suggestion of how we may understand Christ in terms of the "paradox of grace." Just as the Christian man for all his active striving after goodness of character is compelled to confess "It was not I but God," so we see in the New Testament Christ ascribing the goodness to God in such wise "that the life of Jesus, which being the perfection of humanity, is also, and even in a deeper and prior sense, the very life of God Himself."

Some further issues centering about the interpretation of Christ in contemporary thought will be briefly listed. They are likely to be occupying the attention of theologians for the next generation.

1) How is the doctrine of Christ to be related to our understanding of the Trinity? There is a distinct revival of interest in stating the Incarnation within Trinitarianism.

2) What is the significance of Christ for man's knowledge of God? Barth's radical christocentricism has forced theologians not only to question the old distinction between a natural and revealed knowledge of God but also the newer distinction between general and special revelation.

3) How is the classic christological confession of Chalcedon to be understood with respect to the atoning work of Christ? Increasingly there is an effort to find an overarching point for integrating the many theories of atonement (patristic, Anselmian, penal, moral-influence, etc.) with a christology defined less in terms of "substance" and "nature" and more in terms of "the Christ-event" (John

Knox). "Jesus Christ *is* what He does and *does* what He is" (*No Cross, No Crown,* p. 199).

4) What is the relation of Christ to the Church? This problem comes increasingly to the fore in the ecumenical movement in which the churches that "accept Jesus Christ as God and Savior" meet in conversation and for common action.

WILLIAM J. WOLF

Bibliography

Donald Baillie, *God Was in Christ.*

Walter M. Horton, *Christian Theology: An Ecumenical Approach,* pp. 169-203.

CHURCH

1) The recovery and elaboration of the doctrine of the nature of the Church is one of the chief aspects of Protestant theology in this century. It was preceded by a long period of unrestrained individualism, which regarded the Church as being extraneous to the Christian faith and a strictly human, mundane organization. For this important change there are at least three reasons: the wide consensus of biblical scholars that the Church belongs to the saving work of Jesus Christ; the struggles of Christians during the two world wars and under tyrannical persecution and their need to distinguish the Church from the rest of mankind; the encounters of the divided denominations in mission fields and in the ecumenical movement. This recovered doctrine has to do not merely with what the Church *does* in the world, but with what it *is.*

2) An adequate concept of the Church must arise from the biblical sources rather than from sociological inquiry or theological speculation. The Church is essentially a people, a religious society; and there is no doubt that the whole Bible is concerned with the distinct society called "the People of God." The Old Testament presents the history of the People of God as delineated by tribal and

national characteristics. God made a covenant with Abraham (Gen. 17:19) which was reattested to in the history of Abraham's descendants (Is. 43:21; Jer. 31:33). Because of the infidelity of Israel, however, God narrowed the dimensions of the People to those of the faithful Remnant (Is. 10:20-22), which was the predecessor in history of the Church of the New Covenant constituted in Jesus Christ (Gal. 6:16; Rom. 11:1-5; I Pet. 2:9-10). The testimony of the Bible thus presupposes both an historical break between the Jewish People of the Old Covenant and the non-national People of the New, as well as an unbroken continuity between these Peoples insofar as God's saving work is concerned.

Recognition of this continuity rests upon faith in the revelation of God as the New Testament presents it. But there is also an internal verbal evidence which reveals at least what the Christians of New Testament times believed about their relation to the Old Israel. This is found in the relation of the Greek *ekklēsia*, which refers to "Church" in the New Testament, to the Hebrew *qāhāl*, which means the "assembly of the congregation of Israel" in the Old Testament. The Greek version of the Old Testament, the Septuagint, translated *qāhāl* by *ekklēsia*. The writers of the New Testament in Greek readily chose *ekklēsia* as the word to designate the new community of those who believed in Jesus Christ. This choice certainly implied a continuity between the Christian Church and Israel. And the importance of that implication for Christians lies in the knowledge that God's revealing and saving action in Israel has been decisively sealed and extended universally through the work of Jesus Christ and the reconstituting of the Church by Him.

Present-day biblical scholars also recognize the centrality of the Church in the mission and message of Jesus Christ. Although he uses the word *ekklēsia* only in Matt. 16:18 and 18:17, Jesus clearly formed about Him a community which was the nucleus of the Church. And those who looked for the Messiah would have expected, according to Jewish belief, that the Messiah would constitute his "messianic people." The portrait of Jesus as a religious teacher directing His message just to separate individuals, whether in His own time or now, is untrue to the Gospels. Neither can there be a Christian apart from the Church.

Apart from Jesus' intention to form a community, the events recorded in Acts are unintelligible. At Pentecost God's Holy Spirit was given to the apostles. A new divine power thereafter directed the Christian community. And all who confessed Jesus Christ as risen Lord, whatever their nationality or race or tongue, were banded together in a loving, worshipping, serving, witnessing and expecting fellowship. Their communal life was characterized by adherence to the teaching of the original apostles, the mutual sharing of material goods and spiritual gifts (Gr. *koinōnia*), the practice of breaking bread together (probably in the light of the Lord's last supper), and common prayers (Acts 2:42).

The exact pattern of organization of this early Church is not described in the New Testament, although there is abundant evidence that there developed quickly some forms of ministry and order. Every Christian belonged to the "royal priesthood" of the whole Church, but some were recognized as having diverse spiritual gifts and so appointed to various kinds of service (I Cor. 12:28; Eph. 4:11). As to the distinctive authority of the apostles there was no doubt. But disputes arise today concerning the normative character of church organization in the New Testament. Some insist that the early Church's expectation of the end of history and the ushering in of the Kingdom of God was so imminent that organization was a secondary matter. Others claim to see in the New Testament a perennially valid pattern for organization, but among themselves they differ as to its nature, some seeing the three-fold order of bishop, priest and deacon, others recognizing only an essential presbyterate, and still others discerning the autonomous local congregation within which the kinds of ministry were only for convenience.

From the outset this early Church practiced two Sacraments which Jesus Christ had commanded them to continue. The common way of entering the fellowship was by Baptism with water, the laying on of hands, and prayer. The central act of worship and love was the Lord's Supper, celebrated with bread and wine and the words by which Jesus instituted it.

The New Testament Church was never a static society. Its essential nature lay in the oneness between the living Lord and the community, as well as the unity of the members of the community one with another. But its essential function was to bring the Gospel of Jesus Christ to the world at large. Both the oneness and the mission of the Church are interpreted largely by means of numerous figures of speech, which indeed are the characteristic ways of referring to the Church in the New Testament. Christ is the Vine, the church members the branches (John 15); He the Shepherd, they the sheep (John 10); He is the Head of His Body, the Church, of which believers are organic members (I Cor. 12:12-27; Eph. 4:11-16). But these figures of corporate unity and solidarity with the living Christ have also the active reference to the mission and extension of the Church. The whole vine grows; there are "other sheep" who must be brought in; the Body increases in growth and is inwardly built up until the "fullness of Christ" is attained in the time of consummation of God's Kingdom.

3) The biblical evidence requires extensive treatment because it is the common basis of varying confessional concepts of the Church as they have developed through the centuries. However much these differ, each denomination holds its view to be in accord with the biblical teaching, even though not necessarily to the exclusion of another denomination's conviction. The major types of concepts of the Church are the following:

a. The Orthodox Church, whether Greek, Russian, Serbian, etc., holds that it alone maintains the full teaching, tradition and order of the "one true and visible Church of Christ on earth." This is not considered by the Orthodox to be an arrogant assertion, but an honest confession of faith and appeal to history. Other Christian bodies are not dismissed as being heretical, but are adjudged to lack the requisite fullness. Of course, this is similar to the teaching of the Roman Catholic Church about itself, except that the Papacy is believed by Roman Catholics to be indispensable.

b. The Old Catholic Church of Europe, the Polish National Catholic Church (largely in America), and the Churches of the Anglican Communion likewise believe that they have maintained the pure Christian teaching, the proper ministry in apostolic episcopal succession, and the true Sacraments. While recognizing the integrity and validity of other episcopal communions, these churches usually regard the non-episcopal churches as being not false but deficient.

c. Lutheran Churches have a clear statement in the Augsburg Confession to the effect that the Church "is the congregation of believers, where the Gospel is purely preached and the Sacraments rightly administered." Forms of ministry and order are secondary, even though some, such as Scandinavian churches, have bishops. Lutherans generally permit full sacramental fellowship at "pulpit and altar" only with those who agree with them on the meaning and interpretation of the Gospel and the Sacraments.

d. The Reformed or Presbyterian Churches also teach that the Word of God (the Gospel) and the Sacraments are the essentials which make a congregation a Christian church, but they add the necessity of an order of discipline.

e. The Methodists, being derived historically from the Church of England and influenced by the Reformed, have a comprehensive doctrine of the Church which permits them to recognize readily and fully most other Christian communions.

f. Congregationalists hold the distinctive view that the local congregation is the essential and autonomous unit of the Church. Congregations in covenant and fellowship with one another constitute the whole Church.

g. Baptists and Disciples of Christ are also congregational in polity, but lay down the added requirement that only persons baptized as believers, rather than as infants, may be members of the Church. Many such churches require further the Baptism by total immersion as being in accord with the New Testament practice.

h. The Society of Friends (Quakers) witness to a Christian fellowship independent of creeds, orders, and Sacraments.

i. Various other denominations find their views of the Church expressed in one or more of the above categories. In recent years there have come into being by mergers a number of United Churches, combining distinct elements of their constituent bodies. Only the Church of South India has united churches of episcopal, presbyteral, and congregational ministries, although such an attempt is being made in several countries. The force of the contemporary ecumenical movement lies not in its insistence that denominations should merge according to a common pattern, but that they seek freely in their particular circumstances to overcome divisive barriers, to renew the corporate life and services of the churches, and to find effective means for extending the Christian mission to all persons.

J. ROBERT NELSON

Bibliography

R. N. Flew (editor), *The Nature of the Church.*
J. R. Nelson, *The Realm of Redemption.*
A. Nygren (editor), *This Is the Church.*

CONGREGATIONALISM

Congregationalism is that type of church government which promotes and protects the spiritual values which lie in the regular meetings (Latin: *congregationes*) of Christian groups.

Congregationalism has been implicit in the Christian Church from the beginning. It was not until the early seventeenth century in England, when the values in congregations were being threatened by forces inside and outside the Church, that Congregationalism emerged as a separate denomination with its own corporate organization.

The Pilgrim Fathers who landed at Plymouth in 1620 were Congregationalists. So also were the far greater company who presently settled about Massachusetts Bay. The direct spiritual descendants of these early Americans today are the members of the churches known as Congregational Christian. They total slightly over one million and a quarter.

Baptists and Disciples of Christ also employ congregational forms of church government, as do many other smaller denominations. In the United States there are in fact more Christians who worship in churches of the congregational type than there are of any other kind.

The Congregational Christian Churches in the United States are members of the world-wide confessional organization called the International Congregational Council, which includes constituents from many nations in the world, such as the Congregational Union of England and Wales, the Mission Covenant Church of Sweden, and the Remonstrant Brotherhood of the Netherlands.

Congregational Christians are at home in the ecumenical movement—the organized attempt at cooperation among the denominations. Such ecumenical bodies as the World Council of Churches and the National Council of Churches are congregational in structure.

The Congregational Christian Churches, with the exception of a small and undetermined number of congregations which disapproved the step, united with the Evangelical and Reformed Church in June 1957. This is the first instance, on so large a scale, of a union between a denomination dominantly congregational and one dominantly presbyterial in structure.

The theology of the Congregational Christian Churches has always been that of the Christian Church in general. Its ministers keep *au courant* of the thinking of leaders not only in their own denomination but in all of them. The theological seminaries at which its prospective ministers receive their training are chiefly of the interdenominational type, where the young men learn to know and appreciate the best thought of the many communions.

Congregationalism derives its policy from its theology. The living Christ is the center of every congregation. His presence lends the congregation its spiritual importance. It also lends it its importance as a unit of government: the congregation through prayer and study keeps itself open to the wisdom of Christ and, for decisions regarding its own affairs, allows no extraneous force, not even the will of bishop or higher presbytery, to intervene between itself and the will of Christ as it understands the latter.

Because of the acknowledged presence of Christ in each congregation, Congregationalism at its best is never exclusive and individualistic. Each congregation, recognizing Christ in other congregations as well, is drawn to cooperation with those congregationalists under their common Lord. This is a powerful factor making for ecumenicity, for though there are denominations without bishops and those without presbyters, there are none without congregations. The congregation therefore becomes a universal key to mutual understanding and reciprocal respect not only within the Congregational Christian denomination but between it and other denominations.

It is because of the immediate presence of Christ, cultivated in each congregation, that Congregational Christians have often been moved in His name to apply themselves to causes of social amelioration. They were active protagonists of emancipation in the middle nineteenth century as they are active de-segregationists today. Their mission boards, the oldest in the country, are oriented at once to the worship of God and the welfare of man.

DOUGLAS HORTON

Bibliography

Douglas Horton, *Congregationalism: A Study in Church Policy.*
Daniel Jenkins, *Congregationalism: A Restatement.*

CONSCIENCE

Conscience, in the New Testament, would seem to be regarded as that faculty which reminds us, by stimulating feelings of guilt and shame, when we are doing wrong. Of course this faculty needs educating, and normally we may say that it is trained and developed by the moral influence of the society to which we belong and in which we live. Hence the emphasis placed by the New Testament writers on the importance of living in the Church rather than in the world.

With the development of the doctrine of natural law, and in more modern rationalist philosophers like Butler and Kent, conscience becomes a faculty of reason by means of which we recognize, as rational beings, what conduct is befitting our true human nature and calling. The Reformers were suspicious of any doctrine of this latter kind. They did not go as far as did later sectarian Protestants, especially the Quakers, in identifying conscience with the "inner life" or inward prompting of the Holy Spirit, making of it thereby something absolute and independent of church and society. The scriptural basis for the view of sectarian Protestantism would appear to be those episodes in which God speaks directly to the prophets, or directly inspires apostles and evangelists in the New Testament. It is doubtful, however, whether such examples of a divine initiative have anything to do with a faculty like conscience, which is supposed to be a permanent part of man's natural endowment. Modern relativistic psychological and sociological approaches to the problem would seem to be closer to the general New Testament idea of conscience as something primarily negative in its testimony, and in constant need of social education. The dangers of rationalization and ideology, wherever conscience is taken to be a source of absolute and positive guidance, are clearly very great. Even those who say that conscience requires nurture and education through participation in the life of the Church do not necessarily sunder conscience from the activity of the Holy Spirit, for they would claim that the Holy Spirit is normally operative in the life of the Church.

The association of conscience with feelings of guilt and shame would also find some support in contemporary psychology. The Christian would claim that guilt and shame are not necessarily pathological, still less useless and ineffective. The whole Christian tradition is well aware that guilt feelings are sometimes unhealthy, but it would claim that when such feelings are aroused by an objective guiltiness they amount to a wholesome and stimulating experience of reality which often leads to a positive amendment of life. Such an approach would recognize that in its actual workings conscience is often a relative instrument, and that it can never safely be regarded as absolutely infallible. Nevertheless, the well-trained conscience remains a factor of the utmost importance in the moral life.

J. V. LANGMEAD CASSERLEY

Bibliography

K. E. Kirk, *Conscience and Its Problems.*
Pierce, *Conscience in the New Testament.*

COVENANT

In the course of Christian history "the Covenant" comes to the fore as a theological category whenever the Church becomes seriously aware of being involved in an encounter on two fronts at once—with God above and with the world around about. At such times the Church has often been led to recover the biblical Covenant theology of history as the frame of reference for dealing with the issues of her life. She is reminded that her life in the grace of the Lord Jesus Christ separates her from the world and yet involves her in a responsibility to and for the world. Notable examples are St. Augustine in the fifth century, *The City of God and the City of the World,* and John Calvin in the sixteenth century, *Institutes of the*

Christian Religion. These churchmen have left an indelible mark upon subsequent theology by their interpretations of the Christian life as a "Covenant of Grace." Later variations of this heritage in Reformed theology include the *Heidelberg Catechism* (1563), the *Westminster Confession* (1647), the Scottish Covenanters, English and American Puritans and the continental Federal theology.

The current revival of interest in the Covenant reflects the recovery of biblical categories in Christian theology generally and the use of such tools as "historical event," "dramatic encounter," and "existential communication" to interpret the biblical revelation. Thus, life in biblical history (*Heilsgeschichte*) and Christian theology (confession of the Mighty Acts of God) swing on the same hinge, the divine-human Covenant (O.T., *berith;* N.T., *diatheke*).

Both the prophets and the apostles tell the story of God's continuing covenant encounter with His people as a divine-human dialogue of revelation and faith- (or unfaith-) response.

Through His *Word* and in His *Acts* God has established with His chosen people a permanently binding personal relationship whose fundamental troth is "steadfast love." From the time of our father Abraham (Gen. 12; 15; 17) to the consummation of the Church in the New Jerusalem (Rev. 21) the Word by which God announces His steadfast love and sovereign righteousness is the same:

> *You shall be my people*
> *and I will be your God.*

The key historical events through which God has acted to judge and redeem His people are, according to prophetic and apostolic witness, the deliverance of Israel from Egyptian bondage at the Exodus (Deut. 6:20-24), and the deliverance of all mankind from the dominion of evil through the New Covenant in the life, death and resurrection of Jesus Christ (Acts: 2:22-36). In both instances

God has acted definitively to establish a servant-people (the Church in Israel and the universal Church of Jesus Christ, respectively), and has given them the task of proclaiming His righteousness and of mediating His love to the nations.

God's Covenant is by many dimensions a deeper kind of personal relationship than a contract and must not be confused with any form of bargained pact. In the Covenant of Grace the Church's life is rooted in the mystery of the divine election of a chosen people, and points toward the destiny of human history in God's everlasting Kingdom. Just because this intimate personal bond with God is *a gift* with promise, it involves *a task,* i.e., the people's responsible participation in the servant life of God's covenant-community. Therefore, between the beginning (Creation) and the goal (Eschatology) of the Mighty Acts of God, the Bible tells the story, generation after generation, of God and His people in dramatic encounter. The plot runs through three Acts: 1) God's righteous government and His people's rebellion (the Law and our sin), 2) our judgment and redemption by the grace of God (Christ and our new being), and 3) our recreation by the gift of God's own Spirit, restoring us to covenant responsibility (the Church, her mission, and our Christian vocation).

This formulation of the biblical *Heilsgeschichte* offers an outline of a Covenant theology that is relevant to both aspects of today's ecumenical encounter of the churches: a) of the Church with her Lord (Faith and Order) and b) of the Church and her Mission to the world (Life and Work). Moreover, it gives each churchman the theme around which to compose his life.

ALLEN O. MILLER

Bibliography

B. W. Anderson, *Rediscovering the Bible.*
John Bright, *The Kingdom of God.*
F. W. Dillistone, *The Structure of the Divine Society.*
Allen O. Miller, *Invitation to Theology.*
G. Ernest Wright, *God Who Acts.*

CREATION

Protestantism is becoming increasingly sensitive to its doctrine of creation. The Reformers understood that their first task was to protect theology from human inventiveness and to return it to its proper concern—revelation. Luther and Calvin sought to define theology, not as metaphysics, but as the description of the dynamic relation between faith and grace. As a result Protestantism placed its emphasis almost solely upon God's *redemptive* activity. Man was stripped of every power that would tempt him to forget that redemption was supernatural. The central doctrines of *justification by grace* (Luther) and *predestination* (Calvin) saved the Church from sustaining itself by feeding upon its own flesh. As a result, Christendom (both Protestant and Roman Catholic) was availed of the opportunity of rediscovering the power of the Pauline-Augustinian view of grace. The historical task of the Reformation was to direct attention not to the creation but to the Creator, not to the order of the world but to the faithfulness of Him who had redeemed it.

A high price was paid for this victory. Although new vigor was given to the doctrine of redemption, the idea of creation was all but lost. In the Lutheran tradition, to be sure, a view of faith emerged which displayed the grandeur of man's response to God. It could also be argued that Calvin's doctrine of vocation gave more significance to human life than did the medieval view of natural law. At the same time Protestantism was forced into a fixed position regarding the *total depravity* of man's nature. Thus Reformation theology repudiated St. Thomas' view of natural reason without developing an alternative view.

As Protestantism hardened into a tradition it attempted to incorporate faith and grace into a system. Hostile to medieval thought and indifferent to classical culture, Protestantism lost its ability to maneuver. Tragically, it failed to recognize the indebtedness of theology to the logic and philosophical curiosity of the ancient world. It was inevitable that Protestant theology be driven into the one area which it could exploit—the Bible. The Bible was forced to become what it had not been in the Reformation, a compendium of truth, an encyclopedia of the arts and sciences. Truth came to mean the doctrines which logic projected into the Bible. As theologians were unable to sense the Logos in creation, it was inevitable that genuine intellectual activity would be replaced by adherence to the supposedly fixed tenets of the Bible. With such an abdication of responsibility, Protestantism began to enter its own version of the dark ages.

The Protestant tradition has not, of course, been uniform. There have been voices and movements which sat in judgment upon obscurantism. Friedrich Schleiermacher (1768-1834) insisted that theology be responsive to the world. Great pressures came from the revolutions of the nineteenth century. The questions of Darwin, Freud, and Marx challenged the parochialism of the Church. As a result of these forces, Protestantism was forced to "justify" itself before a culture which did not depend upon the Church for its vitalities and structures of meaning. The Church began to concern itself less with its purity and more with the relevance of the gospel to the economic, political and philosophical dimensions of human existence. Theology discovered that the Church needs the world as much as the world needs the Church. A new orientation came into being.

Protestants owe a great debt to Sören Kierkegaard. More than any other thinker Kierkegaard has helped Christianity to take man seriously as creature. It is the Danish theologian who has taught Christendom that it must impregnate all thought with existence. With this strange and powerful thinker, Protestantism comes full circle. It began with a doctrine of redemption. Through Kierkegaard it has come to realize that no man can understand Christ if he does not also understand himself as creature.

It cannot be said that Protestantism has a clear doctrine of creation. As yet there is no Protestant equivalent of natural law. There is, however, movement in that direction. Protestantism has emerged from a weary scho-

*l*asticism into a world which receives God, into a world which has been marked by God as eternally His own. To understand those markings without forsaking its doctrine of redemption is surely the next task of Protestant theology.

FRED DENBEAUX

Bibliography

Emil Brunner, *Revelation and Reason.*
Reinhold Niebuhr, *An Interpretation of Christian Ethics.*
William Temple, *Nature, Man and God.*

CULTURE

The term "culture" is used in the context of three frames of reference: the pedagogical, the anthropological, and the theological. Theological interpretation and evaluation may be applied to both of the others.

"Culture" in the pedagogical sense refers to the knowledge, moral integrity, and sensitivity acquired through the disciplines of education. In its classical form it originated with the Greek conception of the cultivation of mind and character implied in Plato's humanistic ideal of "tending the soul" or "minding one's own business" and in Aristotle's aristocratic view of the "serious-minded man" who by habit acquires the intellectual and moral virtues and who employs his leisure for self-development. This conception of the shaping of the person was understood within the context of the city-state and the obligations of citizenship. From these roots has grown the university tradition, a tradition that has aimed to provide the humanistic disciplines that define and shape "the educated man" and that in the course of its development has received support and qualification at the hands of Christian groups both Catholic and Protestant. In the modern period, however, conflict and creative tension have emerged between the various ingredients of the university tradition, particularly as a consequence of the new place occupied by the natural and social sciences, of the debate between the humanist and the "specialist," and of the inescapable (if ambiguous) role of religion in higher education. Today increasing attention is being given to the issues involved here: What is the place of theology in the university? To what extent and in what ways should religious and anti-religious presuppositions be taken into account? What is Christian higher education?

"Culture" in the anthropological sense is today sometimes defined in contrast to "civilization," the body of practical and intellectual knowledge, and the technical means, for controlling nature. Generally, however, it is understood to include these things and to refer to the total human effort manifest in the language, habits, customs, beliefs, artifacts, institutions, technical processes, normative value preferences and sanctions which are characteristic of a territorial group and which are promoted for the sake of human fulfillment. In a dynamic society it comprises the individual and social materialization, criticism and transformation of values under the aegis of freedom and authority, of tradition and innovation, and all of this in some relation to other societies and cultures. Moreover, stagnation, failure of nerve, anomie, and nihilism as well as creative courage may appear.

It is difficult to determine the status of religion in the context of these cultural phenomena. In general it is erroneous to distinguish religion from culture; for the dominant religion among men is cultural religion, an aspect of the anthropocentric enterprise devoted to the promotion of human good and interests. In contrast to cultural religion the rare phenomenon of prophetic religion is (in a special way) theocentric rather than anthropocentric. For prophetic religion the chief end of man is to know God, to serve Him and enjoy Him— what Hosea means by "the knowledge of God"; and culture, including its ostensibly religious elements, is under judgment from beyond culture.

Insofar as Christianity is prophetic it stands in tension with the culture. According to the New Testament, culture is "of the world" (*kosmos*), and "in Christ God was reconciling the world to Himself." "The world" is by no means without religion: the powers that rule in it belong to God's creation, but they are fallen, demonic powers. In their superindividual strength they hold men in their sway. Christ frees men from this bondage. In the End these powers will be brought under subjection. Thus Christ and His saving power are in the world and for the world, but not of it. In response to the power of God-in-Christ the Christians form a community in the world. As a community they not only enter into conflict with "the world," they also become a cultural group dependent upon the order and vitality they find there; at the same time they are commissioned to bear witness to the power of God which is beyond culture and which works towards its conservation and transformation.

From this beginning, with its Old Testament prophetic background, there develops the paradigm of relations between Christ and culture which constitute the forms of conflict, synthesis and compulsion, of protest and tolerance, of accommodation and transformation, reaching from the early small community to the extensive *corpus christianum* commencing in the Middle Ages, on to the various forms of established church, sect and denomination within the context of modern social and religious pluralism. Here the culture of the West is profoundly affected, for example, in certain of its major presuppositions (the doctrine of creation, the conception of the person), in social organization, and in the understanding of vocation. In all of these periods extra-ecclesiastical culture exercises influence upon the churches. The cultural influence is ambiguous, as is examplified in the decisively effective social tradition of Greco-Roman antiquity (including the idea of natural law), in the precise and systematic intellectual dialectic stemming from the Greeks, in the modern development of higher criticism of the Bible and tradition, and also in the intrusion within the churches of highly destructive class or nationalist or racial loyalties and demonries. At times the cultural forces offer protest against these loyalties and demonries of cultural religion, in the name of freedom or humanity or intellectual integrity; or they provide the technology which makes possible the industrialized urban society that in turn secularizes and also radically alters the situation of the churches; or they produce the nihilism that reflects the dissolution of values. The churches for their part reveal analogous ambiguity in face of culture and cultural religion. But God and Christ are not bound to culture or cultural religion or churches.

It is the role of prophetic Christianity in humility and audacity to witness to and respond to that which lies at the depth of both culture and cultural religion and which is never in their possession: the creative and formative power of God and Christ in relation to which the cultural "good for man" is always at best only a proximate, ambiguous good unreliable as the ultimate object of faith. The Christian understanding of this total situation has been contributed to by characteristically modern cultural insights reflected in every theology except perhaps that of the Fundamentalists. It is the merit of contemporary (Christian) process philosophy, for example, that it attempts to illumine our understanding of the ways in which the more-than-human good actually functions when men give themselves to its working and keeping. This understanding of course has an important bearing on the evaluation of culture in the pedagogical sense.

JAMES LUTHER ADAMS

Bibliography

W. John Baillie, *What is Christian Civilization?*
Bernard E. Meland, *Faith and Culture.*
H. Richard Niebuhr, *Christ and Culture.*

DEATH

From the biologist's point of view, death is no more than a phase in the rhythm of organic existence— "Nature's dodge to secure abundant life"—as Goethe called it. But death takes on a new significance when it is the death of the biologist himself. As organisms, we men share in the common mortality. But unlike other organisms we are *conscious* of our mortality, we *know* we are destined to die. The shadow of our inevitable end is thrown backwards over our entire human experience. "In the midst of life we are in death"—and contemporary philosophies like that of Heidegger read off the deepest meaning of our life as an "existence-unto-death."

Man finds it hard to reconcile himself to dying. He believes—and this is perhaps the oldest of his beliefs—that something in him survives the death and decay of his body. From the first this belief has been linked with religion, but in itself it is a "common-sense" inference from such data as are provided by dream-experiences, in which the human spirit seems to live and range at large independently of the sleeping body which houses it. In due course this primitive inference is given philosophical status in a doctrine of the indestructibility of the soul-substance, and is also incorporated into religion as faith in a future life in which rewards and punishments are meted out according to the deeds men have done in their present earthly existence.

The Bible teaches that God created man by breathing His Spirit into the dust of the earth, and so bringing into existence the *nephesh,* or living personality. When God withdraws His Spirit man dies and returns to the dust. Thus man's life is lived by favor of God. Nowhere in the Bible is the human soul regarded as naturally immortal. The only way in which man can live again after death is by a resurrection—a miracle. It is true that death does not mean utter extinction. The departed Israelite was thought to be in Sheol—where, as in the Greek Hades, the bloodless wraiths eked out a joyless existence. Sheol was not originally conceived to be a place of punishment. But it was a place of exile from God. It lay beyond the frontiers of His realm and its inhabitants were banished from His presence and denied the opportunity of worshipping Him.

This helps to explain why death was dreaded by the pious Israelite. But so long as the conception of "corporate personality" held the field, and the individual Israelite had his value and significance only as a member of his tribe or nation, death encountered at the end of life's natural span was not without its compensations. A man, when "gathered to his fathers" and buried in the family grave, went on living, as it were, in his descendants who perpetuated his name and kept his memory green. Premature death was another matter. To die before one had had time to found a family was calamity indeed, which could only be regarded as God's signal judgment on wrongdoing. But with the rise of individualistic ways of thinking the penal element in premature death attached itself to death in general, as the result of a darkening and deeping of the conception of sin. As symbolized by the story of Adam's transgression, death has come upon the race as the punishment of man's sin.

The idea of *unnaturalness*—the abnormality—of death begins to appear. If God created man in His own image in order that man might glorify Him and enjoy Him forever, then death is a contradiction, not only of man's hopes and longing for life but also—it seems—of God's gracious purpose in creating him. Man "thinks he was not made to die." But it is his consciousness of deserving this dread punishment that makes man fear death and dread its inexorable approach. From the point of view of the Bible, man's fear of death is the sign of a bad conscience.

In the New Testament, the solidarity of mankind in sin is the dark presupposition of the gospel of salvation in Christ, the second Adam. "The wages of sin is death." But death is not an arbitrary penalty which a celestial despot chooses to inflict on transgressors. According to the Bible, the root of all sinning is *unbelief*, which is not an intellectual skepticism but man's refusal to acknowledge God by trusting and obeying Him as Father and Lord. Thus, by its very nature, sin disrupts the relationship in which man stands to God. By his sin, man cuts himself off from the source of Life and dooms himself to perish. Apart from the grace of the forgiving God, there is no hope for him. For he can be saved only by being raised from the dead. Not a natural immortality of the soul, but resurrection from the dead by the power of God, is the message of the Bible.

In the light of the Christian gospel death appears both as the penalty of sin and as the means of salvation. As the penalty of sin it brings estrangement from God. Not spatial separation from Him—as in a Sheol lying beyond the frontiers of His Kingdom—but spiritual and moral remoteness from God which makes the sinner's inability to escape from God a torment. For not even man's sin can abolish the relationship in which God destined him to live. It is true that God could annihilate the sinner; but the sinner cannot annihilate himself. Nevertheless, by his sin he distorts the relationship between himself and his Creator, turning its positives into negatives. He still knows God—but with a knowledge that is infected with error and delusion. The face of God is averted from him. The Father has become the Judge.

The death of Christ, the second Adam, transforms death, sin's penalty, into a means of deliverance from its guilt and power. Because Christ "has tasted death for every man," He has made death the gateway into eternal life. The crucified Son of God has drawn the sting of death—which is sin. The believer must still undergo "natural" death, but he has been delivered from "the second death" of final estrangement from God. He lives in newness of life, because by the saving grace of God in Christ *he has learned how to die*. His faith is itself a daily dying, in which the "old man" of sin is crucified and dies, in order that the "new man" may be raised from the dead by the same power of God that raised Christ. Baptism is the symbol of this daily dying.

The believer, therefore, has already begun his new life in the Spirit. He now "lives unto the Lord." The Apostle Paul presents this truth in noteworthy phrases: "Ye died, and your lives are hid with Christ in God." . . . "We were buried therefore with him by baptism into death, so that as Christ was raised from the dead by the glory of the Father, we too might walk in newness of life." And the whole matter is summed up for us in the words of Jesus in the Fourth Gospel: "He that believeth *hath*" (even here and now) "eternal life."

H. F. LOVELL COCKS

Bibliography

J. Baillie, *And the Life Everlasting.*
E. Brunner, *Eternal Hope,* Chapters 11 and 12.
H. F. Lovell Cocks, *By Faith Alone,* Chapter 5; *The Hope of Glory.*

DEMONS, DEMONIC, AND THE DEVIL

Demons (Greek *daimōn,* Latin *daemon*) are ethereal beings of varying magnitude and power which have worked various degrees of mischief in the lives of men. They have been imagined as possessing human mentality and feelings, and responding to man in human ways. They have been treated as sheer potencies which needed to be recognized and placated with offerings; as powers which could be used against enemies by means of magical practices; as *numens* or lesser deities resident at given places (marked by trees, waters, stones) who acted as oracles and patrons of diviners; in general as co-habitants of the world with men, who were implicated in men's good and especially evil fortune.

The ubiquity of demons and their persistence through the ages indicate that they owe the attention they have received to some deep-seated traits in man himself. Man has always projected himself into his environment and attributed his character and powers to objects around him. He has lived in a world of powers like his own, and tried to enjoy good and prevent evil by entering into a manageable relationship with them. If man is to have security in this world he must understand the powers around him, and the notion that these powers are akin to his own is profoundly reassuring in spite of the wilfulness of the demons.

Demons are ghosts and ghosts are men without their bodies. Demons are often the dead hovering near their former habitation who, free from the limitations but not the passions of the flesh, enter into a troublesome but not altogether unwelcome relationship with the living. Without doubt death, and the dread and hope of man in relation to it, has been a constant source of demonism.

But above all demons are evildoers. Demonism must therefore be understood as an expression of man's dread in the presence of evils and the perils of evil. In spite of the intermittent joy we find in human life, one cannot escape the fact that man's brief life is "but toil and trouble" (Ps. 90:10). The demons both objectify and mitigate man's "tragic sense of life." They make evil manageable and the sting of death tolerable.

Popular piety in ancient Israel seems to have paid due attention to demons. *Numens* of trees, stones, wells were recognized. Divination was practiced and there were sundry kinds of magic (Deut. 18:9-14; Is. 8:19). Such practices seem to have flourished under Canaanite, Assyrian, and Babylonian influence and in times of unrest and disaster (Is. 2:6; 2 Kings 21:1 f; Is. 44:25; Jer. 27:9; Zech. 10:2). The Law and the prophets regarded demonism as idolatry and a denial of the living God. "Should not the people consult their God? Should they consult the dead in behalf of the living?" (Is. 8:19). To seek a remedy for the misery of human life in fictitious powers or any power other than the Lord was adjudged both sin and folly. Therefore, biblical and Christian theology is an absolute repudiation of demonism, and according to it demons or gods are without power of their own and are as nothing (Deut. 32:17; Is. 2:8; 18:20; 44:1 f; Jer. 2:11; Ez. 30:13). "For all the gods of the peoples are idols, but the Lord made the heavens" (Ps. 96:5).

The New Testament presents us with a lively belief in demons as "unclean spirits" which entered men and made them insane. The Evangelists tell us that Jesus, as an integral part of His ministry, cast out demons (Mark 3:10-15; Matt. 9:34; 12:22-28; Luke 7:18-20). This was due partly to popular conceptions of the day and partly to a new sense of the conflict between God and the evil one and his demonic servants (Matt. 12:27). Persian and Hellenic influences were both operative. Jesus' own concern was to exhibit the sovereignty of God over the evil powers which infest human life. God's kingdom came through the overthrow of spiritual powers set to destroy men.

This sense of a world harassed by evil powers was strong in the early Church. The enormity of the struggle with evil and man's helplessness in it; the knowledge of the power of the living God who overthrew evil by the might of His Word and Spirit, by the cross and resurrection of Jesus Christ, gave this new demonism a validity and vitality which is evident in the New Testament, especially in the Pauline epistles (1 Cor. 2:6; 5:1-5; 8:1-6; 10:14; 2 Cor. 12:7; Gal. 5:16 f; Eph. 2:1 f; 6:10; also 1 Tim. 4:1; Heb. 2:14; James 2:19; 3:15; 1 John 4:1; Rev. 9:20-21).

At this point it is well to observe that in the Old Testament Satan belonged to the heavenly court of God. Although he meant mischief and set out to undo man by tempting him to do evil, he had none of the virulence of Satan in the New Testament, where he is still the tempter (Luke 4:1-13; 22:3; Acts 5:3; 1 Cor. 7:5; 1 Tim. 5:15; Rev. 12:9). In the latter, Satan is a world power, the father of lies and deception (John 8:44-45), the Antichrist, the anti-God, the Destroyer, who, even though overthrown by Christ, continues to work against the Church and will do so until the end when he, with death and sin and this world, shall be overthrown.

The Church gradually repudiated the demons, and replaced sundry deities with angels. But the devil as anti-God, even though serving God against his own will, remained in Christian theology, and received renewed recognition whenever the Church became aware of the depth and virulence of evil.

In our own day, after several centuries of eclipse, the devil has returned as the "demonic," expressive of the depth and mystery of evil in the world, as against the view which sees evil as either caused by physical forces or as willed malevolently by men (Tillich, Berdyaev, R. Niebuhr). So long as men try to think adequately about temptation, the devil will be acknowledged for what he is, the quasi-personal father of lies, allied with death and sin, and a power in the world which only the living God can and does overcome by the gospel and "the Spirit of truth."

JOSEPH HAROUTUNIAN

Bibliography

Edward Langton, *Essentials of Demonology, a Study of Jewish and Christian Doctrine, Its Origin and Development.*
C. S. Lewis, *The Screwtape Letters.*
Denis de Rougemont, *The Devil's Share.*
Paul Tillich, *The Interpretation of History.*

DESTINY AND FATE

By destiny and fate, which for most purposes may be considered synonymous, we ordinarily understand one or another of three different things: 1) the ultimate principle or reality by virtue of which things are as they are or events happen as they do (as in "What fates impose, that men must needs abide"); 2) the actual state of things or course of events which is thus determined (as in "I am the master of my fate"); or 3) the ultimate end or final outcome of things or events (as in "The fate of the bill in the lower house is undecided").

Upon reflection, however, it becomes clear that the original and primary meaning of these concepts is existential. That is, they refer in the first instance to either 1) the objective power which (or who) determines human existence; or 2) that existence as actually determined; or 3) the final end or goal toward which man's existence ineluctably moves. Thus, with reference to the three illustrations cited in the preceding paragraph, the first and second statements, rather than the third, more nearly express the primitive and still fundamental meaning of the words. For it is really only by way of analogy that we ever speak of the "fate" of a bill or, for that matter, of the "destiny" or "fate" of any other non-human thing. In this sense, then, the notions of fate and destiny are very like the idea of creation. For just as what is primarily at stake in the latter concept is not an answer to a scientific question, but rather an answer to the very different question of the meaning of human existence, so also in the case of the former notions the first meaning intended is entirely existential.

Furthermore, it also becomes evident that the concepts as above defined have a purely formal significance. For however true it may be that, as they are customarily employed, they have a very specific material meaning (i.e., presuppose some particular understanding of human existence), it is no less true that they may be used and indeed actually are used to express very different existential self-understandings. In this respect, of course, they are exactly like all the other basic concepts (e.g., God, good, evil, sin, etc.) which pertain to the phenomenon of human existence. Therefore, if they are to be defined more specifically than we have previously defined them, it is an unavoidable necessity that such definition take place from the standpoint of some particular self-understanding. For our present purpose, it must suffice to specify the meaning which the two concepts have for the uniquely Christian understanding of human existence.

Their first meaning may be stated very simply. For, from the standpoint of Christian self-understanding, the ultimate principle or reality by reason of which human existence is as it is and, by analogy, all other things are as they are, is none other than the God and Father of our Lord Jesus Christ. That is, it is neither the "gods many" or "lords many" of the various heathen mythologies (cf. I Cor. 8:4 ff.), nor some indifferent necessity to which even these "powers" themselves are finally subject, but, on the contrary, is a holy will of love whose sole purpose is the good of all His creatures and whose special gift and demand to man in every situation is that of personal fellowship with Him. It is precisely because this is so, of course, that the concepts destiny and fate in this first sense play so negligible a role in traditional theological reflection. Even so, however, this should not lead us to overlook the fact that the existential question out of which these concepts arise and to which, in various ways, they seek to give an answer is the same question to which the God who makes Himself known in Jesus Christ is the only really valid answer.

It directly follows from this, however, that the second meaning which these terms may have is also significantly different for the Christian understanding of existence. For if it is true that the ultimate determining power is a personal will who in every moment offers and demands fellowship with Himself, then it must also be true that the existence which is thus determined is itself a personal existence. That is, whatever may be the case with respect to non-human creation, man at least is destined to be free. He is neither the plaything of an inscrutible necessity nor is he ever "without excuse" for what he actually makes of his life (cf. Rom. 1:20). Thus, unlike all ultimately dualistic understandings of human existence (e.g. gnosticism), Christianity knows of no destiny or fate within the terms of man's existence which is not at the same time determined by his own free decision. In its view, man is never simply the product of certain inescapable conditions and circumstances, but, on the contrary, is constantly confronted with the necessity of deciding how he is to live in the situation in which God in His providence has placed him. He must determine, in other words, whether he will accept the things and events of his life as the good creatures of God and as tokens of His loving concern, or whether he will anxiously embrace or flee from them in the futile attempt to escape the nothingness with which both he and they are always threatened.

In either case, however, the ultimate end or final outcome of his life, as well as that of all created beings, cannot be encompassed in wholly this-worldly terms. For, from the standpoint of the Christian understanding of existence as it finds expression in the classic symbols of the resurrection and the last judgment, the final destiny of all things is to be caught up within the everlasting love and judgment of God (cf. I Cor. 15:28). Thus, while Christian theology does indeed make use of the concepts of fate and destiny also in this their third sense, it does so only by giving them a meaning which is uniquely its own.

SCHUBERT M. OGDEN

Bibliography

Roger Hazelton, *God's Way with Man.*
Reinhold Niebuhr, *The Nature and Destiny of Man.*

DOGMA

Dogma is a term ordinarily used to designate the official doctrinal teaching of a Christian church.

Although the Greek word *dogma* appears five (perhaps six) times in the New Testament, the only passage in which it has this connotation is Acts 16:4; and there it would seem to be primarily ethical and ceremonial decisions, rather than doctrinal ones, that the writer has in mind. In Ignatius, *Magn.* 13, the word begins to acquire its later meaning, which is also evident in Origen and other Fathers. But only when the councils of the Church actually began to formulate doctrine could the term begin to acquire the official, almost legal, significance it now possesses.

In the strictest sense, nothing less than the whole of the Church is qualified to define dogma. Therefore the only dogmas in the most precise sense of the word are the dogmas of the Trinity and of the person of Christ, as these were defined in the first four (or seven) ecumenical councils. But the term is usually employed in a looser sense for the particular doctrinal decisions of a church body. Its applicability varies with the degree of canonical status and the amount of enforcement that such decisions carry in the church body. For example, the formulations of the Cambridge Platform or of the Thirty-Nine Articles might be termed "dogmas" on the ground that they were officially promulgated by church bodies; but because in many parts of those church bodies they have become a dead letter, the term does not apply to them. On the other hand, the doctrine of the immaculate conception or, more recently, of the assumption, can be called "dogma," even though something less than the whole of the Church was involved in their promulgation, because of the canonical status of these teachings and their enforcement on pain of excommunication.

In Protestant theology since the Enlightenment, the term "dogma" has acquired a primarily historical connotation, being used especially in the study of the "history of dogma." It was the original function of that study during the eighteenth century to demonstrate that the doctrines of the Church had been conditioned in their formulation by the circumstances under which they arose. At the hands of its greatest practitioner, Adolf Harnack (1851-1930), the history of dogma became the discipline by which the continuing value and authority of ancient dogma was called into question. Concentrating his attention upon the ancient dogmas of the Trinity and the person of Christ, Harnack sought to show that they were the products of Greek influence in Christianity. Although his extreme attitude was reversed by the generation of theologians who followed him, the word "dogma" has not lost the opprobrium it acquired when, as was said, "the history of dogma is the dissolution of dogma." It is noteworthy in this connection that even the most confessionally loyal among Lutheran theologians in Europe and America rarely use the term for the particular teachings of their own symbols, restricting it to the two dogmas of the ancient Church and, in a polemical context, to the particular doctrinal promulgations of the Roman Catholic Church.

The several Catholic churches continue to use "dogma" as a designation of their offical teachings. For the Orthodox, it means the decisions of the seven ecumenical councils, a meaning it also has for some Anglicans. Other Anglicans tend to include the decisions of subsequent Western councils until, but not including, the Council of Trent of 1545-1563. Roman Catholics mean the decisions of the ancient councils, the formulations of later Western councils until and including the Vatican Council of 1870, and the infallible declarations of the Pope *ex cathedra*. It is required of Roman Catholic theologians, particularly since the Modernist controversy, to subject themselves to this dogma and to carry on their theological work within the limits set by it. It is therefore not permissible for a Roman Catholic New Testament scholar to come to any conclusions about the life of Jesus that would contradict the offical dogma of the two natures in Christ.

Because the second third of the twentieth century has seen a deepening of the catholic consciousness in the Protestant churches, the possibility exists that dogma will begin to acquire more status among them than it once had. But their central doctrinal concerns—like the atonement and justification by faith—are not part of dogma, as this is usually interpreted. It would therefore seem that only through the reinterpretation of their own history and of its connection with Christian history as such will these churches be able to repossess the dogmas of the Christian past.

JAROSLAV PELIKAN

Bibliography

Henry Denzinger, *The Sources of Catholic Dogma.*
Adolf Harnack, *History of Dogma.*

DOGMATICS

Dogmatics may be defined as the organized and systematic presentation of the dogmas of the Christian Church.

The determination of the proper scope and method of Christian dogmatics depends upon the conception one holds of Christian doctrine and of its status in the Church. In those churches and periods of church history where Christian doctrine is thought of as something given in a relatively stable form, the task of dogmatics is to demonstrate the correctness of the Church's dogmas in the light of Scripture, reason, and tradition, and to refute the critics of the dogma on the same grounds. Men like Francis Turretin (1623-1687) for the Reformed tradition and John Gerhard (1582-1637) for the Lutheran tradition are representatives of this conception of Christian doctrine and this interpretation of the task of dogmatics. With a thoroughness and precision matching that of medieval scholasticism, Protestant dogmatics organized the doctrines of the Reformation confessions into a systematic theology of unrivaled comprehensiveness. In order to accomplish this feat, Protestant dogmatics depended upon the existence of given dogmas and upon the acceptance of a general philosophical framework—usually, but not always, the Aristotelian—within which those dogmas could be systematized.

But the challenge of the Enlightenment both to the dogmas of the Church and to the particular philosophies with which those dogmas had been linked called forth a revision of the assignment that dogmatics was expected to carry out. Symbolic of that revision is the change in the titles of books on dogmatics; from names like "Theological Commonplaces" (*Loci*), "System," and "Institutes," theologians turned to "The Teaching of Faith" (Glaubenslehre) and similar designations. With the dogmatic works that appeared during the period of the Enlightenment there begins that process of reconstruction which is still associated with the work of the Protestant systematic theologian. No longer was it possible to take dogmas for granted, and therefore it was also impossible to write a dogmatics whose content had been predetermined by the propositions of scripture and/or the confessions of the churches. Instead, the dogmatician was faced with an apologetic assignment in relation to culture and a task of salvage in relation to the dogmas of the Church's past. Dogmaticians varied widely in the extent to which they sacrificed aspects of the past to the exigencies of their apologetic assignment; but the Protestant dogmatics of the eighteenth century was affected throughout by this revision of its assignment, and the discussion of what was left for dogmatics to do was perhaps the principal item of theological controversy in that period.The work of S. J.

Baumgarten (1706-1757) is representative of that discussion.

A new and decisive change of emphasis in dogmatics came with the theology of Friedrich Schleiermacher (1768-1834). He sought to escape the dilemma of Orthodox and Enlightenment dogmaticians by a two-fold reconsideration of what dogmatics is and does. He introduced the data of the Christian consciousness into the purview of dogmatics, and he called upon dogmatics to be the reflection of the status of Christian teaching in a particular church at a particular time. Thus he sought to achieve the advantages of both subjectivity and objectivity in dogmatics. His more radical followers concentrated upon his view of the Christian consciousness, while his more conservative pupils combined his two insights into one by their contention that the task of dogmatics was the formulation and systematization of that which was the content of the self-consciousness of the Church. This enabled them to incorporate into their systems more of ancient dogma than had Schleiermacher himself, without negating the significance of the individual Christian consciousness. Protestant dogmatics since Schleiermacher has been permanently affected by his redefinition of its work.

Among the attempts at a dogmatic since Schleiermacher, several deserve more than casual mention. While he never wrote an entire dogmatics, Albrecht Ritschl (1822-1889) attempted in his monumental work on justification and reconciliation (1870-1874) to show how dogmatics could make the Bible its source and Christ its center without involving itself in the situation of Orthodoxy. He had many pupils; but their major accomplishments were in the field of history, especially the history of dogma (q.v.). The dogmatics of the Reformed theologian Charles Hodge (1797-1878) and of the Lutheran theologian Francis Pieper (1852-1931) were among the most ambitious efforts at a systematic theology in the American churches; but there were many other efforts, most of them, like these, denominational in character.

There are two contemporary dogmatic works that claim the attention of all serious students, those of Paul

Tillich and Karl Barth. Although other theologians—Emil Brunner, Regin Prenter, Gustaf Aulen, Lionel Thornton, Paul Althaus, to name a few—have had some following, Tillich and Barth are reaching a wide audience. Tillich employs the insights of philosophy to raise the questions and the teachings of Christianity to supply the answers in a carefully stated attempt at correlation. His is, therefore, one of the few systematic theologies since Schleiermacher to call forth a significant response outside the Church. Barth, meanwhile, has written an explicitly ecclesiastical dogmatics, ecclesiastical both in its source and in its object. His work may therefore be called a "dogmatic" in the historic sense of the word.

Whatever their orientation, systematic theologians tend to agree that three elements are involved in a dogmatics: the biblical, as an account of the events of revelation and of the witness of the primitive Church to those events; the historical, as a description of the processes by which that witness was transformed into dogma; and the philosophical, as the critique and corrective of the culture upon these given elements. But the relative weight and value of these several factors would vary from dogmatician to dogmatician, some even disclaiming this title on the grounds that dogma has no hold upon them.

JAROSLAV PELIKAN

Bibliography

W. Gasz, *Geschichte der protestantischen Dogmatik.*

EASTERN CHRISTIANITY

There are two groups of Eastern churches: 1) those forming together the *Orthodox Church* (including the ancient Byzantine Patriarchates of Constantinople, Alexandria, Antioch, Jerusalem, and the national churches of Russia, Greece, Yugoslavia, Bulgaria, Roumania, Georgia, etc.) and 2) the churches which rejected the Byzantine "canon" of Orthodoxy during the great christological controversies of the fifth through the seventh centuries (the Coptic Church of Egypt, the Armenian Church, the Nestorian communities in Iraq, etc.). In this article we will deal exclusively with the Eastern Orthodox Church. "Eastern" by its historical development, the Orthodox Church is no longer confined to one geographical area; not less than five million Orthodox Christians live permanently in the New World, and Orthodox communities exist today in nearly each country and region of the world. Although organized as "autocephalous," i.e., independent-national or territorial bodies, all the Orthodox churches hold the same doctrine, have the same tradition of worship and an identical canonical structure. Each church is governed by its own hierarchy (bishops, priests, deacons) with the highest authority and the final decision in all matters belonging to the Episcopate. The Patriarch of Constantinople has in the whole Church a primacy of honor. The laity forms an active element of the Church for, according to the Encyclical letter of the Eastern Patriarchs (1848), the "preservation of Truth belongs to the whole body of the Church."

The Orthodox churches include today a great variety of national traditions, languages and local particularities. But they all have a common *historical background;* the Christian Orthodox world of Byzantium. It is in Byzantium, in the "Christianized Roman Empire of the East" (G. Ostrogorsky), as it developed after the conversion of the Emperor Constantine (312), that the churches of Asia Minor, Greece, Syria, and Egypt acquired that common pattern of life, those thought-forms and that tradition of worship and spirituality which still shapes their organization and life. It was from Byzantium and in its Byzantine form that Christianity spread to the Slavs of the Balkans and to Russia (ninth and tenth centuries). And though each national church had of course its own "spirit" and made important contributions to the common tradition (cf., for example, the spiritual and theological creativeness of the Russian Church, which after the collapse of Constantinople in 1453 and until the Revolution of 1917 occupied a position of leadership in the Orthodox world), Byzantine inheritance has remained and still constitutes the pattern and the "canon" of Eastern Orthodoxy.

It is not easy to give a short and simple definition of "Orthodoxy" in its content. The Eastern Orthodox Church has never been challenged by a crisis comparable to that of Reformation in the West and which would have forced it to express its faith and life in *definitions*. On the other hand, the concept of *sacred tradition*, which for the Orthodox Church constitutes the norm of belief, cannot be reduced to a series of doctrinal statements, to a clearly formulated "minimum." It is a "whole" in which all parts are equally vital but whose real significance can be grasped only within the context of the whole. One can distinguish at least three essential elements in the Orthodox Tradition: 1) the *dogmatic tradition*, 2) the *liturgical tradition*, and 3) the *spiritual tradition*.

The dogmatic tradition. The Orthodox Church claims to have preserved the Christian faith in its fullness and to be therefore *the* One, Holy, Catholic, and Apostolic Church. This claim is rooted in the Orthodox doctrine of the Church as the "Pillar and Ground of the Truth," the Body of Christ and the fellowship of the Holy Spirit, which eternally guides her "into all truth." The Church does not possess a single organ of infallibility, but is infallible in its universal agreement, by the impossibility of its accepting as truth anything that is contrary to the guidance of the Holy Spirit. There are two sources of that Catholic faith: the Scriptures and the Tradition, but in Tradition nothing can ever be in contradiction with the Scriptures. Tradition is the "spiritual reading of Scriptures," the *life* of the Word of God in the Church. For varous reasons the Orthodox theologians did not take part in the great Western controversies about the Bible, and so far have not expressed the Orthodox point of view on the main issues of these controversies. The Orthodox Church, however, firmly believes in the Divine Inspiration of the Scriptures in their totality and in the necessity for anyone to interpret the Bible within the Church, i.e., in the light of her Tradition. As to the Tradition itself, it has many "expressions," of which the most important are: 1) The dogmatical definitions of the *Seven Ecumenical Councils* (Trinity, Christology, Mariology, Holy Icons). 2) The testimony of the *Fathers.* They are the theologians whom the Church Universal has recognized as true exponents, interpreters and defenders of her faith. The most important among the Fathers are: St. Athanasius, the Cappadocian theologians: St. Basil, St. Gregory of Nazianzen, St. Gregory of Nyssa; St. Cyril of Alexandria, St. John Chrysostom, St. Maximus the Confessor, St. John Damascene, St. Gregory Palamas. Their testimony is neither dead authority nor an infallible source of truth. It is rather the general spirit of their work, the "catholicity" of their minds and their loyalty to the Church that the Orthodox Church considers as normative for all theological work. 3) The *canons,* as formulated by the Councils and the Fathers. The canons regulate the Church's life but are not juridical norms. They describe and defend Orthodox ecclesiology rather than define it. 4) The *tradition of worship.* Many teachings and doctrines of the Orthodox Church have no other explicit source but the liturgy; i.e., Mariology, the Saints, the prayers for the dead, etc. (Cf. below.)

The liturgical tradition. For the Orthodox the liturgy is much more than the "corporate worship" of the Church. It is above all the "actualization" of the Church herself, her participation in the glorified Body of Christ, in the Kingdom, which for this world is still the "Kingdom to come." "Heaven on earth"—such is an early definition of worship in which the Orthodox recognize their liturgical experience. In and through worship the Church "becomes what she is"—the fellowship of the Holy Spirit, the new People of God. One can distinguish in the Orthodox liturgical tradition: the liturgy of Initiation: Baptism and Holy Chrism; the Eucharist, which is the total and highest realization of the Church in her fullness; the worship that sanctifies the *time:* daily cycle, weekly cycle, and yearly cycle; finally, many rites sanctifying the life of the family and the individual. The Orthodox worship is described and exposited in more than twenty-five liturgical books. The most important are: The Liturgicon, containing the texts of the eucharistic services (St. John Chrysostom and St. Basil) and the sacraments; the Octoechos with the hymns of the weekly cycle, the twelve Menaia (Yearly Cycle), and the two Triodia (Lent and the Easter cycle).

The spiritual tradition. Both the doctrinal and the liturgical traditions of the Orthodox Church point to an *ideal of holiness.* The "cult of saints" is based on the certitude that the grace of God, given in Christ, has a power of transformation and transfiguration; that human nature has through the Incarnation become "adequate" for the reception of the Spirit and "deification" (theosis). The Spiritual Fathers, the saints, are the teachers in this quest for the "acquisition of the Holy Spirit." In this way one of the latest Russian saints, St. Seraphim of Sarov, has defined the goal of Christian life. The spiritual tradition is constituted by the writings describing both the way of man to God and the fruits of his communion with God— his mystical experience, the contemplation of the light of Mount Thabor. From the early Fathers of the Desert: St. Anthony, St. Pakhomius, St. Isaac of Syria, St. John the Ladder, it continues in an unbroken succession to the great Byzantine mystics: St. Symeon the Young (eleventh century), St. Gregory Palamas (fourteenth century); and the Russian saints and spiritual teachers of the eighteenth and nineteenth centuries: St. Tikhon of Zadonsk, Paissy Velichkovsky, St. Seraphim of Sarov, and the "startzy" of Optino. Many classical texts of this spiritual tradition have been collected in the volumes of "Philocalia."

ALEXANDER SCHMEMANN

Bibliography

S. Bulgakov, *The Orthodox Church.*
G. P. Fedotov, *Treasury of Russian Spirituality.*

F. Gavin, *Some Aspects of Contemporary Greek Orthodox Thought*.

J. M. Nussey, *The Byzantine World*.

A. Schmemann, *Historical Road of Orthodoxy*.

ECUMENISM

The term and its use. The word ecumenical is derived from the Greek *oikoumene* which meant originally the whole inhabited world (*oikos* = house). In the course of history we can disinguish seven meanings of the word: a) pertaining to or representing the whole inhabited earth (thus, e.g., in Acts 17:31, Matt. 24:14); b) pertaining to or representing the whole of the Roman Empire (thus in Luke 2:2 and in the writings of the early fathers); c) pertaining to or representing the whole of the Church (the "ecumenical" councils are councils of the whole Empire, but as such they represent the whole Church); d) that which has universal ecclesiastical validity (the Eastern Church speaks of three "ecumenical doctors," and in the sixteenth century the three creeds were first described as "ecumenical" creeds); e) pertaining to the world-wide missionary outreach of the Church (thus the Ecumenical Methodist Conferences since 1881); f) pertaining to the relations between and unity of two or more churches or of Christians of various confessions (this is a modern use of the word which originated in the nineteenth century, especially in the World Evangelical Alliance); g) expressing a consciousness of belonging to the world-wide Christian fellowship and a desire for unity with other churches (again a modern use— In the middle of the nineteenth century Henri Dunant, founder of the Red Cross, spoke of the "ecumenical spirit" of the Y.M.C.A.).

The more general use of the term dates from the 1920's when the Stockholm and Lausanne Conferences brought representatives of many churches together. The Oxford Conference of 1937 stated: "They (the churches) are ecumenical insofar as they attempt to realize the Una Sancta, the fellowship of Christians who acknowledge the one Lord."

It follows from the above that ecumenism has the two following aspects: first, the study of the faith, order, life and work of the churches as they are and of their relations with each other; second, the study of the nature of the unity and universality of the Church and of the ways and means through which the churches may arrive at a fuller manifestation of that unity and universality.

Ecumenism as a descriptive science. Sound knowledge about the real convictions and the actual life of the different churches is the indispensable basis of ecumenical study. In the centuries preceding our own the main preoccupation in dealing with other churches has been apologetical and polemical. It is a great gain that in our century all confessions (including Roman Catholicism) have produced scholars whose first concern in describing other churches is to understand the life of those churches from within. Such objectivity does not necessarily lead to a general relativism. The task of the ecumenist is precisely to combine deep understanding with a fundamentally critical attitude based on his own deepest theological convictions.

This descriptive ecclesiology (*Konfessionskunde*) is closely related to church history, but it differs from the latter in that it deals with the faith and life of the churches as they are today. It must not merely include a study of their confessions, creeds and liturgies, but also an analysis of the message which they proclaim in fact through their preaching, their theological contributions, their church activities, their evangelism and mission, and their attitude to the world around them. At the same time it must seek to ascertain the role which each church plays in the ecumenical movement, and its fundamental attitude to the issues of church unity. Such descriptive ecclesiology must at the same time include a study of the modern ecumenical movement, its origins, its growth, its problems.

The theological dimension of ecumenism. Descriptive ecumenism must be accompanied by a consideration of the basic theological issues involved in the encounter of the churches and their search for unity. The purpose of this theological approach to the ecumenical problem must provide us with clear criteria for our evaluation of the various attitudes of the churches to church unity and for a clarification of our own ecumenical position.

The theological starting point is that the Church as the one, undivided People of God and the unbroken Body of Christ belongs to the fundamental biblical *kerygma*. When the New Testament speaks of churches in the plural it never means self-contained bodies which live largely in isolation from each other and in many cases do not even have altar and pulpit fellowship with each other. According to the New Testament, unity belongs not only to the *bene esse,* but to the *esse* of the Church. And this unity which is given in the fact of the one Lord, must become manifest and incarnate, as the Lord Himself became manifest and incarnate (John 17).

Unity in the context of the whole calling of the Church. Ecumenism is concerned with the unity of the Church, but it cannot be concerned with unity alone. For all depends on the kind of unity which is envisaged. Unity as a goal in itself, in isolation from the total calling of the Church, may and has often proved to be sterile.

Ecumenism must be concerned with that unity which expresses the obedient and grateful response of the churches to their whole calling. A statement issued by the Central Committee of the World Council of Churches in 1951 says that ecumenical "is properly used to describe everything that relates to the whole task of the whole Church to bring the Gospel to the whole world." Thus the unity with which ecumenism is concerned is not merely unity of ecclesiastical organization, but unity in all realms which belong to the mission of the Church: teaching, worship, sacrament, mission, service to the world.

Historically the ecumenical movement arose as, in different ways, the New Testament understanding of the

Church took hold once again of the minds and hearts of men in separate churches. Similarly the ecumenical movement can only arrive at results as that vision of the Church in its oneness, its universality, its world-embracing calling, its uniqueness in relation to the world penetrates more deeply into all the churches.

Constitutive factors of unity. What are the constitutive, indispensable factors of full Christian unity? That is the decisive issue in the field of ecumenism. It is difficult enough to bring together churches which, while differing in matters of faith and order, have the same conception of the conditions which need to be fulfilled in order to achieve true unity. As a matter of fact, there are different confessional conceptions as to what constitutes unity and there are divergences within the confessional families on this subject. Thus the ecumenical discussion is dominated by the question: what unity is required before two or more churches can decide to unite altogether?

The main positions can be briefly described as follows: 1) the main requirement is an agreement concerning the central affirmations of the faith; 2) the main requirement is an agreement on all points which are normally included in the credal or confessional documents of a church; 3) the main requirements are an agreement concerning the central affirmations of the faith together with an agreement on the right order of the Church (historic episcopate); 4) the main requirements are an agreement on all points which have been decided by ecumenical councils and a doctrinal, as well as practical acceptance, of the traditional order of the Church.

It will be seen that the important differences have to do with the degree of doctrinal unity which is required and with the relative emphasis to be given to "faith" and "order."

Closely connected is the question whether inter-communion is acceptable and desirable between churches which have not yet united. According to one position inter-communion is the consummation of full unity and can therefore only be practiced when such full unity has been achieved. According to the other position, inter-communion is an important step on the road toward unity.

The road toward unity. Ecumenism must also be concerned with the steps which the churches are taking or should take on the road toward unity.

a. *Cooperation.* This is a first indispensable step, for churches which have not learned to cooperate in matters of common concern will not arrive at the stage at which unity becomes spiritually possible. Such cooperation may begin with superficial matters, but must lead increasingly to common participation in the fundamental tasks of the Church: common witness, mutual service, common worship, etc. The danger involved in this form of inter-church relations is that it may so easily become a substitute for full unity. In order to avoid this it is essential that churches should also take the next step.

b. *Conversation.* The churches have for a long time lived in isolation from each other. True ecumenism requires that they should enter into serious conversation with each other. This conversation must begin by an effort to get to know each other's convictions, but must lead increasingly to a common confrontation of the question whether they are justified in remaining separate. Whenever such conversations are undertaken with that sense of proportion which the Bible gives, it will be found that there are many differences between the churches which are unimportant or cannot be theologically justified. The question then arises whether the remaining differences are of such importance that to proceed further on the road toward unity would in fact amount to betrayal of deep convictions.

c. *Reunion.* Reunion means that any obstacles toward full unity have been removed and that the oneness of the churches concerned is clearly manifested. But this may take very different forms. It is a grave mistake to suppose that the ultimate goal of ecumenism is a monolithic centralized church structure for the whole world. The churches in the World Council have expressly repudiated such a conception. Manifest unity is perfectly compatible with variety, independence and decentralization. The New Testament Church had remarkable variety and was in no sense a super-church, but it manifested to all who had eyes to see that the People of God were one single family.

The ecumenical movement and the World Council of Churches. When we speak of the ecumenical movement we think on the one hand of all the organizations on the local, national and international level which bring churches and individual Christians of differing churches together, and on the other hand of persons in all churches (even those who do not participate in the World Council) who are working for the unity of the Church.

The ecumenical movement can be characterized as an attempt to express that unity which we have already in our common allegiance to Jesus Christ. This is a very imperfect unity and must never be thought of as a substitute for the full unity described in the New Testament. But it must not be underestimated in that it is a great gift of God and that it enables us to render witness to an important aspect of the Christian message which has been obscured for a long time.

The World Council of Churches is that sector of the ecumenical movement in which the churches as such meet and work together. As the well-known Toronto statement of 1950 states clearly, it is not a super-church; it does not force churches to unite with each other; it does not propagate one particular conception of unity. It is rather a fellowship of churches which acknowledge Jesus Christ as God and Savior and which desire to enter into constructive relations with each other. It is a platform for serious conversation about the issues of unity, a means for cooperation in matters of common concern, an organ of common witness when it is given to the churches to speak together to the world.

Thus the World Council of Churches is not *the* answer to the problem of Christian unity, but an instrument which helps the churches in the fulfillment of their calling to unity in Christ.

W. A. VISSER 'T HOOFT

Bibliography

A History of the Ecumenical Movement (ed. by Rouse and Neill).
The Christian Hope and the Task of the Church (in which the "Toronto" statement of 1950 is reprinted on pp. 9 ff.).
The Universal Church in God's Design (Amsterdam Assembly Series).

EROS AND AGAPE

It is a generally accepted concept in theological circles, at least since the days of St. Augustine, that Christianity is "the religion of love." In using the expression "religion of love," something clear and definite is intended. Love has been spoken of as an univocal and well-known entity, as if the word *love* were always used in the same sense whenever and wherever it appears in the history of Christianity. In other words, Christians have spoken quite unproblematically of love without being aware that behind this term enormous problems and the greatest contradictions lie concealed.

Not all problems which appear in this connection can be taken up in this discussion. Only one, the greatest and most fateful, shall be touched upon here. The circumstance which has contributed to complicate matters was that the Christian message of the love of God, God's love which forgives sins—this love for which the New Testament has formed a special word of its own, God's *agape*—encountered from the very beginning a totally different concept of love, namely, that of the Platonic *eros*. As the Christian message entered the Hellenistic world, it was unavoidable that these two streams, although they flowed from such different sources, would become confluent. A mixture, a fusion, a synthesis of the two love-motives occurred. The most noble result of this fusion was St. Augustine's concept of *caritas*, which not only influenced the Middle Ages but continues to exert influence up to the present day.

One cannot discuss the meaning of the Christian idea of love at all if one has not first analyzed and clarified the

threads twisted together by various internally related motives. The problem of *"eros* and *agape"* is not only an
historical problem, but also a systematic problem of the
present day, inasmuch as contemporary thinking is growing on ground where the mixture of motives has become
meaningful. One cannot talk unproblematically about love
as if the meaning and structure of the Christian idea of
love would self-evidently be clear and univocal and sufficiently defined if one simply uses the term *love*. One has to
learn how to differentiate between *eros* and *agape*.

What does "love" mean in the New Testament? *What
does* agape *mean?* The New Testament uses this new word
because it must communicate a message of a new kind,
namely, God's love revealed through Jesus Christ, given
through Jesus Christ. We can never imagine on our own
what *agape* is, because *agape* does not fall into the framework of human possibilities. *Agape* is the love which God
proved to us by giving His only Son (John 3:16). If that
had not happened, we never would have heard anything
about *agape. Agape* is the love which Christ proved to us
by giving Himself unto death for us. In Romans 5:8 the
Apostle Paul says: "God shows his love toward us in that
while we were yet sinners Christ died for us." And in I
John 3:16 it is written: "By this we know love (*agape*)
that he laid down his life for us." In his love God, the
Highest, enters our earthly human dimension. In Christ
He becomes as one of us. As Christ He takes up our
burden and carries the sins of the world. Christ's love,
Christ's *agape,* means that He descended for us into the
lowest depths; He makes Himself one with the sinners,
with those who have acted against the holy will of God
and therefore stand under the judgment of the law of God.
Agape is God's love which forgives sins. Therefore Jesus
says: "I came not to call the righteous, but sinners"
(Matt. 9:13). God's *agape* does not mean that He searches
for that which is precious as such, but it means that He
looks for what is lost (Luke 15). This is the love which
drives Christ unto death on the cross. *Agape* is "*agape* of
the cross."

This love of God in Christ is what gives everything that is called Christian love its structure. As it was Christ's love which drove Him, the one and only just one, to become one with the many, thus it is the same love which makes out of the many a unity (I Cor. 12:12). *Agape* is that "binding tie" (Col. 3:14) which makes of the many members the one body of Christ (Rom. 12:15) and which accomplishes the result of the various members serving each other in love, each according to the gift given to him. On the whole it is said of *agape:* "It does not look for its own" (I Cor. 13:5). It is selfless, serving, and helping love.

We are transferred into a totally different world if we ask what love means in the Greek-Hellenistic frame of reference. *What does* eros *mean?* We receive the best answer if we turn to Plato. The background is formed here by his teaching of the two worlds: above the world of the senses arches the world of the eternal ideas, this world which at one time was the home of the human soul before it was bound to the body and with it bound to the prison of the world of the senses. The soul, however, retains a memory of its pre-existing mode of being; this is the reason why the soul is conscious of its present misery and is grasped by the longing for a higher world. With this we arrive at the point where *eros* belongs; because *eros* is exactly the longing of the soul upward toward the world of ideas.

The Platonic *eros* is desiring love. As such it is marked by two elements: the consequences of a present want, and the direction of this want toward the freedom of a higher and more blissful state. The first is the starting point, the latter is the aim. *Eros* is rightfully called a "wanting to have." According to its structure it is egocentric; it circles around its own ego, its needs, and its satisfaction. Its desire is, however, not directed toward the nether world of the senses. *Eros* is love directed toward the higher regions; it is the longing upward toward the world of ideas, and in relation to the present world it assumes the form of fleeing from the world. But even in its highest and most sublimated form it never abandons its desiring, egocentric direction.

Eros and *agape* signify two principally different orientations of life, two fundamental motives which compete with each other. Each is the highest of its kind.

Before we proceed, it will be beneficial if we compare these two concepts in their typical differentiation. However, first a comment will have to be made. If we say that *eros* is egocentric love and *agape* selfless love; that *eros* is self-affirmation, while *agape* is self-surrender; it readily occurs that the idea of selflessness and self-surrender is considered valuable, and the idea of self-affirmation valueless. With the influence of the transformation of values through Christianity this conclusion seems unavoidable. For men of antiquity self-affirmation and egocentric action were equally self-understood values. We have to characterize, however, the different structures of *eros* and *agape* and thus place them, in this sense, antithetically side by side.

The history of the Christian idea of love is essentially the history of how these two perceptions of love—*agape* and *eros*—were first joined and then sundered again. The mixture of both is obvious in gnosticism, where even that which Plato called the "vulgar eros" was identified with the *agape* of Christianity. The mixture of motives becomes evident also in Alexandrian theology, culminating in the sentence of Origen, that one can say with equal right, as the first letter of John says, "God is *agape*" and "God is *eros*."

The process of amalgamation is found in its final form in the doctrine of *caritas* in Augustine. Here neo-Platonic perceptions of *eros* and New Testament perceptions of *agape* have undergone a peculiar union. Love is, according to Augustine, an elemental human drive. It is founded upon the essence of man which is always to desire, to seek his *bonum*. If he directs his desire toward perishable, temporal things, desire takes on the character of *cupiditas*, that is, false love. If man directs his desire upward and thus seeks his satisfaction in God and in the eternal, desire is called *caritas*—that is, the right kind of love, because only in higher things can man really find satisfaction for his needs. God is at the same time "the highest good and the good which cannot be lost." Thus the love directed toward God becomes the right kind of self-love. If Augustine moves entirely on neo-Platonic grounds, the element of Christian *agape* in his thought emerges in such a way that *caritas* can occur only through the fact that God descended to us in Christ and became humanly accessible to us.

The main problem of the doctrine of love during the Middle Ages grew out of the inner tension within the doctrine of *caritas:* if love is principally desire, that is, egocentric love, how can one arrive at a really selfless love of God? This is the primary problem for scholasticism as well as for mysticism. As a final offshoot of this problem, the "disinterested" love of quietist mysticism could be noted.

If the Renaissance meant primarily a revival of the *eros*-motive, the Reformation meant an even more decisive revival of the fundamental Christian *agape*-motive. One can discern this most clearly in Luther's central idea of justification by faith alone. In opposition to the scholastic doctrine of the *"fides caritate formata"* which was founded upon Augustine's doctrine of *caritas,* Luther claims that man becomes justified *sola fide* (by faith alone). It is not "faith formed by *caritas*" which justifies. If *caritas* is disjoined from justification, it would seem to an external observer as if Luther had pushed love into the background and was interested only in faith. In reality, what happens here is something quite different: the *caritas*-love, this mixture of *eros* and *agape,* is turned aside to make way for *agape* in the New Testament sense. The community with God has its foundation, not in something in us, but exclusively in Christ. But, says Luther, *"Christus non est caritas mea"*—Christ is not my love (*eros, agape*) but God's love (*agape*). The fact that man is justified and taken into the communion with God testifies, not to his love for God but to God's love for him in Christ. As such, nothing remains which man could win with his love. Non-christocentric love and ethical life are no longer meritorious. Any thought of merit and any form of religious eudaemonism are excluded. The way is cleared thereby for a new ethics, an ethics in the Christian sense of the word, ruled by love which "does not seek its own," but gives itself freely, ready, if it should come to pass, to be "a lost love." With this, love has regained its New Testament meaning and has become "the *agape* of the cross" or —to use Luther's expressive phrase—it has become *"amor crucis ex cruce natus"*—the love of the cross born of the cross.

ANDERS NYGREN
Translated by Werner Rode

ESCHATOLOGY

Eschatology is the doctrine of what is to be expected unconditionally. It has its foundation in the contemporary experience of the unconditioned as encountered by faith. Eschatological hope has its foundation, therefore, in faith. Faith necessarily turns into hope, for faith can retain the certainty of having encountered the unconditioned only insofar as it looks at the unconditioned as also defining and fulfilling the future.

The hope of the Christian faith is rooted in the immediacy of God's action with man through Jesus Christ and, therefore, in the present state of life into which Christ puts man. In a twofold way this state is prophecy (or promise) of that which is to come. On the one hand God's action, and the state in which it establishes us, has *finality;* this is why faith is deeply aware of that which *remains* unconditioned through all catastrophes of personal life or through all catastrophes of the world. On the other hand, God's action through Christ puts us in contradiction with our empirical reality and consequently into a paradoxical position. This position as such has a preliminary character and points beyond itself. In it faith becomes certain of what comes unconditionally. Eschatology speaks thus of that which remains and that which comes.

God acts with mankind within the dialectics of both

the Law and the Gospel. That is to say, we are assigned by God both to the state of responsibility to Him and to the state of salvation: as such we are not rejected by His love in spite of the fact that we cannot justify ourselves before Him. In this state of salvation, we are accepted as His children. From the view of eschatology, the state of responsibility implies that our responsibility never ends, that even at the end we are faced with a responsibility to God (the judgment). Similarly, the present state of salvation means, from the view of eschatology, that the love of God which grasps us through the Gospel remains directed to everybody unalterably and that it will resolve, in the glory of "eternal life," the contradiction that men, although declared to be the sons of God, remain both in sin and before the inevitability of death. Eschatology is therefore within the dialectics of the Law and the Gospel.

Christian hope is concerned with the future of every human being; however, it is not solely preoccupied with this. Although concerned with us as individuals, God's action nevertheless transpires in such a way that we are called, through Jesus Christ, into a communion which is Christ's Church. The Church, however, is engaged in the struggle for the advent of universal salvation—that is, for the dominion of the grace of God. Thus the Christian expectation embraces at the same time both the future of the Church and the goal of the history of mankind; moreover, as individual persons, we are in an indestructible relation and therefore in a communion of fate with that extension of our own physical nature—the whole cosmos. The vanity (*nichtigkeit*) of the natural world (Romans 8:20) is the reflection of the fall of mankind. The hope for man thus includes also the hope for the natural world. Consequently Christian eschatology is personal, universalistic, and cosmic at the same time. The fulfillment of persons, the goal of the history of mankind, and the renewal of the cosmos cannot be separated from one another. Faith expects all this from the one and the same act of God in the elevated Jesus Christ (*Parousia*). All this together makes for the fulfillment of the kingdom of God in Jesus Christ.

The method of eschatology corresponds to this foundation of the Christian hope. Eschatology cannot dogmatize the whole apocalyptic substance of Holy Scriptures in a biblicistic way. The method of eschatology has to present concretely—by listening to the biblical message—the real necessity witnessed in this message, in which the presence of God's action in Christ becomes a promise of the future, and has to apply it as criterion for dogmatic acceptance of biblical thoughts and images of last things.

The hope for man. The grace of God in Jesus Christ transplants, as of now, everyone who has faith into the "eternal life" (The Gospel according to St. John). However, this life is still "hidden with Christ in God" (Col. 3:3), because of the veil of sinfulness which continues to cover our empirical life and because of the inevitability of death. The Christian is called in the power of Christ into the battle against sin. But he knows also that the state of sin which he shares equally with all mankind is not overcome in this earthly life. Man remains as "flesh" until death. He expects future freedom from sin as promised to him by the justice-bearing judgment of God. This happens beyond death by God's power to make new. Man's assurance beyond death is founded upon God's having called him into a strictly personal bond of love: He will fulfill what He has begun (I Cor. 1:9; Phil. 1:6). This certainty is something totally different from the Platonic idea of an "immortality of the soul." The latter idea denies the death of at least the spiritual part of the person, which supposedly is free from evil. Christian faith, however, takes man as a whole, ontologically as well as ethically. We sin as whole beings and we die as whole beings. We expect the state beyond death only in God's act of the resurrection. This act, like death, is concerned with the whole human being. In the question of death and the new life we do not distinguish dualistically between soul (or spirit) and body. But we are concerned with the person and his individual form of being. To die means that God destroys totally the earthly form of the person; to be resurrected means that God gives to the person a new, eternal form of being of body and soul. Thus the resurrection will be a transformation of the whole human being but will maintain at the same time the identity of the person and his history with God.

We cannot expect our entrance into eternal life, which is prepared for us by God's grace, in any other way than by going through a final judgment, because the presence of God's action remains with us always under the Law and the Gospel. As we can attain grace daily only in a penitential surrender to God's judgment, the same applies at the entrance to eternity. The final decision about our life is made here. Beyond this the last judgment will also be a retribution. Grace gives salvation to all who have faith. But this salvation is to be distinguished from the rewards and punishments meted out to those who are saved according to the measure of their earthly triumphs and failures (I Cor. 3:14 f).

Shall all be saved? The Christian can answer this question only by saying that, like himself, so every human being stands in a state of responsibility until death, in the decision between faith and unbelief. Each and every man can become lost; yet in this knowledge we commend ourselves, as does every other human being, to the grace of God which leads us home. Consequently, we are not allowed a theoretical answer to this question. Under no condition can theology teach the *apokatastasis* (the resurrection of all). Were it to do so, theology in its eschatological teachings would fall outside the province of the dialectics of the Law and the Gospel.

The hope for history. In faith we know that our history moves toward its end, because the structure of history stands in contradiction to God's will of salvation as revealed in Jesus Christ. The history of mankind is defined by the laws of competition and the laws of struggle as well as the power of evil. Christianity shall not be idle. It should, in any new historical situation, do what is demanded in order to create a just order and to mitigate the hardships of the existence of mankind. But Christianity will always move within narrow limits: it does not become master of the law of death, of evil, of the demonic in history. As a whole there is no progress in history toward the Kingdom of God. We expect the coming of the Kingdom out of the transcendent: Jesus Christ shall come in "Glory" out of the hiddenness and limitation of his Kingdom. This means that he will break the structure of this world which is destined to perish (I Cor. 7:31). His *parousia* shall be the end and the aim of history. But, as such, this means that the *judgment of history* is an open judgment pronounced on the open and hidden evil in the history of mankind, a bringing into the open, and a bringing to honor of the misunderstood and hidden truth and justice. In this event Christ shall finally make powerless the superhuman power of evil which, in opposition to Him and His Church, came to highest consciousness and power (Anti-Christ; II Thess. 2:7 ff). The fulfillment of the Kingdom of God, according to the witness of the Holy Scriptures, does not happen in chronological progression during history, but happens by going through an acute final battle.

The idea of an intermediate reign, a pre-fulfillment (*millenium, chiliasm*) between our history and the eternal Kingdom of God, cannot be founded theologically and must be rejected as totally contradictory. However, this idea contains the truth that God's eternal Kingdom shall be not only the end, but also the fulfillment and completion of our history with all its toil and struggle.

The hope for the cosmos. This our world of nature is, for faith, the creation of God, but not His final will. We become familiar with the world to the extent that its laws of the struggle of being and death are attached to our sin. The salvation of mankind through Christ will therefore end as well the present lowliness of creation and will free it for a form of glory which corresponds to the glory of the children of God. We cannot hope for the transformation of our own corporeality without hoping also for the whole of nature into which we are so closely woven. In the same manner as we cannot imagine the likeness of our future life in the eternal world of God, so we cannot imagine the new creation. Eschatology must emphasize that God will make an end to this cosmos, but at the same time that His coming creation will be a renewal and a completion of the world as it is now. In this way we may speak of a connection between the two worlds and see in nature, as it is now, a parable and a prelude of the coming world of glory.

PAUL ALTHAUS
Translated by Werner Rode

Bibliography

Paul Althaus, *Die letzten Dinge.*
Emil Brunner, *Das Ewige als Zukunft und Gegenwart.*

ETERNITY AND TIME

Man's knowledge of time and eternity derives from his experience of change. Without change he could neither know anything nor be aware either of the passage of time or the presence of eternity. But change occurs, and he knows things, is aware of time, and, in some measure, knows eternity.

Things occur and events happen in space and time. In contrast to space where we place things by using three pairs of co-ordinates—above and below, before and behind, right and left—time offers but a single and irreversible pair: before and after. That is to say, the characteristic feature of man's experience of time is its successiveness, its passage. But this feature is not, as Kant thought, just a form of man's understanding, but rather a characteristic of things and events themselves. This is most clearly illustrated by a musical phrase of, say, five notes, which, if played simultaneously, might produce an harmonious chord, but would not thus be a melody. Time, succession, passage clearly enters into the very constitution of a musical phrase; the notes must follow each other in a certain order for it to be, and for it to be known. Yet a musical phrase is but a clear example of a quite universal feature of all human experience.

The knower and the known alike are subject to succession, passage, to change and finitude. As Heraclitus said long ago, *"Panta rhei"*—everything is in flux.

But change is not merely temporal. There is more in it, and we experience more, than mere succession, mere passage. To know a musical phrase may involve hearing five different notes in a certain sequence; but it also involves a transcendence of that succession so that the five notes are not known as a mere succession of different notes but as a togetherness, a unity that transcends the succession. Such transcendence involves both the listener and the notes he hears; the listener, or he would not be able to "hold the notes together"; the notes, or they could not constitute the unity that is known as a melody.

What is thus manifestly true of the apprehension of the particular change-sequence we call a melody is true of all experience of change. We can know things only within time's passage, in succession, yet in and with the succession we apprehend something that transcends it, and thus demonstrate our own inherent ability to transcend it also. A sentence, a play, a novel, an historical narrative, an historical event, a scientific hypothesis—these and all other objects of human knowledge illustrate the doubly duplex character of man's experience, in which both man himself and the objects he knows share the successiveness of time and yet transcend it.

Such duplex character of human experience underlies the traditional distinction between time and eternity. The facts of succession have given rise to the view of time as a series of irreversible moments, finite or infinite in number, while the character of that which transcends succession has suggested the idea of eternity as the *nunc stans,* the constant "now." This traditional philosophical distinction of time from eternity has perennially embarrassed the theologian who has to deal with biblical language about God. For the philosopher God is eternal, dwelling in an eternal "now," entirely apart from succession. But the Bible speaks with unashamed anthropomorphism about a God who acts in history and meets with men. But if the twin characteristics of passage and the transcendence of passage are ingredient in all human experience, then a quite new approach is possible to the problems of time and eternity, of God and the world.

When we listen to five successive notes and hear a melody we perceive the transcendent quality, as it were, directly. But not all the transcendental elements of experience can be thus directly apprehended. Some need the help of "clues," elements in the succession where the "meaning" lies particularly near the surface. We read the successive words of a simple sentence and almost certainly apprehend its meaning directly. But when we read the successive sentences of a novel or a play we do not commonly perceive its meaning so directly. We find passages in the book, incidents or speeches in the play, which are especially "bearers of the meaning" of the whole, and which thereby become the starting point of interpretation. The success of an interpreter will vary in proportion to his sensitiveness to the clues, and to his ability to interpret his material in their terms. But because we speak of "clues," "meaning," and "interpretation" it must not be supposed that the transcendent, unifying element is therefore the mere product of the interpreter's imagination. Certainly an interpreter needs imagination to apprehend the clues, as it is necessary to have a "musical ear" to hear five notes as a melody; but the interpretation based on the clues is not in essence the product of subjective imagination any more than the melody from the five notes. We need to repeat our earlier finding, that transcendence belongs both to the subject that knows and to the object known.

The historian also works by "clues." His "book" is the period of history of which he writes; his "clues" events or persons or ideas from that period or elsewhere. The clue does not need to be near the surface throughout the story; incidents may have both positive and negative relationship to the clue (say to the abolition of slavery) which in turn must be able to exhibit the unity of the whole. The "truth" of history does not consist of claiming that the interpretation offered is the only possible and the entirely complete one, but it does mean that the interpretation offered really describes the objective order of history, even if, for a full understanding, the material needs description under other clues besides. We may illustrate this by imagining the difference that would emerge if the history of Britain were to be retold as part of the history of Europe, or observing the differences in the history of the Second World War as it comes to be written in the United States, Great Britain, Italy and Russia! Again, no historian will deny that the use of imagination belongs to his craft, but that does not make his product unreal; rather does his imagination make him sensitive to the clues to history that will unlock its meaning.

The Christian's faith finds expression in a "gospel" or "good news." At the very center of his religion is something uncommonly like a piece of history. Indeed it is history—with some important differences. The most important difference is that the Christian claims finality and completeness for the "clue" with which he unlocks the meaning of the story of the universe. There is, he claims, one central clue, the life, death, resurrection and ascension of Jesus Christ. That central clue has absorbed many clues from the Old Testament and elsewhere into itself. Historical events with already known meanings like the Exodus under Pharaoh are used to interpret the Last Supper and the Cross; historical persons like Elijah are used to point the purpose of John the Baptist; prophecies (i.e., past analyses of historical situations made from a divine perspective and yielding previsions of the nearer and sometimes the more remote future), like Zechariah 9:9 f., are used to indicate the meaning of the entry into Jerusalem. Ultimately this concentration of clues focussing upon Jesus Christ asserts two things: 1) that Jesus Christ is the Son of God incarnate, living, dying, rising, reigning over us, securing us thereby to His eternal kingdom; 2) that He is the transcendent meaning of the whole universe. If we liken Him to the five notes we considered earlier, then He is the melody we hear. Or if, more illuminatingly, we think of Him as the unfinished book of the story of the universe that we are reading, Jesus Christ is its meaning, and we are at least past the place where that has become inescapably plain.

Once more, this is not the projection of Christian imagination into alien material. Just as we have in ourselves the power to transcend, the transcendent element is in the order outside of us. The transcendent character in the history, which is the Christian gospel, must itself be a will, for history is the sphere of the operation of wills. If that operation, which is a succession, is to have a transcendent element in it, it must be a will, just as a melody is musical because it transcends five separate musical notes. The transcendent has qualities of its own, as the melody has qualities that do not belong to the notes.

For the Christian, time is therefore not a long line at the end of which he will come upon eternity; rather is time the passage within which he knows both the passing things of this world, of which he himself is one, and those things that transcend the passage of the world, supreme among which is the eternal, transcendent God, of whom he learns most through the Christian community as it finds its life in Jesus Christ, who was and is the transcendent in the passage, the eternal in temporal, God in man. Not a timeless God and an eternity-bereft man, but a living God, active and incarnate as man in history, is the center of the Gospel.

JOHN MARSH

Bibliography

F. H. Brabant, *Time and Eternity in Christian Thought.*
O. Cullmann, *Christ and Time.*
John Marsh, *The Fullness of Time.*

ETHICS

As reflection on human conduct, Christian ethics aims to achieve clarity and consistency with respect to the ground and goal, the motives and norms, the means and the consequences of right action conceived as the response to and the working of the grace of God. Organically related to theology, it is faith seeking understanding in the realm of moral action, though of course it frequently achieves something other than systematic articulation, as for example in the Gospels. In its practical outcome it is "faith active through love" (Gal. 5:6), in obedience to the Great Commandment, "Thou shalt love the Lord thy God . . . and thy neighbor as thyself." This faith is a response to the living God whose love and righteous purpose are uniquely, if not exclusively, witnessed to in scripture and are manifest especially in the redemptive power of the life, the teaching and the death of Jesus, a power continuingly available through the Holy Spirit at work in and through the community of faith. Ultimately it is the work of God for the overcoming of man's sinful alienation from Him and for the fulfillment of man's personal and social salvation from the powers of evil. This fulfillment takes place only provisionally in history. Again and again through man's alienation it issues in tragedy. The Cross stands here as the tragic consequence of man's alienation, as the earnest of God's outreach to man, and as the openness of obedient love to the divine purpose.

Such formulations as these can denote basic features of the Christian conception of the ground and substance, the posture and the goal of Christian behavior. But they do no more than approximate the common denominator of the numerous forms of Christian ethics which have actually appeared in history. Having developed within the manifold community of the churches, Christian ethics, like Christian theology, has exhibited varying types and degrees of unity and difference; it has also expressed differing forms of piety. This variety is to be observed in the primitive and the early Christian churches, in the Byzantine and later Eastern churches, in Roman Catholicism (medieval and modern), in the right and left wings of the Reformation and their derivatives, down through the Enlightenment and the post-Enlightenment periods to the proliferation of Christian ethical outlooks in our own time. It is to be observed also in the multitude of

Christian social movements such as monasticism, chiliastic and other revolutionary trends, theocracy and other forms of authoritarianism, pietism and revivalism, the Social Gospel movement, and religious socialism.

Major divisions of this composite development may be viewed as "families" of Christendom and of Christian ethical outlook. In one type, for example, sacramental media, where the divine power is seen as present in given social realities or patterns, are emphasized; in another, prophetism, which sees the divine power primarily in the demand for personal and social decision in the name of a coming holy community, is prominent. The Catholic-Protestant split suggests another line of demarcation, a line that finds its analogue in certain non-Christian religions. Another distinction is made between the ethics of conscience, where the purity of inner disposition and motive is stressed, and the ethics of cultural values and responsibility, where action is judged primarily in terms of consequences. Moreover, varying types of church polity, for example, the episcopal and the congregational, tend to develop characteristic social philosophies in which the general structure of the polity itself serves as a model for social organization generally. Each of the different types of Christian ethics has believed itself able to find precedent and sanction in scripture or in the early Church. Thus, apart from any differentiation of types of Christian piety and ethics into "families," these types in general tend to be determined by their respective selection of differing norms or integrating concepts for the interpretation of scripture and of the Christian ethos.

Accordingly, a given form of Christian ethics will usually be an elaboration of some integrating concept, or of a cluster of concepts, drawn from scripture or from other sources claiming traditional or intrinsic prestige. Most familiar among these integrating concepts are: sacramental participation as the nexus of a sacramental society; natural law; the incarnation; the forgiveness of sins and justification by faith; the Two Kingdoms; the covenant; the Kingdom of God; Pentecost and the freedom of the Spirit; discipleship; the reign of Christ; the

new being in Christ; the responsible society; vocation.
Each of these is related in one way or another to love of
God and love of neighbor, and emphasis on one or
another of them is characteristic of the varying types of
piety.

These basic concepts lend themselves to variety of
interpretations; even in a given tradition they are subjected to changing interpretation. Sometimes in a changed
situation a concept will be replaced or radically modified,
perhaps because it appears momentarily to be exhausted,
or because it has acquired connotations ("ideological" or
"utopian") which are deemed unacceptable or perhaps
unchristian, or because a new situation serves to disclose
some latent facet of the concept. The idea of the Kingdom
of God, for example, has been given such a variety of
interpretations as the (inward) spiritualist and the cosmological; the immanental and the transcendental; the
"actualist" and the futurist; the evolutionary and the
revolutionary; we may add to these what is today called
"realized eschatology." Each view has its peculiar validity
and place in the Christian ethos of creation and redemption. The Bible and the traditions, then, provide a re-
pository of integrating concepts which are drawn upon
in the process of creative construction. The innovative
character of primitive Christianity has served at times
as a model for social criticism and reform; on the other
hand, the apparent lack of an articulated social ethics in
the New Testament has been interpreted as a sanction for
quietism, or for stressing the hope for the Second Coming
of Christ, or for withdrawal from "the world," or for
indifference to structural social problems.

The history of Christian ethics, especially in the modern
era and in our time, is a history of the conversations within
and between the "families" of Christian piety and ethos,
and also between certain of these "families" and groups
outside the Church—groups with which affinity is discovered, or groups which are viewed as inimical to Christian faith, or groups which are deemed to offer pertinent
challenge. In the midst of changing situations and of the
ongoing conversation, Christians as individuals and in

corporate groups have been continually confronted with the exigency of responding in new ways to the creative and redemptive power of God. This is particularly true in modern dynamic societies and in times of crisis.

Viewed across the centuries and across confessional boundaries, Christian ethics has not in reality achieved fixed articulation, though certain basic motifs persist or recur. Consequently, it remains always a matter of continuing enquiry seeking new understanding of the faith in a living God. This continuing enquiry and the demand for new response to the living God are particularly imperative in face of new forms of man's alienation from his fellows, from himself, and from God, forms of alienation growing out of class or ethnic, or nationalist and other societal attachments.

In addition to issues already mentioned and in connection with them, the liveliest recent conversations between the "families" of Christian ethos and between these families and groups or positions outside the Church, have had to do with the nature of Christian love (*Agape*), the significance of Christology in Christian ethics, the place (if any) of metaphysics or ontology, the relation of Christian faith to idealism and natural law, the claims of cultural relativism, the challenge of Marxism and of existentialism, and the problems of the application of Christian ethos to specific situations (casuistry). These conversations have been made particularly acute by "the storms of our times," and they have been accelerated by the ecumenical movement, the World Council of Churches, as it has attempted to come to terms with the pressing spiritual and social problems thrown up by "the storms."

The conversations regarding the nature of *Agape*, in face of sentimental perversions of it, have raised the question as to the relative significance of completely sacrificial love and of mutuality (particularly in the context of power relations). Analogous to this question is that of the relation between love and justice. Are love and justice mutually exclusive; or do they stand in creative tension with each other; or is justice the social-institutional expression of love; or is love, more narrowly defined, relevant primarily to person-to-person relations, and does it thus remain only interstitial in the social order? These questions are bound up with the perennial question regarding the relations between law—the Ten Commandments, the prophetic ethos of the Old Testament, justice (*suum cuique*), or positive law—and love, the problem of law and gospel. In some circles the answers to these questions are related strictly to the revelation in Christ (Christomonism); in other circles they are dealt with in a trinitarian manner which gives discrete significance to God the Father and the Holy Spirit, thus providing theological validity for justice or moral law as known apart from revelation through Christ. This latter view impinges upon the problem of natural law, the moral law known through reason. Roman Catholicism pre-eminently and also large sectors of Protestantism have propounded various theories of natural law; the historical provenance of these natural-law theories includes both St. Paul (Rom. 1-2) and pagan antiquity. Christomonist Protestant theologians today deny the validity of natural law, on the ground of the radical sinfulness of man; accordingly, in their view natural law is a form of idolatry or self-worship. The spectrum between Roman Catholic views and Christomonism is crowded with subtle variations. In each view there is an attempt to come to terms with relativism by appeal to sanctions drawn, for example, from ontology, from presuppositions regarding the essential nature of man, or from a trans-relativism that takes cultural diversity seriously and yet recognizes at least the formal validity of an ultimate unconditional demand from on high. A major embarrassment for most natural-law theory is the great variety of ethical demands that have been made in its name, demands that rather obviously reflect local preference, ecclesiastical authority, or ideological taint (conservative or revolutionary). Skepticism regarding Roman Catholic doctrines of natural law rests particularly upon the ecclesiastical guidance (finally depending on power politics) that intrudes itself. On the other hand, a strength of natural-law theory is that it at least seeks a basis for obligation valid in human nature as such.

Existentialism, especially under the influence of Kierkegaard, stresses the threat to Christian faith and to the unique individual which ensues when ethical principles or philosophical systems presumptuously usurp the place of the living God. It also emphasizes the uniqueness of each situation, and therefore insists that the gospel may have its sovereign sway and yield its redemptive power only when it can speak directly and anew to the believer who renounces the false securities of "rational principles" and who is ready to make unique and critical decisions. The living God, the uniqueness of the individual, his situation and his decision—all of these are salutary reminders for the Christian who decks himself out in a pious moralism or who cherishes the cushions that comfortably fit under the elbows of sinners. But the penchant for "uniquity" can readily issue in what is arbitrarily paradoxical and irrational. Every situation is unique, but it lends itself to rational discrimination in terms of persisting social structures or mal-structures. Every decision in order to be relevant must be unique, but in the societal situation it cannot be merely the unique decision of the isolated individual; it must be a decision growing out of social concensus regarding the definition of the situation and its possibilities. Under these circumstances a conflict of values (for example, between freedom and order) and also a compromise of values in face of the actual situation will be inevitable.

Here one encounters the problems of casuistry—the application of norms or of the Christian ethos, the response of faith to the living God, in the concrete situation. Alternative methods or possibilities have been considered here. On the one hand, "middle axioms" are employed to mediate between more general norms and the unique structural situation (cf. the pronouncements and the literature of the Oxford Conference of 1937); on the other, stress is placed on the ostensibly more complex and flexible response of a faith that is skeptical regarding the validity or adequacy of rationally articulated "principles" and that aims to remain sensitive to the ever-shifting contextual situation. (Both approaches today seek assistance from the social sciences for the empirical analysis of the actual situation.) On the one side there looms the danger of rationalism, on the other that of antinomianism or nominalism. The issues are the perennial issues of Christian faith under the paradoxical imperatives of law and gospel. These dangers arise in the encounter with ethical problems of the individual (not dealt with explicitly in the present article) as well as with those of institutions. In either sphere and under both law and gospel, the God of the Christian moves in a mysterious way his wonders to perform; and yet he is not a God of disorder.

JAMES LUTHER ADAMS

Bibliography

Emil Brunner, *Justice and the Social Order.*
Reinhold Niebuhr, *An Interpretation of Christian Ethics.*
Paul Tillich, *The Protestant Era.*

EVIL

In careful usage, Christian theology would restrict the use of the word *sin* to those states, acts, and situations in which the whole self is involved, and involved especially as *will*. Sin is not always deliberate—for example, there are sins of blindness and insensitiveness, sins of omission as well as sins of commission—but sin is always *culpa,* implying what we call *culpability*.

The term *evil* is broader. It includes the havoc wrought by man's prideful will, but it includes also that area where ugliness, frustration, pain, and death spread despoliation beyond the reach of man's mastery and clear responsibility. It is not an area of entire meaninglessness, as the following examples indicate:

1. It is apparent that some forms and varieties of evil are the fruit of culpable acts or culpable neglect.

2. It can be argued that good takes its meaning only in relation to evil—that good is recognized in implicit contrast with evil, beauty in contrast with ugliness, fulfillment in contrast with frustration.

3. Evil can and at times does provide the occasion for endurance, so that it appears to function in a disciplinary fashion. It is said of Christ (Hebrews 5:8) that "he learned obedience by the things which he suffered."

It could thus be argued that the threat or the presence of evil is the condition of responsibility and that creativity may serve to lift the weight of a meaninglessness; but biblical faith refuses to attribute finality to a history in which suffering is the precondition of creativity. It thrusts toward a consummation in which "righteousness and peace have kissed each other" (Psalm 85:10), and it is no longer needful to build righteousness at the price of breaking the peace.

Evil seen as an aspect of the consummation of history is, in the strict sense, a *mystery*. That does not mean that all *available* explanations are inadequate: it means that in the nature of the case *every* "explanation" must be an oversimplification, a falsification. The word *mystery* (*love* is the prime example) refers to something which is itself beyond explanation, yet which, if it is properly *looked into,* if it is taken with seriousness and without compromise of its reality, endows areas of life with meanings which remain otherwise opaque.

Human reflection on the problem of evil moves in two directions: either the agonized acceptance of the reality of evil breeds the denial of meaning in existence; or the strong conviction of the fact of meaning breeds the denial of the reality of evil. "If evil is real, then God is not good: if God is good, then evil is not real." It is worth noting that the Bible consistently avoids both options. It affirms, on the basis of revelatory events which to the men of the Bible were sufficient, that God is faithful (*good* is too ambiguous a word to be used without explicit context); but with illogical conviction it affirms also that evil is real. The conviction that God is faithful was

wrought precisely out of the worst evil; out of the captivity of Israel in the Old Testament, out of the death of
the Christ in the New. In such fashion there is retained
the full dimension of the mystery, in order that no violence be done either to the truth of revelation or to the
truth of experience. The men of the Bible will neither
deny the reality of evil nor identify it with the will of
God in such fashion as generates only resignation.

In Christian theology the figure of the Devil (Satan,
the Evil One, the Adversary) in one aspect serves to
locate an origin of evil which recognizes its reality outside
the will of men, yet avoids identifying it with the direct
will of God, and keeps it always and finally subordinate
to Him. Historically, theology has made a distinction,
with the same intention, between God's *ordinance* and
His *will*. God's ordinance denotes that which is, including
that which is the work of the Evil One: Paul, for example,
declares it to be the ordinance of God that Nero rules
in Rome (Romans 13:1); but that evil rulers do rule,
and rule in some sense by God's ordinance, fixes only the
occasion of the Christian's obedience, but does not define
its form. The form of obedience is determined by the
command of God in the Gospel, which in historic fact
may require that the evil ruler be endured, resisted, or
subverted. Thus, while God can bring good out of every
kind of evil (Romans 8:28: "in everything God works for
good with those that love him"), and particular good
out of particularly atrocious evil, the evil in the situation
is still the work of the Devil. To acquiesce in the evil
as if it were the will of God (cf. the falsely pious opposition to the use of anesthesia) or (Romans 3:8) to "do
evil that good may come" (cf. the suggestion that society
needs to retain or manufacture insecurity for the sake of
virtue) is to serve the Devil rather than God.

For biblical faith, then, the presence of evil is an occasion for obedience rather than for speculation (cf. the
words of Jesus about the man born blind, John 9:3; and
about the men on whom the Tower of Siloam fell, Luke
13: 4-5). The mind must do what it can with the problem:
but the solution of the mystery is not an intellectual solu-

tion, since the question is not an intellectual question.

The archetypal response to the presence of evil is the identification of the Christ with the suffering of the world, enduring a sorrow like no other, afflicted with all the afflictions of men. In the Christian understanding of the matter this is the archetypal case of suffering accepted for love's sake, and of the harvest sprung from a seed content to die. It is in this light that we see light on the problem of evil: that to be afflicted by evil is not to be afflicted by God, but to be appointed to fight the Holy War on a crucial part of the front.

ALEXANDER MILLER

Bibliography

C. S. Lewis, *The Problem of Pain.*
Richardson (editor), *A Theological Word-Book of the Bible,* articles on "Evil," "Suffering."

EXISTENTIAL PHILOSOPHY

It is not possible to understand the inner development of Protestant theology during the past thirty years without confronting existential philosophy and its basic ideas. Although it is still too early for the entire story to be written, one can easily see the impact of this type of thought upon almost every branch of current Protestant thinking. The influence stems not only from the ideas of the existentialists, but also from their approach to thinking, and especially from their emphasis upon relating the destiny of the individual thinker to the ideas he is engaged in thinking. The concern for the nature and destiny of the individual self common to all philosophers of existence forms one of the most important links between these philosophers and Christian thought.

Before proceeding to the ideas basic to existential thinking and to those theological interpretations stemming from them, a brief historical sketch will help to clarify the background. There can be no doubt that the ultimate source of existentialism, especially in its religious and theological aspect, is Sören Kierkegaard (1813-1855), the Danish "religious writer" as he liked best to describe himself. In many brilliant writings (*Either/Or*, 1843; *Fear and Trembling*, 1843; *Philosophical Fragments*, 1844; *Concluding Unscientific Postscript*, 1846; *Sickness unto Death*, 1849) capable of engaging and holding the attention of even the most unsympathetic reader, Kierkegaard set forth his understanding of the human predicament—despair, indecision, vanity, pleasure—and of the resolution offered in Christianity—hope, faith, love.

Although Kierkegaard must stand as the fountainhead of existentialism, we should not overlook the fact that the German philosopher Friedrich Schelling (1775-1854), whose lectures of the 1840's were attended by both Kierkegaard and Marx, was already developing the metaphysical background for an existential philosophy. Schelling's ideas have borne fruit in the theology of Paul Tillich (1886-   ), and this fact has been decisive in many ways for the American theological situation. Kierkegaard has, nevertheless, been much more influential than Schelling, both because of the availability of his writings and the dramatic form in which they are cast. Kierkegaard's use of descriptive, introspective psychology communicates itself to a reader sensitive to his own experience even though he may be unfamiliar with the language in which theological or philosophical ideas are usually expressed.

The translation of Kierkegaard's writings into German at the beginning of this century, together with the movement of *Lebensphilosophie* and the method of phenomenology, gave rise to an existential philosophy which first became powerful in Germany after the First World War. Martin Heidegger's (1889-   ) epoch-making work, *Sein und Zeit* (*Being and Time*) which made its appearance in 1926, together with the writings of Karl Jaspers (1883-   ), provided an impetus for existentialism which showed itself in full force at the end of the Second World War. It was in this second period that the works of Kierkegaard came most opportunely and powerfully into the English language through the devoted labors of

David and Lillian Swenson and Walter Lowrie. It is these writings and the approach to man and God contained in them that have shaped recent Protestant theology chiefly through the works of Karl Barth (1886-   ), Reinhold Niebuhr (1892-   ), Nicholas Berdyaev (1874-1948), Rudolf Bultmann (1884-   ) and Paul Tillich. A more complete account of existentialism in its theological bearings would call for discussion of the works of Gabriel Marcel (1887-   ), Unamuno (1864-1936), particularly his *Tragic Sense of Life,* and Martin Buber's (1878-   ) little classic, *I and Thou.* For existentialism in its general bearings much would have to be said about J.-P. Sartre (1905-   ), Merleau-Ponty (1908-   ), Camus (1913-   ) and others.

There are at least five features which serve to define existential thought and to distinguish it from other philosophical positions. Since it is not possible to describe these features from the standpoint of each of the thinkers concerned, we shall have to take them as indicative of the *main drift* of existentialism. *First,* there is the fundamental distinction between the *essence* of something and its *existence* and the assigning of the priority to existence. In the philosophical tradition a distinction had been made between the essence of a thing—its "what" or nature as known—and the existence of a thing—its "that" or the fact of its having a place in the world of changing and developing things. Hegel in his all-embracing philosophical system had tried to relate these two aspects to each other in a new way, but Kierkegaard and others attacked the solution on the ground that existence was swallowed up by essence. Existentialism, in opposition to rationalism which tends to equate everything with essence or with the thing as known, stresses existence, the fact of having a place in a dynamic and dangerous world (cf. Heidegger's term for "existence," *"Dasein"* or "being there"). *Secondly,* having singled existence out as basic, existentialists go on to give to it a most singular meaning. Starting with the assumption that each individual self-conscious being can grasp his own existence in reflection, they go on to identify existence with the individual's own immediate experience of himself and his situation as a free being in the world. Furthermore, the self intended is a very rich one indeed; it is very far from being merely a knowing self, but is a hoping, fearing, believing, willing, concerned self, aware of its need to find a purpose, a plan and a destiny in life. *Thirdly,* instead of presenting what may be taken by the reader as one more philosophical theory to ponder, the existentialists, and Kierkegaard in particular, literally try to drive men back to an awareness of their existence through the rhetoric of their style. It is imperative that each individual grasp his own existence for himself, and this can only be done by engaging him. In a neat but perfect illustration, Kierkegaard pointed out that a man who knows that "all men are mortal" knows a piece of the universal essence of man, but what is needed is that he draw the singular conclusion in his own case, "I, too, must die." And Kierkegaard's aim was to help men to draw that conclusion and thus to experience the impact of the truth in their own individual existence. *Fourthly,* and as a direct result of the preceding, it is essential that man abandon the attitude of theoretical detachment when confronting the problems that involve the ultimate purpose of his own life and the basis of his conduct. Concern and engagement of the self are called for; the significance of human life remains closed to the one who refuses to participate in it. It appeared to Kierkegaard as comical that a man should try to take an "objective" view, i.e., a view which leaves the individual out of account, towards moral and religious questions, when these questions have as their central meaning the life of the very individual considering them. This emphasis upon the involvement of the self forms the most important link between existential philosophy and religion. *Fifthly,* the common opponent of existentialism is rationalism (for many, but not all, existentialists this has meant the rationalism of Hegel) and, in modern thought, rationalism has frequently meant some form of idealism. Kierkegaard launched bitter attacks against idealism because to him it meant a dwelling in the sphere of thought (possibility) alone, and an escape from existence (actuality). Moreover, he stressed the "absurdity" of Christianity when taken as a faith that might be proved by rational argument, in order to "offend" the reader and shock him into a more than intellectual consideration of Christian belief. He made a vigorous use of paradox ("God does not exist; he is eternal") as a means of confounding rational solutions to theological issues, and laid the greatest emphasis upon those aspects of human life—failure, evil, sin, folly—which cannot easily be fitted into a rational system. The anti-rationalist and idealist thrust in existentialism has had a subtle but decisive importance for Protestant theology.

Every attempt to reassert a position must begin by distinguishing it from other alternatives and from doctrines that tend to obscure its uniqueness. Since many current Protestant theologians have taken the view that Christianity has been disastrously identified with idealism since the end of the nineteenth century, the drive to reassert classical Protestantism has taken the form of a "Christian realism" and an attack upon all idealist associations. In the interest of dissolving idealist ties, theologians have given new emphasis to the tragic aspects of life defying rational explanation. The anti-idealist tendency in existentialism fitted it well in this respect to serve as a basis for Protestant theology. And this remains true even if, as few existentialists and even fewer theologians suspect, existential thought is heavily tarred with the idealist brush.

Thus far attention has been focussed upon existential philosophy itself; its special connection with Christian theology must now be made plain. This can best be done by singling out several theological ideas and tendencies most clearly rooted in existential doctrines.

Behind the thought of virtually every theologian dependent upon the philosophy of existence is some form of the conviction that the human predicament to which Christianity is relevant can most adequately be expressed through this philosophy. Nicholas Berdyaev, the Russian theologian, has been more outspoken on this point than any thinker except Bultmann. The idea, more simply expressed, is that if any philosophical concepts and categories are essential for theology they must be existential ones.

In considering the impact of existentialism on Christianity, Kierkegaard would, of course, present us with a special case in view of the fact that in his thought the inner connection begins. His point of view, nevertheless, serves as an illustration in several directions. He gave a new and profound emphasis to *faith* by underscoring the inwardness of the self and the element of risk and adventure which faith involves. Faith in the Christ was represented by him as a "leap" engaging the whole self in commitment. In calling faith "subjective" Kierkegaard meant to show how it is related to the individual's own realization of having involved himself in the most ultimate decision. Faith means the giving and risking of the self; it is no mere provisional acceptance of a formula or a passive allowance that some ancient events may really have taken place.

Moreover, Kierkegaard dramatized the urgency of the situation of existence by pointing up the *limited* character of human life; limited, that is, not only spatially and causally, but also temporally. Man has but a finite time to find and appropriate his salvation, and this means that it is a grave error to view the issues surrounding the life and death of the soul as they might appear to someone who could take an infinite time to resolve them.

Of great importance in current Christian thought is Tillich's philosophical or mediating theology and the central use made by him of the existential concept of concern or *Angst*. In both sermons and systematic treatises he has tried to show that concern, for his own ground and goal is at the root of man's nature as the essentially religious animal. For him, man is the being who is incomplete, who is uneasy about himself in his guilt and separation from God and who betrays this separation in a life that is fragmented and futile. Starting from a description of the human situation, Tillich goes on to portray God in His reality as the New Being or Christ who is able to overcome the broken character which existence must suffer when left to itself. Tillich's enterprise of reinterpretation by means of ideas and language originally derived from an existential philosophy has done much to give to classical Christian content a contemporary relevance it might otherwise fail to have.

No account of the influence of existential thought on Protestant theology would be complete without mention of Barth's early thought, particularly his *Epistle to the Romans* (1918; English translation, 1933). It is necessary to say "early" because in his subsequent development, Barth has tried to dissociate his dogmatic theology frcm all philosophical influence, even that of existential philosophy. Nevertheless, it remains true that his fresh and vigorous presentation of Pauline theology through the medium of Kierkegaard's analysis of despair and the leap of faith was one of the potent influences instigating the current revival of classical Protestant theology.

The idea of paradox and the "realistic" view of life as found in Kierkegaard have been used in a most brilliant and skillful way by Reinhold Niebuhr in his many influential writings aimed at showing the relevance of Christianity to moral, social and political problems. Driving a middle road between naturalism, which reduces man to his animal conditions, and idealism, which identifies him with spirit, Niebuhr has tried to show how Christianity in a realistic faith transcends the alternative and leaves the two poles in a paradoxical balance. Man is a being of spirit, to be sure, but he is also a sinner bound to earth who must be redeemed from beyond his own resources. Niebuhr interprets the Kingdom of God, for example, in a way which brings out the paradoxical approach very clearly. On the one hand, man stands under the religious and moral imperatives defining Christian duty and he can bring these to bear upon the historical situation; on the other hand, the Kingdom is not identical with any historical state of affairs but transcends history and belongs to God. Thus the Kingdom both is and is not in the world; insofar as it can actually shape history it is in the world, and insofar as it cannot be fully achieved in history, it is not in the world. Or again, in seeking to retain both the freedom of man and the doctrine of original sin, Niebuhr has proposed that sin is to be taken as "inevitable but not necessary." Kierkegaard himself has no more arresting paradoxes than these!

Nicholas Berdyaev, the Russian philosopher and theologian coming out of the Eastern Orthodox tradition, has not only constructed his own theology with existentialist notions (especially the concept of freedom), but he has insisted in the most vigorous way upon the indispensability of existential philosophy for sound theology. In his analysis of revelation (*Truth and Revelation*, 1953) he states a view that would meet with the approval of many theologians:

> If we are to look at the relation between truth and revelation philosophically, it can only be done by a philosophy which is inwardly based upon religious and spiritual experience, not by a rationalist philosophy but by an existential philosophy which recognizes that spiritual experience is primary (p. 8).

The existentialist theology of the German biblical critic and religious thinker Rudolf Bultmann is most significant because of the singular use made by him of Heidegger's existential philosophy. Heidegger's *Sein und Zeit*, 1926, (*Being and Time*) still stands as the most impressive single work in the philosophy of existence since the discourses of Kierkegaard. Starting with the experience of "being thrown into" the world, Heidegger sought to describe man's actual situation as a being whose very nature drives him to find a purpose for his own individual existence. According to Heidegger, man is a being of concern or care and he is confronted by death; his problem is to find a significant existence in the face of these limitations. In a variety of works, Bultmann has employed Heidegger's chief categories for interpreting the religion of the New Testament, especially the Pauline theology of sin, grace and faith. In this way, the human situation to which Christianity speaks is made to stand out in bold relief and Christian faith is exhibited as the answer to the "dead end" which human existence would reach if left to its own devices.

JOHN E. SMITH

Bibliography

Helmut Kuhn, *Encounter with Nothingness*.

Gabriel Marcel, *The Philosophy of Existence*.

David E. Roberts, *Existentialism and Religious Belief*, ed. R. Hazelton.

John E. Smith, "The Revolt of Existence," *Yale Review* (Spring, 1954).

Paul Tillich, "Existential Philosophy," *Journal of the History of Ideas* (January, 1944).

FAITH

In Protestant theology, the term "faith" refers to the dynamic and vital context of man's meaningful dependence upon the activity of God in Christ. Because of this comprehensive scope, the expression "the Christian faith" is frequently used as a synonym for Christianity. Insofar as faith defines the living center and has implications for every Christian affirmation, such usage is understandable. More precisely, however, the concept "faith" should be confined to the living confidence and trust in God which results from, and is therefore in part also identical with, the experience of His active presence. Faith is that relation to God in which final dependence rests upon the reality to which one is related.

Because the relation depends upon the object, faith is said to be a gift. But it is important to note how the giving is defined. In more orthodox accounts, the mystery of faith is affirmed by emphasizing the initiative of God apart from the reception of God. In more liberal, and sometimes pietist traditions, the aspect of decision is affirmed to such an extent that faith appears as an act of the will or a decision of reason. In a more mediational but equally unsatisfactory frame of reference, decision was defined as the capacity to accept the grace by which one is redeemed. Frequently the capacity to make the decision was itself declared to be grace. Such ways of focusing the issue do violence to one side or the other. Faith as the gift of God is the confession of the believer that in his depths he knows the foundation and source of his decision to be of God, that the decision itself is authentic, validating the self, precisely as it has been known to lie somewhere else than in the self. Hence, the priority of God can never be defined apart from the reception or the experience of God.

Faith is, as such, neither objective nor subjective. These are interrelated in the complex of faith, with the ontological priority, as distinguished from the chronological priority, lying in the mystery of God's activity. But once the foundation is affirmed, the descriptive or more subjective side can come into focus.

The experiential side has also suffered distortion. The experiential aspect of the faith relation is not identical with general religious experience. Nor can it directly be described in terms of the various elaborations of religious experience. In various degrees, an emotional element is included in religious experience, but it cannot be reduced to emotion. There are aspects of reason in all experience, but the nature of faith and its formulation cannot be reduced to reason. Where reason is narrow, faith and reason are in opposition; where it is broad, reason belongs to the total matrix of faith. There are aspects of decision, usually described as will, in faith. But in faith, the mystery is not the cancellation of the self, but its redirection; this happens neither by an act of will, nor without the affirmation of the will. It was a mistake to define faith as the movement of the will by which one assents that the Church's dogmatic declarations concerning revelation are true, as was done in various periods of the Church. It removed faith from its central position, psychologized it, and tended to make truth propositional. Knowledge, too, belongs to faith. If it is God whom one encounters in the context of faith, cognitive elements are included. Just as reason and will are included, so is the concept of knowledge. The form of knowledge, of course, is not identical to that of the empirical world. Nor is it total knowledge—but it is knowledge nevertheless, namely, the type of knowledge which is appropriate to God.

Descriptively most adequate is the conception of faith as trust and confidence in God. The instinct of liberal theology was correct in identifying faith and trust. It was on dubious ground when it defined the relation in such a self-evident fashion as to do violence to the mysterious but gracious activity of God, on the basis of which experiential reality the possibility of trust is predicated. In more classical thought, it was the mystery and miracle of God's love in Christ, confirmed in the heart of the believer by the Holy Spirit, which was the basis of trust and confidence. Hence, trust or confidence was the disposition of the believer who had known and continued to live by the redemptive reality and promise of God.

In Protestant thought, the crux of faith is frequently expressed in the Pauline formulation made central by the Reformers, particularly Luther, namely justification by faith. For Paul, justification or righteousness (to justify is to be put or made right) is the inexplicable mystery of a justice by which God is faithful and merciful in spite of the continued sin of man. To be justified by faith, therefore, is to be considered as having that justice or righteousness which emanates from God Himself, given and known in the reality of faith. The express statement that such justification is through or by faith guarantees the source of righteousness and its dynamic character.

Historically, there has been disagreement as to how the righteousness was to be understood in respect to the life of the believer. In one way of understanding it, the righteousness was said to be imputed or ascribed to the believer. It was the cloak which covered him in his sins. But there were also those who interpreted justification to mean an actual transformation of the self in the context of faith, so that one could, in varying degrees, speak of the righteousness of the believer. Even in the latter conception, the source of the righteousness was declared to be that of Christ, the agent and reality in the transformation. Nevertheless, it was the first position which seemed more adequately to guarantee the necessity of justification in every moment of the life of the believer. But it is also obvious that faith makes a difference, and it was this which the second position, in its various forms, was concerned to affirm. The difficulty arose in that any statement which does more than affirm the difference inevitably seems to overstress the righteousness of the believer, thereby threatening the very sharp focus on the sole dominance of God's mercy in the redemptive activity.

In order to explicate the two sides of this problem, the terms "justification" and "sanctification" were used increasingly and became a more accepted terminology than the debate concerning the nature of righteousness in relation to the believer. Justification referred to the foundation of the faith of the believer, and sanctification, to the new life of the believer. Wherever these states were considered successive rather than simultaneous, the dangers in the previous formulations were repeated. Then sanctification became a work of righteousness, now in the very citadel of faith, and the freedom of man under Christ became a new bondage. It is only when justification and sanctification are affirmed simultaneously, that the continued trust in the righteousness of God is held as the freedom by which the believer lives the Christian life; it is only then that his destiny has the certitude of trust in God rather than in himself. It is then that the new life in Christ is seen in its proper perspective, as the first fruits, not as an object of achievement or contemplation. Because the Christian is saint and also still sinner, sanctification must, at every point, be encompassed by justification. It is for this reason that faith remains the central concept.

This same point is reiterated in the discussions concerning the relation of faith and works. The polemic against works was not that works were irrelevant but that they could not become determinative for one's relation to God. If man must fulfill conditions prior to faith as a precondition, even in the minimal sense of a sign of seriousness, man must contribute to his redemption. Then calculation enters and psychological uncertainty ensues. Where works are insisted upon in the context of faith in a way which indicates that the accent falls upon what is being accomplished, the focus of orientation is such that the gospel inevitably becomes a new law. Here false conceptions of sanctification and works coalesce. One can be under the burden of works also as a Christian. It is more adequate to speak of faith, not without works, than to speak of faith and works. The former points to faith as the encompassing reality rather than that to which something else is added.

Faith, then, is the dynamic center of a relation to God and consequently to man, anchored in the given and mysteriously received mercy of God. As such, as has been noted, it determines the context and defines the relation to various other concepts in Protestant theology. Calvin's definition still provides us not only with the various ingredients which comprise faith, but also with their proper relations. ". . . We shall have a complete definition of faith, if we say, that it is a steady and certain knowledge of the Divine benevolence towards us, which, being founded on the truth of the gratuitous promise in Christ, is both revealed to our minds, and confirmed to our hearts, by the Holy Spirit" (Institutes, II, III, VII).

JOHN DILLENBERGER

Bibliography

Karl Barth, *Dogmatics in Outline.*
Paul Tillich, *The Dynamics of Faith.*

THE FALL AND ORIGINAL SIN

The story of man's fall in the third chapter of Genesis is an early Hebrew myth which has profound theological meaning. It, and similar myths, may be understood in one of two ways. C. S. Lewis, for instance, understands the story as a "Socratic myth," that is, as "a likely story" which says, in spite of the absence of exact historical details, that something like this happened. Lewis contrasts a "Socratic" definition of myth to a "Niebuhrian" definition of myth. The latter describes something which is true but which makes no pretense to speak about past events even in "likely" terms.

"Original Sin," a phrase which comes from Augustine, describes the condition of every man by reason of the fact that he is born into, and participates in, the fallen world. Thus, the Genesis myth, and the idea of a "fall," can be used to express the human situation as it is experienced by both Christians and non-Christians. Albert Camus in *The Fall* unveils an egocentric self, Jean-Baptiste Clamence, who closely resembles Thomas Becket in T. S. Eliot's *Murder in the Cathedral* but who lacks the divine help which Thomas enjoys.

Christianity uses the Genesis myth to express the fact that man's basic malady is sin rather than finiteness with its concomitant aspects of weakness, ignorance, and mortality. As the story stands, Adam's disobedience to God issues in his expulsion from Eden and his loss of access to the fruit of the tree of life. "The wages of sin is death" (Rom. 6:23). Sin brings not only death, but also a loss of dominion over the animal order, existence in a disordered physical world from which bread is wrested by overexertion, and in which woman is subordinated to man and suffers in childbearing (Gen. 3:14-24). This is a mythical expression of man's alienation from God, from himself, from social harmony, and from harmony with sub-human nature. Since the malady is rooted in man, he cannot save himself but must be saved by God's action of love in Christ which evokes in him a response (faith or love) toward God which is impossible for man without God.

Original sin is the world's condition of faithlessness to God. Faithlessness is lack of trust in and obedience to God which either denies God entirely or rebels against Him because He is encountered as "another" who stands against man as a tyrant, benevolent or cruel. Sin, therefore, is always two-sided. On the one side man rebels against God, pretending to be God, and on the other side, he asserts his tyranny over God's creation, that is, over other men and the sub-human orders of existence. Self-realization for sinful man becomes not creaturely self-realization but autonomous realization and self-deification. The self is often magnified to represent the master race, the absolutistic political order, the world-saving culture or some comparable idolatry.

The usurpation of God's sovereignty and the assertion

of one's own may be expressed in terms of external power domination (Hitler) or in the solipsist's domination of a private world into which he has retreated. Both aspects of sin are to be seen in every overt sinful act, that is, in every trespass or transgression. The murderer, for instance, whatever his immediate motivation, desires, insofar as the murdered one is concerned, the world entirely for himself. He exalts himself (*superbia, hybris*) and depresses the other into nothingness. So also the liar creates a partial world of his own making, the logic of which is an infinite universe of lies to support the original lie. The liar usurps the place of God as Creator and Preserver of the universe. And, since the lie is told to be believed by others, the liar seeks to draw others into his falsified world. The liar seeks to dethrone God and to reign in God's stead. The devil is a liar and, therefore, the father of lies, as well as a murderer (John 8:44). "Pride is the beginning of all sin; and the beginning of man's pride is a falling away from God" (Augustine, Tractate XXV, 15 *On the Gospel of John*).

Self-exaltation and tyranny over others are radically exposed by Jesus in Matthew's Sermon on the Mount. They are the dual aspects of the sin which underlies murder, adultery, selfish divorce, perjury, vindictive retaliation, and hate of enemies (Matt. 5:21-48). Even more searchingly, however, Jesus exposes this same sin as it may prompt good works. One may give alms (Matt. 6:2-4), pray (6:5-6), or fast (6:16-18) to exalt the self and win praise from others. Self-righteousness, therefore, becomes the special expression of original sin for those who do righteous deeds. Every overt good work, even the acceptance of martyrdom, may be corrupted by self-exaltation.

An understanding of the Myth of the Fall and of the Christian doctrine of Original Sin transforms man's question, "How shall I save myself," into the question, "Who will deliver me?" For the Christian there is only one ultimate answer, "Thanks be to God, through Jesus Christ our Lord" (Rom. 7:24-25).

A. T. MOLLEGAN

Bibliography

C. S. Lewis, *The Problem of Pain,* chap. 5.
N. P. Williams, *The Ideas of the Fall and Original Sin.*
Reinhold Niebuhr, "The Truth in Myths," in *The Nature of Religious Experience.*

FINITUDE

The word finitude, used in the basic sense that is common to both philosophy and theology, implies the infinite, not in the sense of the boundless but of the perfect (aseity). The finite is that substance which cannot exist in and through itself.

In Platonic thought, however, finitude also refers to the distorted way in which such substances reflect or participate in their forms. Finitude, particularity, essential ontic distortion, and temporality are virtually synonymous in such a view. Aristotelian metaphysics, on the other hand, conceives of the finite not as that which necessarily distorts its essence, but as that which requires a completely active final cause (the Unmoved Mover) to draw it toward the complete realization of its own form. Over against these traditions, the distinctively theological understanding of finitude was achieved primarily by Augustine in his conception of finite or creaturely selfhood set forth in his *Confessions* and *On the Trinity.* But Augustine's genius was made possible only by the long and painful struggle of the Church to articulate the doctrine of the Trinity and the full significance of the dogma, *creatio ex nihilo,* which he then so penetratingly elaborated.

The Christian doctrine of creation *ex nihilo* posits the self as essentially creaturely, as finite or dependent upon God, but, unlike Aristotle who derived the goodness of the finite from its proximity to divine aseity, Augustine derived the goodness of the creature from God's creative fiat, from communicative love, not aseity. In a similar fashion Augustine derives the vitality and form of the creature from the same source, but it is the belief in God as Triune, as fount of being, logos, and love, that enables

Him to create *ex nihilo*. Only if power (God), logos (the Son) and communicative or relational goodness (the Holy Spirit) are all involved together in the creative fiat, is it possible to hold a realistic view of the creature on other than tragic terms. The trinity of vitality, structure, and meaning are not subjected to an unbearable inner tension by virtue of any ontological disparity among those elements.

With Platonism, the theological view of the creature does include a recognition of the essential distortion of the creature. But this is not due to the fact that the finite is merely dissipated being (Plotinus) but to an intra-mundane "fall" of man away from God's presence. Only within the context of the doctrines of the Trinity and creation can this fall be regarded as significant but not fateful.

Since the seventeenth century, and particularly since Kant's critique of metaphysical theology and the rise of evolutionary theory, the classical Christian doctrine of creation has become an atrophied and perfunctory paragraph in systematic theology. Concomitantly, the doctrine of the Trinity has fallen into a kind of limbo. As a result, the philosophical or tragic idea of finitude has been assimilated into the body of Christian thought by many thinkers. The influence of Hegel and Kierkegaard betrays itself in virtually every contemporary treatment of finitude. According to the former, the significance of the finite creature, and particularly of *homo religiosus,* lies in the role it plays in the self-enrichment of the Absolute; the finite is really a movement within God. This attitude toward finitude is expressed again in Heidegger's conception of human existence as being completely within the power of death and totally dependent for significance upon the acknowledgment of death as its own ultimate possibility. Rudolf Bultmann, who employs Heidegger's analysis of human existence, is bound to the same understanding of finitude. Kierkegaard introduced into theology the psychological concepts of anxiety and despair and at least prepared the way for Paul Tillich's treatment of finitude in which anxiety is given an ontological root, in conformity with his definition of finitude as a mixture of being and non-being. Karl Barth, on the other hand, has placed the doctrine of the Trinity at the head of his *Church Dogmatics* and given extensive consideration to the doctrine of creation. However, there is still suspicion that Barth, by reducing anthropology to Christology, has counteracted the effectiveness of this procedure and so reproduced an essentially Hegelian logic. Perhaps the most serious and productive effort to grasp the meaning of finite creatureliness in contemporary theology is that of Austin Farrer, whose definition of a natural theology is ultimately dependent upon Augustine's analogical method. In general Farrer's thesis, even within its strict, self-imposed limits, incisively argues the judgment that the relation of finite and infinite, nature and grace, needs to be examined theologically, yet not exclusively in a Christological context.

RICHARD R. NIEBUHR

Bibliography

Austin Farrer, *Finite and Infinite*.
Paul Tillich, *Systematic Theology*, Vol. I; *The Courage to Be*.

FORGIVENESS

Forgiveness is the act by which God brings sinful man into a right relationship to Himself. It is an act of grace, that is, of undeserved favor, on the basis of the work of God in Jesus Christ, and is offered to the repentant sinner who trusts God's word of promise.

Its chief exponent is St. Paul, who teaches that the significance of the work of Jesus as Messiah is the declaring righteous of the sinner who responds in faith to the revelation in Jesus Christ. There are two main factors in St. Paul's development of this doctrine.

The first is his experience of the condemnation of the law. Christ intensifies the law's demands and reveals its true import as requiring the total devotion of the whole person to God. Man is thus no longer able to assume that he can earn acceptance with God, but confronts the devastating fact that the law condemns him, and that he can do nothing to rescue himself from his plight. Unless help comes to him from outside he is doomed to despair.

The second element in the Pauline doctrine is the prophetic teaching of the righteousness of God. This involves not only the righteousness which God requires of all men, but also the activity by which He establishes righteousness among men, His vindication of the covenant people. Paul sees the fulfillment of this soteriological aspect of righteousness in the life of Jesus Christ. He is the revelation of God's saving activity directed toward the covenant people and through them to the entire world. The righteousness which man cannot achieve for himself is offered to him by God in Jesus Christ and can be effectually received by faith, by the trusting acceptance of the word of promise in Jesus Christ.

Two objections have consistently been made against this teaching. First, that it involves God in the unethical business of treating man as righteous when in fact he is not. Unless some arrangement can be made so that man actually achieves some measure of righteousness, he cannot enter the divine Presence. But the view of St. Paul is that there is no contradiction between God's love and His holiness. Love is the instrument through which God's holiness attains its objective of establishing righteousness in His creation. To be united by faith with the Christ who is the revelation of God *is* righteousness. Man cannot deserve or earn God's approval. It can only come to him as a gift. Trust in God is the proper relationship to God, and this relationship is righteousness.

The second objection is that justification by faith destroys ethics. "Let us continue in sin, that grace may abound." If man is accounted righteous apart from ethical accomplishment, he will have no concern for ethics. But this ignores both the cross and the judgment. In the cross God has demonstrated His hatred and condemnation of sin. In the judgment faith is assessed by its fruits. Indifference to sin and evil or neglect of the responsibilities of the life in Christ cannot be defended. Ethical indifference is not a valid inference from justification by faith, but is

the substitution of an impersonal moral or legal relationship for the true religious, personal relationship to God
which is offered to man in the Gospel.

WARREN A. QUANBECK

Bibliography

Alan Richardson (editor), *A Theological Word Book of the
Bible.*
Ethelbert Stauffer, *New Testament Theology.*

FREEDOM

Both human and natural history enter into the formation
of events, in that both the free actions of men and natural
necessities are involved.

The distinguishing mark of human history is that men
superimpose their desires, ambitions, and ends upon the
limited ends of nature. They have the freedom to do this
because they possess the conceptual capacity to apprehend not only single events and objects but to comprehend
the flux of events in its general patterns and essential
character. Consequently they can lift themselves above the
immediacies of events and project ends more inclusive
than those for which the creatures of nature strive.
Another facet of human freedom is man's capacity to
retain past events in his memory. He is thus delivered
from the immediate course of natural events and is able,
by remembering history, to affect history. His memory
enables him to record not only natural recurrences but the
unique and contingent events which, by virtue of man's
unpredictable freedom, constantly occur.

Man, despite his unique freedom, never ceases to be
a natural creature, driven by natural hungers and necessities. But human freedom can enlarge, for both good and
evil, the scope of every natural desire. Insofar as man is
a creature and his actions are determined by previous
events, they are subject to scientific analysis. They can
be sorted out in categories and can be predicted as natural
events can be predicted. But insofar as human freedom is

woven into the events of history, historical events are not exactly predictable. Even a scientific analysis of the motives which prompt human action cannot become the basis of a prediction, for of many motives and of many causes, it is impossible to prove which is the determining or dominant one in a given situation.

The historical sciences are in a different category from the natural sciences. Since historical events produce an endless variety of configurations and patterns in which the historian may discern, at best, inexact analogies and recurrences, he is inescapably preoccupied with the problem of distinguishing invariable from variable factors. The good historian is therefore half artist and half scientist. He is a scientist in that he may analyze causes and historical trends. He is an artist in that he must interpret the meaning of an historical structure according to a general system of meaning, which his imagination partly imposes upon them and partly elicits from them.

Since the ultimate freedom of the person beyond all psychological, economic, political, geographic and other determining factors is always hidden and can be known only introspectively, and since every event or action, once having taken place, can be plausibly interpreted as the inevitable consequence of a previous event or action, there is a natural temptation for all students of historical events to be more deterministic than the facts warrant. The freedom of persons, which is evident particularly in the biographical pinnacles of the mountains of history, remains a threat to every scientific account of historical events. It cannot be charted and remains a mystery to the observer of the drama of history, who must be content with statistical averages for the description of the main currents of history. Yet the endless variety and unpredictability of the historical drama are proofs of the reality of that freedom, supporting the introspective evidence of the actors themselves, who know that they make free and responsible decisions, though they are also conscious of all the determining factors which prompt and occasion decisions.

The social and political freedoms which modern democratic communities accord the person express the belated convictions of modern communities, gained after desperate struggles, that the community must give the person a social freedom which corresponds to the essential freedom of his nature, and which enables him to express hopes and ambitions and to engage in interests and vitalities which are not immediately relevant to the collective purposes of the community, but which in the long run enrich the culture and leaven the lump of the community's collective will and purpose.

The unique and radical freedom of man, and the resulting endless variety of historical configurations, which can only be partially reduced to rational systems of meaning, give validity to the biblical account of history and of the relation of the individual to the divine source and end of meaning, which transcends the coherences of nature and history. The biblical account assumes a divine providence over individual and collective destinies, which establishes meaning on the vast panorama of history without annulling human freedom. The alternative methods of establishing meaning by coordinating historical events into systems of natural or rational coherences, tend to create excessively deterministic or equally excessive voluntristic interpretations of historical events in which either the freedom or the finiteness of men is obscured. On the other hand, it must be admitted that versions of the Christian faith frequently interpret the idea of providence so that the freedom of man is annulled or imperiled and God appears to be an arbitrary despot of the historical drama who creates meanings by special providence, that is, by interference with the natural causalities and coherences which always furnish the foundation upon which human freedom erects the various pinnacles of history. Calvinism has been particularly guilty of the primitive interpretation of the legitimate biblical idea of the sovereignty of a mysterious divine power who is both the creator and providential preserver of the human and historical enterprise.

REINHOLD NIEBUHR

FUNDAMENTALISM

Fundamentalism is an extreme right element in Protestant orthodoxy. Orthodoxy is that branch of Christendom which limits the basis of its authority to the Bible. Fundamentalism draws its distinctiveness from its attempt to maintain status by negation.

Fundamentalism dates its birth from the turn of the present century. Its initial "rugged bursts of earnestness" were among the finest fruits of the Reformation. The theory of evolution and the documentary hypothesis were examined with prophetic courage. Many fine scholars joined battle, publishing a series of essays entitled *The Fundamentals*. They sought to prove that modernism and the system of biblical Christianity were incompatible. They reached their goal.

But in due time fundamentalism made one capital mistake. This is why it converted from a religious movement to a religious mentality. Unlike the Continental Reformers and the English dissenters, the fundamentalists failed to develop an affirmative world view. They made no effort to connect their convictions with the wider problems of general culture. They remained content with the single virtue of negating modernism. When modernism decayed, therefore, fundamentalism lost its status. Neo-orthodoxy proved too complex for it to assess. It became an army without a cause. It had no unifying principle.

This is why fundamentalism is now a religious attitude rather than a religious movement. It is a highly ideological attitude. It is intransigent and inflexible; it expects conformity; it fears academic liberty. It makes no allowance for the inconsistent, and thus partially valid, elements in other positions. This attitude helps to explain its crusade against the Revised Standard Version of the Bible. No study was made by the Fundamentalists of the canons of lower criticism or the delicate shades of meaning in Hebrew and Greek idioms. Such scholarly labor was considered unnecessary. Fundamentalism believes that liberals corrupt whatever they touch; and since liberals shared in the translation of the Revised Standard Version, the work is *ipso facto* heretical.

Fundamentalism is an ironic position. Its distinctives do not even comprehend the leading issue of the Protestant Reformation. The Roman Catholic Church affirms "the five fundamentals"—the infallibility of the Bible, Christ's virgin birth, the substitutionary atonement, the resurrection, and the second coming. Fundamentalism fails to see the irony in its own position because it does not understand the interrelatedness of Christian doctrine.

Fundamentalism is a paradoxical position. It sees the heresy in untruth but not in unloveliness. If it has the most truth, it has the least grace, since it distrusts courtesy and diplomacy. Fundamentalism forgets that orthodox truth without orthodox love profits nothing. The more it departs from the gentle ways of Jesus Christ, the more it drives urbane people from the fold of orthodoxy.

Fundamentalism is a lonely position. It has cut itself off from the general stream of culture, philosophy, and ecclesiastical tradition. This accounts, in part, for its robust pride. Since it is no longer in union with the wisdom of the ages, it has no standard by which to judge its own religious pretense. It dismisses non-fundamentalistic efforts as empty, futile, or apostate. Its tests for Christian fellowship become so severe that divisions in the Church are considered a sign of virtue. And when there are no modernists from which to withdraw, fundamentalists compensate by withdrawing from one another. They dispute whether the rapture takes place before or after the tribulation. Status by negation must be maintained or the *raison d'être* of fundamentalism is lost.

Many fundamentalists have taken refuge under the aegis of "dispensational theology." But this affords only provisional security. The distinctives of dispensational theology are the postponed kingdom of the Jews and the parenthesis view of the Church. These distinctives are too far to the right to enjoy classical status.

EDWARD JOHN CARNELL

Bibliography

Stewart G. Cole, *The History of Fundamentalism.*
Norman F. Furniss, *The Fundamentalist Controversy, 1918-1931.*

GNOSTICISM

The gnostic movement of the first centuries A.D. manifested itself mainly—at least for the surviving historical record—in the form of heretical teachings within, or closely related to, emerging Christianity; actually it had wider ramifications in the Hellenistic and Eastern world, and origins in part independent of the Judaeo-Christian tradition. In applying the name, it is now usual to go considerably beyond the listing of the Church Fathers and to classify, e.g., the Mandaean and Manichaean religions in the East, and part of the Hermetic literature in the West, as "gnostic."

Gnosis (Greek, "knowledge"), from which the name is derived, denotes in this context an initiation into the higher truths of religion that supasses mere faith on the one hand and natural reason on the other. The main topics of this "knowledge" are the mysteries of the beginning, the genesis of the world, the transcendent origin and present condition of man, and the nature of salvation. These themes are elaborated in extensive symbolic myths, and in practical precepts for the securing of redemption. The possession of the "knowledge" itself, in its transforming effect upon the soul, is considered to be an essential factor toward the attainment of the ultimate goal.

Theology. A cardinal feature of gnostic thought is the radical dualism of God and world, correspondingly of man and world, and again of man within himself. The deity is absolutely transmundane, its nature alien to that of the universe, which it neither created nor governs and to which it is the complete antithesis: to the divine light, the cosmos is opposed as darkness. The world is the work of lowly powers which do not know the true God and obstruct the knowledge of Him in the cosmos over which they rule. The transcendent God Himself is hidden from all creatures and is unknowable by natural concepts. Knowledge of Him requires supranatural illumination, and even then can hardly be expressed otherwise than in negative terms.

Cosmology. The world is like a vast prison whose innermost dungeon is the earth. Around and above it the cosmic spheres (most often seven, but sometimes multiplied to vast numbers) are ranged like concentric enclosing shells. The significance of the cosmic architecture lies in the idea that everything which intervenes between here and the beyond serves to separate man from God. The spheres are the seats of the Archons (rulers), especially of the seven planetary gods borrowed from Babylonian astrology. The Archons collectively rule over the world, and each individually in his sphere is a warder of the cosmic prison. Their tyrannical world-rule, called Destiny, is physically the law of nature, morally the law of "justice" as exemplified in the Mosaic law which issued from the "world-creating angels" for the enslavement of man. As guardian of his sphere, each Archon bars the passage to the souls that seek to ascend after death, in order to prevent their escape from the world. The Archons are also the creators of the world, except where this role is reserved for their leader, who then is called *demiurge* (artificer) and often painted with the distorted features of the Old Testament God.

Anthropology. Man, the main object of these vast dispositions, is composed of flesh, soul, and spirit. Of these, not only the body, but also the "soul" is a product of the cosmic powers, which shaped the body in imitation of the divine Primal Man and animated it with their own psychical forces: these together make up the astral soul of man, his *psyche.* Through his body and his soul man is a part of the world and subject to destiny. Enclosed in the soul is the spirit, or *pneuma,* a portion of the divine substance which has fallen into the world. In its cosmic exile, thus immersed in soul and flesh, the alien element is unconscious of itself, stupefied, asleep, or intoxicated by the poison of the world: in brief, it is "ignorant." Its awakening and liberation is effected through "knowledge."

Eschatology. The goal of gnostic striving is the release of the "inner man" from the bonds of the world and his return to his native realm of light. The condition for this is that he *knows* about the transmundane God and about himself. This knowledge, however, is withheld from him by his very situation, since "ignorance" is the essence of mundane existence. Hence the necessity of divine revelation. Its bearer is a messenger from the world of light who penetrates the barriers of the spheres, outwits the Archons, awakens the spirit from its earthly slumber, and imparts to it the saving knowledge "from without." (In the Christian systems, this savior-figure is identified with Christ.) Equipped with this *gnosis*, which also comprises the potent formulas for overcoming the "gate-keepers," the soul after death travels upward, leaving behind at each sphere the psychical "vestment" contributed by it: thus the spirit stripped of all foreign accretions reaches the God beyond the world and becomes reunited with the divine substance.

Morality. In this life, the general principle of gnostic conduct is hostility toward the world. From this principle, however, two contrary conclusions could be drawn: the ascetic and the libertine. The former deduces from the possession of gnosis the obligation to avoid further contamination by the world and therefore to reduce its use to a minimum; the latter derives from the same possession the privilege of absolute freedom: to the pneumatic all things are permitted, since the law as representing the will of the demiurge does not obligate the *pneuma*, which is "saved in its nature" and can neither be soiled by actions nor frightened by the threat of archontic retribution. In argument, this antinomian nihilism is sometimes curiously blended with the Pauline antithesis of works and grace.

Of major theological and philosophical significance is the gnostic division of spirit and nature, the radical extrusion of the divine from the universe, and the consequent distinction of an unenlightened creator or world-cause from the true God. In the teaching of Marcion this anticosmic dualism became a particular challenge to the Church in that he denied the identity of the Father of Jesus Christ—the "unknown," "new," and "alien" God—with the God of Moses and the prophets—the "known" world-God—though not denying the latter's reality, and strove to exclude the Old Testament from the Christian canon. Claiming to follow St. Paul, he thus sundered and distributed to two mutually exclusive gods that polarity of justice and mercy whose very togetherness in one God determines the whole dialectic of Pauline theology. Crypto-Marcionite tendencies have been recurrent in the history of Christianity. In modern times, a modified Marcionite dichotomy has become tempting to theology—by enabling it to concede to natural science the complete autonomy of the physical realm and to retain a God dealing merely with the soul and no longer charged with the role of cosmic providence.

HANS JONAS

Bibliography

Robert M. Grant, *Gnosticism.*
Hans Jonas, *The Alien God: Gnostic Religion at the Twilight of Antiquity.*

GOD

The starting-point for an examination of contemporary Protestant thought concerning God is necessarily the conception of God in original Protestantism. Indeed, the development of Protestant theology since the Reformation may be most usefully—and truly—interpreted in terms of a three-stage movement not without analogy to the familiar Hegelian triad of *thesis, antithesis,* and *sythesis.* Its origin was in the teaching of the Great Reformers. The second phase was direct response to the impact of "modern thought," the dominant trends in the intellectual culture of the nineteenth and early twentieth centuries; this was largely a movement of accommodation and adjustment. Theology today is in sharp reaction from the whole outlook of the "modern mind"; its most extreme spokesmen seek to call Protestant faith back to Reformation dogma unmodified; its more moderate exponents aim at a reformulation of the traditional conception of God which shall both conserve the authentic gains of the modern period and hold current interpretations in living relationship with present-day thinking.

The "Great Reformers"—Luther, Zwingli, Calvin, and Melancthon—introduced no innovations in the interpretation of God which they inherited from the catholic tradition. To be sure, they differed in their major stress, Luther upon the love of God, Calvin upon God's majesty and sovereignty; but both emphases were derived directly from opposite sides of Augustine's thought. Representative of the classic Protestant definition of God is that of the Westminster Confession of Faith:

> There is but one only living and true God, who is infinite in being and perfection, a most pure spirit, invisible, without body, parts, or passions, immutable, immense, eternal, incomprehensible, almighty, most wise, most holy, most free, most absolute, working all things according to the counsel of his own immutable and most righteous will, for his own glory; most loving, gracious, merciful, long-suffering, abundant in goodness and truth, forgiving iniquity, transgression, and sin; the rewarder of them that diligently seek him; and withal most just and terrible in his judgments, hating all sin, and who will by no means clear the guilty.

Clearly, this is a definition of God which lays major emphasis upon His transcendence. It is worth noting that, although it professes to be a *Christian* definition, there is no explicit reference to Jesus Christ, let alone to the Trinity.

In this as in most other matters, the truly original contributions of the Reformation are not to be found in "classic Protestantism" (Lutheranism, Calvinism, and Anglicanism), but in the thinkers of "radical or sectarian Protestantism" (Baptists, Congregationalists, Quakers, etc., and, later, Methodists) who sought to press behind the theological formulations of the centuries and recover the "pure" faith of primitive Christianity. However, only in the present period has their influence begun to become significant within the main stream of Protestantism.

By universal acknowledgment, the title of Father of Modern Theology belongs to Friedrich Schleiermacher. His position and influence are comparable to those of Francis Bacon and Descartes in philosophy. However, Schleiermacher is significant not primarily for the content of his teaching, but as a symbol of transition and precursor of a movement.

The ruling purpose of the theological development which stemmed from Schleiermacher was to bring Christian belief into confrontation and, so far as possible, into accord with the prevailing outlook of the "modern mind" which was rapidly taking shape. All Protestant theologians confronted a common problem: the interpretation of inherited belief in the face of new knowledge and new philosophies. But it is important to note that their response to this common problem followed either of two alternative lines. Some took up a position resolutely within historic Christian faith and, from that viewpoint, attempted adjustment to the new and bewildering modern world; in its climactic and most worthy expression, this was the intention of theological "liberalism." Others, however, willingly surrendered the traditional standing-ground, launched forth boldly upon the new currents, made themselves at home within them and, discovering a position there, sought to reclaim and redefine as much as possible of the old faith; this was the essence of "modernism."

Whichever of these alternative courses was preferred, the outcome was a definition of God in accord with the premises and language of contemporary thought. The definition which resulted was, therefore, in radical contrast to class Christian formulations, whether Catholic or Protestant. These were among the more important features of the modern viewpoint to which the traditional Christian conception of God had to be adjusted and, if possible, reconciled:

The *scientific outlook*, with its portrayal of a vastly expanded universe, its conception of universal law, its emphasis upon process, its attention to uniformities rather than to diversities and originality, its predilection for understatement rather than overstatement, its disdain of the past and partiality for the new.

The *historic perspective*, with its critical interpretation of all tradition including the Christian, its radical reconstruction of Christian origins and Christian developments, its sense of advance encouraging a presumption of progress, its suspicion of all claims to finality and absoluteness.

The *global consciousness*, with its growing awareness of the omnipresence of religion among all peoples and a consequent skepticism toward exclusive claims and alleged uniqueness, its catholicity and tolerance toward all faiths.

Perhaps, most subtle but also most pervasive, the *spirit of the modern age*, with its lofty confidence in man, his achievements and his capacities for boundless future achievement, and in consequence its preoccupation with the interests and affairs of this world.

The upshot of the attempt of Protestant theology to come to terms with these features of modern thought was a vast variety of definitions of God. At one extreme stood Hegel's *Absolute Spirit*, who comes to self-knowledge only through and within man's consciousness of Him, and Herbert Spencer's *Infinite and Eternal Energy*. Later, came Alfred North Whitehead's *Principle of Concretion* and Henry Nelson Weiman's elaboration of Whitehead's suggestion:

God is that feature of our total environment which most vitally affects the continuance and welfare of human life, that character of events to which man must adjust himself in order to attain the greatest goods and avoid the greatest ills—this most subtle and intimate complexity of environmental nature which yields the greatest good when right adjustment is made. (*The Wrestle of Religion with Truth*, pp. 14, vi.)

At the opposite extreme was the simple definition of a naive liberalism: *"God is the Father of Jesus Christ."* Yet, with all their diversity and contrasts, most definitions of God in the modern period were at one in stressing His active presence within His world, i.e., his *immanence*.

Clearly, the two dominant features of contemporary Protestant thinking are, on the one hand, recoil from the prevailing outlook of the recent past and, on the other hand, a "theological renaissance" of extraordinary vigor and power. As Schleiermacher was the prophet and precursor of the earlier development, so Karl Barth stands as the most formative mind in initiating the theological renaissance of today. As Schleiermacher was important less by virtue of his own distinctive teaching than as the forerunner of a movement, so likewise Barth may be found to have been less influential in his specific teachings than as "prophet of a new Christianity."

The current phase in Protestantism's definition of God is to be understood less as reaction to the "modern mind" than as revulsion from the "modern world"; it is one expression of the widespread disillusion over contemporary society, "the collapse of the optimistic hope that modern science and human good will would bring the world into an era of peace and justice." For that reason, it has not yet achieved a precise or generally accepted formulation which can be readily defined. Indeed, what we confront, no less than in the modern period, is no single Protestant definition of God but rather a congerie of contrasted and unreconciled alternative interpretations.

At the same time, it is possible to identify some of the more representative and important features of current Protestant thinking:

1) The most powerful voices in theological interpretation today are often characterized as "neo-orthodox"; but none of these spokesmen will accept the designation. Indeed, its inappropriateness is testified to by the fact that the move-

ment for which they speak is less a reaffirmation of classic Protestantism as typified by the Westminster Confession definition quoted above, than a return to "the strange new world within the Bible." Contemporary Protestant theologians seek a recovery of "Biblical theology" and its conception of God, even though they profess to accept to the full the new understanding of the Bible which was among the notable achievements of the modern period.

2) Like all current thinking, theology is strongly under the influence of "existentialism." "Existentialism should be of compelling interest to the Christian thinker today. . . . It is a protest against all forms of rationalism. . . . It embodies a deep-seated distrust of all efforts to compel religious belief through the devising of arguments or so-called 'proofs' for the reality of God." (David E. Roberts, *Existentialism and Christian Belief,* pp. 4, 6, 344. Cf. also, John McQuarrie, *An Existentialist Theology.*) This results in a profound disinterest in, as well as distrust of, attempts at precise definitions of Ultimate Reality, of what God is in His essential being in contrast to the meaning which God holds in man's "existential experience."

3) Theologians are also under the sway of the prevailing preoccupation with the inner problems of the soul, and of the teaching of psychology and psychotherapy regarding the bearing of religious faith upon self-fulfillment. This makes for an extreme subjectivism and consequent relativism in theological statements.

4) On the other hand, theology shares with the contemporary mind an intense interest in human history, and in the vast and baffling complex of problems regarding God's relation to history. One aspect of this concern is an intensified, and presently unresolved, divergence as to the distinctness, uniqueness, and finality of Christianity in comparison with the other living religions of mankind, and as to the absoluteness of the Christian definition of God. This, likewise, induces modesty and relativism in advancing distinctive Christian claims.

5) Lastly and most important, there is, in view of the widespread recognition that the realities apprehended in religious faith exceed the powers of the human mind and human speech to describe and define, skepticism regarding *all* "definitions" of God. Positively, this encourages recourse to symbolic representations of trans-rational realities through the employment of "myth," one of the favorite instruments of contemporary interpretation. The fusion of these several elements is well illustrated in these characteristic sentences from the leading contemporary theologian: "The religious myth points to the ultimate ground of existence and its ultimate fulfillment. . . . The true import of myth is not to give a picture of the objective world. It expresses rather the way in which a man understands *himself* in his world. . . . The gospel is proclaimed in the language of mythology." (Reinhold Niebuhr, *An Interpretation of Christian Ethics*, pp. 12 ff.)

We have proposed that the history of Protestant thought from the Reformation to the present day may best be interpreted as a three-stage development, and that this development suggests the Hegelian triad of *thesis, antithesis,* and *synthesis.* The first two of these terms well describe the relation of Reformation theology to that of the modern period. But it is by no means certain that what we are now witnessing can be rightly described as a "*synthesis,*" or even the beginnings of a "synthesis." One of the most acute interpreters of the current scene, Daniel Day Williams, argues that "our time is not favorable for theological synthesis." Indeed, the achievement of synthesis may be recognized as the claimant task confronting Protestant thought in the days immediately ahead.

HENRY P. VAN DUSEN

Bibliography

William Hordern, *A Layman's Guide to Protestant Theology*.
Daniel D. Williams, *What Present Day Theologians are Thinking*.

GRACE

Grace is God's personal attitude toward man, His action and influence upon him. For Christians grace is concretely manifested in, and communicated through, the historical person Jesus Christ. St. Paul was the first Christian writer to make grace a central theological word. The word *charis*, which means *favor*, was used by him as a synonym for God's love. The attitude of spontaneous, uncaused favor with which God regards man expresses itself fully in the life, words, deeds, death and resurrection of Jesus of Nazareth. "God shows His love for us in that while we were yet sinners Christ died for us" (Romans 5:8). This love evokes from us a response, faith, which is our self-giving trust in, our commitment and obedience to, God in Christ. The full Pauline formula appears in a sentence probably written by one of St. Paul's disciples: "For by grace you have been saved through faith; and this is not your own doing, it is the gift of God—not because of works, lest any man should boast" (Ephesians 2:8). Grace (love), manifest in Christ, elicits from us faith by capturing our wills, not by infusing into us a new faculty. Faith is a gift in that it is evoked beyond our mere willing. This saving faith is not to be confused with the special faith which is a gift of the Spirit (a *charisma*), a "faith that moves mountains" (I Corinthians 12:9, 13:2) nor with the faith which is an aspect of "the fruit of the Spirit" (Galatians 5:22) which is faithfulness (R.S.V.) or fidelity. Saving faith enables us to participate in grace. "Through him (Christ) we have obtained access to this grace in which we stand. . . ." (Romans 5:2).

We stand in grace because faith binds us to Christ in His death, burial and risen life (Romans 6:1-11). This union with Christ shapes our lives into likeness to Christ. Grace as the personal shaping influence of God in Christ becomes a synonym for the Spirit of Christ (the Spirit of God, the Holy Spirit). Grace as Holy Spirit is the operative power of God's personal influence recreating us, fulfilling our created potentialities and moving us toward

that which God intends us to be. St. Paul credits grace
with his new existence as an apostle in contrast to his
former existence as an enemy of the Church. "For I am
the least of the apostles, unfit to be called an apostle,
because I persecuted the Church of God. But by the grace
of God I am what I am, and his grace toward me was not
in vain. On the contrary, I worked harder than any of
them, though it was not I, but the grace of God which is
with me" (I Corinthians 15:9-10). In brief, God's personal
attitude of grace expressed in Christ and participated in by
faith becomes operative in us as a transforming personal
influence, enhancing our talents, giving us new marks of
character and a new task. Yet this is also our own doing
in that grace does not override our wills in an authoritarian
way. The grace-filled man is the free man who does what
he desires and wills to do since he desires and wills the
purpose of God which has become his own purpose.

Because participation in this grace (divine favor) restores and completes our original nature, grace is understood to be the ground and source of all existence. Creation as well as redemption is by grace. All contingent
existence is supported by the grace of God. We literally
move and have our being in God's grace. Grace, therefore,
becomes also a word for our thanksgiving to God as when
we say "grace at meat." *Charis* appears in the word
eucharist, a name for the central service of Christian
worship in which God's grace in creating, preserving and
redeeming us is answered by our thankful gift to God of
ourselves and all that we control.

The Bible is a record of the mighty acts of God's grace.
This action of God is both for and within man. The
Church, by the proclamation of these mighty acts, culminating in Christ and the communication of the Spirit,
enables men to participate in grace. Grace comes to us
and becomes operative in our life through "the means of
grace," the speaking, the living witness and the sacramental actions of the Church for which the Bible is
normative.

Christians may speak of the grace of Creation and
Preservation, the grace of the Incarnation, the grace of the

Atonement, the grace of the Holy Spirit, the grace of the Word and Sacraments, the grace of final Consummation, but we must always remember that grace is the personal attitude, action, and influence of God. There is only this one grace within its many manifestations, the grace of our Lord Jesus Christ.

A. T. MOLLEGEN

Bibliography

James Moffatt, *Grace in the New Testament.*
Norman Powell Williams, *The Grace of God.*

HEILSGESCHICHTE

The term *Heilsgeschichte* (holy history, or, literally, history of salvation) was coined in the middle of the eighteenth century in pietistic circles of Southern Germany. Its first representative was the Swabian theologian Bengel (1687-1752). He pointed out that in order to understand the meaning of the historical books of the Bible, it was necessary to see the divine purpose of redemption that was brought to a gradual actualization in them. The historical events narrated in the Bible did not only follow a chronological principle, as Archbishop Usher had demonstrated, but also a teleological one. Consequently the last events, with which particularly Daniel and the Apocalypse were dealing, were no longer to be considered as an abrupt and whimsical termination of the world, but rather as the necessary conclusion of God's saving work. Bengel felt therefore that he could predict with absolute certainty the date of the End.

In the nineteenth century, Bengel's view came to new life. The development followed two different lines, however. With Darby and particularly his follower Scofield, whose annotated Bible did so much to popularize his views, *Heilsgeschichte* became Dispensationalism. God's plan, according to this school, can be divided into a number of periods of "dispensations," each of which serves a specific end. Believers are particularly interested in the last phase, because they are to be taken from this world in the "Rapture" (I Thess. 4:17) and be spared the dispensation of the Great Tribulation. Great hopes are held out for the literal fulfillment of all the divine promises given to the Jews, and in Dispensationalist circles, the establishment of the state of Israel in 1948 was considered as an infallible sign that the End is rapidly approaching.

An entirely different development of the idea of *Heilsgeschichte* was conditioned by certain trends in German theology. Hegel's philosophy was combined with *Heilsgeschichte* by J. T. Beck, who insisted that the teleological character of God's dealing with His people required a logical connection between the various stages. *Heilsgeschichte* is like a tree or some other organism, where all the stages of the process are equally important, because they become part of the organism. Beck attempted to distill a divine logic from the biblical records. Such an interpretation was a wholesome antidote against a one-sided interest in the apocalyptic portions of the Bible.

The modern approach to history, ushered in by Ranke, induced the Lutheran theologian J. Chr. K. Hoffmann of Erlangen to offer another revision of the understanding of *Heilsgeschichte*. In a teleological view of history, the earlier elements cannot have the same function as the later ones. However, over against those liberal theologians, who wanted to dispense altogether with the Old Testament because they believed to find the whole truth in the New Testament, Hoffmann pointed out that the superiority of the New Testament is lost when it is studied in isolation. It is only when we see in Jesus and the New Testament the fulfillment of the prophecies given in the Old Testament that we have a right to say that in the New Testament we have the completion of God's redemptive work.

Hoffmann's significance lies in his having set in relief the religious value of the historical material in the Bible. The majority of the Protestant theologians had treated the Bible as a textbook of theology, or, if they disliked the traditional theology, as a textbook of morals or the philosophy of religion. Hoffmann was able to show that for the writers of the New Testament the gospel was not confined to the birth and death of Jesus, but rather they proclaimed the whole story of Jesus and showed, furthermore, that that story was the outcome of God's former dealings with His chosen people Israel. Moreover, Hoffmann taught that the life of Jesus is interpreted by the New Testament writers as forming the basis of the Church. It is not a self-contained unit. Consequently the Book of Acts is not an anti-climax to the Gospels, but rather it records the continuation of God's saving work. Over against a purely sociological view of the Church, which was then prevalent in Protestant circles, Hoffmann pointed out that, notwithstanding its human character, the Church is the place in history where Christ's spirit is at work.

In recent days, the idea of *Heilsgeschichte* has been used to overcome the dilemma into which historicism had brought the theologians. When the principles and methods of modern scientific research are applied to the Bible, it is reduced to a purely human work sharing the relativism of all the rest of history. Yet the principal reason why the Bible is studied is the conviction that it is the Word of God. Some theologians, e.g., Tillich, Brunner, Barth in his earlier phase, Bultmann and his school, have disclaimed any interest in the historical contents of the Bible and in history itself, and they treat the historical narratives of the Bible as symbols of timeless truths. Others, however, such as Cullmann, Piper, Dodd and the majority of the younger English theologians, have turned to *Heilsgeschichte* again. According to them the biblical records, notwithstanding their human origin, show an amassing agreement throughout the centuries. They point to an increasing awareness of God's saving work in history, and thereby make us sure of the ongoingness of that work. Thus every believer is confronted in his daily work and in contemporary history by a divine challenge, to put himself obediently at God's disposal. *Heilsgeschichte* makes us sure that Christ is not far away from man, but rather is present here on earth, so that men can be "in Christ." The life of faith does not exhaust itself in approving of theological propositions or in obeying commandments which tell us to be good, but rather faith is the awareness of the ongoing work of

Christ, and man's collaboration in that work. Likewise, *Heilsgeschichte* offers a new view of the Bible. It is not a book that the Holy Spirit dictated to various authors; but it is not, either, merely a collection of subjective views on religion. Rather God has used human beings, notwithstanding the limitations of their persons and their age, to become aware of what He was doing for the salvation of mankind, and obediently to record it as they understood it. The interpreter, in turn, will grasp the truth of the Bible only when, in addition to his scholarly studies, he is himself a living participant in God's dealing with human history in and through the Church.

Finally, recent theology has given thought to the relation between *Heilsgeschichte* and the rest of history, whereas the earlier schools treating the problem in a supranaturalistic way had failed to see any connection. Biblical history was a realm all by itself in which God worked in a miraculous way. Under the influence of Hegel, on the other hand, *Heilsgeschichte* was considered evolutionistically as the supreme development of all history. Human nature would have reached its climax in Jesus Christ. Contemporary theology rejects either view. *Heilsgeschichte* is interpreted as the organizing center of all history. The latter is destined eventually to take part in it, and *Heilsgeschichte* is the power by which purely human history is gradually transformed into a history with God.

OTTO A. PIPER

Bibliography

Oscar Cullmann, *Christ and Time.*
Otto A. Piper, *God in History.*
E. C. Rust, *The Christian Understanding of History.*
Erick Sauer, *The Dawn of World Redemption and the Triumph of the Crucified.*
Gustav Weth, *Die Heilsgeschichte.*

HERMENEUTICS

Hermeneutics designates the scholarly attempt to clarify principles pertinent to an adequate understanding and interpretation of texts as well as monuments. Since all sources for the study of the past can be similarly interpreted, one may speak, for example, of the hermeneutics of fine arts. The fundamental problem posed by hermeneutics is: how can sources of the past be understood in their own historical environment *and* their meaning for the present be adequately perceived? This problem becomes theologically relevant when applied to the Bible. On the one hand the Bible is an historical book, written by human beings for men. On the other hand, the Church regards the Bible as the canonical document of the Word of God. Would this imply that two concepts of hermeneutics should be employed in biblical research—one for the neutral historian and another for the Christian understanding of God's word? To this question there are a variety of answers.

The first examples of biblical hermeneutics are to be found in the New Testament itself: in the allegorical interpretation of Old Testament passages (Gal. 4:24 ff.) and the typological interpretation of Old Testament events (Rom. 5:14; I Cor. 10:1-6). In the third and fourth centuries the Alexandrians introduced a more spiritualized method of interpreting the Bible, while the schools of Antioch tended toward a more historical interpretation. The turning point and basis for medieval hermeneutics was Augustine. In his work on *The Christian Doctrine* (III, 2, 2) he formulated principles for the interpretation of Holy Scripture and established the doctrine of the Church as the touchstone to hermeneutics. With the Reformation prior principles were changed. The Church was no longer the key to biblical truth; rather, biblical interpretation became the key to the doctrine of the Church. Luther's rule that "the Holy Scripture is its own interpreter" was understood to mean that obscure passages should be understood in the light of principles articulated by clear ones.

With the Age of Enlightenment the Bible is viewed as an historical document, whose interpretation must differ in no wise from that of any other historical source. Faith and revelation were henceforth to be evaluated by reason. It was, however, the hermeneutics of Schleiermacher which exerted decisive influence on the nineteenth and twentieth centuries. Reviving Aristotelian theory, Schleiermacher enlarges its scope and establishes four principles: 1) a formal analysis of the style and composition of the whole is needed: as the single verse is to be seen in its context, the whole is to be assessed in the light of the single verse; 2) when dealing with foreign languages philological knowledge is required in order to come as close as possible to an adequate translation of the text; 3) since sources must be understood in their cultural and political context, a knowledge of history is requisite; 4) and, lastly, to insure the affinity of the scholar to his subject psychological understanding is desirable.

W. Dilthey, building on the principles of Schleiermacher, stresses the point that all literary sources are the expression, even confession, of individual life and personal experience. The historian must wrestle with his hermeneutical principles in order to rediscover the individual life concealed beneath the language of his sources.

The present theological and philosophical situation is marked by a new awareness of the problem of hermeneutics. The theologians of crisis, existentialists, and the philosophers of history reflect this awareness most profoundly. The new approach results from the attempt to overcome mere historicism, and its aim is to reconstruct the past; namely, "to retell it," in Ranke's phrase, "as it actually was." It is characteristic of the new approach that personal interest in the subject matter of the source is stressed as a prerequisite for the full understanding of the whole. Thus Bultmann demands a fifth principle, in addition to those of Schleiermacher: a personal interest must lead and define the hermeneutic questions of the scholar.

With regard to biblical hermeneutics in the present period, there is a general tendency to overcome the positivistic and merely archaeological interpretation of the Bible as well as the Barthian principle of the "Word-of-God" as regulative. It is agreed that the Bible does not require a special hermeneutics, but is rather an instance of general hermeneutics. The Bible as such does not require for its hermeneutic understanding a method formed by Christian principles; since all scholarly methods are profane and Greek in origin, what is required is only the affinity and interest of the scholar. Such open-mindedness as is required cannot employ such conceptions as "Word of God" or "justification by faith" or *Heilsgeschichte* as exclusive principles. Nor is it possible to concentrate upon the *kerygma* and thus restrict the variety of possible texts from the outset. Biblical hermeneutics demand a constant dialogue of the exegete and his texts: he who questions is as well aware that he himself is questioned.

ERICH DINKLER

Bibliography

Rudolf Bultmann, "The Problems of Hermeneutics," *Essays, Philosophical and Theological.*
Erich Dinkler, "Principles of Biblical Interpretation," *The Journal of Religious Thought,* Vol. XIII, pp. 2-30.

HISTORY

Christianity has always been an historical religion, both in the sense of believing in the historical character of Jesus as the Christ and in affirming an intimate connection between the activity of God and the course of human history. The idea of the Kingdom of God and the doctrines of eschatology (See "Eschatology," Paul Althaus) have served to express this continuing tie with the historical order. Christianity is, in this respect, distinguished from many other religions in which historical life and the course of history are undervalued in favor of a reality essentially indifferent to time and standing apart from all relation to historical change.

The idea of history has been especially important for Protestant theology during the past three quarters of a century for two main reasons. First, the development of the historical sense and the historical treatment of every part of life in the later nineteenth century gave rise to a quest for the historical foundations of Christianity. Out of these studies came a new understanding of the importance attached by Jesus and the primitive Church to the Kingdom of God and its bearing upon the course of history. Secondly, world events of the present century, by casting grave doubts upon the validity of progressivistic views of historical change, have once again directed attention to the biblical view of history and to its elaboration in Christian theology.

The first of these two motives is expressed in the work of Albert Schweitzer, *The Quest of the Historical Jesus* (English translation 1926), the chief importance of which was to disclose Jesus' own consciousness of His mission and the role of the Kingdom of God in shaping history. The second motive is expressed in the universal concern among Protestant theologians to recover essential Christian teaching about the meaning of the historical process.

The best way to gain an understanding of the meaning of history in modern Protestant thought is to pay attention to the chief ideas of the leading contemporary theologians—Reinhold Niebuhr, Paul Tillich, Karl Barth, Emil Brunner, Nicholas Berdyaev and Rudolf Bultmann. These thinkers are all united in a common belief that history is central for Christian faith, although there are sharp divergences among their views both in doctrine and emphasis.

Reinhold Niebuhr has contributed more than anyone else in America to a Christian understanding of the historical order. Above all to him must go the credit for having leveled a decisive criticism against all progressivistic theories of history in which man is envisaged as able to control his historical destiny through technological progress and thus to save himself through his own ingenuity. Niebuhr's views are outlined in many books, but of chief importance is his *Faith and History* (1949). Here he elaborates the biblical interpretation of history as rooted in two ideas: first, the idea of a universal history over which God is sovereign and through which His purpose is achieved, and, secondly, the idea that history testifies to man's misuse of his freedom and his consequent to deny the divine sovereignty by setting himself up as god. Essential to his view is the conviction that the divine pattern in history must be worked out in spite of and in opposition to this human rebellion, with the result that history becomes a mixture of both darkness and light which cannot be understood from a simple moralistic perspective. His view is that the final purpose of history—the Kingdom of God—is not achieved within history as we know it, but that the divine standard is nevertheless relevant to human events, illuminating them and judging them at the same time. Man cannot achieve the "kingdom of God upon earth" because only God can fulfill the historical process.

Paul Tillich has laid great stress upon history both as the medium of divine revelation and as the sphere of human freedom. He has insisted that history has its own peculiar character and that it must be understood in a way that does not reduce it to the cyclical pattern of the world of nature. Central to his view is the idea that, from the Christian perspective, history has a special pattern—a beginning, a "center" or decisive point, and an end or final fulfillment. The meaning of the whole is given in the "center"—the appearance of Jesus as the Christ—because it is this event in history which reveals its pattern. The *beginning* is found in the first expectation of the Kingdom of God and the *end* in the realization of the Kingdom. The Christ, as the revelation of the new form of life, points to the ultimate meaning of all life in a Kingdom where the fragments of our life are unified and all evils are purged. Tillich's writings about the dynamics of history have given great impetus to Christian action seeking to achieve historical goals.

Karl Barth, the leading doctrinal theologian of the neo-Reformation revival, has centralized in his theology the biblical conception of God as revealing His nature to man in history through a series of "mighty acts," the most important of which is the appearance of the Christ as the mediator of God. In addition to joining others in attacking the adequacy of all philosophical and secular attempts to understand the course of history, Barth has concentrated upon two main themes. First, he has insisted upon the *unique* character of the event through which God breaks into history in Christ, and, secondly, he has sought to reconcile the two aspects that have always troubled theologians seeking to understand the Christian doctrine of the "last things." On the one hand, he maintains that God has already established His Kingdom in and through Christ, but on the other he holds that "at present the glory of the Kingdom of God is held out to us only as a hope." This means that God has still to guide the course of history in His Providence to the "second coming" of Christ in which, as St. Paul says, "God will be all in all." Barth has insisted more than any other thinker upon the need for God to break into history to reveal Himself to man, and he has consistently rejected all human attempts to understand either God or history from this revelation.

Nicholas Berdyaev, representing one strain in the Eastern Orthodox tradition, has exerted considerable influence upon current Protestant thinking. Of primary importance is his idea of the uniqueness of the historical order and of the need for the individual to *participate* in an historical tradition in order to understand its meaning. A religion cannot be understood from a vantage point beyond it and cannot be approached through speculation; all history is made up of the individual and the concrete and can only be grasped from within. The course of history itself can only be understood in relation to a supra-historical goal which is the divine life itself. The movement toward this goal is a dynamic process encompassing necessity (the fixed conditions of historical life), freedom (man's self determination), and transfiguring grace (the power of God in history).

Emil Brunner views history as the scene of the encounter between God and man. Seeking to reestablish the primacy of biblical conceptions, Brunner has laid great stress upon God's confronting man in his historical life through the medium of the Word, in the sense both of the Bible and of Christ Himself. For him the principal feature of the coming of Christ is the "once-for-allness" of the event as an historical happening, implying both the sufficiency of the mediator and the rejection of any other possible revelation of the nature of God. Of great importance is Brunner's belief that Christianity can and must enter into the fabric of civilization, transforming and elevating it, but not allowing itself to become identical with any cultural situation. The Kingdom of God may thus be a leaven in civilization but it cannot be said to be fully realized in any historical state of affairs.

The thought of Rudolf Bultmann presents something of a puzzle. On the one hand he is concerned, as a New Testament scholar, to preserve the results of historical scholarship and to show their importance for contemporary faith, but on the other he is inclined to express considerable skepticism about the extent to which God can actually be known in and through the course of history. The real significance of history for him consists of the fact that the individual must confront the choice which decides his destiny in the *present;* history can speak to us if we know how to listen to it critically. This we can do only if we are already aware of God's demand upon us. Thus Bultmann is more concerned with the individual's relation to God in history than in the disclosures of God through the course of history.

The main problem behind all these conceptions is whether the history of salvation, expressing "God's time," is regarded as so completely other than human history, or "man's time," that the two will remain indefinitely irrelevant to and incompatible with each other.

JOHN E. SMITH

Bibliography

Herbert Butterfield, *Christianity and History*.
Karl Löwith, *Meaning in History*.
H. Richard Niebuhr, *Christ and Culture*.
Roger L. Shinn, *Christianity and the Problem of History*.

THE HOLY

Perhaps the best clue to the meaning of the word *holy* is its liturgical use. Hymn Number One in many hymnals is "Holy, Holy, Holy, Lord God Almighty." One of its lines is, "Only thou art holy, there is none beside Thee." Similarly the traditional "Gloria in Excelsis," in addressing the triune deity, says of God the Son, "For thou only art holy."

These two ascriptions share a double implication. 1) God is "the Holy One." Here is the declaration of the majesty, the glory, the sovereignty, the unfathomable mystery that mark the divine. Holiness is so inherently a quality of God as to belong to the very definition of deity. Thus holiness is a more elemental quality of God than any other, e.g. than even justice or love. To declare that God is love is to announce something revealed or discovered, something that has often been questioned or denied; for conceivably God might not be love. But to deny God's holiness is to deny the sacred nature that constitutes deity.

Hence Paul Tillich describes the holy as "the *quality* of that which concerns man ultimately." And Gustaf Aulén says that holiness is not one of the attributes of God, but "the background and the atmosphere of the conception of God," which colors every attribute.

2) God alone is holy. His holiness is unique to His being and belongs to no other person or thing, save as He imparts it. Holiness may be ascribed to created things only in a derivative sense. When the Bible refers to holy places, men, angels, etc., it means that these are "holy unto the Lord." That is, they belong to God or are the

channels of God's relation to men. To attribute independent holiness to any created thing is idolatry.

In customary use the idea of the holy combines two
meanings, taking its primary shading from one or the
other. It is necessary, therefore, to distinguish the two.

The *basic* meaning of the holy is purely religious rather
than moral. It refers to the sacred as against the secular
or profane. It testifies to the inscrutable mystery and
otherness of God, to the separation between the Creator
and the creaturely. It is exemplified in the taboos of many
religions and the element of awe in reverence. The Old
Testament tradition that "no man may look on God and
live" expresses the fear that holiness inspires. A cultic
counterpart is the belief that anyone who touches the
Ark of the Covenant, however reverent his motives, must
die. The very Hebrew word *Qadosh* and its Aramaic
equivalent have the root meaning of *that which is
separate.*

A *secondary* meaning of the holy is the pure as against
the corrupt or unclean. Here the holiness of God is less
His majesty than His perfection. The classical biblical
passage in which the holiness of God becomes united to
His purity is Isaiah 6, where the prophet's terror before
God's majesty is removed by divine cleansing. The
Psalmists and Prophets often emphasize the ethical meaning of holiness, and the "Holiness Code" within Leviticus
(Chapters 17-26) combines elaborate ritual law and
moral law ("you shall love your neighbor as yourself").
The effect of this moral emphasis is evident in the fact
that *profane,* which originally meant simply the non-
sacred (literally, outside the temple) has come to imply
the corrupt.

Either of these meanings in isolation from the other
loses the theological significance of holiness. The original
meaning with no ethical significance can degenerate into
crude superstition, magic ritualism, and irrational fear.
The secondary meaning by itself has often become a
trivial moralism, lacking the reverence which marks the
original conception.

In modern theology the attitude toward the idea of the holy has varied widely. The Enlightenment, fearful of all irrationalism, reduced the meaning of holiness to the grandeur of the first cause of the universe and of morality. The Ritschlian wing of liberal theology limited holiness almost exclusively to its significance for ethics or values. Ritschl himself rejected the Old Testament conception of holiness and absorbed the meaning of holiness in goodness. Many of the Ritschlians, in their conception of the evolution of religion, relegated to primitive stages all conceptions of the holy except the moral.

Liberal theology, however, in the wing influenced by Schleiermacher, took a different line. Schleiermacher, who based religion upon the "feeling of absolute dependence," and the later theologians of "religious experience" often recover some of the meanings which rationalism and moralism had purged from the holy. Rudolf Otto in his classic work, *The Idea of the Holy* (*Das Heilige,* 1917), gave currency to many of the phrases which have marked later discussions; e.g., the numinous, *mysterium tremendum,* the "wholly other." He showed particularly how the idea of the holy combines the experience of overpowering awefulness with insistent fascination. Otto drew his data from many religions. But by calling attention to his theme in the Bible and in Luther, he led many Protestants to greater concern for the holy.

In recent religious thought and practice three other factors have contributed to increased preoccupation with the idea of the holy. 1) Anthropologists have shown persuasively that amidst the great diversities of religion, something akin to the holy has been a universal element in the religions of widely-varying cultures. 2) The dominant movement in Protestant theology (variously called post-liberal, neo-orthodox, or biblical theology) has emphasized the transcendent glory of God. 3) The widespread liturgical movements in the churches have shifted the interest of many congregations from a service of moral edification to worship of a God whose glory is not solely His moral value.

Yet the ambiguity of the idea of the holy persists. All

the variations in its traditional meaning are preserved in the colloquial uses of the word to include Holiness (Pentecostal) sects, holy days, the Holy Grail, the Holy of Holies, holy orders, holy men, holy water, Holy Week, the Holy Scriptures, the Holy Catholic Church, and many others. The only common element in these phrases is some conception of a holiness derived from God, "the Holy One."

ROGER LINCOLN SHINN

Bibliography

Rudolf Otto, *The Idea of the Holy.*
Paul Tillich, *Systematic Theology,* Vol. I (see index).

HOLY SPIRIT

The doctrine of the Holy Spirit is at once the most central and the most neglected doctrine of the Christian faith. It is the most central in the sense that everything in the Gospels is energized and motivated by and through its agency. The New Testament, as one commentator puts it, "is preëminently the book of the Holy Spirit" (R. Birch Hoyle, ERE, Vol. xi, p. 791 b). It may be put even more dramatically: whereas we may be permitted to sin against Jesus Christ, the sin against the Holy Ghost is unforgiveable. Yet while Christianity is thus as firmly *pneuma*-centric as it is Christo-centric, the doctrine has remained peripheral for the most part in the long history of doctrinal thinking.

The reason for this seeming neglect is not difficult to see. One of the *Fragments* from the lost writings of Irenaeus, for example, opens as follows: "Know thou that every man is either empty or full. For if he has not the Holy Spirit, he has no knowledge of the Creator; he has not received Jesus Christ the Life; he knows not the Father who is in heaven . . ." (*Fr.* xxvi). The Holy Spirit is something to be experienced, and is not subjected, therefore, to the criteria of formal thinking: the doctrine remains as a numinous, if always somewhat nebulous, presupposition of any Christian experience or meaning whatsoever. To neglect it, however, always leads theology either into intellectualism or dogmatic positivism, and the faith becomes legalistic and brittle. "Grace" is set over against man as sinner, and "God" is set over against the "world" in such a way as to surrender these terms to causal and naturalistic patterns of thinking, and in such a way as to deprive God of any immanent relation with his world.

In the Old Testament the word for spirit is *ruach*, or breath. It is the life-giving breath of God. It is the primal power of God in all things. Without the life-giving spirit of God man is but dust of the earth. At times it is used almost as a synonym for *nephesh*, the breath-soul in man. At others it is almost interchangeable with *leb* (*lebab*), standing for the innermost and deepest sense which the self has of itself. But at the same time it may appear in the divine conjunction, *ruach-Adonai*, the spirit of the Lord, the life-giving and energy-declaring power of God as manifested in human life and the world.

In the New Testament the term "spirit" is accented differently in the Synoptics, in Paul and in the Johannine writings. It is significant that in the Synoptics Jesus claims the anointing of the Holy Spirit as commissioning His work. The Holy Spirit's power is credited with the driving out of the possessing demons (Mt. 12:28); and at the same time all the goods of the Kingdom (of which the expulsion of the demons is an evidence) are summed up in the Holy Spirit (Lk. 11:13, Mt. 7:11). The Holy Spirit as God's power is affirmed. Similarly in the Pauline literature the place of the Holy Spirit is central. It may indeed be held to be the pivotal concept around which all his specific understandings turn. It is the Spirit which comes to man and delivers him from sin, death, and the law and opens the way to freedom and all the fruits of the Spirit—faith, righteousness, joy, peace. The work of Christ makes possible the renewal of the spirit within us. The Spirit becomes the mode whereby the Christ becomes the indwelling and dynamic principle of productive power within us. In the Johannine literature it is the life-giving aspect of the Spirit that is emphasized. As such the Spirit becomes almost a metaphysical principle and Spirit and truth are identified (I John 5:6).

Clearly the notion of the Holy Spirit is intended to convey our sense of God's activity toward us. This activity and power must assume a variety of forms. It must be assigned to God's primal creative act as well as to the exultant sense of power moving through us. It is also that power which is perverted into demonic forms by the rebellious creature, just as it is the redeeming power "from on high" made available to us in the witness of Jesus as the Christ. It is perhaps significant, therefore, that the Apostle Paul does not attempt to define the term, but is content to observe its presence and the manner of its working. For in terms of Trinitarian speculation it clearly risks distortion the moment it is hypostatized or affirmed as a "Person": for clearly it is the one term of "immanence" with which the "I-Thou relation" formula cannot dispense. Nor can its inherence in man as "spirit" be dispensed with, albeit spirit may be carnalized. For spirit remains a depth-dimension rather than a dimension of transcendence. A theology of "Grace" which neglects this tends to become intellectualistic and barren, just as a theology of the "Word" which confines the operations of spirit to the spoken or preached word tends to become magical. The obvious danger on the other side is the temptation to extend the Spirit's immanence into a monistic and immanental mysticism in which other distinctions proper to the Gospels are dissolved. What we discover is that we "live" in worlds projected from our ego-centric wilfulness, and hence do not dwell in the real world but in a world where reality and illusion are confused: our "spiritual" awakening must be an awakening into the real world which the Spirit sustains and into true experience which is not empty but full.

STANLEY ROMAINE HOPPER

Bibliography

R. Birch Hoyle, "Holy Spirit," *Encyclopedia of Religion and Ethics.*
Regin Prenter, *Spiritus Creator* (Trans. by John M. Jensen).
Charles Williams, *The Descent of the Dove.*

"I-THOU" AND "I-IT"

"I-Thou" and "I-It" are terms coined by the contemporary Jewish philosopher and theologian Martin Buber to describe man's two primary attitudes and relations. These terms are first employed in Buber's classic exposition of the "philosophy of dialogue," *I and Thou* (1923). Although the "I-Thou" relation was already adumbrated in the late eighteenth and the nineteenth centuries by such thinkers as Friedrich Heinrich Jacobi, Ludwig Feuerbach, and Sören Kierkegaard, it is only in the twentieth century that it has flowered into a full-scale philosophy and philosophy of religion through largely independent and more or less contemporaneous elaboration by the Jewish philosophers Martin Buber, Hermann Cohen, and Franz Rosenzweig, the Protestant philosopher Eugen Rosenstock-Huessy, and the Catholic philosophers Ferdinand Ebner and Gabriel Marcel. Of these it is Martin Buber who gave the I-Thou its classical form, and who clarified the difference between the I-Thou and the I-It relations and worked out the implications of this distinction in a systematic and thorough-going fashion. Largely through the influence of Buber on such key Protestant theologians as Emil Brunner, Karl Barth, Reinhold Niebuhr, H. Richard Niebuhr, Paul Tillich, John Macmurray, John Baillie, Herbert H. Farmer, Friedrich Gogarten, Karl Heim, and J. H. Oldham, the "I-Thou" philosophy has become, in Paul Tillich's words, "a common good of the Protestant world." It has also penetrated deeply into the thought of such Catholic thinkers as Erich Przywara, Ernst Michel, Romano Guardini, Theodore Steinbüchel, and M. C. D'Arcy, as well as Ebner and Marcel, and into that of the Russian Orthodox existentialist, Nicholas Berdyaev.

"As I become *I*, I say *Thou*." The "I" of man comes into being in the act of speaking one or the other of the two primary words—Thou or It. "The primary word *I-Thou* can only be spoken with the whole being. The primary word *I-It* can never be spoken with the whole being." The real determinant of the primary word in which a man takes his stand is not the object which is over against him but the way in which he relates himself to that object. *I-Thou*, the primary word of relation and togetherness, is characterized by mutuality, directness, presentness, intensity, and ineffability. *I-It*, the primary word of experiencing and using, takes place *within* a man and not *between* him and the world. As exemplified in the typical subject-object relationship, whether in knowing, feeling, or acting, it is subjective and lacking in mutuality.

To Buber, I-Thou and I-It alternate with each other in integral relation. The Thou must continually become It, and the It may again become a Thou; but it will not be able to remain one, and it need not become Thou at all. Man can live continuously and securely in the world of It, but he can only actualize his humanity if he interpenetrates this world with the relation to the Thou. Real communication, likewise, is a fruitful alternation between I-Thou and I-It. The "word" may be identified with subject-object, or I-It, knowledge while it remains indirect and symbolic, but it is itself the channel and expression of the direct and reciprocal knowing of I-Thou when it is taken up into real dialogue. This applies equally to the religious word and the religious symbol which may point man back to a dialogue between man and God, when taken up into real meeting, but may obstruct that dialogue when taken as a reality in itself.

Buber's distinction between I-Thou and I-It has been applied by H. and H. A. Frankfort to that between mythical thinking and discursive thought. It has also been fruitfully applied by Buber and many others to ethics, education, and psychology, in all of which the presentness, uniqueness, and awareness of the other found in genuine dialogue have made possible a more concrete and discriminating approach to the understanding of interpersonal relations and of the methods appropriate to the study of man. Its most revolutionary effect, however, has been in the field of philosophy of religion and theology. Buber's concept of God as the "Eternal Thou" who cannot become "It" has redirected the approach to philosophy of religion from the objective—concern with questions as to the existence and nature of God—and the subjective—questions as to the pragmatic effects and psychological or emotional accompaniment of religious belief—to the dialogical—the relation *between* man and God. Man knows God in relation and *only* in relation. The true God can never be an object of our thought, not even the "Absolute" object from which all others derive. God, to Buber, is "the Being that is directly, most nearly, and lastingly over against us, that may properly only be addressed, not expressed." The "eternal Thou" is not a symbol of God but of our relation with God. God *is* not a person, but He *becomes* one in order to know and be known, to love and be loved by man. Man cannot discover God through philosophical speculation, but he can meet the eternal Thou in his direct, reciprocal meeting with man and nature. Man becomes aware of the address of God in every meeting with the concrete and the everyday, if he remains open to that address and ready to respond with his whole being. God is always present. It is only we who are absent. Evil for Buber is not I-It, but the predominance of the I-It relation that prevents the turning to the Thou. Good is not pure I-Thou, but the permeation of the world of It by the I-Thou relation.

There are many Christian interpretations of the I-Thou philosophy, some of which see Christ as Thou (Gogarten), some as I (Guardini, Barth), some as both (J. E. Fison). Many of the Protestant Neo-Orthodox thinkers and theologians who have adopted the I-Thou philosophy have recast it, in contrast to Buber, in the form of a radical dualism between I-Thou, understood as good, and I-It, understood as evil. Writers like Gogarten, Brunner, and

Barth, in varying degrees, equate I-It with man's sinful nature and I-Thou with the grace and divine love which are only present in their purity in Christ. The consequences of this dualism are often a de-emphasis on the possibility and significance of ethical action, an emphasis on the primacy of grace, the belief that God is always the addressor (I) and man always the addressed (Thou), and a view of ethical choice as between I *or* Thou.

MAURICE S. FRIEDMAN

Bibliography

Martin Buber, *I and Thou,* translated by Ronald Gregor Smith.

Martin Buber, *Between Man and Man,* translated by Ronald Gregor Smith.

IDOLATRY

Few biblical terms are more widely misunderstood than the concept of idolatry. According to popular interpretation, it is merely an exaggerated symptom of primitive exclusiveness. Arnold Toynbee, for example, regards the ancient Hebrews as simply more stubborn than their neighbors in clinging to their particular war god. In his view, idolatry was a term of abuse applied to the "outgroup," and especially to anyone who dared abandon narrow, tribal loyalties for a more broadminded attitude.

The trouble with this conception is that a careful reading of the Bible does more to confound than to confirm it. It can scarcely make sense of the prophet's strictures against national pride as *itself* a form of idolatry. Nor can it account for the continual chastisement of Israel by her allegedly chauvinistic God: "You only have I known of all the peoples of the earth: therefore will I punish you for your iniquities" (Amos 3:2).

Instead of examining its biblical context, Professor Toynbee's definition superimposes upon idolatry some of the favorite clichés of the twentieth century. Its original meaning derives from a very different world of thought.

It is not necessarily out of date on that account, however. Since truth is not bound by time or place, idolatry, like any other concept, ancient or modern, can be judged by its contemporary relevance.

The definition of idolatry as "the worship of a false god" presupposes an understanding of the word "god." The Bible uses it as a strictly functional term. It stands for that point of reference, external to himself, which serves the individual as both his criterion of truth and his standard of value. For a child, his parents usually function as his god. The Bible further contends, however, that having a god is by no means a phenomenon of childhood alone. On putting away the gods of his youth, the adult does not become godless; he merely substitutes one object of worship for another. The Bible never charges a man with being irreligious. It conceives the human being as "worshipping animal" who necessarily has some object of primary allegiance which functions as his guide to truth and his norm of conduct. Though free to adopt the god of his choice, no man is free to avoid this decision. Every attempt to do so turns out to be not a renunciation but an exchange of gods.

At the suggestion that he worships a god, the man of the world is incredulous. But the absence of a label need not alter the contents of the package. In fact, some enterprises are more successful when anonymous. The gods of the twentieth century are simply more sophisticated than graven images of wood and stone. Baal and Moloch have learned to masquerade as the various "-isms" and "-ologies" which compete for modern man's allegiance.

Nor do they always require the incognito. A surprising number of moderns openly acknowledge that they have in fact exchanged the biblical God for another. One of today's reigning deities was recently paid the following public homage:

> Men bet their lives on it [science] as they do on other gods, and on the record, it *functions* no less divinely than any other . . . "God" is no less fitting an appellation for this [science] than for any that

churchmen so name and require laymen to bet their lives on, worship, and adjure. (Horace M. Kallen, *Democracy's True Religion*, p. 10.)

Science, of course, is by no means the only deity to which modern man has looked for deliverance. Today's pantheon is as liberally populated as those of Greece and Rome.

Its patrons provide case studies in the effect of idolatry upon the individual. If a man's character is the reflection of his values, and if his values are derived from his god, then the kind of person he becomes depends directly upon the object of his worship. As the psalmist puts it:

> Their idols are silver and gold, the work of men's hands. They have mouths, but they speak not; eyes have they, but they see not . . . *They that make them are like unto them;* so is everyone that trusteth in them (Psalm 115).

If a man is made in the image of God, then the key to personality is religion. It would consequently never occur to a biblical author to write either the biography of a man or the history of a nation apart from a thorough account of their respective gods.

The religion of science, for example, leaves its trademark upon its devotee in the form of that humorless, fact-centered literal-mindedness which so readily lends itself to caricature. The same inner logic is at work in another modern cult, that of deified democracy. Explicitly embraced as their religion by numerous intellectuals, it casts its followers in the mold of an undistinguished mediocrity, without style or manners. Carrying "democratic equality" beyond the political sphere, where it properly belongs, into the whole of life, they tolerate no distinction between the superior and the inferior. Under the dominion of this god, the cultivation of a fine sense of discrimination and taste, once recognized as the very spice of life, threatens to become an un-American activity.

Of course, a person need not confine himself to a single god. But he who tries to divide his ultimate loyalty also splits himself. No longer integrated about a single center, his personality becomes equivocal and ambivalent. In its extreme form, this phenomenon is known clinically as schizophrenia. Its diagnosis, in biblical terms, is polytheism.

This biblical analysis provides an easy explanation of the frustration most people have experienced in arguments over moral questions. If a man's moral values are the consequence of the god he worships, he will never change them without first changing gods. Until he does, all criticism of his standards will appear to him as treason.

That a man's god is the keeper of his conscience is beautifully illustrated by Communism. A book by six former Communists demonstrates how this movement, point for point, fits the biblical definition of religion. Bearing the significant title *The God That Failed* (Harper, New York, 1949), it gives a vivid, first-hand account of the way in which this idol washes not only the brain but also the conscience. Lenin spoke for all its victims when he declared that had he not purged his own closest comrades he would have been guilty of treason to his ideals. He thereby revealed that the cleavages which divide the world are too deep to be resolved by moral indignation. Now, as in ancient times, they represent a battle of the gods.

If the abstract deities of modern times are less crude than their predecessors, they have demonstrated no less a capacity to visit destruction upon believer and unbeliever alike. The consequences of idolatry, not content with their damage to the individual personality, find expression in physical destruction as well. This is nowhere more evident than in the worship of the German nation, openly preached by Heinrich von Treitschke and subsequently put into practice. This fearsome deity not only molded the Nazi character, not only hypnotized the conscience of the world's most scientific nation, but, with its mystique of war, exhibited the same appetite for human sacrifice as the pagan gods of Babylon.

The destructive consequences of idolatry provide the touchstone by which the Bible distinguishes the true God from impostors. At this suggestion that one religion is true and the others false, the modern reader recoils in horror. Like Professor Toynbee, he has been conditioned to respond to any such claim with cries of "intolerance" and "bigotry." But this is hardly the kind of reaction which befits a scientific age. When the prophet invokes the distinction true and false, he is merely applying the same principle with which science has so successfully *combatted* dogmatism. The scientist's basic premise is that, under specified conditions, a given question may have millions of false answers, but only a single true one. Far from encouraging dogmatism, this distinction between true and false enables men to resist claims of infallibility, whether advanced by church, political ideology, or intellectual doctrine. Yet, by a curious inversion of logic, the very principle which prevents authoritarianism in science is thought to promote it in religion. To maintain that there is but one true God among a host of pretenders raises in people's minds the specter of inquisitions and witch hunts.

Some contemporary theologians have been so frightened by this mistaken charge of bigotry that, in their zeal to avoid it, they take a position which ironically enough can lead straight to it. For, in their haste to agree that it is impossible for one religion to be truer than another, they deny that Christianity finds corroboration in either reason or experience. Christian loyalty is a leap in the dark, closed to tests of any sort. It is completely gratuitous and, therefore, in the last analysis, arbitrary. Such theology is consequently more open to bigotry than that which acknowledges an objective criterion by which it can be refuted. And it is the open acknowledgment of just such a criterion which the God of biblical theology demands.

The prophets of the Old Testament were not afraid of being refuted by either experience or reason. The Bible is not a collection of dogmatic fulminations and unverifiable pronouncements, but a book of *evidence*. Far from exhorting men to believe what they cannot see, it taunts them for their veritable genius for not believing what they do see: "Ye have eyes to see but do not perceive; ye have ears to hear but do not understand" (Is. 6:9). The prophets challenge false gods and their worshippers to a trial of strength, and invite them to choose their own weapons.

The victor will be determined on the basis of performance. The true God is He who actually accomplishes what His rivals only claim to do. All gods provide the individual with a standard of truth, reality, and goodness, upon which to base the day-to-day decisions of ordinary life. He who entrusts himself to a false standard therefore flies in the face of reality. His behavior will resemble the drunkard's in its incongruity with the facts of life. Hence the prophet's derision:

> Every man is brutish in his knowledge, every founder is confounded by the graven image. For his molten image is falsehood, and there is no breath in them. They are vanity, and the work of errors. In the time of their visitation they shall perish (Jeremiah 10:14, 15).

The idolater has been duped by a promise which only the true God could fulfill. Having bet on illusion instead of reality, he is sure to be confounded. In the end his idol will visit him with the exact opposite of what he had expected. Two recent books provide dramatic illustration of this thesis as it applies to two of America's favorite idolatries, the cult of individualism and the cult of sex.

Individualism, of course, is one of the watchwords of America. From pioneer days to the present, it has been invoked as an infallible guide to economic, political, and even moral decisions. One would therefore expect America to be the incubator of strong, independent personalities. Yet studies by Erich Fromm and David Reisman indicate unmistakably that we are fostering instead a mass-produced citizenry whose greatest desire is to emulate, whose greatest fear is to deviate, and whose greatest skill is to be all things to all men. Most recently William Whyte, in *The Organization Man*, has detected one of the strongest pressures for the rubber-stamp mentality in that bastion of free enterprise, private industry itself. While consciously doing obeisance to the god of rugged individualism, the American corporation often dictates to its executives their taste in dress and automobile, their choice of friends and clubs, and even their ethical and political views. Exactly as the prophet would have predicted, the more desperately individualism is pursued as a good in itself, the more it is belied by the facts.

A similar fate is in store for the worshipper of sex. Americans are so notorious for exploiting it at every opportunity, from art to advertising, that one might expect to find them oversexed. Psychologists have long suspected that the opposite is the case. The façade of sensationalism, they contend, is a screen for sexual failure, the daydream of people who betray by their fantasies what they have failed to achieve in fact. The prodigies recorded in the Kinsey Reports do not suggest fulfillment, but rather a frantic groping for the right combination. A contemporary theologian, Robert E. Fitch, has diagnosed this ironic phenomenon in his *The Decline and Fall of Sex*. Analyzing the treatment of sex in such so-called "daring" and "honest" books as *Peyton Place* and *Bonjour Tristesse*, he finds not vitality but tedium, not joy but cynicism, not exaltation but degradation. The hero is the person who goes through with it as an act of fidelity, even of sacrifice, to Aphrodite. Promising its followers salvation through sex, this god destroys their capacity to enjoy it.

As a man repeatedly barks his shins upon these recalcitrant facts, he may see through the duplicity of his idol, and recognize that he has been the victim of a "god that failed." Like any intoxicant, however, idolatry has an element of the vicious circle about it. Since he cannot recant without loss of face, the idolater resolutely fortifies himself against the rude awakening. This inability to come to terms with reality, of course, is one of the surest symptoms of neurosis. It reaches an extreme in philosophers like Nietzsche and his followers, who pride themselves on the "courage" to believe in illusion, who scorn success and who court catastrophe. This willful blindness underlies the prophet's description of idolatry as the "primordial stupidity."

In addition to this self-deception, however, there is also a touch of pathos about idolatry. Its victim has also been duped. In St. Paul's words, "When ye knew not God, ye were in bondage unto them which by nature are no gods" (Galatians 4:8). More often than not, these gods are able to deceive a man by appealing not to his baser instincts but to his sense of goodness. Science, democracy, patriotism, and the rest are all creative in the service of God. Only when permitted to usurp His place do they run amuck. Most idolatry is thus not simply the fruit of sheer perversity, but of good intentions gone wrong. The idolater may even set an example of sincere and courageous devotion. The biblical analysis enables one to sympathize with his bewilderment when his self-sacrificing exertions boomerang.

The final arbiter between gods is pragmatic: the true God is He who keeps His word. But it is also objective: the true God can fulfill His promises only because He is the Lord of all reality. The biblical writers tell of a God whose promises to men far exceed those of the most extravagant idol. They also invite men to behold the mighty acts by which He fulfills them. The prophet summons every idol to a trial of strength, secure in the confidence that "God is not mocked."

E. LA B. CHERBONNIER

Bibliography

Abraham J. Heschel, *God in Search of Man.*
Claude Tresmontant, *Essai sur la Pensée Hébraïque.*
G. Ernest Wright, *God Who Acts.*

IMMORTALITY

Immortality is a concept relatively rare in biblical thought, occurring only in Rom. 2:7, I Cor. 15:53-54, I Tim. 6:16, and II Tim. 1:10. It came into the stream of historic

Christian faith chiefly through the Greek tributary. Although there are many varieties of belief in immortality in Greek thought, the chief emphasis is upon a dualism in the human person between body and soul. The body is mortal, subject to corruption, and will decay after the moment of physical death. The soul, on the contrary, is immortal, not subject to corruption, and will continue in unending and eternal existence, apart from the body. Hence immortality, or deathlessness (the Greek *thanatos,* death, is transformed into *athanatos,* deathless, by the addition of the *alpha* privative, from which comes *athanasia,* immortality) is a possibility for the indestructible soul, but not for the mortal body, which is sloughed off and discarded. This notion pervades Orphic thought in Greece, and is developed by Plato, particularly in the Socratic dialogue on death and immortality of the soul, the *Phaedo.*

In the life of the early Christian community, as it came into contact with Greek culture, the notion of immortality of the soul made its way into the faith of Christendom, sometimes as a specific attempt to describe the Christian hope in eternal life by means of Greek categories, and sometimes as a broad term to describe the Christian hope in general. It is clearly to be contrasted with the more distinctively Hebraic strain of Christian thought, which stresses resurrection (q.v.) as opposed to immortality. An early Christian confession of faith, usually called the Apostles' Creed, affirms, for example, belief in "the resurrection of the body," the body [see "Soul (body)"] being understood as the total personality, which dies, and is then raised up by the power of God, rather than by its inherent deathlessness, to newness of life with Him. It was partly in reaction to literalistic interpretations of the phrase "resurrection of the body" that the phrase "immortality of the soul" became for many centuries of Christian history a more common and acceptable way of speaking of life after death. The recent recovery of "biblical theology" in Protestant thought, however, has rendered the term "immortality of the soul" suspect on two counts: 1) as failing to convey the fullness of the biblical concern with the ultimate fulfillment of the *total* life of man, and

2) as stressing rather the negation and ultimate worthlessness of a part of that life (e.g. the discarding of the "corrupt" body).

Whatever its linguistic origins, and whatever its final inadequacies as a symbol, it is nevertheless true that the conception of "immortality" is used today in popular Christian thought simply as a convenient synonym for "everlasting life," "life eternal," etc. Disassociated from its Greek origins, the broader contemporary understanding of the term indicates a belief, not subject to empirical evidence but following as a corollary from faith in a good and loving God, that the "threescore years and ten" of man's existence do not exhaust the meaning of that existence, but that that which has been begun by God during man's life on earth, the creation of sons fit for full fellowship with Him, will be continued and completed by God, in His own time and in His own ways, beyond the confines of earthly life. It is further contended (with considerable biblical support, especially from the Fourth Gospel and the other Johannine writings) that this dimension of life is not reserved for a time after the moment of physical death, but that life can be lived eternally in the present, as a kind of foretaste of what will be fully realized after death. For the Christian, the sign and seal of this power of God over death is found in His conquering of death in the resurrection of Jesus Christ.

But in all of this, any Christian view which bases itself on the power of God over the fact of death, separates itself rather clearly from the notion that "immortality" is an inherent right, as Greek thought supposed, and insists that it is by the power of God alone that the believer is raised up to newness of life and given a gift which he in no wise deserves.

ROBERT MCAFEE BROWN

Bibliography

J. Baillie, *And The Life Everlasting.*
E. Brunner, *Eternal Hope.*
A. E. Taylor, *The Christian Hope of Immortality.*

THE INCARNATION

The doctrine that God became man in Jesus Christ is authoritatively defined by the ancient Christian creeds. Newman is representative of Eastern and Anglican theology in considering the incarnation the central truth of the gospel, and the source whence we are to draw out its principles. Indeed, the originality and uniqueness of Christianity consists of this: "that unique and absolute truth has in Christianity the form not of a rule, a law, *Dharma,* nor of ideas or theologies; Christian revelation has the form of a man" (Söderblom).

It is significant that it was not until after Christianity had broken with Judaism and become a church of the Gentiles that its "consciousness of the Deity of Christ became free and unrestricted" (Dorner). The doctrine of the incarnation arose with the Hellenization of Christianity, which replaced the Pauline-eschatological conception of the dying and rising again with Christ with the Hellenistic-mystical conception of the union of flesh and Spirit (Schweitzer). Spirit becomes flesh in the Person of Christ and therein flesh becomes capable of immortality and resurrection. This transformation is complete by the time of Ignatius, who also thought of the sacraments as a mediation of the Incarnate Spirit. In the Fourth Gospel, a Hellenistic conception of redemption through union with the Incarnate Word has wholly replaced the Jewish-eschatological expectation of redemption which underlay the Synoptic Gospels. It shows the historic Jesus preaching the mystical doctrine of redemption through rebirth in the Logos-Christ, and thus makes possible a "biblical" doctrine of incarnation.

Irenaeus, Athanasius, and the Cappadocians extended the doctrine by conceiving the incarnation as the restoration of the human race to the divine life. Athanasius thought of the result of the incarnation as the transformation of human corruption into incorruptibility by the renewal of the divine image in man and its consequent participation in the life of God. The incarnation also resulted, as had been held by the Apologists, in the restoration of the knowledge of God. This knowledge had not only been lost in the Fall (the emphasis of Western theology), for the creation itself was not sufficient to admit of the creature perceiving the Creator. Eastern theology centered upon the incarnation as God's way to man which makes possible the deification of human nature through the mystical-sacramental advent and presence of the Incarnate Word. Anselm is representative of Western theology in conceiving of the work of the incarnation as the union of man with the Person but not with the nature of God.

Hegel thought of Christ as the full incarnation of the Idea in the form of conscious Spirit. Christ is the supreme appearance "in the sensuous form appropriate to history" of the unity of man with God. The Spirit appeared in fullness in Christ that from Him the whole of humanity might be set free and made conscious of its divine state. Kierkegaard reversed Hegel by conceiving of the incarnation as the absolute paradox of an eternal and infinite God becoming a temporal and finite man. Jesus Christ is the Eternal made "Paradox," whose historical garb is accidental. He is only to be apprehended through the suspension of history and in the immediacy of the Incarnate Moment which becomes present through a leap of faith. Strangely enough, Barth has returned to the rational spirit of Anselm by rejecting Kierkegaard's conception of the incarnation as a breach between the being of God in Himself and His activity as reconciler of the world. God's incarnate acts are in accordance with His divine nature, for His omnipotence is such that it can assume the form of weakness and in that form can triumph. Bultmann rejects the doctrines of the pre-existence of Christ and His incarnation as the cosmic Son of God as mythological. He insists that what the New Testament says of the pre-existent Christ as the mediator of creation expresses the faith that creation and redemption are one: "The love of

God which encounters the hearer is the word of proclamation originated before all time."

THOMAS J. J. ALTIZER

Bibliography

J. A. Dorner, *History of the Development of the Doctrine of the Person of Christ.*
A. Harnack, *History of Dogma.*
H. A. Wolfson, *Philosophy of the Church Fathers.*

JUDAISM

Judaism, as the distinguished theologian Solomon Schechter has observed, is a "catholic" religion. This is to say that its concerns, however its historical manifestations to the contrary, are not narrowly parochial, exclusivist, or legal.

Judaism is formed of two abiding and contending elements: one which, in the spirit of the prophets, protests against the complacencies and idolatries of the world ("Therefore we trust in thee, O Lord, our God! speedily to behold thy glorious power, to remove abominations from the earth and cause all idols to be utterly destroyed, and establish the universe under the dominion of the Almighty"—from the *Alenu,* Hertz Edition of the Prayer Book); while, at the same time, persevering in obedience to the liturgical, social, and personal *way* (a more proper translation of *halakhah,* usually rendered as *law*) which the Talmudic Age detailed and the medieval codes popularized.

The dialectic of protest and order necessitates that Judaism be manifest in the following aspects: ecumenical, in that masses of dispersed and culturally different peoples are bound into community by a defining commitment to a creating, revealing, redeeming, and transforming God; catholic, in that the Torah is understood to be universal, complete, and true for all mankind (whether it is accepted directly or under the form of what Maimonides terms "imitating" creeds). Both aspects are dynamic, in that community and authority may always be challenged and modified by the witness of greater wisdom, more profound piety, and more reasonable understanding of the person of God and the ways of Torah.

Modern Judaism finds the challenge of its ecumenism and catholic universality rendered suspect before the modern insistence upon sheer novelty—a quality too often mistaken for vitality. The knowledge of tradition within the Jewish community is, at the present moment, so insufficient as to make all authority and principles of unity subject to cavil. Where once each Jew was a "learner" of Torah, or at least a disciple of those who "learned," he is today increasingly proud, and correspondingly independent, in his ignorance; moreover, those who continue to "learn" are split off by the content and language of their study from those most desperately in need of their findings. The consequence is that Jewish religious life is weak. Despite this situation, the claim of theological question has once more been asserted. The challenge of non-Jewish religions, the appeal of secular society, and anarchic disorder within the faith have provoked new interest in philosophic and theological apologia. Jews have come increasingly under the influence of Christian theological movements and have sought to assess Judaism in the light of more easily accessible Christian sources (the influence of Reinhold Niebuhr, for example, is more pronounced in the work of Will Herberg than is any classic or contemporary Jewish thinker); the language of Christian theology has come to assert a claim upon Jewish thinkers seeking a language in which to gain access to Jewish religious concerns (the early writings of both Buber and Rosenzweig witness to the more immediate impress of Christian literature than of Jewish sources). Notwithstanding such attempts to recover Judaism by first passing through Christianity, such authentically Jewish theologians as Franz Rosenzweig and Abraham Heschel (both vastly contrasting minds) have emerged. They, perhaps more than others, have acted to reformulate the primary axes on which Judaism turns: Jewish life, as experienced through the daily liturgy, the sanctification of the profane, the way of study; and Jewish thought, as realized in commitment to fundamental postulates of faith—the revelation of the Torah, the Covenant with Israel, the redemption of Israel, and the establishment of the Kingdom of God.

Judaism is neither clear, coherent, or explicable at the present moment. The evidence is profound, however, that an intellectual renascence is in process. Though such renascence must inevitably pass through peripheral phases (witness the establishment of institutional colloquia on such impractical themes as the derivation of a universal ethics from Talmudic authority) it will inevitably direct itself to realistic religious needs. Where theology and philosophy were once considered ancillary and posterior to concrete observance of the Torah (to the question posed by a Christian scholar of the court of John II of Aragon as to whether he was a Jewish philosopher, R. Abraham Bibago replied: "I am a Jew who believes in the Torah given to us by our teacher Moses, though I have studied philosophy"), the situation is currently reversed. The optimism, emancipation, and secularism characteristic of the recent past rendered unnecessary the insulation which fear and defensive pride had forced upon European Jewry. The popular assumption that Torah was valid only in the ghetto, but invalid in the emancipated salons of Western Europe, has produced in our day the consequence that neither Torah nor liturgy are considered a quite suitable preoccupation for "liberated" and "equalized" Jews. The only way which contemporary Jewish thinkers have found to reapproach the community is to subject it to the challenge of prior questions—to hold up to the individual the mirror of his finitude and deception. Not the appeal of ancient claims but the devices of existential insinuation become the viable bases of apologetics (Cf. Rosenzweig, *Understanding the Sick and the Healthy*). In this Judaism stands together with Neo-Orthodox Christianity and the dialectical paradoxes of "Crisis Theology." Out of such theological confrontation of the community, the biblical way, and the liturgical statements of traditional Judaism may, one hopes, be recovered; as well, the never-ending, but suspended conversation of Judaism with Christianity and Islam may be resumed.

ARTHUR A. COHEN

Bibliography

Arthur Cohen, *The Making of the Jewish Mind.*
N. N. Glatzer, *Franz Rosenzweig: His Life and Thought.*

JUSTICE

In Christian ethics the idea of justice has, as in philosophical ethics, three major referents: 1) God's justice or righteousness (comparable to a norm of absolute justice in the philosophical tradition), 2) the right ordering of life among men (social justice), and 3) the virtue of justice (being the just man).

The Bible tells of God's righteousness. God is holy and just; the content of His righteousness is disclosed in part in the Law. God requires fidelity and obedience to Himself; the wicked and the just man each will receive his due recompense. Yet even in the Old Testament God's love and mercy are never separated from the wrath of His righteousness. In the New Testament God's righteousness appears to refer to His character, His action, and includes His merciful justification of man.

Biblical literature also knows human justice as it is urged by the eighth-century prophets. Amos, for example, says, "Let justice roll down like water," and speaks specifically to the situation of the people of Israel. God requires a right ordering of social relationships. To some extent this is described in the law code, in part it must be discerned in the particular situation.

The biblical idea of the just man is one who is obedient and faithful to God. External conformity to the law is not enough (Jeremiah, Jesus); the law must be written on the heart, internalized in motivation. Yet finally man's just and righteous life is not enough (Paul); man is saved by God's righteousness (which includes His mercy).

Contemporary Christian ethicists deal with several aspects of the problem of justice. Some persons work on justice in relation to its ultimate source and ground. Thus the Roman Catholic Jacques Maritain and the Anglican V. A. Demant base their understanding of right order among men on a theory of the moral law of nature that is rooted in the classic traditional Plato and Aristotle and became a major part of the Christian tradition in St. Thomas Aquinas. A created order and purpose exists in the essence of man and human relations. This purpose seeks fulfillment in the restoration of man and society to their true nature. Jesus Christ is morally important in part because through Him and the Church this restoration has begun to take place. The right order of life in contemporary society is grounded in and reflects the right order that is given in creation and continues to exist in essential form in spite of sin and human disorder.

The Protestant Paul Tillich understands justice, like love and power, to be the "form of Being"; i.e., the social category of justice is grounded in the "cosmic hierarchy" of ultimate reality. Love, power, and justice are inseparable both ontologically and historically. There are various levels of human justice, e.g., proportional justice and creative justice. Fundamental to these, however, is "the intrinsic claim for justice of everything that has being."

Unlike Maritain, Demant, and Tillich, all of whom speculate about the ultimate ground of justice knowable through human reason, other important contemporary theologians eschew such theories. They are concerned with a more "biblical" interpretation of justice. In the Reformation tradition the law and the major institutions of life exist to maintain justice in a world of sinful and unfaithful men, to lead men to repentance (they can never fulfill the law), and to be a form of discipline and action even for the man who in God's grace lives a life of love. Thus for Emil Brunner justice is necessary because we cannot have a society of spontaneous loving relationships in history. There are "orders of creation," e.g., the family, work, and the state, in and through which we can act justly, and which become a "school" for the true community of love. Love, compared with justice, is free, spontaneous action in community. In the life of divine love, to be fully known only in the Kingdom of God, the forms and structures of justice are overcome. Thus one has in Brunner a sharp separation of love and justice.

Reinhold Niebuhr also eschews a positive theory of natural law and the ontological ground of justice. Man stands as one condemned under the law of love given in Jesus Christ. The life of perfect realization of love is an impossibility in man's state of unfaithfulness to God and to consequent sin. Thus in the most intimate human relationships relative justice is involved, e.g., a definition or understanding of the limitations of the rights and privileges of others. In the impersonal social structures the Christian is called upon to engage in power struggles, knowing that relative justice is the best that can be achieved. He can do this because he knows the justification of God, i.e., that in the end one's failures are redeemed in God's mercy.

Other theologians see justice and love in immediate relation to each other both as qualities in human relations, and as ultimately grounded in the unity of God, the Creator-Redeemer, e.g., in Karl Barth on the one hand, and D. D. Williams on the other.

JAMES GUSTAFSON

Bibliography

E. Brunner, *The Divine Imperative.*
V. A. Demant, *Theology of Society.*
J. Maritain, *True Humanism.*
R. Niebuhr, *Interpretation of Christian Ethics.*
P. Tillich, *Love, Power, and Justice.*
D. D. Williams, *God's Grace and Man's Hope.*

KAIROS

Kairos is one of the two words created by the Greeks to designate time. The other is *chronos*. Their difference is characteristic of the genius of the Greek language, which is able to reveal dimensions of reality which remain unnoticed in modern languages. While chronos designates the continuous flux of time, kairos points out a significant moment of time. Chronos points to the measurable side of the temporal process—clock time—which is determined by the regular movements of the stars, especially the movement of the earth around the sun. Kairos points to unique moments in the temporal process, moments in which something unique can happen or be accomplished. In the English word "timing" something of the experience which underlies the term kairos is preserved. Timing means doing something at the right time. One can formulate the difference between chronos and kairos by saying that chronos brings out the quantitative, calculable, repetitive element of the temporal process, while kairos emphasizes the qualitative, experiential, unique element. One of the main differences between man's encounter with nature and his encounter with history is that the former can be mainly, though not completely, expressed in terms of quantitative time—chronos—while the latter must be expressed mainly, though not exclusively, in terms of qualitative time—kairos.

This is why the term kairos did not show its full significance in classical Greek. It was used for the contingent moments of time in which a finite transitory event could happen, or a finite, relatively insignificant action could take place. One could say that now is the right time to go to war or to build a house or to accept a disciple or—in a more banal use—to buy a special meat or to sell a piece of cloth. The same banalization can be observed in the use of the English word "timing" (for which there is no German or French equivalent). Therefore, no reason would exist for an article on kairos to appear in a *Handbook of Christian Theology* if the word had not been used in a context in which it received a profounder meaning and a more far-reaching significance. This happened when the predominantly historical view of the universe in Christianity expressed its historical concern with the help of the Greek word *kairos*. When this was done by Christianity (as early as in the synoptic Gospels) the meaning of kairos was not changed, but focussed on a unique event in time —the appearance of the Christ.

Kairos, for the biblical writers, is fulfilled time—the time in which the appearance of the Christ was possible because, in spite of actual rejection, all the conditions of His reception were prepared. The one real kairos is the moment of history in which the preparatory period of history comes to an end because that for which it was preparation has become historical reality. In this sense, kairos implies that the central event—the appearance of the Christ—is not an isolated happening falling, so to speak, from heaven; but that it is an event which is prepared for by history and by the "timing" of historical providence. One can express this by saying that "the great kairos" presupposes many smaller *kairoi* within the historical development by which it was prepared. From this statement one can derive the other; that in order for "the great kairos" to be received many smaller kairoi are required in the historical development following it.

The latter point has become important for the Christian interpretation of history in former centuries as well as in our own. Again and again in the history of the Church, prophetic minds such as the Reformers interpreted their historical task as the demand implied in a particular kairos. Mostly they were aware of the fact that their own kairos depended on the central kairos—the appearance of Jesus as the Christ. Sometimes they declined to subject themselves to the criteria implied in the central kairos. But there can be no doubt that Christianity needs not only the consciousness of the central kairos, but also of smaller kairoi and their prophetic interpretation. Otherwise, the central kairos loses its concreteness and applicability to future history.

It was the Swiss-German Religious Socialist movement in which both a concrete kairos and the universal meaning of the kairos were rediscovered. The idea of kairos became the principle of a Christian interpretation of history. The German Religious-Socialist movement found itself between two opposing attitudes, none of which it could accept. On the one hand, there was the traditional attitude of the German Protestant churches (predominantly Lutheran) which denied any particular kairos other than the one universal kairos—the appearance of the Christ. Consequently, they rejected the prophetic criticism of the present period of history and restricted the prophetic voice to the criticism of the doctrinal and ritual distortions of Christian message in the Roman Church. Before the end of history nothing new in history was demanded or expected by traditional Lutheranism. Fulfillment lies above time and only in the one moment of the appearance of the Christ within time. Prophetic criticism of social abuses was impossible from this point of view. There was no kairos for such a criticism.

On the other side there was the powerful socialist movement which believed that the great kairos was imminent and the kingdom of God as classless society was around the corner. The kairos was understood as the beginning of the final fulfillment of history within history. In contrast to the Lutheran pessimism about history, utopian optimism prevailed. The result was a profound existential disappointment and the rise of indifference in the masses, cynicism or fanaticism in the few. Religious socialism discovered and used the term kairos in order to overcome this alternative. It spoke about a particular kairos in the period after the First World War. It saw occasions of creating a new social and personal reality. But it did not believe that this is the central kairos and that the kingdom of God is imminent. It knew that the demonic forces in history (the structures of destruction) can be attacked and partly conquered, but that they can never be eliminated. There are kairoi, but there is no utopian fulfillment. Fulfillment is possible only insofar as the central kairos is the final criterion of all smaller kairoi. But history cannot be fulfilled within history: The eternal can break into the temporal; and where this happens there is a kairos. But the eternal does not remove the temporal.

Kairos, which first was used as meaning "right time" in the sense of good timing, and which secondly was used as meaning the *one* right time, the fulfillment of time in the appearance of the Christ, is now used to signify a category of a prophetic interpretation of the "signs of the time" and of history universal.

PAUL TILLICH

Bibliography

Paul Tillich, *The Interpretation of History*.
Paul Tillich, *The Religious Situation*.
Paul Tillich, *The Protestant Era*.

KINGDOM OF GOD

The Kingdom of God is one of the most fruitful yet controversial concepts in Christian theology. It has been employed to uphold the status quo, and it has been a revolutionary ideal used to break social forms and customs. Although appropriated from Judaism, it was radically transformed by Jesus and so reinterpreted by the early Christian community.

It is clear in the New Testament that the concept signifies the kingly rule, the sovereignty, or the rule of God. Its basic intention is to affirm the fact that God reigns in all aspects of personal and social life. It is not a general, but a unique, kind of rule or reign. Whereas Judaism encountered the rule of God through obedience to the Law and looked forward to the full and complete establishment of God's rule, the New Testament asserted that in a new and peculiar way the Kingdom of God had already come.

Jesus said that if He cast out demons through the power of God, "then the Kingdom of God has come upon you." The Gospel of Mark takes its departure from the assertion that the time has reached fulfillment and that the Kingdom of God has come—"repent and believe the good news." This is not merely a statement of living under God's commandments and so living under His rule. Rather, it is a new manifestation of God's power and sovereignty in which His nature, power, and will are brought to bear.

The early Christian community believed that in Jesus

of Nazareth the Christ or the Messiah was encountered, and God's Kingdom was made manifest. Man could either repent and believe or he could reject it, but regardless of man's response, the Kingdom had come. It is not a series of isolated passages which establish this point of view in the New Testament. On the contrary, it is the central motif for Mark and John and strongly reinforced in Matthew and Luke. That for which Israel had hoped and prayed had come to pass in Jesus the Christ. God's freedom and rule expressed itself in a new and an amazing way—in the life, death, and resurrection of Jesus the Christ.

Nevertheless, there are also in the New Testament references to the Kingdom of God as still to come. Some references are apocalyptic visions, and others are predictions about future particular historical events. Together they provide a source to interpret the Kingdom of God as still to come. At different periods in the Church's history stress has often been laid on the Kingdom as primarily future. This point of view moved in one of two directions. Either it tended to uphold the status quo under the direction of the Church, or it tended to revolutionize the forces of society in the name of the coming Kingdom.

The first position was that taken by the Roman Catholic Church. It tended to identify the Kingdom of God with the Church as opposed to the world or the Kingdom of Satan. Insofar as the world was good, it was under the direction of the Kingdom of God through the Church. This life was but preparation for a life to come which would be lived in the presence of God. Meanwhile, man's relation to God's rule was mediated through the Church. Emphasis was not upon a fresh breaking in of the Kingdom or upon a final cataclysmic judgment of the world.

Throughout Christian history another interpretation of the Kingdom of God constantly reappeared. It did not believe that the Kingdom was really present, and particularly it did not believe that the Kingdom of God could be equated with the Church. It stressed the Kingdom as imminent or as about to break in. The Montanist movement represented such a protest against the early Catholic

Church's attempt to spiritualize and indefinitely postpone the coming of the Kingdom of God. Throughout the Middle Ages various protests, those of the Francisco Spiritualists being the most thoroughgoing, were made on behalf of an immediate return of the Christ, bringing with Him God's Kingdom.

Wherever this interpretation of the Kingdom of God appears, it demeans the role of the Church and pronounces a negative judgment against culture and society. It condemns social institutions as instruments of the Kingdom of Satan. It sees little or no relation between God's rule and life as it is being lived at a given moment. The object is not to transform life within history so as to bring it into conformity with an ever-present dynamic will of God. Rather, the object is to negate history through a total judgment, as God ushers in His Kingdom through a new heaven and a new earth.

In addition to the New Testament itself providing diverse sources for a variety of interpretations of the Kingdom of God, the very concept itself is so dynamic that it constantly brings forth a series of options. The fact that the symbol is that of a Kingdom implies a close relationship to analogous structures of life and history. Of necessity such a concept must deal concretely with the day-to-day affairs of living men and women. Furthermore, this symbol, by its very nature, must include the personal and social aspects of life; since to be less inclusive would do violence to the symbol of "kingdom" or of "rule."

Insofar as it is the Kingdom of God, it stresses the freedom and the sovereignty of God the creator, sustainer, and the redeemer. It transcends the totality of this life, both personal and social, and demands that the Christian take a stand against this life. It appears as a completion of this life, as a fulfillment, as the final meaning of history; yet it is God's Kingdom, God's work and not man's. In this sense the Kingdom of God is never the inevitable consequence or development of human life and history.

Thus, the concept of the Kingdom of God posed a number of the central theological problems with which Christian theology still wrestles. If one affirms that the

Kingdom of God has already come, then one must make clear what this means. How is the Kingdom of God in operation? Is it through a series of laws or commands? Are these primarily moral and personal or are they onto-logical? How is God's rule to be discovered in and for culture or the state? Is the Kingdom of God directly operative in personal and social life or is it mediated through the Church or through other forces? Can it be mediated differently through the Church on one hand and through the structures of life on the other? Is it possible that the Kingdom of God is already present as a special perspective through which men are called to new life? If so, what is the content of this perspective, and on what is it based and how is it maintained?

If one affirms that the Kingdom of God is present, but that its real meaning is hidden and the Kingdom is still to come, then one faces an additional set of creative possi-bilities. How is the Kingdom of God to come? Is it to mean the end of all history as we now know it? If so, what is the relation of the Kingdom of God to history and the partial meaning of life as one now experiences it? Is the Kingdom of God related to some kind of perfection of our present social and cultural order? It must include the personal but must equally include the totality of life. How is the com-ing of the Kingdom of God to be related to the life of the Church? Does the Church fully embody the Kingdom of God? Does it not also embody the forces of evil? Does not the Church, in some sense, have to be the bearer of the Kingdom of God? In doing this, does not the Church have to embody the presence of the Kingdom and yet point beyond itself to God and His fulfillment of the Kingdom?

At present theological discussion remains torn between two basic emphases. One stresses the reality of the presence of the Kingdom of God transforming this life through judgment and mercy. The Kingdom is here as a new reality in life, but it is engaged in a life-and-death struggle with satanic forces and demonic powers. History is thus a great stage on which the drama of redemption is fought. However, the battle, though desperately real, has been won in the victory of Jesus the Christ. History has a positive meaning because it has a beginning, center, and ful-fillment. But in and of itself history has no meaning. Only in relation to the dynamic presence of the Kingdom of God can it be seen as meaningful. Thus the minor motif is the Kingdom of God still to come.

The other point of view stresses the Kingdom yet to come. Though it is recognized that God rules, for He is sovereign, the demonic forces are so great that nothing but suffering can be anticipated. In theory history must be important, but, in actuality, one cannot expect much from it. Only a new divine manifestation of salvitic power will suffice. The Kingdom of God really has yet to come in any power of genuine significance.

It is to be noted that both emphases recognize the dual stress of the Kingdom of God—it is here, it is yet to come. Each emphasizes one point as a major motif and the other point as a minor motif. Between these two poles the present interpretation moves. No longer does the opti-mistic view persist that the unfolding of history itself is bringing closer the final stages of the Kingdom of God. It is no longer understood as an evolutionary concept or primarily as a moral-ethical concept.

JERALD C. BRAUER

Bibliography

John Bright, *The Kingdom of God.*
Rudolf Otto, *The Kingdom of God and the Son of Man.*
H. G. Wood, et al, *The Kingdom of God and History.*

LANGUAGE

Language is a system of vocal and visual signs for the expression and communication of meaning. Meanings so entertained and presented include both "pointers" (signals having little or no intrinsic meaning save as directives for attention) and symbols. Symbolic meaning includes both *images* and *concepts*. Religious language is both imaginal and conceptual. The day-to-day life of a religious person or community characteristically employs a language rich with image. Theology as such is concerned with conceptual language; and even where the theologian examines the relationships of image and concept to each other, or studies the various patterns of images, or propounds a theory of the relation of image and concept to revelation, he habitually uses conceptual symbols as his analytical instrument and his mode of communication.

Christian theologians have expressed a lively interest in certain of the problems of language almost from the beginnings of the Church's existence. Much of this interest from the earliest Christian times has centered in the interpretation of scripture. On the one hand the Old Testament had to be given an interpretation favorable to the Christian faith; and on the other hand both Old and New Testaments had to be defended against opinions in the Church felt to be detrimental to the historic faith. This situation was also profoundly complicated by the great influence in the culture of religious philosophies, such as Neo-Platonism and Stoicism, which exploited conceptual patterns of the Greek tongue for their own purposes. Christian thinkers had not only to use that tongue but also to employ many of the same philosophical concepts. Thus Christian thinkers were compelled to show that the meaning of concepts, and, beyond that, the meaning of the language as a whole, was controlled by the revelation of God in Jesus Christ. In essence this program was not altogether novel, since mystical philosophers and sectarians had long since been pointing out the radical defects of language for the expression of divine truth. But Christian thinkers believe that language can be relieved sufficiently of certain of its defects to make it a faithful instrument for the communication of such truth. Under systematic elaboration this means that certain terms (both concepts and images) have an appropriateness of attribution to God that other terms lack. It means also that the criteria of appropriateness of attribution are apprehended in the revelation of God rather than in the analysis of language itself. But the implication is unavoidable that the uses of language are controlled and directed by the being or kind of being which the particular use or system of language is calculated to express or communicate.

In recent times a great deal of philosophical and scientific attention has been given to the genesis of language and to the inter-relationships of symbolic forms. Theology appears to have more at stake in the latter question than in the former one; but whether or not this is actually so, certainly there is a lively contemporary discussion continuing on such questions as the relations of scientific language to religious language, whether religious discourse is entirely symbolic, whether the ultimately important symbols of religion are imaginal rather than conceptual, etc.

Much of this discussion concerns the status of biblical tradition. Is the Bible to be understood as mythological at decisive points? Or are the myths imaginal interpretations of recoverable historic events? A consensus of opinion on these matters among Protestant theologians is very hard to discern. A consensus is much more clearly apparent and important on the question of symbolic meanings in the Christian faith. Furthermore, the fact has come home that all symbolic systems are creatures of historic accident at many points. The truth expressed in such languages is itself not such an accident. But the question thus remains in all its native force, how to express that truth in the historically conditioned language in which indeed it must be expressed.

JULIAN N. HARTT

Bibliography

E. Cassirer, *The Philosophy of Symbolic Forms.*
A. Farrer, *The Glass of Vision.*
W. M. Urban, *Language and Reality.*

LAW

Law is the principle and operation of order in the world. As principle, law is expressed in the form of prescriptive statements. As operation, law expresses the fact that diverse and changing relations unfold in a dependable and an intelligible pattern. In this broad sense, law has a meaning which is common to the cosmic, social, moral, and religious forms of order in the world. Law has, however, also a broad and particular meaning for man. The human aspect of law is a double one: externally, law operates in terms of some form of restraint or coercion. Internally, the response of man to this restraint or coercion is the sense of obligation, the root of the conscience.

For Christian theology, law raises a special problem, owing to the tension introduced by Christianity between the principle and operation of order in the world and the activity and purpose of God as creator and redeemer of the world. Christianity raises the question whether it is really "the law" or whether it is really "the gospel" which determines how the principle and operation of order in the world is to be interpreted and responded to. In sum, in a world whose creator and redeemer is God, is law a self-evident expression of God's will and purpose or is law instrumental to another and different or higher expression of God's will and purpose? If the law is the self-evident expression of God's will and purpose, then it is hard to see how the gospel relates to the principle and operation of order in the world except as an interruption or suspension of order by a higher "order" altogether. If the gospel is a "higher order" in terms of which to understand and respond to the principle and operation of order in the world, then, it is hard to see how the gospel can take prescriptive and directive form or structure in the world without being reduced to law. In order to avoid two "laws" or two "gospels," theology must explore the precise nature of the relation between law and gospel in the world.

The initial form assumed by this problem in theology was the question of the relation between the law of Moses, especially the Ten Commandments, and the religious, ceremonial, and juridical laws of peoples other than the Israelites. And the general answer given was that the law of Moses was the clear and manifest expression of God's will and purpose and thus, of the principle and operation of order in the world, whereas the laws of the peoples were expressions of man's sense of obligation responding to the prescriptive arrangements for his life in the world, a kind of "natural law" or "law written in the heart" (Rom. 2:15-17). The second form of the problem of the relation between law and gospel in the world was that of the relation between the "law of Moses" and the "law within the heart," on the one hand, and the "law of love" enunciated in the teachings of Jesus and uniquely expressed in His life, death and resurrection, on the other. The general answer given to this question has been that "the gospel" or "love" is the fulfillment of the law.

In dealing with the question: in what sense love is the fulfillment of the law, Christian theology has fluctuated between a more dominantly biblical-soteriological interpretation of the relations between love and law, and an interpretation based upon natural law.

As Ernst Troeltsch has shown, the concept of natural law was adopted by Christian thinkers from Greco-Roman Stoicism in order to try to bridge the gap between what appeared to be the purely spiritual love, individualism and universalism of the religion of Jesus and the competing claims and complex structures of life in this world. The law of Moses and natural law thus gradually found a common point of prescriptive significance in the principle of justice expressed in the maxim of the *suum cuique*, the obligation to give every man his due.

It was, of course, easier to correlate natural law and the law of Moses than it was to relate the law of love to natural law.

Natural law, being a divinely established principle of reason and human nature; and the law of Moses, though revealed, being not contrary to the sense and intent of human obligation defined in natural law; it could be argued that there was a providential correspondence between the Decalogue and natural law. But the law of love required another kind of explanation. St. Thomas, to note the most influential instance of such an explanation, argues that both natural law and law of love are forms of eternal law. Eternal law is the way God orders and governs all things in accordance with His wisdom. Natural law is that form of eternal law according to which man is directed to his earthly end. Divine law is that form of eternal law according to which man is directed toward his supernatural end. Divine law consists of the "Old Law" and "The New Law," the "Decalogue" and the "law of love" respectively.

A different way of relating natural law to the law of love was launched by the theology of the Protestant Reformation. The Reformation really broke, in principle, with the whole tradition of natural law. It drew a rather sharp line between the structural and prescriptive forms of law (the so-called first, or political, and second, or pedagogical, uses of the law) which were derived in the tradition from natural law, and the (third, or didactic) form of the law which was really operative for Christians. This was the law of love. It fulfilled the natural law and the law of Moses by deriving the motivation and direction for Christian behavior from the redemptive action of God in Jesus Christ which forgave man his sins and "set him free from the law of sin and death" (Rom. 8:2).

But while the Reformers broke, in principle, with the tradition of natural law, they did not do so in practice. When it came to relating "the gospel" to the order of nature and society, the Reformers did not see the way forward and fell back upon the theory of natural law. Protestant theology has, in consequence, been caught in a paralyzing contradiction between its soteriology and its ethics. Its doctrine of redemption made the forgiveness of sins primary and central, as the fulfillment of the law. Its guidance of behavior in personal and public affairs has been prescriptive.

It has remained for the theology of the mid-twentieth century to try to overcome this contradiction by taking up afresh the break with natural law in principle which was launched at the Reformation. Some theologians, those most directly influenced by Karl Barth, have rejected natural law as a valid theological possibility. Others, like Reinhold Niebuhr and Emil Brunner, have contended that natural law may have a limited prescriptive usefulness as a formal principle but that its application to concrete problems is less universal than the tradition, particularly in Roman Catholic theology and ethics, supposed. The unsolved problem in contemporary Protestant theological discussion of law is whether a biblically derived understanding of God's redemptive and providential ordering of human and world affairs can provide a frame of reference for dealing with the structural and directive aspects of life in this world according to which love transvalues all law and law acquires an indicative rather than a normative, a descriptive rather than a prescriptive, a functional rather than a regulative significance.

PAUL LEHMANN

Bibliography

Reinhold Niebuhr, *Christian Realism and Political Problems.*
Ernst Troeltsch, *The Social Teaching of the Christian Churches.*

LIBERALISM

"Liberalism" as applied to a type of theological thought needs to be understood in the same broad terms which are necessary when it is used to characterize modern social and political movements. In its theological context it designates the spirit and attitude of those who sought to incorporate in Christian theology the values of freedom of thought, tolerance, and the humanitarian motives in modern Western culture. Theological liberals have always asserted the claims of reason against a petrified orthodoxy, and have sought freedom for diversity of belief in the Church. In the modern period they have declared the need of theology to incorporate the basic values, aspirations, and attitudes which are associated with modern democratic culture. Insofar as theological liberalism emphasized the need to establish the relevance of Christian faith to the scientific and rational understanding of life it was closely allied with the theological methods of modernism. It might be said with some accuracy that all theological liberals were modernists; but not all those who used modernist methods of interpretation shared the faith of the liberal theology, especially its optimistic estimate of human nature.

The most characteristic theme of liberal theology, one which has been asserted throughout Christian history in various forms, is the emphasis on the freedom of man, his capability of responding to God and shaping his life in accordance with the divine will. Christian liberals share with their classic forerunner Pelagius the insistence that even in his freedom man cannot be saved without the grace of God; but with Pelagius against St. Augustine, and against the later views of Calvin, liberals have rejected the doctrine of the total depravity of man, and have condemned theories of predestination as destroying man's freedom.

Liberals have taken a positive attitude toward the achievements of democratic culture, and have generally stressed the ethical imperatives in the gospel. In the nineteenth century, liberal interpretations of the life and teachings of Jesus stressed His prophetic expression of spiritual victory and ethical perfection. The German theologians Ernst Troeltsch and Adolf Harnack at the turn of the century formulated the gospel in relation to a critical understanding of Christian history and the problems of modern culture. Harnack's summary of the essential message of Jesus is a classic expression of liberal faith: "Firstly, the Kingdom of God and its coming. Secondly, God the Father and the infinite value of the human soul. Thirdly, the higher righteousness and the commandment of love." (Adolf Harnack, *What is Christianity*, p. 51.)

Anglicans such as Frederick Denison Maurice, and, later in the nineteenth century, Charles Gore, with the other authors of *Lux Mundi*, developed liberal themes in interpreting the Anglican tradition. Both Roman Catholic and Anglican movements of social criticism and reform have incorporated in many instances the liberal democratic outlook while remaining critical of its secular expressions.

The social gospel movement, which is the most characteristic expression of liberal Protestant theology in American Christianity, had as its greatest interpreter and prophet Walter Rauschenbusch, Professor of Church History at Rochester Theological Seminary. In his thought the prophetic ethical impulse was welded together with the social democratic faith. Concepts of social sin and social salvation were developed in rejection of the tendencies toward individualism and quietism in pietistic Christianity. In Rauschenbusch and others who followed, the liberal theology participated in, and sometimes led, the shift in social theory from individualism to democratic collectivism. The religious education movement, strongly influenced by the philosophical liberalism and pragmatism of John Dewey, was another expression of the interaction of liberal Christianity with modern culture.

In American theology of the twentieth century, in addition to Rauschenbusch, theologians such as William Adams Brown, William Newton Clark, Shailer Mathews, and Robert Lowry Calhoun stand in the liberal tradition.

It is the fate of liberal theology in the mid-twentieth century to have undergone radical criticism both from within its own ranks and from those who have broken with it, or who stand outside it. Since Albert Schweitzer's book, *The Quest of the Historical Jesus* in 1907, the liberal reliance on the view of Jesus as proclaiming an ethical message for the gradual reconstruction of human society has been radically shaken. The theological critique of Reinhold Niebuhr and of Karl Barth, both of whom came through the liberal tradition, has judged the liberal view of man as having a too shallow view of the nature of sin, and a false optimism about human history. The facts of twentieth-century history and the corresponding mood of tragic realism have led to a reaffirmation of the Pauline doctrine of justification by faith as central to the redemptive truth of the gospel, and thereby to a radical correction of the liberal faith. Yet the liberal defense of freedom of critical thought in the Church and society, and the emphasis upon the social and ethical imperatives in the gospel, remain valued elements in theological reconstruction. [See also *Modernism*.]

DANIEL D. WILLIAMS

Bibliography

Robert L. Calhoun, *God and the Common Life*.
Walter Rauschenbusch, *A Theology for the Social Gospel*.
David E. Roberts and Henry P. Van Dusen (editors), *Liberal Theology, An Appraisal*. Essays in honor of Eugene W. Lyman.

LITURGY

In Christian contexts, the term "liturgy" (from the Greek, "work of the people") refers to the official, authorized forms and rituals of public, corporate worship and ministration of the sacraments in the Church. The basic patterns of liturgy in Christianity were derived from Judaism, such as the sacramental actions of Baptism and the Lord's Supper, the use of the Psalms, and ritual forms of confession of sin, thanksgivings and blessings, prayers of intercession and dedication. Transfused with specifically Christian beliefs about the person and saving work of Jesus Christ, these Jewish forms of liturgy were gradually developed and elaborated by the Church into the classic rites of Eastern and Western Christendom that reached their definitive formulation in the fifth and sixth centuries A.D. In this process of development, the Church's liturgy was also influenced by ideas and usages of worship familiar to Christian converts from Greco-Roman paganism.

At the time of the Reformation in the Western Church during the sixteenth century, the various Christian bodies that separated from allegiance and obedience to the Roman papacy revised and re-ordered their liturgical traditions, but differed one from the other in the principles applied to their several reforms. They were agreed only in an insistence upon the use of vernacular in the worship of the Church, and in the appeal to the Bible as a norm and standard of what was permissible in the Church both in belief and in practice.

The Lutherans in Germany and Scandinavia and the leaders of reform in the Church of England were conservative in their treatment of the inherited, medieval Latin rites, and confined themselves for the most part to the excision from the liturgy of those aspects of customary usage that they considered specifically contrary to scriptural teaching. But whereas the Lutheran "Church Orders" that outlined the revised liturgies were advisory and permissive, the liturgy of the Church of England, embodied in the Book of Common Prayer, was imposed and enforced by authority of the State. The Reformed Churches of Zwinglian and Calvinistic persuasion, however, were more radical, in that the forms of worship produced by their leaders were based upon a principle that only those elements in corporate worship that were explicitly enjoined in the New Testament were to be observed and used. They did not, however, reject the principle of prescribed norms of public worship, though in general the tendency of these bodies was to leave the direction and content of such worship largely in the hands of the officiating ministry. The more extreme reforming groups, such as the Anabaptists and the separatist Puritan congregations in England, opposed all liturgical usages as a non-scriptural restraint upon the free inspiration of the Holy Spirit in Christian worship, often carrying their objections to the point of rejecting even the corporate use of the Lord's Prayer, and the due observance of such traditional holy days and festivals as Easter and Christmas.

The twentieth century has witnessed to date an extraordinary revival of interest in the appreciation of liturgical worship in almost all Protestant churches. This has taken the form of extensive revisions of official liturgies in Anglican and Lutheran bodies, the issuance of recommended books of common worship in Presbyterian, Reformed, and Methodist denominations, and widespread adoption of liturgical elements in the worship of many Baptist and Congregationalist churches. The movement in this direction is worldwide. Perhaps the most notable, single example of the trend has been the enthusiastic acceptance of liturgical forms issued by the Church of South India, a body formed in 1947 by the union of Anglican, Methodist, Presbyterian and Congregationalist traditions.

It is only fair to say that much of the renewed interest in liturgical worship, particularly in America, has been concentrated upon external and less essential aspects, such as the revival of medieval forms of church architecture and ornamentation, altar-centered rather than pulpit-centered arrangements of church sanctuaries, the use of vestments, processions, choral responses and litanies, and, in general, a more dignified and artistic setting and ceremonial conduct of public worship. This development has been in line with the passing of frontier conditions in American life and a greater degree of sophistication in the appreciation of American society generally with respect to history, art, and music. But there have been factors at work that penetrate more deeply into fundamental re-orientations of modern Protestant Christianity.

A major influence has been the change of perspective with respect to the Bible produced by modern historical criticism and research, out of which has come a larger appreciation and understanding of the liturgical elements in the worship of the Church in New Testament and early Christian ages. Another potent factor has been the contemporary ecumenical movement looking towards the reunion of the churches. It has become increasingly apparent that the several "ways of worship" in the churches are divisive forces, whether theologically or psychologically, keeping Christians separated from full inter-communion. The recognition of this fact has fortunately led to a greater tolerance and willingness to learn, not only from the distinctive traditions of all the several churches, but also from the riches of past ages of Christian devotion. It is also admitted that churches with a fully developed liturgical heritage are less inclined to be thrown off balance, theologically speaking, by changing fads of doctrine and fashions of biblical interpretation, and are more able to preserve through continuing generations the fullness of the Christian faith in its essentials.

Nor should one overlook the fact that the modern revival of liturgical worship in Protestantism is in great measure a reaction to the excessive individualism that has characterized Western society since the close of the Middle Ages, with the ultimate loss on the part of many people in the modern age of satisfying social relations and communal values. A liturgy is in principle an instrument of group participation and responsibility. It does not depend upon individual gifts of leadership or inspiration, however valuable these may be when available. At its best, liturgical worship provides the poorest member of the Church with the full richness of faith and devotion of the whole Church in time and in space, and at the same time gives an opportunity to the humblest member to make a maximum contribution, to the full extent of his talents and abilities, to the community of faithful people.

The chief problem that has engaged ecumenical discussions of worship to date is the discovery of a due balance and complement of liturgical forms that are responsive to Christian tradition and the freer, more spontaneous elements that are open to immediate inspiration of the Spirit. Into this larger context comes the search for a better integration and harmony between ministries of the Word and of the Sacraments, so that neither is emphasized at the expense of the other. Each must enhance and support the other: objectively, in the proclamation of the gospel and the creation of a redeemed community, and subjectively, in the communication of saving grace to each and every member and the sharing of spiritual gifts to the greatest edification of the whole Church. Needless to say, the ecumenical discussions of liturgy and worship, in their search for fundamental unities which all Christians can accept and share, have no design or desire to create uniform patterns or rites that would be imposed upon either a reunited Church or any particular congregation of Christian worshippers.

MASSEY H. SHEPHERD, JR.

Bibliography

P. Edwall, E. Hayman, and W. D. Maxwell (editors), *Ways of Worship*, The Report of a Theological Commission of Faith and Order.

D. H. Hislop, *Our Heritage in Public Worship.*

LOGOS

Logos, in Christian theology, is the name given to the pre-existent Christ, the second of the three persons of the Trinity. According to the creeds established during the period of the Church Fathers, the pre-existent Christ or Logos was generated eternally out of the substance of God the Father and is true God of true God. It is this eternally generated Logos in the sense of the pre-existent heavenly Christ of whom it is said that He was made flesh in Jesus, the Christ born among men.

Each of these points in the established Christian doctrine about the preincarnate Logos has a history.

The conception of a pre-existent Christ, derived from the Jewish conception of a pre-existent Messiah, was introduced by Paul, who calls him Wisdom, a term which in Judaism was applied to the pre-existent Law. In Paul's conception of the pre-existent Christ, the Jewish conceptions of the pre-existent Messiah and pre-existent Law were combined. The name Logos, given to Paul's pre-existent Christ by John, is taken from Philo, by whom this term as well as the term Wisdom is used primarily as a designation of a pre-existent mind which contained the intelligible world of ideas, and secondarily also as a designation of the pre-existent Law.

Though Paul describes the pre-existent Christ as God's "own son" and John describes the Logos as the "only begotten son" of God, it is not quite certain whether these descriptions were meant by them to be taken literally as an indication of the manner in which the pre-existent Christ or Logos came into existence. The Fathers of the

Church, however, from earliest times took these descriptions literally as meaning that the Logos was generated out of the substance of God and not created by Him out of nothing, after the manner of His creation of the world.

Similarly, though Paul speaks of the pre-existent Christ as being "equal with God" and John speaks of the Logos as being "God," it is not quite certain what they mean by these statements. Here, again, the Fathers of the Church from earliest times took these statements in their literal sense. This was a logical consequence of their view that the pre-existent Christ or Logos was generated out of the substance of God. In the process of generation, they reasoned, that which is generated must be of the same species as that which generates.

But, with regard to the belief that the generation of the Logos from the substance of God was an eternal process, such a novel view was introduced by Irenaeus and Origen. Before them, the prevailing view among the Church Fathers was that the Logos existed from eternity in God Himself and only prior to the creation of the world was He generated out of the substance of God as a real personal being. This early view of the Fathers regarding a two-fold stage in the existence of the Logos, though it ultimately disappeared, was never formally anathematized at any of the ecumenical councils. In fact, the principle of the eternity of the process of the generation, though undoubtedly assumed, is never explicitly expressed in the creeds.

In opposition to this view of the Logos, which constituted the established creed of Christianity, there appeared during the period of the Church Fathers two heretical views.

First, there was the view that the Logos was created by God out of nothing and consequently was not God. This is known as Arianism, which was anathematized at the Council of Nicaea in 325.

Second, there was the view that the Logos was not a real personal being but was only a power of God. This view had many exponents, but it is best known, after the name of one of its exponents, as Sabellianism. It was anathematized at the council of Constantinople in 381.

H. A. WOLFSON

Bibliography

B. J. Otten, S.J., *A Manual of the History of Dogmas.*
R. Seeberg, *Text-Book of the History of Doctrines,* translated by Ch. E. Hay.
H. A. Wolfson, *The Philosophy of the Church Fathers,* I: *Faith, Trinity, Incarnation.*

LOVE

The single word "love" must, by lingual necessity, serve to express the infinite range of love in all its human and divine aspects. The desire and fulfillment of sexual life, the ethical spirit of good will toward one's neighbor, the aspiration of the mind for the ultimate good, the gracious spirit of God's redemptive action—all these are meanings which the word "love" suggests and which it must embrace. This very complexity points to the central theological problem in interpreting love, insofar as all the "loves" manifest in human experience bear some analogy and relationship to one another, and the problem of understanding this relationship is involved in all our thought about God and His creatures.

The flexibility of the Greek language, with its several words for love, facilitates the drawing of certain theological distinctions. The Greek word *eros* means aspiration for the good. It is the power which leads men toward fulfillment through union with the object of desire. The word *agape,* in its New Testament usage, means the love which God shows in the giving of His Son for mankind. The theological problem may be stated, therefore, in broad terms as the problem of relating and distinguishing *eros* in man's created nature and the *agape* of God's redemptive purpose.

The New Testament usage of *agape* points to the ulti-

mate nature of love in God and in human life. It both
gathers up the meaning of the righteousness, mercy, and
love of God expressed in the Old Testament and makes
redemptive love the foundation of the Christian understanding of love. So St. Paul declares, "God commendeth
his love for us in that while we were yet sinners, Christ
died for us" (Rom. 5:8). And the Johannine writer concentrates the entire doctrine of God in the one statement
that "God is love (*agape*)" (I John 4:8).

The requirement laid upon man by a Holy God is the
complete response and self-giving which is summed up in
the two commandments reemphasized by Jesus: "Thou
shalt love the lord thy God with all thy heart, and with
all thy soul, and with all thy mind," and "Thou shalt love
thy neighbor as thyself" (Matt. 22:37-39). In the light of
the revelation in Christ, the Christian obligation toward
the neighbor is to give the same love which Christ has
shown to us. Thus the *agape* of God is the foundation of
man's ethical obligation. The spirit of love cannot be
fulfilled as obedience to a command, but must be expressed as personal response. St. Augustine can say, therefore, that if one first loves he may then do as he will.
Ethical love in the New Testament is not devotion to an
abstract ideal, but the concrete meeting of the neighbor's
need. The word *philia*, also used in the New Testament,
usually means brotherly love, though it is sometimes used
for the love of God for man.

The word *eros* is never used in the New Testament,
probably because in the Hellenistic period it had acquired
a connotation of sensuality and degradation. But the
teaching of Jesus does not require an ascetic renunciation
of human desire. Paul enjoins attention to the things
that are "lovely, true, and of good report" (Philippians
4:8). The foundation for marriage, according to the
Christian faith, is laid in the law of God expressed in
the family as a created order of life, with monogamy as
its ultimate intention; and in the personal aspect of *agape*
which leads each partner to seek the fulfillment of the
other in freedom, equality, and reverence for the divine
intent in the relationship. For the Christian churches

which regard marriage as a sacrament, and also for those which do not, the analogy between the love of God and of Christ for the Church and the love in the marriage relation is held to show the spiritual foundation of sexual union.

The history of the Christian idea of love through the centuries, as Bishop Nygren has shown in his *Agape and Eros* [see article *Eros and Agape,* Anders Nygren] is largely a series of attempts to show how the two loves can be synthesized in a union of grace and nature. In St. Augustine the Latin *caritas,* which the Vulgate prefers as translation for *agape* and which survives in the English "charity," receives its definitive statement as a synthesis of man's search for the good and God's search for sinful man. God's love is the secret of the mystery of all being. As the Spirit is the bond of love between Father and Son, so all love participates in the truth and goodness which alone fulfills human striving.

Augustine's doctrine became the primary resource for Christian mysticism through later centuries. The mystical union of the soul with God is often described with symbols drawn from sexual ecstasy, though the supernatural virtue of love transcends all human virtue and knowledge. In *The Divine Comedy* Dante records his spiritual pilgrimage as having its awakening in romantic love. Led by the mystery and beauty in the eyes of Beatrice he begins the journey which ends only in Paradise, where again her eyes lead him close to God; yet at the end all eyes of the creatures and angels are turned toward the One Source of Light in the depth of God Himself. Thus in Dante the vision of love becomes not the apotheosis of romantic love but its transmutation.

Bishop Anders Nygren, whose great work on love has been referred to, regards the Augustinian doctrine and its subsequent mystical expressions as invalid syntheses of *agape* and *eros,* which weaken the full meaning of *agape.* He believes that the uncalculating and unmotivated love of *agape* which God pours out upon the sinner stands in final contrast to the *eros* which always seeks the fulfillment of the self. Nygren argues that the Protestant Reformers, especially Luther, saw the weakness in the traditional synthesis and broke it in favor of a radical doctrine of *agape* as grace given to man.

A somewhat analogous thesis is presented by Denis de Rougemont in his *Love in the Western World*, which seeks to trace the origins of modern romantic love in the heretical religion of love in the Middle Ages. Here the love relationship between men and women reached its idealization especially in adulterous attachment and harbored a secret longing for death. The ecstasy of desire and immolation which is celebrated in the legend of Tristan and Isolde becomes an important key for understanding the violent emotion and self-destructive spirit in modern romanticism.

Most interpreters of Christian love, both Catholic and Protestant, while recognizing the danger of reducing *agape* to human desire, seek to preserve a positive place for *eros* within the goodness of man's created nature, and thus provide for its fulfillment within the purpose of God, though that purpose becomes clear only in the light of *agape*. Theological discussion in the twentieth century has taken account of modern psychological theories of the development of human love in the interpersonal relationships especially of the primary group. Psychological understanding has been of especial value in exposing the emotional roots of many false interpretations of religious experience. Ethical problems related to love appear in the discussion of justice in human society and in assessing the relevance of forgiving love to problems of freedom and equality in human relations. The relation between the sacrificial spirit in *agape* and the requirements of human self-affirmation has provided much ground for discussion, including analysis of the problem of the meaning of a right self-love and its limits as viewed from the Christian perspective.

Neither *agape* nor *eros* nor their relationship can be captured in a doctrinal formula. The richness and complexity of human existence in all its aspects is gathered into the vitalities of *eros*. The mystery and depth of the divine power and goodness are present in *agape*. The unity of the Christian view of love as the meaning of existence can be secured only through the recognition that the same God who is Creator is also Redeemer. Man's striving toward the good with its misdirection and perversity consequent upon estrangement from God is met and fulfilled by the suffering love of God who through forgiveness opens the way for man to walk by faith.

DANIEL D. WILLIAMS

Bibliography

M. C. D'Arcy, *The Mind and Heart of Love.*
James Moffatt, *Love in the New Testament.*
Anders Nygren, *Agape and Eros.*

LUTHERANISM

Lutheranism is an interpretation of Christianity. The name derives from Martin Luther (1483-1546), though he himself deprecated its use in designation of the movement he initiated in the Church. Born and educated in the medieval Latin Church, he never thought of himself as founder of a new church, much less of a sect within Christendom. His followers were called Protestants, especially in the political repercussions which followed the religious changes, but Luther and his colleagues were most intent on a reformation of and within the Church. Luther in fact never left the church of his childhood, but was expelled from it by the hierarchy which refused to countenance the changes he called for. Belatedly the Roman Church effected some reforms in the Council of Trent.

Since Lutheranism is a reforming movement within the Western Church, there is still an area of agreement which was not challenged by the Reformer. Indeed, as late as 1530, when the basic confession of the Reformation, the Augsburg Confession, was formulated, the authors still hoped for a reconciliation with the hierarchy at Rome on points at issue, and declared that on important questions there was no disagreement. On the trinitarian doctrine of the ancient creeds, on the important doctrine of the incarnation, on the necessity of liturgical forms of worship, the reformers were in the tradition of the ancient Church. Even with regard to "the things in the Scripture which on either side have been differently interpreted or misunderstood," the authors of the Augsburg Confession (in Latin, *Confessui Augustana*) hoped that "these matters may be settled and brought back to one perfect truth and Christian concord that for the future one pure and true religion may be embraced and maintained by us, that as we all serve and do battle under one Christ, so we may be able also to live in unity and concord in the one Christian Church."

The hope proved futile, and the reforming movement was forced to organize itself outside of the hierarchal structure of the papacy. The crucial point of difference was that of authority. Whereas the Roman Church had already tended to make the papacy the absolute center of authority in doctrine and morals (a tendency reaching its culmination in the nineteenth century), the Lutheran position considers the ultimate authority a revelation of God, not only recorded in scripture of the Old and New Testaments, but brought home to each new generation by the Holy Spirit as the Word of that scripture is proclaimed. Of the seven Roman sacraments the Lutheran Church retained only those two which had distinct scriptural basis—baptism and the Lord's Supper. The Roman Church makes its very organization a divine order. Lutheranism denies that there is any final authority in an episcopate that stands in succession to the apostles and to St. Peter. The authority of the clergy derives from no constitutional organization, but from the proclamation of a gospel and the administration of sacraments in accord with scriptural revelation.

Whereas the Roman Catholic Christian lets the papal church determine doctrine for him, the Lutheran judges the church by its loyalty to the word of scripture. The congregation calls its pastor, who must have this sanction of the church in order to teach. Lutheranism does not, therefore, permit the individualism allowed by some Protestant communions. But it does not consider the call of the pastor any more sacred than the call of each Christian to witness to the lordship of Christ in his life and work. The universal priesthood of believers does not make all men priests, but makes the vocation of every man a holy calling, and gives every believer the responsibility of ministering in his way to his neighbor. Faith in Christ thus issues in love to one's fellow man.

The elaboration of the doctrines which thus became fundamental for Lutheranism is found in the Book of Concord (1580) which in whole or in part is everywhere accepted as the teaching of the Lutheran Church. The most succinct statement of Lutheran doctrine is to be found in Luther's Small Catechism.

While Lutheranism developed its teaching and worship as opposed to Rome, it had at the same time to define its position as differentiated from other churches which resulted from the Reformation. One of the important distinctions related to the sacrament of the altar. Here the Lutherans, who had found no biblical basis for the Roman doctrine of transubstantiation, took their stand on the scriptural text which demanded the belief in the real presence of the body and blood of Christ, as opposed to Protestants who made of the communion only a memorial. The Lutherans retained the traditional mode of child baptism, though holding that the manner is indifferent. In general the Lutherans were conservative and were inclined to preserve churches, altars, music, festivals, forms of worship (divested of all veneration of Mary and the saints as unbiblical), while the followers of Calvin and Zwingli tended to eliminate whatever the Roman Church had possessed. Luther defended whatever was not opposed to scripture; many other Protestants accepted only what was commanded by scripture.

The placing of the center of the evangelical faith in the experience of the forgiveness of sins by faith in the atoning work of Christ as revealed in scripture (a doctrine called "justification by faith") left all other matters to the freedom of the congregation. The result was a variety of organization in Lutheranism. In the nations of Europe that accepted the Reformation a form of incorporation of the church within the structure of the state became common (state churches in Scandinavia and Germany). In America, where Lutheran congregations date from 1638, the presbyterian form of church government was adopted, congregations forming synods, and synods gradually entering into relations with each other in conferences or in united bodies. The Augsburg Confession claims that uniformity is not necessary in anything except the fundamental doctrines of scripture. This flexibility has enabled Lutheranism to adjust its external forms to any political condition, and the Lutheran Church today is the largest Protestant communion in the world. Within the past decades it has found a medium of communication in the Lutheran World Federation. Holding firmly to its doctrinal unity, it has recognized that the Christian Church is truly ecumenical and catholic, and has taken a leading part in the ecumenical movement. It considers itself a co-heir of the ancient Christian Church, reformed in accordance with the gospel of the New Testament and witnessing to the One Lord of the One Church until the Coming of Christ which will consummate the meaning of God's revelation to man.

CONRAD BERGENDOFF

Bibliography

Gustaf Aulen, *The Faith of the Christian Church.*
Concordia or *Book of Concord*. The Symbols of the Evangelical Lutheran Church, with Indexes and Historical Introductions.
The Works of Martin Luther. 6 v. Holman Edition.

MAN

The Hebrew-Christian scriptures affirm a view of man which, while it finds room for all that can be known of man by any useful procedure, sets what we know of man in a perspective which provides it with final depth and meaning. It takes with utmost seriousness all that we learn of man by, for example, *measurement, reflection,* and *introspection.*

Measurement. At one important level of his existence man is susceptible to being handled by normal scientific procedures of description and analysis: much can be learned by anatomy, physiology, psychology, and sociology. Christian theology has every interest in the conclusions, and no interest in dictating the conclusions, which may be reached by the methods proper to each of these.

Reflection. Scientific method has not displaced that philosophy which sought to establish general truths about man by abstraction from particular details about particular men, seeking to reach by reflection an essential *humanness* which is constitutively present in all men, though variously embodied. The procedure is still fruitful, though psychological and social science has taught us that it is highly precarious and subject to prejudice, as witness the persistence in the history of thought of *rationalism* (man is his reason), *naturalism* (man is an organism), and *romanticism* (man is a dynamism, generally the will, which dominates both mind and body).

Introspection. Introspection is the peeling away of the superficial levels of consciousness, generally to discover an indestructible intuition of freedom and responsibility, of a "self" which is in some sense transcendent over every expression of the self in thought and action.

Christian theology finds itself in especial sympathy with the renewed emphasis upon an insight which has seldom been absent from the history of thought, and never absent from it where it has been affected by Christian theology. It has been reaffirmed by thinkers as diverse as Karl Marx, in his too-simple formula, "Man is the ensemble of the social relations"; and Martin Buber, who insists that the truth about man is neither rational nor organic but *dialogic,* that is, man is man only in "a living relation with other individuals." For any full account of man it is necessary not only that he be *dissected* (whether by anatomy or by psychology) but that he be *located.* We acknowledge this in common usage: if I ask "Who are you?" you do not normally reply, "I am an introvert weighing 178 pounds," but, rather, "My name is so-and-so, I live in . . . and work for. . . ." You identify yourself, that is to say, not by reference to your *structure* either anatomical or psychical, but by your *relations,* since it is in relationship that you are defined in your personal and social being. It is the personal encounter that is *revealing,* in the strict sense, of the character and quality of our existence, as when we say, "So-and-so makes me feel inconsequential," or "I did not know what life could be like until I met. . . ." Yet clearly no human encounter can be finally determinative; it is the "divine-human encounter" (a phrase of Emil Brunner's) which illumines man's life in its final dimension. The long and broad consensus of Christian theology is that the Bible is the transcript of such an encounter and that the believing community is its continuing *locus.*

The Bible is written out of a stance of faith which can take seriously the natural vitalities of man without suggesting that the meaning of his life is exhausted in the relation between the organism and its environment; it makes room for reason and exalts its function without finding in it the distinctive quality of man's existence or the sole ground of his dignity. Summarily stated, the biblical account of the matter is somewhat as follows. It affirms the organic character and quality of man's life ("the Lord God formed man of the dust of the ground," Gen. 2:7) while it endows him with special worth ("God created man in his own image, in the image of God created he him," Gen. 1:27; "What is man . . . thou hast made him a little lower than God," Psalm 8:5; "The very hairs of your head are all numbered," Matt. 10:31; Luke 12:7). It has to be noticed that here the worth of man is grounded, not in his wisdom (the *image* is never equated with the reason: it refers to man's *confrontation* with God, the living encounter in which man is summoned—"elected"—to freedom and responsibility), but in the status which he has "in the eyes of God"; which means, God being who He is, in the love of God. As distinct, therefore, from Hellenic philosophy, which made much of man's wisdom and little of his worth apart from his wisdom, the Bible makes little of man's wisdom, and much of his worth irrespective of his wisdom. This is an insight of crucial importance for democracy (cf. Reinhold Niebuhr, *The Children of Light and the Children of Darkness*). Man is to be greatly loved but not greatly trusted.

He is to be greatly loved for his worth in God's sight; he is to be distrusted because of a fundamental distemper which poisons all his life. And when the men of the Bible look for the source of this distemper, they locate it not in the body, as if the pure mind were weighted with the corrupt flesh; nor in the mind, as if the fault were ignorance to be healed by sophistication or pedagogy. They located it, as on the basis of their account of man's nature they must, in a rebellious will or a self-idolatry ("Ye shall be as Gods," Gen. 3:4) which wrenches man out of his wholesome and loving subordination to God, and radically distorts his existence at every level and in its total range. It can be healed neither by adjustment, as if man were an organism, nor by sophistication, as if he were disembodied mind; but only by a transaction of love.

This biblical account of the matter finds its quintessential expression in the story of the Christ, who is not only the perfect embodiment of the righteousness and the mercy of God in terms of which man measures his own wretchedness and his worth in spite of his wretchedness; but the *proper* Man (a phrase which is not only Luther's), the second Adam who represents the dignity which is recoverable for man at one price only—the price of giving up his rebellion.

ALEXANDER MILLER

Bibliography

E. Brunner, *The Divine-Human Encounter*.
R. Niebuhr, *The Nature and Destiny of Man*. I. Cha. 6, 7, 8.

METAPHYSICS

Metaphysics is philosophic enquiry into and proposal about the nature of reality. As such it was for a long time one of the principal fields of philosophic thought. At first glance metaphysics appears to be a natural ally of theology, since theology has also certain teachings about God, the world, and the human soul. Actually Christian theology has frequently drawn heavily and wittingly upon metaphysics; and some Christian theologians believe (and a long tradition supports them in this) that a particular system of metaphysics is a necessary theoretical foundation for Christian theology. Other Christian thinkers have rejected this notion of partial dependency upon metaphysics; and still others have seen in metaphysics something to be rejected altogether.

In the most recent philosophic epoch metaphysics has been harshly treated and in many quarters suffers ill repute. Among the reasons for this treatment of metaphysics we find several of particular interest for Christian theology. For one, metaphysics in the nineteenth century became strongly tinctured with *ideology*, meaning by *ideology* a rationalization of a cultural order. Thus in the philosophy of Hegel the ideological strain is present and active and, for a great deal of subsequent thought, decisive. But when metaphysics ceases to be science and becomes ideology, nothing is easier for the Christian preacher than to decry it as self-justification and sinful pride. Furthermore, the scientific character of metaphysics had already been effectively called into question by David Hume and Immanuel Kant. Thus metaphysics, either as ideology or as disqualified science, was widely judged to be no fit foundation and ally to Christian theology.

A positive ground for the theological rejection of metaphysics was found in the claim for Jesus Christ as a divine revelation requiring and allowing no metaphysical presupposition. But here too an animus is evident, directed against the *systematic* character of metaphysics both in its scientific and ideological modes. For system seems inevitable where men are trying to think reality as a whole.

At present skepticism, both naturalistic and theological, enjoys ascendancy over metaphysics. Methodological problems have latterly been receiving far more attention both in philosophy and theology than have metaphysical problems. In Protestant theology specifically, more attention is still being given to the question of the meaning of revelation than to the question of the existence and nature of God. And where the influence of Kierkegaard is positively embraced, *faith* is interpreted in such a way as to make a philosophic doctrine of reality either impossible or irrelevant for Christian thought.

On the other hand, Roman Catholic theology maintains its traditional sympathetic relationship to metaphysics in the "scientific" mode; and continues to recognize in such metaphysics at least an important ally if not a necessary theoretical foundation of Christian doctrine. Thus in Catholic theological circles philosophical theology remains in good odor.

We should note that a kind of analogy of metaphysics can be found in certain contemporary Protestant theologians. Revelation is thought to be a foundation for doctrines whose intent is to interpret and elucidate aspects of reality of greatest interest to faith, notably and naturally God and man. The meaning and truth of doctrine is judged insusceptible either to common-sense or to traditional philosophic criteria of meaning and truth; but the doctrines are nonetheless proposed as interpretations of reality. On these conditions it is perhaps possible (though not necessarily desirable) to speak of a "metaphysics on the grounds of faith."

Finally, the reduction of classical metaphysics to an ontology concentrated in man's being (rather than in being as such) is finding important reflection in Christian theology.

JULIAN N. HARTT

Bibliography

E. Brunner, *Revelation and Reason.*
D. Emmet, *The Nature of Metaphysical Thinking.*

J. Maritain, *Introduction to Metaphysics.*
W. H. Sheldon, *God and Polarity.*
P. Tillich, *Systematic Theology*, Vol. II.

METHODISM

Contemporary Methodist theology can best be understood as 1) the attempt to reformulate the traditional Methodist emphasis on salvation in terms which take account of twentieth-century psychology, sociology, and philosophy, and 2) the many-sided attempt to re-appropriate in contemporary terms the ecumenical context of this emphasis which Wesley, in refusing to break with Anglicanism, presupposed, but never adequately formulated for the early Methodist societies.

John Wesley (1703-1791), an Anglican priest of high church persuasion, who taught logic and classical languages at Oxford, had been prepared for his conversion by a devout and strict upbringing, his sense of failure in the search for Christian perfection through mystical and ascetic practices, and a period of missionary service in Georgia which left him convinced that he did not know the salvation which he preached. Under the influence of the Moravians, and especially of Peter Böhler's teaching that justification by faith could be experienced, Wesley felt his "heart strangely warmed" (May 24, 1738, "about a quarter before nine"), while listening to Luther's preface to Romans. Wesley's description of the experience emphasizes its content—the world of Romans 8 now becomes personally meaningful to him. Within a year Wesley began field preaching in Bristol, and there the Wesleyan revival may be said to have begun. For the next fifty years Wesley traveled incessantly, preaching, organizing, directing, winnowing his societies, and supervising his growing conference of lay preachers. His brother Charles (1707-1788) wrote more than six thousand hymns, from which the revival drew much of its hymnody. George Whitefield (1714-1770), far the most eloquent preacher of the revival, became leader of a "Calvinist" wing. William Fletcher

(1729-1785)—had he lived, Wesley's chosen successor—
was the systematic theologian of the revival, especially
during the second controversy over predestination (ca.
1770), during which he developed a position which he
himself and others somewhat inaccurately labeled "Armin-
ian."

The themes of the Wesleyan preaching can be pictured in
three concentric circles. 1) At the center was the *order of
salvation,* understood as a process involving justification
by faith, regeneration or conversion, and sanctification.
Justification by faith, understood as acceptance and forgiveness, but not primarily as imputation of Christ's righteousness, was heavily emphasized in Wesley's conversion
and the beginning of the revival, and remained the cardinal
presupposition of Methodist preaching. Recent studies have
illumined Wesley's use of the Puritan doctrine of second
or final justification by faith alone at the last judgment.
Somewhat more explicitly, the preaching concentrated on
regeneration and sanctification, with two closely related
doctrines—the assurance of salvation through the direct
witness of the Holy Spirit, and striving for perfection (an
experience of perfection in love, attained by faith)—
providing a characteristic Methodist accent. In relation
to sanctification special reference was often made to ethical
and social questions of the day. 2) Circling around this
homiletical core are several more or less *explicit presuppositions.* God's eternal decree—the Wesleyan answer to
predestination—offering salvation freely to all men on condition of faith; original sin understood as total depravity;
prevenient grace; the moral law as the norm of sanctification and the standard of divine judgment; the atonement,
emphasizing Christ's passive obedience and His penal substitution; the means of grace resolutely used as defense
against quietism; and a final forensic judgment. 3) In the
widest circle are not so much explicit doctrines as persistent and deep-lying motifs drawn from the *ecumenical
tradition,* as passed on through the Anglican formularies,
but nonetheless essential to the Wesleyan message. Here,
e.g., are the remarkably thoroughgoing, but never explicitly
formulated, Wesleyan Trinitarianism and Christology. Wes-

ley was fully aware of this ecumenical doctrinal background, and it is significant that when the American Methodists separated from Wesley subsequent to the revolution and organized themselves into a church, Wesley went to great pains to supply them with an abridgement of the Thirty-nine Articles and the Book of Common Prayer.

English Methodism formally separated from Anglicanism and became a Church four years after Wesley's death. Richard Watson wrote the first English Methodist systematics, his *Theological Institutes,* in 1823-1829. William B. Pope's *A Compend of Christian Theology* (1875-1880), a wide-ranging exegetical, historical, and dogmatic study, stands as the representative nineteenth-century English Methodist theological work.

In this country, under the leadership of Francis Asbury (1745-1816), Methodism's first bishop (and so titled against Wesley's will), the new church threw itself into the expanding frontier with an almost military efficiency, and only slowly, toward the end of the nineteenth century, did a widespread suspicion of theological training begin to wane. The importance of this period, when theological libraries had to fit into saddlebags, can hardly be overestimated in judging the refraction of the original Wesleyan message in nineteenth- and twentieth-century American Methodism. Early nineteenth-century theology was occupied, not too fruitfully, with debates about predestination and perfection until the establishment of seminaries began about 1850. Outstanding among early writers was Miner Raymond of Garrett, whose three-volume *Systematic Theology* (1877-1879) is the first American Methodist systematics. Thomas O. Summers, first dean of Vanderbilt, published a notable two-volume *Systematic Theology* in 1888. Borden P. Bowne (1847-1910), with his philosophy of personalism, influenced to some extent by Ritschl and Eucken, inaugurated a new era of Methodist theology whose influence reaches into the present day (E. S. Brightman, 1884-1953, A. C. Knudson, 1873-1953). Much contemporary Methodist social concern—one of the characteristic marks of the Methodist Church—has been reformulated and nurtured anew in this personalist tradition

(F. J. McConnell, 1871-1953). On the other hand, H. F. Rall (1870-   ), influenced by Ritschl, and Edwin Lewis (1881-   ), influenced at one time by Barth, have been harbingers of a contemporary Methodist eclecticism. The fundamentalist-modernist controversy (the "essentialist controversy" of 1910-1924) stirred Methodism less deeply than other denominations.

Present-day Methodist theology in America, while continuing much of the older tradition, and especially its social concern, is striking out in several new directions. 1) The revival of biblical theology has influenced theology on both sides of the Atlantic, and has provided a language for ecumenical discussion (C. T. Craig, V. Taylor, D. T. Niles). 2) The ecumenical movement is challenging Methodism to become conscious of its relation to the ecumenical theological tradition, and more particularly to develop its own characteristic view of the Church (C. T. Craig, in England R. N. Flew). 3) Existentialist thought, secular as well as religious, has made a considerable initial impact in the seminaries (S. R. Hopper, C. Michalson), and may offer a new language for much of the core of the Wesleyan tradition. 4) Depth psychology is both demanding and inspiring a new evaluation of the Methodist teaching about the experience of salvation (A. Outler). 5) The last three decades have seen the emergence in England and America, as well as on the Continent, of a many-sided theological evaluation of Wesley and his contemporaries (G. C. Cell, M. Piette, W. R. Cannon, J. E. Rattenbury, H. Lindström, D. Lerch).

Methodism in this country has a Wesleyan heart but an American head. Its characteristic emphases remain those of the core of the Wesleyan preaching—"heart religion" and moral renewal. Its theological articulation of this central emphasis has tended to lack stability and continuity, and to be unusually open to stimulus and influence from without. In part this situation roots in a characteristic Methodist attitude toward theology as subordinate to experience. Wesley, himself, had occasional scorn for "mere opinions." At a deeper level, this Methodist theological eclecticism bears witness to the fact that

Methodism was born not as a church but as a movement and emphasis within Anglicanism, and that the Wesleyan heart needs again and again to reach beyond the "Methodist doctrines" and renew its living contact, first of all, with the scriptural revelation, which Wesley emphasized, but also with the ecumenical theological tradition in which, through the Anglicanism which Wesley presupposed, it originally learned to know its own mind.

JOHN W. DESCHNER

Bibliography

W. K. Anderson, *Methodism*.
Henry Carter, *The Methodist Heritage*.
H. Lindström, *Wesley and Sanctification*.

MODERNISM

"Modernism" in Christian thought designates those theologies which are concerned with reinterpreting traditional Christian beliefs so as to make them intelligible in the light of the scientific understanding of the world and of historical knowledge. Modernism thus seeks to establish the relevance of Christian doctrine to the experience of modern man. It seeks to conserve the essential elements in the historic faith by showing that the content of Christian truth is not bound to the supernatural world picture of ancient man which forms the background of the biblical writings. The Christian beliefs about creation, sin, the fall of man, the incarnation and resurrection of Christ, and redemption through grace, must be understood as expressing the reality of man's dependence upon God, estrangement from God, and the saving act of God; but these can be interpreted in relation to contemporary perspectives upon the nature of man and his experience.

It may be said with some justice that modernism is a method of interpreting Christian scripture and tradition, not a particular set of beliefs. "Modernizers" are found in every period of church history, and in most of the

Christian communions. Their interpretations of the Christian faith reflect the diverse contexts of experience and thought in which the modernist method is used. All modernists of the nineteenth and twentieth centuries, both Catholic and Protestant, share, however, the conviction that scientific knowledge and the application of historical criticism to the biblical record have created real issues for Christian faith, sufficiently so that a major task of interpretation must be performed if the saving truth of the gospel is to be grasped in its relevance to contemporary life.

As an ecclesiastical designation of a theological position the term "modernist" has its origin in the papal encyclical *Pascendi*, 1907, in which Pius X condemned the position of a group of Catholic theologians among whom were George Tyrrell and Alfred Loisy. These thinkers had sought to show how the dogmatic tradition of the Roman Church could be regarded as a symbolic expression of eternal truth which can never be expressed in literal form. Since human formulations of the truth are always inadequate, they argued, freedom for interpretation and for new understanding should be allowed. The early Catholic modernists sometimes stated this position in such an extreme way that all objective reference of dogma seemed to be dissolved, and its rejection by the Roman Church was inevitable.

In Protestant theology the modernist movement took other forms, and while some extremists appeared here also, Protestant modernism generally attempted to preserve a synthesis of the objective content of faith and the necessity for reinterpretation, though the degree of success in this endeavor is differently judged depending upon one's theological standpoint. F. D. E. Schleiermacher, who is sometimes called the "father of modernism," laid down in his *Glaubenslehre* in 1821 the fundamental principles by which all later modernism in Protestant thought developed its method. He sought to exhibit the contents of the Christian belief as expressions grounded in man's religious consciousness, and particularly the consciousness of redemption through Christ. This reliance upon religious experience was developed in nineteenth-century theologies through the conception of the immanence of God. Theologians attempted thereby to meet the problems raised for Christian belief by theories of evolution. The activity of God was manifest in the emergence in the creative process of higher orders of life and value.

In the later nineteenth century the Ritschlian theology showed less interest in metaphysics; but stressed the conquest by spirit and emphasized the moral content of faith as the essential key for theology. Thus modernist theology allied itself with the ethical aspirations of the nineteenth-century liberal doctrines of historical progress, and the need for social reconstruction.

The work of the modernists in establishing the rights and methods of historical criticism of Christian origins remains of fundamental significance even for the later theologies which have passed beyond the modernist perspective. Theologians like Paul Tillich and Rudolf Bultmann in the mid-twentieth century show a continuity with the modernist spirit in their assertion of the necessity for an interpretation of the biblical message which is correlated with man's contemporary self-understanding, especially as expressed in existentialist philosophies. But these theologians find a realism in the existentialist view of man quite different from the idealisms and moralisms of nineteenth-century thought. Further, the revelation of God proclaimed in the gospel is asserted to be a disclosure to man which transcends the experience in which he appropriates it. Thus Schleiermacher's tendency to equate revelation with man's religious experience is qualified, and the modernist theological method may be regarded as having passed into a post-modernist phase.

DANIEL D. WILLIAMS

Bibliography

O. C. Quick, *Liberalism, Modernism, and Tradition.*

A. R. Vidler, *The Modernist Movement in the Roman Catholic Church.*

MYSTICISM

Mysticism is a term that describes the condition of being overwhelmingly aware of the presence of the ultimately real. "I have met with my God . . . I have felt the healings drop upon my soul from under his wings" is the way that the seventeenth-century Quaker mystic, Isaac Penington, refers to his first-hand experience of being inwardly swept by the presence of the Lord. His French contemporary, Blaise Pascal, describes such an experience in the words, "Fire, God of Abraham, God of Isaac, God of Jacob, not of the philosophers and the scientists. God of Jesus Christ. Joy, joy, joy, tears of joy."

All of the great world religions acknowledge this direct encounter with the real. The names of Sankara within Hinduism; of the Zen movement within Buddhism; of Laotze and Taoism within Chinese religious aspiration; of the Cabalists and Hasidim within Judaism; of Al Ghazali or Rumi and the Sufis within Islam; or of Augustine, Bernard of Clairvaux, Eckhart, Boehme and the Quakers within the Christian company are all reminders of this fact.

With such a variety of religious cultures serving as lenses for this experience, identity in the reports of it or in the subsequent life-responses of the mystics is neither to be expected nor does it occur. Nevertheless, there is much common ground among the mystics of different world religions and a capacity for understanding across boundaries that is a highly important religious phenomenon. It becomes peculiarly important in a period of religious inter-penetration such as the second half of this century is witnessing. In such a time the mystically minded in each religion may serve as sensitive antennae that can reach across barriers and seek to understand and to interpret those from which they are separated. It is not by accident that such mystically minded Christians as Francis of Assisi, Raymond Lull and Nicholas of Cusa were drawn to a radically different approach to Islam than Christians of the crusade mentality.

Within each faith, when the mystical element is present

and active, it serves as a source of renewal to the other elements of the faith; and as long as it flourishes, it constitutes a continual challenge to what William James calls "a premature closing of accounts with reality" in terms of an exclusively ethical, institutional, theological, or intellectual presentation of religion.

There seems to have been a period in the early Christian Church when the direct experience of the Holy Spirit was the common expectation of all. Ascetic specialists then appear to have taken over, and the expectation of the mystical experience was narrowed down to a small élite. The great authorities on Christian mysticism have uniformly repudiated this drastic shrinkage of the perimeter and have insisted that the mystical experience in some degree is open to all. "The wind of God," Fenelon insists, "is always blowing, but you must hoist your sail." Augustine Baker speaks of "All conditions capable." Evelyn Underhill writes, "The spring of the amazing energy which enables a great mystic to rise to freedom and dominate his world, is latent in all of us; an integral part of our humanity." There could scarcely be any greater symptom of vitality in the religion of an age than the restoration of this common expectation of a direct experience of ultimate reality.

The mystic's witness to the fact of continuing revelation has led to his concern that others may share in this direct experience of the presence and be irradiated by its light and power. In fact, the name of mysticism has often been associated with the steps of preparation of the soul for this experience. There is *purgation*, the ridding of the soul of those practices which disperse it and prevent it from paying attention. There is *illumination*, the mobilization of the preliminary disclosures that focus attention. And there is *contemplation*, the final stage in which the presence penetrates the beholder.

In acknowledging this conventional description of the inward steps of preparation for mystical disclosure, the mystics have echoed Augustine's words that "We come to God by love, and not by navigation," and have been the first to insist that grace cannot be bound by any describable patterns and that this "gift of gifts" may appear suddenly and elude any and all of the wisdom contained in these well-meant instructions for preparing the way. This insistence, however, has not seemed to inhibit the mystics in the least from continuing to lay down suggestions for proper preparation, and those very suggestions in themselves often provide a highly important source of material for studying the character of the reality which the mystic has experienced. For, in spite of his reluctance to speak of what has happened to him and his language of concealment that may go as far as negative theology in trying to express that he has felt a plenitude which no conceptualization can ever do justice to, his concern that others may share this experience and the counsel he gives them for getting ready, change his alleged ignorance into a "learned ignorance" and one from which we can learn much.

The mystic's witness to the accessibility of the living presence and of its continuing revelation of itself in the hearts of contemporary men and women has been an enormous encouragement to the religious yearnings of men. It points to the neglected sector of the Incarnation teaching, namely, that God became man in order that men might be lifted to God. It has given to men here on this earth a foretaste of eternal life and has kindled their powers of thought and expression by showing them how thin is the membrane which separates us all from the illumined life of common joy.

DOUGLAS V. STEERE

Bibliography

W. R. Inge, *Christian Mysticism.*
R. M. Jones, *Studies in Mystical Religion.*
R. Otto, *Mysticism East and West.*
Evelyn Underhill, *Mysticism.*

MYTH (DEMYTHOLOGIZING)

Myth. The term myth is used in several ways. It signifies 1) that which is a fable, a tale, a figment (I Tim. 1:4);

2) a literary form which describes other-worldly matters in this-worldly concepts; 3) a method of interpreting ultimate truth and, therefore, a method of thinking. Contemporary theologians, although no longer concerned with myth in the first sense, are preoccupied with myth as both literary form and method of thought.

In the late nineteenth and early twentieth centuries the historians of religions began to consider myth as an historical problem. Since the beginning of the European enlightenment, philosophical and theological criticism has been leveled at the dogmatic conclusions which had been drawn from biblical myth. At present biblical scholars, on the whole, consider the biblical view of the cosmos as not only pre-Copernican but mythical.

The narrative myth originated in Greek and oriental antiquity. In reaction to the pluralism of pagan mythologies, the religion of Israel had a transforming influence, speaking, as it does, not of a plurality of gods but of a single and unique God. This transformation can be seen in the mythical stories of creation (Gen. 1), of the paradise (Gen. 2-3), the flood (Gen. 6-7), the tower of Babel (Gen. 11). These stories all present a revised version of Babylonian myth and still retain some anthropomorphic features alien to the old religion of Israel. Besides nature-myth (the interpretation of the rainbow, Gen. 9:12 f), we encounter, especially in Jewish apocalyptic writings, mythical expositions intermingled with the visions of the prophets (Is. 6; Ez. 1).

The New Testament continues the mythical pattern introduced in Jewish tradition, but connects it closely with the Christian message. The New Testament portrayal of the cosmos retains the three-storied conception of antiquity: heaven, earth, and hell. Though the New Testament, as a whole, is not concerned with detailed descriptions of the worlds above or beneath, it is clear that Satan and the demons inhabit Hades (or Gehenna) and that Christ is enthroned with God in heaven; and that terrestrial man is poised between divine and demonic forces.

In addition, mythological elements appear in the Christology and eschatology of the New Testament. The Messiah, come down from heaven, was pre-existent (Phil. 2: 6 ff.), was born of a virgin (Matt. 1:1-18 ff.), descended into limbo, walked on earth, and reascended to heaven. As evidence of mythic concepts in eschatology we read in I Thessalonians 4:16 f., ". . . for the Lord himself will descend from heaven with a cry of command, with the archangel's call and with the sound of the trumpet of God . . ." and men, both alive and dead, will rise to meet the Lord in the air. Such a concept of a world-drama is taken over from Persian and late Jewish traditions and is used as a vehicle for interpreting the significance of Christ to the ancient world. Myth supplies a vehicle of communicating eschatological truth in its cosmic dimensions, while pointing to and disclosing God's salvation in Christ Jesus.

Demythologizing. How is it possible to preserve the very essence of Christian faith, namely, that God acted with man in and through Christ Jesus, without demanding the acknowledgment of the mythological pattern of its presentation? To believe in Christ Jesus as our Lord and Savior is it necessary to believe in the physical resurrection and the empty tomb, in the events of the "Last Day" as the end of this-worldly history, in the virgin birth, etc.? Is it not a pious self-deception to pretend that we believe literally in the Apostle's Creed? Why do we often repeat the biblical myth without explaining its deeper meaning, thereby putting before the man of today obstacles of mere form, without stressing the central stumbling block given in Christ Jesus as the revelation of God?

It was Rudolf Bultmann who, for the first time, dealt with the foregoing issues in a systematic way, and opened a discussion which continues to the present hour. Bultmann's point of departure is that biblical mythology expresses a truth in an obsolete way. It is impossible and meaningless to sanction the preaching or dogmatizing of the mythological elements of the Bible. It is impossible because our picture of the universe has changed radically —neither the biblical conception of "above" and "below" nor the tripartite division of the universe any longer obtain. It is meaningless because the mythological elements of the Bible are in no way an inherent part of our Christian message—they are but time-bound clothes of thought. To overcome the obsoleteness and preserve at the same time the deeper truth of the Bible we must interpret the *meaning* of the myth. Demythologizing means the interpretation of the myth, and must be seen, therefore, as a particular application of biblical hermeneutics.

The student may ask what lies beneath such mythological setting, behind the time-bound and historically conditioned forms? This question should be further defined: what is said about man's existence before God? In order for the interpreter to rediscover the specific concept of man's self-understanding veiled by myth, an *existentialist interpretation* must be employed. Bultmann uses the defined categories of Heidegger's philosophy, being aware, to be sure, that the language of the scholar must be other than the poetical or symbolical speech of the preacher or oracle. It may be asked whether or not such interpretation might result in a dangerous modernization or even falsification of the biblical message. To this Bultmann responds in a twofold way: 1) The New Testament demands, even begins itself, with an interpretation of the myth. It demands it because it teaches different and sometimes contradictory mythological concepts; moreover, it, itself, begins by interpreting the eschatology of a final drama in which the decisive action of God has already occurred. 2) The method of existential interpretation does not eliminate mythopoetic language and substitute for it abstract thought. It is aware of the abiding realities inherent in biblical mythology; yet it demands that the exposition of its values be done in a consistent and methodical way. It aims not at making Christian faith easier for the modern mind, but to radicalize the question of faith as such. The existential interpretation does not merely imply the diminution of the quantity of the assumptions of faith, but rather the awareness that to believe means qualitatively something other than the acceptance of a greater or smaller bulk of credal formulations.

The program of demythologizing—or positively: existentialist interpretation—may be seen as well under the categories of *kerygma* and myth. It has as its intention the exposition of the abiding truth, the kerygma, contained within myth. The Greek word *kerygma* means the action of proclamation. In the New Testament, *preaching* is its primary meaning, the proclamation of Jesus of Nazareth as Christ, Lord, and Savior for us (*pro nobis*). While theology is a human explication resulting from our thinking about faith and its content, the kerygma is the authoritative word kindling faith and coming, in its absoluteness, close to revelation. One may say that in the New Testament the word kerygma implies that God and the Lord Christ Jesus reveal themselves encountering man. Bultmann consistently distinguishes between myth and kerygma. He does the same with respect to theology and kerygma, although he is aware that kerygmatic passages in the New Testament are embedded in theological or mythological formulations. Existentialist interpretation focusses, therefore, on two points: the lifting up of the kerygma from the traditional text-pattern as the divine call, and the laying bare of man's response in faith as manifest in his new self-understanding.

The basic concept of demythologizing was formulated by Bultmann in an essay published in 1941. His radical approach was partly welcomed and partly criticized. On the one hand Bultmann seeks to overcome the liberalizing tendency to eliminate mythical concepts while selecting, quite arbitrarily, theological key-passages and, on the other hand, the fundamentalist proclivity to take myth at face value and to sacrifice all intellectual criticism. Although Bultmann is basically a liberal (though today he is often called neo-orthodox), he insists, against old-fashioned liberalism, that one would dissolve kerygma by excising its mythological presentation. The existentialist interpretation that he supports aims at the preservation of the ultimately paradoxical truth of Christian faith. To fundamentalism he insists that the human, historical origin of biblical literature must be acknowledged, and points out the necessity of its critical interpretation; as well, he asks for the recognition that the biblical world-view can no longer be literally retained.

Critical questions of those sympathetic to Bultmann's basic intention have been raised and should be noted. 1) Is not mythology somehow indispensable to the language of religion? Is not a cipher language needed to make a transcendent reality transparent (Jaspers)? Is not myth, like symbol, always needed to express or reflect transcendency (A. N. Wilder)? 2) If one considers all texts from the viewpoint of "what is said about man before God and man's self-understanding" is it restrictive of the biblical content? Is there not an inherent danger in such a formulation that the cosmic dimension of the event of Christian salvation would be dissolved? 3) Is there not a danger in the use of Heidegger's existentialism that faith in Christ would, by the use of a rational system, result in the dismissal of the abiding value of symbols?

Although these questions cannot be resolved here, it should be remembered that Bultmann's concern is not epistemological but hermeneutic. How to cope with such a concern Bultmann demonstrates in his *Theology of the New Testament* and *Primitive Christianity*.

ERICH DINKLER

Bibliography

Rudolf Bultmann, *Kerygma and Myth.*
Erich Dinkler, "Existentialist Interpretation of the New Testament," *Journal of Religion*, XXXII (1952).
Amos N. Wilder, "Mythology and the New Testament," *Journal of Biblical Literature*, LXX (1950).

NATURALISM

Naturalism is defined by two claims: 1) all actualities are temporal, meaning that they occur in time even if they are everlasting; 2) all knowledge of actualities must be gained by empirical methods requiring observation of predicted consequences. Human experience is vastly deeper and richer than knowledge.

Naturalism in theology results from an understanding of the religious problem. The religious problem is: What operates in human life to transform man, as he cannot transform himself, to save him from evil; to bring him to the greatest good, provided that he give himself to this transforming power with that wholeness of the self which is called religious faith?

Nothing can transform man unless it actually operates in human life. It may "come from" beyond human life; but regardless of from where it "comes," it can do nothing for man unless it operates in the human personality and between persons, in society and history. Therefore it must operate in the time and space where human life is lived and in the form of existence which distinguishes humanity. This excludes Being as such from religious significance. Also, knowledge about it must be, like all knowledge, in the form of statements confirmed by observation of predicted consequences; but art and symbols can bring to conscious awareness a depth and fullness of its reality far exceeding the abstractions of propositional truth.

What saves man from evil, as he cannot save himself, is properly called God, no matter how different it may be from traditional conceptions of God. The operative reality is more important than any cherished belief about it.

Until a person gives it centrality, this divine reality is only one thread amidst counter processes in human life. When it becomes a major preoccupation it may exercise its saving power.

Good and evil are determined not by conscious wants and desires, but by what is required 1) to unify the individual and 2) to satisfy the realized wholeness of his being. What accomplishes this is a kind of interchange between individuals which 1) creates in each an appreciative understanding of the real self which is hidden beneath the pretenses imposed by social adjustment; 2) enables each to learn from the other person's original experience; and 3) integrates into the self what is learned in order to create one's own individuality. This process begins with the newborn infant and progressively creates in him the human level of existence.

Many counter processes in human life oppose this creative interchange. To the measure that it prevails (which

is never complete) it saves the individual from inner conflict, sense of futility, irresponsibility and loneliness; unifies
the individual and satisfies this wholeness of his being;
magnifies the importance of the individual in all social
relations; enables one to enter into appreciative understanding of more people across greater barriers of diversity
and estrangement; increases freedom by substituting mutual control in place of domineering and coercive control;
expands the range and enriches the content of what each
can know, control and appreciate; creates and increases
intelligent love.

Naturalism of this sort is Christian not because creative
interchange is cosmic (it is not cosmic); nor because it is
found in animal life other than human. It is Christian
because this saving power is revealed in Jesus Christ. Individuals brought into relation with Jesus were transformed
by interchange with Him. It was not the man Jesus but
this creative interchange which saved. First the disciples
were transformed and by interchange between them and
others this power of God unto salvation was transmitted
to wider circles. Thus a fellowship was formed continuing
down through the ages. Obviously all this could occur only
by creative and transforming interchange between individuals.

For naturalism this statement about Jesus is not dogma.
It is considered true only on the ground that historical
research indicates such a process of transforming interchange did emanate from Jesus. Regardless of how much
or how little it depends upon Jesus, this kind of interchange is actually present in human life and becomes a
saving power when given priority over all else.

Giving it priority is called commitment of faith. Commitment requires that one confess, repent and repudiate
everything in himself which resists this transforming
power. This resistance (sin) is not eradicated by its repudiation; but when confessed and repented, it ceases to
be an insuperable barrier between oneself and the saving
process of transformation.

Religious naturalism rejects the self-contradictory claim
which asserts that man is saved by a timeless and change-

less Being. It claims rather to find in the processes of human existence this creative interchange which creates, sustains, saves, and transforms into the ways of love and justice, provided that men accept it as Lord and Master of their lives. It alone can overcome the major evils threatening our existence.

HENRY NELSON WIEMAN

Bibliography

Henry Nelson Wieman, *Man's Ultimate Commitment.*
Henry Nelson Wieman, *The Source of Human Good.*

NATURAL LAW

Contemporary Protestant thought is fundamentally critical of natural law theory, even though it does not repudiate the doctrine entirely. The ground of this critical attitude is that the doctrine of natural law is originally the product of rational philosophy, which rests upon certain notions of the nature and capacities of man which Protestantism does not accept. The bold Christianization of this ancient doctrine, particularly in the Middle Ages by Thomas Aquinas, was criticized by the Reformers for reasons similar to those found in contemporary Protestant thought. Aquinas had defined natural law in relation to eternal law, holding that the eternal law is God's reason which governs the relations of all things in the universe to each other. The natural law is that part of the eternal law which pertains to *man's* behavior. This concept of natural law rests upon Aquinas' notion of analogy, by which he meant that while God and man are not identical in nature, neither are they totally unlike, wherefore man's reason and God's reason also bear some likeness to each other. Catholic natural law assumes that the human reason is capable of deriving ultimate norms for contingent behavior, for it assumes that there are in man and his institutions certain stable structures produced by God's reason which man's reason can know to be normative. Thus, the basis of marriage, property, the state and the content of justice are held to be available to man's natural reason. The rules of positive morality and positive civil law are held to be valid only insofar as they conform to the natural law. Not only is man capable of knowing the natural law, but he is said to be capable of obeying it and thus fulfilling his natural, as compared with his supernatural, self. All this rests on the notion that man possesses a mode of freedom which makes it possible for him to deviate from the conduct required by his essential nature.

With some of these premises most contemporary Protestant theologians would agree, but probably not one of them would accept this Thomistic version of natural law, without some qualification. The most severe criticism of it comes from those who, like Karl Barth and Jacques Ellul, would hold that sinful and fallen man cannot have any direct knowledge of God or God's reason or will without the aid of revelation. They would argue that there are no trustworthy analogies between nature and God, hence no amount of knowledge of man's nature or his institutions can give us any knowledge of what God intended either of these to be. The image of God in man was shattered by sin, thus rendering all human thought relative, never to be confused with the ultimate and eternal. Reinhold Niebuhr's criticism is not so severe, for he accepts the natural law premise that there is an essential and universal structure in the human moral constitution as evidenced, for example, in the almost universal prohibition against murder. He also accepts the validity of certain principles of justice, rationally conceived, as the perspective from which to criticize the achievements of justice of actual governments. Niebuhr's chief criticism of the doctrine of natural law is that its principles are too inflexible and that, while they are the product of unique historical circumstances, they are viewed as absolute and eternal. That is, these natural law principles, according to Niebuhr, are historically conditioned and are therefore biased and relative and must not be taken as "natural" in the sense of being normative for all men at all times. Another dominant view is that of Emil Brunner, who retains much of the doctrine of natural law which he has transposed into the doctrine of the "created orders." He distinguishes between the formal and the material image of God in man, holding that while sin has destroyed the material image, the formal image remains. This means that there is some analogy between God and man, for God is more like man, for example, than like a stone, and in particular man still retains the capacity to be addressed by God. God reveals himself to man through His creation as well as in Jesus Christ. Thus creation is the basis of the law, for creation is God's primal allocation of man into particular relations as, for example, in monogamous marriage. But Brunner makes much of the notion that these created orders are known as the product of God's creation only when seen from the perspective of biblical revelation, for the Bible makes clear that certain relations between male and female, man and property and man and the state are not simply the product of man's will or reason but the consequence of God's creative and redemptive activity. From a more philosophical point of view, Paul Tillich holds that without the ontological grounding of law and justice there could never be the sense of wrong or injustice, for the natural law is the structure of reality including the structure of the human mind. Thus Tillich would see in natural law the discovery of structures of human relations which are universally valid.

The real force of the Protestant reconception of natural law comes from its emphasis upon the revelation of God as love through Jesus Christ. The ground of ethics is love, even for the natural man. Love is the fulfillment of the law, and love and grace are not reserved for the supernatural aspect of human history only, but rather the whole concept of justice is infused with the norm of love. This leads to the distinctly Protestant notion of natural law, for it speaks of man as encountering the God of judgment and love commanding him, not in terms of abstract principles, but subjecting him to the imperative of love. Love is the natural law because it is the law of man's essential nature.

SAMUEL ENOCH STUMPF

Bibliography

Emil Brunner, "The Community of the People and of Law,"
  The Divine Imperative.
Paul Tillich, *Love, Power, and Justice.*

NATURAL THEOLOGY

The historic origins. We owe the phrase "natural theology" to the Roman antiquarian M. Terentius Varro
(116-27 B.C.), who meant by the term "the doctrine about
things divine taught by philosophers as an integral part
of their account of reality." But natural theology itself is
considerably older and seems to have had two sources:
Plato and the Stoics.

In the tenth book of his *Laws* (893 ff.) Plato (427-347
B.C.) argues that there are certain truths about God which
can be strictly demonstrated. The essence of his argument
is that all motion is either spontaneous or communicated.
All communicated movement is in the last resort derived
from spontaneous movement, which is originated by soul
or mind. Since order has the upper hand in the universe,
the supreme Cause is a good Soul, or God.

The Oxford English Dictionary defines natural theology
as "a theology based on human reason apart from revelation," and this speculative theology of Plato, which
Aristotle was to develop, and which after a long history
was to receive its most impressive formulation from
Aquinas, satisfies this definition.

On the other hand, there is a second type of natural
theology, which originates in the thought of the Stoics.
Here a contrast is made between the positive theologies of
various cults and peoples, which differ considerably among
themselves, and what is claimed to be a common measure
of theological belief native to humanity. "What the gods
are, is a matter of dispute," says the Stoic in Cicero's
treatise on the nature of the gods, "but that they are is
denied by nobody." Here is an argument which proceeds
from the witness of universal religious experience and the
nature of man, and not an argument claiming to demon-

strate truths about God from the character of external reality.

The development of natural theology. 1) The first, or speculative form of natural theology finds its most remarkable expression in the work of Thomas Aquinas (1227-1274), who held that some truths about God could be strictly demonstrated by philosophy, but that "it was necessary for man's salvation that there should be certain knowledge by divine revelation" besides the study of philosophy which is worked out by human reason. By reason we cannot know God in His essence, but we can know that He exists as the Prime Cause, and all that pertains to Him as such, in distinction from all His creatures. Beyond this we are dependent on revelation, which also gives to man a more available and more reliable knowledge of the truths necessary for salvation which fall under the competence of reason.

The natural theology of Thomas Aquinas culminates in the famous "Five Ways," which are forms of what is called the Cosmological Argument. This argument starts from facts of everyday experience, facts about the empirical world which, it is claimed, necessarily imply the existence of God.

The First Way is similar to the theistic proof given by Plato in the *Laws*. It is the argument from movement to an Unmoved Mover. Every movement or change presupposes another movement or change without which it would not come to be. But there must be an end to this regress, otherwise there would be no First Mover, and therefore no other mover. But there is movement, so there must be a First Mover, and this is what we all understand God to be.

The Second Way is the argument from finite causes to an Uncaused Cause. This differs from the First Way in that the Unmoved Mover is thought of as existing in the present, while the Uncaused Cause is referred to the past.

The Third Way is the argument from contingency to necessity; the Fourth Way argues from the comparative to the superlative, from "more" to "most"; while the Fifth

Way argues from design in the world to a Designer. This is the famous Teleological Argument, later expounded in the *Evidences of Christianity* of Paley (1743-1805) and assailed brilliantly in the *Dialogues on Natural Religion* of David Hume (1711-1776).

The Five Ways cannot be here examined in detail. They have been under careful examination for several centuries, their chief critic being perhaps Immanuel Kant (1724-1804). Put very briefly, the line of Kant's criticism is as follows. The categories of thought which we necessarily employ in all our knowledge of the empirical world are incompetent to deal with the transcendent realities. When the attempt is made to employ them beyond these frontiers, the mind is led into insoluble antinomies. The cosmological and teleological proofs of Aquinas, Kant asserts, are illegitimate uses of thought-forms suited only to deal with empirical reality. Kant's First and Fourth Antinomies cover more or less the same ground as Aquinas' Second and Third Ways, and he claims that in each case it is possible to argue also the contrary, his conclusion being that both arguments, e.g., for and against Necessary Being, are without convincing power.

On the other hand, there have always been and still are philosophers who maintain the validity of the Five Ways; and many others who, in more general terms, are willing to assert the validity of the arguments of speculative natural theology.

This position is held today by the Roman Catholic Church, which in the Dogmatic Decrees of the Vatican Council (1870) declared that "Holy Mother Church holds and teaches that God . . . may certainly be known by the natural light of human reason, by means of created things."

2) The second stream of natural theology, which took its rise in Stoicism, appeals, it will be remembered, to the idea of God which, it is claimed, is innate in mankind. In other words, appeal is made to the common ground which is asserted to underlie the varieties of belief and practice in the various religions. Reference is made to religious experience in the heart and mind of man rather

than to facts in the external world. The tendency is to show men that they already believe, rather than to prove to them that they must believe. It must be conceded, however, that there is always an emphasis on the rationality of natural theology, which prevents us from distinguishing this form of it too sharply from the first.

The famous Ontological Proof of Anselm (1033-1109) must be classed rather with this form of natural theology than with the speculative type. Arguing that the *concept* of God is "that than which nothing greater can be conceived," Anselm proceeds to say that, if there is no reality which accords to such a concept, then the concept would lack at least the perfection of existence, and so would not be the concept of Perfect Being. The validity of this proof was denied both by Aquinas and by Kant, but it can be restated in a modified form, which asserts that, unless men were confronted by a revelation of God, they would not possess the idea of the absolute, the unconditioned, and the infinite at all.

It is on the whole to this form of natural theology that the work of the English Deists, Toland (1669-1722), Tindal (1656-1733) and others belongs, together with the writings of the men of the Enlightenment on the Continent. There is here a profound difference from the thought of the Schoolmen, in that for these writers natural theology tends to be the only type that is regarded as permissible or, at any rate, is the standard by which claims to revelation are judged. Perhaps the most famous name in this second group is that of Lessing (1729-1781). The English Deists thought of natural religion as underlying the positive religions, as their rational basis, and perhaps original form. Lessing thought of the education of the human race as leading toward a rational religion in the future, when the provisional irrational element or revelation would no longer be necessary.

More recent developments. In the last century the terms of the problem of natural theology have been restated. In the past, natural theology has been considered the counterpart, sometimes the rival, of revealed theology. The former

contained those truths which could be discovered by unaided reason, and the latter those for which we are dependent on revelation. The reason for the reformulation
has been twofold.

First, it was generally felt that, if God is known at all,
then it must be because of His desire to be known. This
necessitates a change in the conception of natural theology. It too must be dependent on a revelation.

Secondly, the conception of revealed theology suggests
that what is revealed is a system of truth about God, and
that scripture is chiefly to be regarded as an authoritative
source of doctrine, whereas what is in fact revealed is
God Himself in His personal approach to men and in His
historical saving acts. It is no longer possible to speak of
dogmatic theology as revealed. Thus the tendency, at
least in Protestant theology, is to conceive of two spheres
of revelation: first, the general revelation, or the revelation
in creation; and, second, special revelation, that historic
revelation to which the writings of the scriptures bear
witness. There are differences of opinion as to whether
these two kinds are definitely different in kind, but the
majority view is that there is such a distinction. The problem of natural theology, however, remains.

Recent discussion on the problem of natural theology.
A brief sketch of the recent sharp controversy between
Barth and Brunner on natural theology must now be
given. Brunner has consistently drawn a distinction between general revelation, or the revelation in creation, on
the one hand, and natural theology on the other. God is
truly revealed through the created world, and, indirectly,
through the moral law. But this revelation has never been
truly grasped save in the light of the revelation of God in
Christ. On the contrary, where Christian faith was absent,
it has constantly been more or less misinterpreted and misunderstood. Brunner's position may be summed up in a
phrase: There is a true revelation of God in creation; there
is no valid natural theology (although the fact of natural
theology no one can deny).

Brunner claims that these positions are solidly based on

scriptural foundations in both Testaments; the most important passage perhaps being Romans 1:19-20, which unmistakably asserts both of them. He claims that both Luther and Calvin support these views, and in the opinion of the present writer his case is unanswerable.

Brunner's argument, as at first expounded, was confused by the use of a term, "Christian natural theology," to describe a discipline which, starting from explicitly Christian presuppositions, sought for evidences of the revelation in creation in the world and man. This term he has now given up, using the term "eristic" to describe this discipline. But the use of the earlier term may in part (though only in part) have led to Barth's attack upon him.

This attack was vehement, but, on his side, Barth was confused by an inability to see, or an unwillingness to distinguish, the difference between the revelation in creation and natural theology. Thus he defined the latter as "the doctrine of a bond with God which exists apart from God's revelation in Jesus Christ," which is not far different from Brunner's definition of the revelation in creation.

Barth's motives are perhaps two. First, he argues that any knowledge of God must be saving knowledge, and if we admit a knowledge not mediated through the incarnate Christ, or a capacity for knowing God still inherent in fallen man, we have destroyed in the first case the claim that only through Christ is salvation given, and, in the second case, suggested that man can do something to save himself.

Secondly, such knowledge as is averred for natural theology is a knowledge which does not lay claim to our obedience as does the knowledge of faith, but is speculative and leaves our will untouched. In both ways the centrality and lordship of Christ is assailed.

To this Brunner and his supporters answer that no claim is made by them to stand outside the revelation or lordship of Christ. And, further, they claim that both the Bible and the Reformers hold that the revelation in creation is necessary to make man responsible and guilty before God. If the special revelation clearly reveals man's guilt, and, when accepted in faith, removes it, there must be a revelation in creation to which it appeals. Otherwise the special revelation does not *reveal* man's guilt, but actually *creates* it.

The question of the validity of natural theology. Who is to judge of this question? The Vatican, or the skeptical philosophers, or some other court of appeal? It may be that only in the context of a whole fabric of Christian presuppositions, consciously or unconsciously held, do these arguments appear convincing. As men move farther away from their Christian background, it is a fact that philosophical theism appears to disintegrate into speculative idealism, atheism, deism, or agnosticism. What is the cause of this undeniable phenomenon? May it not be that what is claimed as a part of natural theology convincing to all reasoning beings may in fact really be a part of Christian apologetic or eristic in disguise? Such Christian apologetic is, in fact, the thinking out in various fields of the consequences of Christian presuppositions, and can expect no universal agreement.

Further, the Stoic and Deistic reasoning which argued that there was a demonstrable common ground in all religions is not borne out by a fuller investigation of the phenomena. What is true is that Christian believers can see in these phenomena evidences leading to a faith in the common revelation in creation behind all of them, from which each of them, in greater or less degree, deflects. Seen in this way even idolatry is a witness to God, for only he to whom God is revealing himself can have an idol! But the unity behind these religions cannot be exhibited by any phenomenological method. It is visible only to faith.

While a position like this may be held with some degree of confidence by a number of Christians, there is nothing to prevent repeated attempts to state and reformulate arguments of natural theology, and nothing to prevent skeptical or Christian thinkers from criticizing them. Each one must be considered on its merits.

DAVID CAIRNS

Bibliography

John Baillie, *Our Knowledge of God.*
Karl Barth, *Nein! Eine Antwort an Emil Brunner.*
Emil Brunner and Karl Barth, *Natural Theology.*
Emil Brunner, *Offenbarung und Vernunft.*

NEO-ORTHODOXY

Neo-orthodoxy can most easily be comprehended as a response to the developing crisis of the Western world in the last four decades. In the theology of the nineteenth century, usually called "liberalism," Christianity had become increasingly wedded to the then successful democratic, industrial and scientific culture of the West. When, therefore, the self-confidence of that culture began to wane, and its foundations to collapse after the First World War, an understandable response occurred from the more sensitive Christian leaders. This response (e.g. in Karl Barth and Emil Brunner) was a passionate attempt to locate the sources of the Christian message and the ground of its hope beyond a culture in crisis. The fear that a Christianity dominated by the thought-forms of a disintegrating culture could not survive, and, even more, that a "culture religion" could have no message of hope to a society that despaired of its powers, was the driving force in this creative effort to reestablish Christian faith on the foundations of God's revelation in scripture rather than on the foundations of Western scientific, political or social thought. The earliest emphasis of the neo-orthodox movement, therefore, was a radical criticism of the "liberal" union of culture and Christianity, and a corresponding assertion of the discontinuity of Christianity in all its aspects from the dominant though-forms of Western life (cf. Barth, Brunner, Reinhold Niebuhr, Aulen and Nygren).

The central theological motifs of the neo-orthodox movement stem from this basic drive towards discontinuity and separation of religion and culture. In the place of the liberal emphasis on the immanence of God in the life of nature and of human society comes the vigorous affirmation of the transcendence of God, of His unknowableness and His consequent difference from all our thoughts about Him in cultural terms. In the place of the liberal faith in man's inherent goodness and wisdom appears the categorical insistence that salvation must come to man and to culture from beyond themselves. Thus the liberal conception of history as a gradual, progressive development of the inherent powers of man towards the good life is transformed into a view of history that is "dialectical" and "catastrophic" in character. Man is and remains a sinner in both his personal and social existence; thus history exists in a tension between God's judgment on man's sin and God's grace which alone will redeem man in this situation. The only hope for man, therefore, lies not so much in the liberal program of education and an enlargement of man's benevolent powers, but rather in the "crisis" of faith when man repents before God, lives in a new state of forgiveness, humility and obedience, and looks to the final fulfillment of God's purposes beyond history (see especially the writings of Reinhold Niebuhr).

All across the theological spectrum this theme of the "crisis" of man's natural powers, of the discontinuity of the gospel and the cultural life of mankind, is the dominant motif of neo-orthodox thought. Hence the neo-orthodox insistence on the radical disparity of religious and cultural truth (e.g. the Word of God in scripture versus the word of man in culture, and revelation over against philosophic reason and natural theology); the new emphasis on the seriousness and universality of sin (e.g. the recrudescence of the doctrine of sin as a central aspect of the Christian understanding of man); the clear distinction between the religious or good man at his best and the Incarnate Lord (e.g. the "Jesus of History" versus the "Christ of Faith"); and finally, the neo-orthodox denial that even the best society is more than an approximation to the Kingdom of God (e.g. the renewed interest in 1) the Church as the unique bearer in history of God's purposes and grace, and 2) in eschatology as the sole object of ultimate hope in history). These have been the central themes of neo-orthodox theology interpreted in a variety of ways by many diverse thinkers from the more "ortho-dox" Barth to the more "liberal" Tillich. In each case, however, we can see the desire to reinterpret Christian doctrine in terms of the transcendence of God and of His grace, and in terms of the inability of the natural and cultural man to save himself.

The Reformation as a theological movement has also been characterized by a vigorous protest against a syn-thesis of culture and Christianity, namely the whole Cath-olic union of classical, feudal and biblical influences which made up the religion of the Middle Ages. The Reforma-tion had expressed with unique power, therefore, the same basic theological motifs, i.e. a transcendent revelation, a divine judgment and a divine grace as solely competent for salvation. Thus it was largely from Reformation sources that the neo-orthodox thinkers, seeking to protest against the nineteenth century's "culture religion," drew their inspiration and theological materials. This move-ment can, therefore, validly be called "neo-*orthodox*" or even "neo-Reformation." We should understand, however, that these men returned to this "orthodox" tradition, not in order merely to be dogmatically orthodox, but because they found there the most compelling and relevant theo-logical writing.

Neo-orthodoxy, however, cannot be understood solely as a return to the Reformation perspective; as its name implies, it is also genuinely "neo" in character. As it has increasingly realized, the movement is also a child of the liberalism against which it reacted, for it retains many of the most important affirmations and principles of liberal Christianity.

Neo-orthodoxy agrees with liberalism that the whole area of spatio-temporal fact and event is the valid object of scientific inquiry, with the result that the hypotheses of science in the area of natural and historical fact are re-garded as authoritative. Thus, although such doctrines as "Creation out of Nothing," and the "Fall of Adam" have again become important theologically, neo-orthodoxy does not quarrel with scientific explanations of the origin of nature and of man's life. Likewise, although the Incarnation has become the central theological doctrine of all neo-orthodoxy, the factual manifestations and explanations of the Incarnation (e.g. the miracles, the Virgin Birth, and the Empty Tomb) have not played such a central role in contemporary theology as they did in "orthodoxy." In other words, to the contemporary thinker theological doctrines are statements containing symbolic rather than literal truth, propositions pointing to the religious dimensions of events rather than propositions containing factual information about events (See Niebuhr's use of "myth," Tillich's use of "symbolic language" and Dodd's "fact and interpretation"). The intricate relation between the historic fact and the religious, "mythical" or symbolic interpretation of the fact remains as an important and as yet unresolved problem for neo-orthodoxy.

Secondly, neo-orthodoxy affirms with liberalism that all of the activities and products of man's religious life (scriptures, creeds, churches) are historically conditioned. From this contemporary theology draws two "liberal" conclusions: 1) these scriptures and institutions can and must be studied historically and critically in order to be properly understood; 2) none of these products of man's religious life is in itself infallible or a direct, unmediated result of divine activity. But still, as we have noted, for the neo-orthodox thinker Christian truth is not merely relative human wisdom, since it contains the Word of God; and the Church is not merely another social institution since it is also the Body of Christ in history. Hence arise other problems peculiar to neo-orthodox theology: e.g. what is the relation of the Word of God in scripture to the words of men which make up the scriptures; and, what is the relation of the Word and Spirit of God, which establish and constitute the Church, to the relative, even sinful historical institutions which we call churches? Out of this same combination of orthodox and liberal elements, however, comes also the unusual grace of neo-orthodox Christianity at its best: namely, that it at once emphasizes the uniqueness of Christian belief and the importance of a sound theology, without at the same time being intolerant or creedal in its spirit.

Finally, the union of culture and religion in liberalism had given to liberal Christianity a passionate concern to relate the Christian gospel creatively to man's social existence, and to find in Christian faith a basis for an improved social environment for man. This emphasis on the social relevance of the gospel to the problems of war and peace, and to the problems of economic, political and racial justice, neo-orthodoxy, at least in its Anglo-Saxon forms (i.e. in Niebuhr, Bennett, Tillich, and a host of others), shares and perpetuates. Instead, however, of referring to social reform as "the building of the Kingdom of God," it speaks of the call to manifest Christ's Lordship over all aspects of a sinful world, and of the necessity of Christian obedience in love to one's neighbor in all the facets of life. It should be noted that the presupposition of this neo-orthodox social concern is an important liberal idea, namely that social institutions are a historical development and so not directly ordained in their present form by God's providential will. In seeing the actual structures of society as permeated by sin and therefore as fit objects for Christian reformation, the neo-orthodox thinker is again dependent on his liberal heritage and running counter to the Reformation view of social institutions.

Thus neo-orthodoxy is a new synthesis of two widely divergent interpretations of the Christian religion, that of the Reformation and that of nineteenth-century liberalism. A movement rather than a "school," neo-orthodoxy has influenced almost every contemporary theologian. It presents, therefore, a variety of emphases and characteristics, but its central themes of the divine transcendence, of the human predicament and of the total relevance of the Christian faith are almost universal today. So far this synthesis of the old and the new has been immensely creative in reestablishing a concern for the religious message of the Bible, for the unique history and traditions of the Christian Church, for the essential theological elements of the Christian faith and message, and for the relevance of that message to the totality of man's life, personal and social.

LANGDON B. GILKEY

Bibliography

G. Aulen, *Christus Victor.*
K. Barth, *The Word of God and the Word of Man.*
E. Brunner, *The Theology of Crisis.*
R. Niebuhr, *An Interpretation of Christian Ethics.*

PARADOX

The term *paradox,* as used in Christian thinking, has come into great prominence in contemporary theology. Not that it is new. It abounds, for example, in Pascal: "The extremes meet"; "there are reasons of the heart that the reason knows not of," etc. It is the clue to the "learned ignorance" of Nicholas of Cusa, as well as to his "coincidence of opposites." It is involved in the *credo ut intelligam* of the Schoolmen; and it has seldom been employed with greater violence than by Tertullian: "I believe, because it is absurd; . . . it is certain, because it is impossible."

Tertullian's violence will be mitigated somewhat, however, the moment we consider how characteristic is paradoxical statement in scripture, as well as in theology. It is in Saint Paul's "foolishness of God" that is "wiser than men" (1 Cor. 1:20 f.); in the notion that he who would save his life must lose it; and even in Job's "though He slay me yet will I trust Him," when profoundly understood. Contemporary theology tends to hold with Kierkegaard that Christianity is "precisely the paradoxical"; or, to put it in other terms, all discourse about God—and particularly Christian discourse about God—tends to be, perhaps must be, paradoxical.

This is apparent the moment we consider that the terms of Christian discourse are precisely those of the divine and the human. But such discourse is necessarily of the divine from the standpoint of the human, of the infinite from the standpoint of the finite, of the perfect from the standpoint of the imperfect, of the eternal from⁻ the standpoint of the temporal, together with such other terms as must juxtapose the absolute to the relative.

Were the problem merely one of formal reasoning, an appeal might be made to the principle of the *analogia entis,* the analogy of being, after the pattern of scholastic metaphysics. But it is precisely *not* the formal relationship that is at stake here; it is the existential one. Hence the stringency of Kierkegaard's claim (so like that of Pascal): "It is the duty of the human understanding to understand that there are things which it cannot understand, and what those things are. Human understanding has vulgarly occupied itself with nothing but understanding, but if it would only take the trouble to understand itself at the same time it would simply have to posit the paradox. The paradox is not a concession but a category, an ontological definition which expresses the relation between an existing cognitive spirit and eternal truth" (*Journals,* Dru, 633).

Putting aside, now, Kierkegaard's elliptical rhetoric, the problem reduces to the following: the "eternal" and the "temporal" are, *by definition,* incommensurate; but Christianity holds that the Eternal *has come into time*—a *logical* impossibility, or absurdity (but true nevertheless, and therefore a paradox to formal thinking).

This Christian claim makes faith also paradoxical. For faith becomes an appropriation of the true as found in Christ (the Paradox); but this is an offense to the "reason." The "reason" seeks formal or reflective coherence of an objective kind: faith is a subjective appropriation of a relationship to the Eternal based on decision rather than reflection.

But the paradox drives us further. Reason is limited not merely by the formal character of its "logic," not even by its finitude; it is also limited by "sin"—our alienation from or separation from God. Since we are antecedently in the condition (metaphorically speaking) of "falling" away from the relation, all our reasoning about the nature of God, or of reality, or of knowledge and the ways of knowing, does not restore us to or reinstate us in the former context of the love relation. Pascal recognized how deeply this doctrine of the fall offends us; but yet, he went on, without this "mystery, the most incomprehensible of all, we are incomprehensible to ourselves" (*Pensées*, Brunschwig, ed., #434). With it, we recognize the contradictoriness of the human creature. Man is "the little creature who is for ever seeking himself, and therefore also fleeing from himself; one who is for ever being drawn and attracted by something higher, and yet is ever seeking to release himself from this higher element; the creature who is both aware of his contradiction and yet at the same time denies it" (Emil Brunner, *Man in Revolt*, tr. by Olive Wyon, p. 24-25). This contradictoriness becomes apparent the moment we grasp the nature of the Christian claim that "in Christ God was reconciling the world unto himself." The contradictoriness that is polemic against God and which sews itself into all our relationships, is itself contradicted by the Contradiction of the Cross—in the Paradox of Jesus as manifesting the Christ (Tillich), as showing forth the nature of the condition of man and the nature of God's intending love toward us.

STANLEY ROMAINE HOPPER

Bibliography

Emil Brunner, *Man in Revolt*.
Sören Kierkegaard, *Concluding Unscientific Postscript*.

PERFECT—PERFECTION

The Greek words for "perfect" and "perfection" are found forty-eight times in the New Testament. But even this enumeration fails to do justice to the dominance of this concept in the teaching of Jesus and indeed in the whole of the New Testament. The word perfection has become suspect over a wide area of Protestantism, and on the Continent of Europe the word perfectionism is a term of reproach. But the word perfection is honored in the Roman Catholic communion. If we admit that it stands for the goal of the Christian life, both social and individual, we shall be forced to study it in the richer term, "the Reign" or "Kingly Rule of God." Jesus said (Luke 12:32) to His disciples: "Fear not, little flock; for it is your Father's good pleasure to give you the kingdom." This is perfection; only it is translating an abstract noun into active, personal, loving deeds in the company of One who will never fail the little flock.

According to St. Matthew (19:21 and 5:48) Jesus used the word twice. To the rich young ruler He said, first, "Why do you call me good? No one is good but God alone." The point of this is often missed. Only once in all the Talmud is any Rabbi (teacher) called good (ágathos). Jesus wants to know why He is being called good. Second, "If you would be perfect, go, sell what you possess, and give it to the poor; and come, follow me." Mark (10:21) tells us that the eyes of Jesus had searched the man's face lovingly. The question that Jesus put, the answer given, the great refusal made—all showed the immaturity of the youth. "If you would be perfect" might in this instance mean, If you want to be full-grown in the spiritual life. Chrysostom notes the tact and delicacy of Jesus shining through this very brief interview. "He leads him on, little by little. He teaches him. He fastens him on to God. . . . He shows him the prize, saying *If thou wilt be perfect . . .* before he says *Sell all that thou hast.* Then the treasure in heaven, and a place in his company." Here the young ruler is suddenly flung back upon God. He is meant to face the impossibility of answering any question which balances eternal life over against a decent, respectable moral life in this age. There is only one way. He is offered, at once, for he has much to learn, intimate fellowship with Jesus and His friends. He will learn about God and this Kingly Rule from a teacher immeasurably greater than all the Rabbis of whom he has ever heard. But he must cleanse himself from the luxurious life he is living. It is no comfortable mission on which Jesus is traveling. But when the decision is made, we see an unhappy figure, solitary despite his wealth— or because of it. He has turned away from the Perfect

One. In the haunting phrase of Mary Coleridge, he is the "Man with his back to the East."

As an introduction to the Sermon on the Mount, we need a warning, first, that in the Old Testament the prophets as well as the lawgivers issued law (*tora*) which they expected to be carried into act. In the second place, Jeremiah's conception of the New Covenant implies that the true *tora* is not any written code nor prophetic message but something which has been partly expressed in these ways yet transcends them—the revelation of the essential ethical will of God. If Jesus expects great things from God, it is because He Himself has been preparing the disciples and expects them to learn in His company what the perfect life is.

The key to any teaching of perfection is the passage on love of enemies in the Sermon on the Mount (Matt. 5:43-48). Jesus seems to make an impossible demand: "You, therefore, must be perfect, as your heavenly Father is perfect." This saying, coming at the end of the most drastic demands (as they seem) in the teaching of Jesus, has the sound of a thunderclap. Yet the command had been, partly at least, anticipated in the Old Testament. "Before the Lord your God you must be blameless" (Deut. 18:13. In the LXX the word is *teleios*). "You must be holy, for I, the Lord your God, am holy" (Lev. 19:1). But the boldness and originality of the link between perfect love of God to us, and our consequent forgiveness to the uttermost, had never been more exquisitely sung. However difficult the verse and its translation into act may be, it does clearly mean that men ought to love as God loves. "Jesus teaches an excess in virtue, an excess in forbearing, an excess in forgiveness, an excess in gentleness, an excess in giving and yielding. He does—and here there is originality—very often oppose the principle of measure for measure, as He is doing here" (C. G. Montefiore).

Teleios *in the Pauline Letters*. The first passage, according to many continental scholars, must be interpreted in the light of the contemporary mystery-cults. *Teleios* is a technical term and would mean "initiated"; the phrase "wisdom in a mystery," a wisdom which has been hidden, a wisdom which God decreed before the ages, would mean that Paul was initiating a few "spiritual" folk into the higher mysteries which the "babes" could not share. This is an attractive interpretation, but will not completely fit the facts.

1) There is an antithesis in the passage between the *teleioi*, or spiritual people, and the "babes." But in the mystery-cults this antithesis does not occur. You are either initiated or you are not. There are no babes.

2) There is another vital distinction between the use of the word mystery in the Hellenistic cults, and the biblical use of the term. In the mystery religions, there are secrets which must not be divulged to any outsider, mysteries in the English or classical Greek sense. In the New Testament there are secrets, but they are being proclaimed. A mystery is something which has been hidden but is now being revealed. Chrysostom saw this distinction clearly enough. "Mystery is a secret long hidden but now everywhere proclaimed from the house-tops. It is a mystery because the Principalities and Powers never knew of it before it happened, but now they know. It is still a mystery, though for three or four centuries it has been preached." Those who care only for carnal things do not understand and those who have a veil upon their hearts do not see. The Christian mysteries are revealed not by human wisdom but by the Holy Spirit.

We must turn to the later Stoics and to Philo for light on the Pauline use of *Teleios*. Philo places the *teleios* after the two earlier phases, the beginners, and those who are progressing. The word is used of the culminating stage of the good life, toward which the philosopher is called to strive. In his *Encheiridion,* or popular Handbook, Epictetus appeals to his reader for action: "You are no longer a lad, but already a fullgrown man (*teleios*). . . . Live as a mature man (*teleios*) who is making progress (*prokoptôn*).

It is noticeable that "full-grown" is the culminating stage of the good life, and that in the popular Stoic speech the same person may be called "full-grown" and as "making progress." This explains why Paul can speak of himself (Phil. 3:12-15) and some of his readers as at once *teleioi* and as not yet having attained the goal of the Christian life.

But Paul is no Stoic, even if he did borrow popular Stoic language. What content did he read into the word *teleios*? He answers our question that the *teleioi*, whom he identifies with the "spiritual" men, can share with him the wisdom that cometh from above by the Holy Spirit. They can understand, first, that the dark forces which influence human history, the evil spirits who still have power though their days are numbered, have been decisively defeated by the Crucifixion of Christ; they can understand, too, that a new and glorious way has been opened by the Resurrection of Jesus Christ from the dead, and that they will share the wisdom of which Paul speaks and which God has revealed to us through His Spirit: "What no eye has seen, nor ear heard, nor the heart of man conceived, what God has prepared for those who love him."

"The dark forces of evil could not fathom the bold magnificence of this method of God's wisdom—The Cross the path to glory!" (W. F. Howard). The *teleioi* owe a perpetual debt to the Spirit of God, and that debt will be eternally increased.

There are several passages in the New Testament in which the word *teleios* has an air of finality about it. This is noticeable in the Hymn of Love (I Cor. 13:9,10): "Our knowledge is imperfect, and our prophecy is imperfect. But when the perfect comes, the imperfect will pass away." Both knowledge (which there includes "meditative study"; cf. Phil. 1:9) and inspired preaching (prophecy) are the gifts of the Spirit, and the whole passage is dominated by the thought of intimate fellowship with God. "Now I know in part: then I shall understand fully, even as I have been fully understood." The word "knowledge" carries with it the thought of personal interest, friendship, and affection here and now; and the perfection of such an intimacy in the life to come.

Conclusions. 1) The full Christian perfection is only attainable in the other life beyond the grave. This means that we dare not lose our hearts to any temporal good. This life is good because it can be made a ladder to the life beyond.

2) No limits can be set to the sanctity attainable in this life, because that would be setting limits to the grace of God.

3) Holiness is given in response to faith. Faith is no mere single response, but a continuous succession of responses to the Divine Giver. It follows that the Christian life is a moment-by-moment holiness.

4) The consciousness of personal unworthiness is one inevitable mark of genuine holiness. Yet the ceaseless aspiration after the unattainable is not without consequences. "All I could never be—This I was worth to God."

ROBERT NEWTON FLEW

Bibliography

W. E. Sangster, *The Path to Perfection.*

POWER

The connection between power and religion arises from the relation of each to reality. Reality is experienced as at once dynamic and binding. The dynamism of reality is the relentless intensity of change in the world of nature and society and in the efforts of man to find himself at home in both. The binding or limiting character of reality is the relentless persistence of pattern and direction, of order and meaning, in, with, and under the intensity of change. Religion, as the stem of the word suggests, is man's recognition of the fact that he is bound, and his response to this fact. Power is concerned with the dynamics of change. The primitive world rightly discerned the religious character of the boundaries within which change occurred. But what the primitive world did not grasp was that the dynamics of change are a question of energy, not of divinities. The modern world rightly sees that the organization of energy is a matter of technics, not ritual. But the modern world has not understood that technics without a religious context are devoid of a sense of purpose and responsibility adequate to control the use, as well as to organize the control, of power. In a word, power without religion is destructive; religion without power is superstitious; for power is a religio-technical phenomenon.

The religio-technical phenomenon of power may be defined by saying that: *power is the energy and the authority by which whatever happens in the world occurs.* And since there is a corruptive as well as a constructive relation between the religious and the technical aspects of power, power is a problem for theological criticism and concern.

Religion has corrupted power in two main ways. On the one hand, religion has coveted power for the sake of preserving and furthering the ideas and institutions of religion. On the other, religion has made possible the worst forms of power for the sake of power. The core of this corruption is the conception of power as sacred energy and its sacerdotal organization and control. Such corruption achieves a hold upon the energies and authorities of life, quite at variance with the authentic function of religion in the world.

The constructive relation between religion and power is defined by the role of religion in giving motivation and meaning to the energy and the authority by which whatever happens in the world occurs. It is this enabling and enlightening function of religion which integrates the organized energies and the insistent purposes of existence, the relentless momentum of change with the equally relentless persistence of pattern and direction, of order and meaning, in, with, and under change. This integrating function of religion is the religious solution to the problem of power.

When the energies and the sovereignties of existence are organized and exercised with reference to the enabling power of meaningful purpose, the problem of power is resolved. The problem of power is resolved because the exercise of power corresponds with its nature. The possession and use of power are divested of both deification and self-justification. Technics and politics make sense because they serve the meaning and direction of reality.

Such a resolution of the problem of power is the unique achievement of Christianity. The Christian analysis of power is based upon the monotheistic assertion that the dynamic and the delimiting aspects of power belong to God alone and that every existing organization and exercise of power, including the power of religion, is subordinate to the divine purpose and subject to the criticism of the divine will. The Hebrew prophets are the architects of this view and break new ground in the analysis of power in the world. In this prophetic tradition Jesus stands, and upon it He builds. In the New Testament, as well as in the thought of the Church, Jesus is viewed not only as the unique revelation of God and the savior of men and the world. He is also acknowledged as the lord of life. It is this integration of deity, deliverance, and lordship in the person and work of Jesus that gives to Christianity its constructive relation to the problem of power.

Theology has undertaken to give continuity and contemporareity to the Christian analysis of power by formulating a doctrine of the renewing and enabling power of grace. The Protestant Reformation took up the creative suggestion of Augustine that grace is the power to love which sets aside the love of power in the souls and the societies of men. In doing so, the Reformation set new terms for loyalty and responsibility in the common life of men. The Protestant interpretation of power means that men are to live where they are set down with an eye single to the divine will. Starting from there, two courses of action are open. For one thing, there can be no retreat from the world and no totalitarian domination of the world. Secondly, men are to move from where they are to where God's power and purpose have already begun to define new possibilities and new necessities. God's next move is always in the making where the struggle against the deification and the self-justification of power, whether in the self or in society, makes conflict bitter and reconciliation indispensable. Since power is a religious as well as technical phenomenon, the distintegrating dynamic of its technical organization in the contemporary world requires the integrating dynamic of a relevant faith.

PAUL LEHMANN

Bibliography

Lord Acton, *Essays on Freedom and Power.*
Paul Tillich, *Love, Power, and Justice.*

PREDESTINATION

Predestination is a Christian theological doctrine developed commonly on the basis of the Old Testament conception of an elect people and the Johannine-Pauline teaching that God continues to redeem His people by choosing individuals to receive the gift of faith in Christ. This motif is usually combined with a concept of the pre-determination of all things by the omniscient and omnipotent Creator. Generally in the Roman Catholic form of this doctrine, God is said to foresee the future faith and merits of believers and to predestine salvation according to what He thus knows to be their free choice. Aquinas (along with Bellarmine in a minority of Catholic teachers) affirms the gracious election by God of the smaller number of mankind, without respect to human merit; but he affirms divine reprobation only by "permission" or "conditional necessity," so as not to remove the guilt of the lost (*Summa Theologia*, I, xxiii). Augustine affirms the double predestination of a fixed number of souls to salvation and the remainder to damnation. Luther and Calvin develop the doctrine in an Augustinian manner, but with an even stronger accent on divine grace and denial of meritorious works. "Predestination we call the eternal decree of God, by which he has determined in himself, what he would have to become of every individual of mankind. For they are not all created with a similar destiny; but eternal life is foreordained for some, and eternal damnation for others. Every man, therefore, being created for one or the other of these ends, is, we say, predestined either to life or to death. This God has not only testified in particular persons, but has given a particular specimen of it in the whole posterity of Abraham" (Calvin, Institutes, III, xxi, 5). Calvin's "use" of the doctrine is to promote gratitude, humility, and hope. Predestination is to be viewed solely through faith in Christ, and in no case does it allow designation of the elect and the reprobate in society. In variation from Calvin, the Calvinist tradition makes the "decree of God" a creedal article which describes the total relation of divine omnipotence to creation: "God from all eternity did by the most wise and holy counsel of his own will freely and unchangeably ordain whatsoever comes to pass: yet so as thereby neither is God the author of sin, nor is violence offered to the will of creatures" (Westminster Confession, ch. iii). Here the central motif of God's saving grace offered to individuals is so transmuted into a general metaphysical determinism that it falls into contradictory utterances about freedom and guilt, both human and divine. The twentieth century has produced two major interpreters of the doctrine. Rudolf Otto found it to be "intensified 'creature-feeling' in conceptual expression," useful analogically, but of no religious value when taken literally as divine determinism. Karl Barth offers a radical restatement meant to continue the grace motif within the Reformed tradition, whereby the themes of election and reprobation converge in the divine election and rejection of Jesus Christ, in whom no man is finally rejected. (See article on Calvinism.)

EDWARD DOWEY

Bibliography

K. Barth, *Dogmatik,* II, 2.

PRESBYTERIANISM

Presbyterianism, which arose during the Reformation in England and Scotland, is essentially an understanding of the nature and function of the Church Catholic. Although the formative influences which shaped this understanding were English and Scottish, many of the basic insights of Presbyterianism first came through the Continental Reformers, especially Zwingli, Bucer, Bullinger, Martyr, Calvin, Ursinus and Olevianus at centers such as Zurich, Basel, Strassburg, Geneva, and Heidelberg. Consequently, the churches of Presbyterian persuasion regard themselves as part of the group known as the Reformed Churches of Switzerland, Holland, France, Germany, Hungary, etc. Since the Presbyterian, and the Reformed, Churches regard their differentiating characteristics as being ways of understanding the nature and function of the one and only Church of Jesus Christ, they regard all other evangelical churches as differing from themselves only in these ways of understanding.

In England the line of creative leadership in Presbyterianism runs from the early Bible translators Tyndale and Coverdale, through the earlier Puritans—Cartwright, Fenner, Perkins, Wilcox, Travers—down to the definitive work of the Westminster Assembly of Divines (1645-1652). In Scotland the line runs from Knox and the two Melvilles, down through the early Covenanters, and to Henderson, Rutherford et al. in the Westminster Assembly of Divines. Most contemporary forms of Presbyterianism are direct or indirect (via North America) offshoots from either English or Scottish Presbyterianism, and follow with adaptations the essential aspects of the constitutional documents worked out by the Westminster Assembly of Divines.

The basis for Presbyterian thinking about the nature and function of the Church Catholic is the gospel concerning Jesus Christ. This gospel proclaims that in the work of Christ God is reconciling a fallen, sinful, and rebelling world to Himself. It is not man who seeks and reconciles an angry God, but God who seeks and reconciles man, when man is truly a sinner. The gospel, therefore, is the "good news" of God's forgiveness and reconciliation in Christ, and it calls for acceptance and reconciliation on man's part in faith and obedience. There can be no private or individualistic reconciliation to God. One can be reconciled to God only as he is also reconciled to his fellow-men; hence the biblical metaphor of being brought into the presence of God only by becoming a member of a body of which Christ is the head.

The Church is that body of people who have been, who are now being, and who yet shall be, thus reconciled to God and to their fellow-men in Jesus Christ. Being bound together in a common reconciliation, the believers are in fellowship, or communion, with Christ and with each other on the basis of God's grace and forgiveness given to each and to all.

The Christian life, the new life in Christ within the Church, is not its own end. This world is the creation of God, and continues in existence despite its rebellion and failure because of God's determination to fulfill, in mercy, His creative purpose and will. Reconciliation to God in Christ means, therefore, reconciliation to God's will and purpose for mankind as disclosed in Jesus Christ. That this will and purpose are truly made known in Jesus Christ leads to the conviction that order and law are given by God as means to responsible common life among men. The structure of society and the form of law and justice are to be shaped, as nearly as may be possible by civil means, to the will and purpose of God in Christ. The Church and the State, however, are not one, but rather two distinct entities separate in nature, in function, and in administration. (Here Presbyterian theory and practice often conflicted in British history.)

The service of God is not the doing of something for the benefit of God, but the service of obedience to God. Ecclesiastical, ritual, or liturgical acts are therefore only contributing factors to the service of God. The social, political, economic, etc., aspects of human life are as "sacred" as that which is usually termed "the sacred."

Rather than a "secular" realm, accordingly, over against a "sacred" realm, there is only an unreconciled realm over against a reconciled realm. The "secular" belongs to God, and has a role to play in the "sacred" purpose of God. To that purpose, or to God who thus purposes for it, the "secular" needs to be reconciled.

The Christian life, the Christian vocation, the religious life devoted to Christ, or life in the fellowship of Christ among his people the Church—all these are synonymous —cannot be equated with any "clergy," or professional religious leadership or group. The Christian vocation is a calling to live in Christ through the Church in every aspect and phase of human life. The areas of human life to which God may call a Christian are as diverse as the extent of God's creative and redemptive intention in Christ. Wherever the Christian is, it is his vocation to bring that part of God's creation into a reconciling fellowship with God which embraces and reconciles also one's fellow man.

Professional office in the Church is but one aspect of the Christian vocation. The "ministry" of the Church is not a group of church officers. Rather, the ministry of the Church is its obligation under God to minister, as His servant, in reconciling the world to Himself. The ministry of the Church is its God-given function, its mission, its apostolate, its vocation. To minister thus, the Church by divine appointment delegates to various officers specific aspects of its function. To some is given the task of preaching, administering the sacraments, and pastoral care of souls. To others, "elders," is given the task of discipline and overseeing. To others, "deacons," is given the care of the poor and the benevolent work of the congregation. These officers function through governing bodies, called church courts. These courts are organized over each congregation (the session) and over larger regional areas of the Church as need may determine (presbytery, synod, general assembly).

These officers are called by the Holy Spirit through the voice or election of the Church. This call is the basis of ecclesiastical office. Ordination to ecclesiastical office is formal ratification of this call, together with the Church's prayer to God that He would indeed accept and use in the ministering of the people of God the officer whom they have elected in response—as they believe— to the guidance of the Holy Spirit. The form of this ordination, prayer with the laying on of the hands of other officers, is followed as being of long-standing in the Church Catholic, and as being wholly appropriate. The officers thus ordained differ from other Christians only in the specific tasks to which they have been elected. Election and ordination confer no unique religious character or status.

That which in the New Testament is central and controlling in the service of God is the presence of Christ, the Head of the Church, by the Holy Spirit given to the Church. The Holy Spirit was given to the Church, not to be a useful possession of the believers, but to possess them in order to direct them, to reveal to them and in them the grace of God in Christ. The "means of grace"— i.e., Word and Sacrament—are not, therefore, means which men may employ in the Church in order to obtain from God salvation, forgiveness of sins, religious strength, etc. They are those divinely instituted media which the Holy Spirit uses within the Body of Christ, to build up the Body, to direct it, to guide it into all truth, to bring to fulfillment and to fruitfulness the redeeming work of Christ.

By the term "word" in the notion of Word and Sacrament is meant "the Word of God." The Word of God is understood to be none other than God Himself, revealing Himself, making Himself known, giving Himself, coming in the flesh; in short, God carrying out in the incarnate Son His redeeming work among men. This self-revelation of God is made alike in preaching, in baptism, and in the Lord's Supper, and calls for one response, faith, which is trust and obedience. God's self-revelation in the Redeemer by the Holy Spirit is redemption. For God's self-revelation is precisely His self-giving to men in reconciliation and communion. The redemptive—revealing—reconciling event of the Word is rooted in the once-for-all event of Christ's finished work, but still looks forward to an eschatological consummation. Therefore the Church lives not from a past Word, but from the Living Word now coming to it, and ever coming to it until the end.

In baptism one is brought, at whatever age, into the Church (that body of people who are now being reconciled to God and to each other in Jesus Christ) by the word of God's promise of free forgiveness in Christ which alone can make him a member of the Body of Christ. This invitation to live in communion with God in Christ is no mere gesture or ceremony. The sacrament is, by divine appointment, used in the Church to bring men to God. As the person baptized grows in both mental and spiritual capacities the significance of that done for him in baptism—calling him to live in newness of life in Christ— will bring forth in him a response either of faith, or of rejection. Since the other means of grace are used by the Holy Spirit through the Church for this one purpose, baptism in itself can never be regarded as essential to salvation. "Emergency baptism," so-called, and private baptism, are based upon a misunderstanding. Baptism properly belongs to the common life and service of the Church, for by this sacrament men are brought into that company of people who together are being made one as they are reconciled to God and to each other in Christ. The element of baptism, water, like the human voice in preaching, is used in the sacramental act by the Holy Spirit without itself achieving any significance.

The Lord's Supper, like baptism and the proclamation of the gospel in preaching, is used in the Church by divine appointment to bring men to God. The sacrament points backward to that time in history when Jesus Christ, by His death and resurrection, opened the way for man's reconciliation with God and with his fellow men. The sacrament is also a common participation of the whole Church in that fellowship with Christ which both binds them together and brings them into the presence of God as forgiven and redeemed. This sacrament looks forward as well to the ultimate reconciliation of the whole of

God's creation in Christ. This sacrament, then, properly belongs in the assembled congregation. It is the *Church's* communion with Christ. The elements of the sacrament are those appointed by Jesus, though in themselves they are only elements of a total sacramental act which gains its significance from Christ's presence among His people by His Spirit. That to which the Church responds in this sacrament, is Jesus Christ, who reconciles men to God and to each other in His own fellowship.

LEONARD J. TRINTERUD

Bibliography

G. D. Henderson, *Presbyterianism*.
Leonard J. Trinterud, "Presbyterian," *Encyclopaedia Brittanica*, 1955 edition, Volume 18, pp. 440-448.

PRIDE

When Madame Grundy speaks of pride she makes it a matter of manners. Pride so considered is at best an admirable self-respect, at worst an unbecoming haughtiness.

When the theologian speaks of pride he now ordinarily means the usurpation, the arrogation by each man of the center of existence and significance. Pride so considered is that overweening self-assertion which tragically distorts men's relationships with God, with each other, even with themselves. This pride is no occasional social *faux pas* but the invariable disrupter of society, human and divine.

A good case could be made for appraising theologies by the place each assigns to such pride. Certainly much of the depth sensed in some ancient mythologies lies below their resonant doctrines of man in which the note of human pride is sounded. The Greek tragedies, for instance, suggest the destructive role of pride, *hybris*, at least in some crises of heroic existence. Back of confusion and calamity lies the insolence of wills which center on themselves, challenge any law outside themselves, obey only their own impulses. Exceptional as were the tragic heroes of Greece, the hard, long dramatic look at their pride gave a seriousness to the implied doctrine of man which the related doctrine of God never matched.

Early Hebrew myth-makers, elaborating their inspired perceptions within their immeasurably profounder theological context, noted human pride as the source of the world's tragic disharmonies. Subsequent Judaic and Christian theologians have not always known what to make of that naive perception, nor where to fit it into their more sophisticated systems. But there can be little doubt now that stories like those of the Fall and of the Tower of Babel, though they may fail as the science or history they were never meant to be, are enduringly valid as descriptive psychologies of pride and as true representations of the universal disharmonies which follow in pride's train.

Nor is the perception limited to myth. Throughout the Old Testament the arrogant presumption of absolute self-sufficiency brings judgment on men and nations. In the New Testament Jesus, as the revelation of true humanity, is, obversely, a revelation of the disruptive pride which prevents men from enjoying the harmony and union for which they were intended and made. The words of Jesus underline the fact of Jesus. Over and over again he commends "the meek" and "the poor in spirit" who follow in the direction of their original and ultimate reality; over and over again he repudiates the self-sufficiency, self-assertion, self-advertisement which are the ugly, visible side of pride.

The Church's theologians have varied in their accounts and descriptions of pride, but all have recognized its role in the complications and desolations of existence. For Augustine it was basic to sin, an obstinate "refusal to humble oneself before God." The scholastic theologians, in their schematic way, all gave pride high place in their lists of mortal sins. The Reformers, less given to lists, reemphasized the priority of pride in the biblical understanding of sin.

The diminished significance of human pride is one mark of the thinning out which wasted Christian theology in the late nineteenth and early twentieth centuries. Taking the rift between God and man less seriously, or at least seeing the rift less dramatically, "liberal" theology had less occasion to give pride primary significance in its anthropology. Where sin is less radical than orthodoxy had thought it, its components are less weighty. Where an improvement in manners and morals can accomplish salvation, pride is deplored—but more because it gets in the way of a man's unselfishness and sweet reasonableness than because it distorts creation and history.

The renewed appreciation of pride's basic role in the human predicament coincides with the contemporary renewal of theology. Biblical myth, depth psychology, current events made common witness to the fact of pride, not as one among many sins but as *hybris,* "self-elevation" (Tillich). Analyses differ, but there is considerable current agreement that pride is the pivot between the grandeur and the misery of man. Men are great in their freedom, their transcendence, their consciousness of self and of self being conscious of self. It is part of their greatness that they know their finitude, their contingency, their dependence. And the anxiety that comes from that knowledge is the panic which drives them to their misery. For in their determination to establish their own security men would be themselves the divinity who alone is independent, not contingent. Each man identifies his own truth, his own goodness, his own creativity with a divine truth, goodness, creativity. The end is always confusion, for each of man's illusions conflicts with the others; and events inevitably smash the whole pretense. Each man reaches out for the power, prestige, property with which to buttress his own existence. The effort is foredoomed to failure.

The pride which Christians are called to repent is not a social nuisance, but a universal tragedy. Such pride is the self's self-defeating, destructive centering upon itself —which self can never even be itself until pride is broken and the self knows its center in God. Appropriate self-respect comes only when there is a real self to respect, when pride is past, when we accept the significance we cannot establish, when we trust God for the ultimate security He alone can guarantee.

Faith, not humility, is pride's antonym.

THEODORE A. GILL

Bibliography

Augustine, *City of God*, Book 14.

Reinhold Niebuhr, *The Nature and Destiny of Man*, pp. 176-207.

Paul Tillich, *Systematic Theology*, Volume II, pp. 44-58.

PRIESTHOOD OF BELIEVERS

Let any element in the Christian truth slip ever so slightly out of the Church's attention, and sooner or later that particular truth is bound to make a stormy reappearance. This, at least, is what happened in the case of the essential New Testament emphasis on the common standing and common responsibility of all Christians. Overlaid for a while by a rigidly categorizing ecclesiology, the fact of Christian commonalty had to hammer and shout its way back into the Church's consciousness in the Reformation. Martin Luther especially made the priesthood of all believers a touchstone for the true Church and a mark of the Reformation's faithfulness to an original Christianity too long subverted.

Looking back across centuries in which the Church had come to distinguish sharply between clergy and laity, between religious and secular vocations, the Reformers could find no scriptural ground for the development. Certainly in the little company of Jesus and His friends there was no division into clergy and laity. In manner, speech and mood Jesus identified Himself as what today would be called a layman. And the disciples, who might look from here like laymen, were really the preachers who were sent out.

When life is set down in writing, the process inevitably articulates living relationships more rigidly and draws distinctions more sharply than reality permits. Even so, in the New Testament there is little sign of the deep vocational difference which would shortly show up in the Church. Quite plainly, the New Testament word for clergy (*kleros*) refers not to a special order among Christians, but to *all* Christians. And the word for laity (*laos*) refers not to a recipient part of the congregation but to *all* Christians. All are called to one service, and all alike are God's people. "And ye are a chosen race, a royal priesthood, a holy nation, God's own people (*laos*), that you may declare the wonderful deeds of him who called you out of darkness into his marvelous light" (I Peter 2:9).

Among the first Christians every man, however he lived and worked, ministered in the parish in which he lived and worked. There were leaders and teachers and special spokesmen, of course. But they did no more than show or set the direction of every Christian's obligation. Then incorrigibly hierarchical humanity began to suspect that some things were too holy, some learning too high, some service too spiritual for just any man to handle. Within Christianity a special order developed and wrapped itself in that New Testament word meant in the beginning to comprehend all Christians—the clergy, the priesthood. Now there were certain Christians set aside to distribute the divine blessing. Everybody else was in the other order of Christian, the laity, who supported and sustained the priests in their performance of the real Christian service and the real Christian worship. The popular temptation was to think of a first-class layman as still a second-class Christian. There was *the* "religious" vocation—and then there were all the other vocations.

The Reformers vigorously assailed this particular distortion. Puncturing what they regarded as the pretensions of the professional clergy came as close as anything to being what the whole Reformation was about. The direct access of each man to the only Mediator demanded the downgrading of all those officers of the Church who had long been interposed between believer and God. A correlative emphasis, of course, was upon the priesthood which devolved on every believer by reason of this direct access. But in polemical turbulence, depreciation of the existing priesthood of a few believers sometimes rang louder than exaltation of the original priesthood of all believers.

The gentle, pastoral doctrine was swung like a battle-axe again in the fight against the political claims of the papacy. Supporting the princes who supported him, Luther challenged the superiority of clergy over laity at any level of governance or on any point of politics. Faithful rulers are priests too, because all believers are priests. And popes have no rights which are based on orders without bases: all believers are laymen.

But the doctrine of the priesthood of all believers had its positive suggestiveness too. Under it there could be no more double standard in Christian ethics. A congregation will select one man to be its leader, but he is priest only as are those who selected him. So one standard of Christian life will prevail in pulpit and in pew. As all Christians are priests before God, God's requirements and expectations will be the same for all. The same principle obtains for Christian knowledge and learning. Typically, this was Calvin's special emphasis. If there is no ultimate distinction in orders, neither can there be a lesser or greater demand for knowledge of and reflection on the scriptures. No man can resign intelligence or inquiry to his priest, for every man is a priest charged to learn and to teach.

Today, in a continuing effort to reclaim the priesthood of all believers, Protestants who note their own repeated failures are putting most emphasis on the common service to which the doctrine bids all Christians. "Every shoemaker can be a priest of God, and stick to his own last while he does it," said Luther. Whoever, wherever we are, whatever we do, we are ministers of God.

THEODORE A. GILL

Bibliography

Martin Luther, "Treatise on Good Works" and "Treatise on Christian Liberty." Cf. *Works of Martin Luther*, Vol. I, pp. 173-286; Vol. II, pp. 297-350.
Gustaf Wingren, *Luther on Vocation.*

PROTESTANTISM

Protestantism, in its emergence as a specific and identifiable movement within the Christian Church, was an immediate consequence of the Reformation of the sixteenth century. It has proven to be the most rapidly expanding movement in Christian history. During the first three centuries of its existence it overspread the northern half of the continent of Europe and the British Isles, and was transplanted to North America. In the nineteenth century and the first half of the twentieth it succeeded—mainly as a result of its missionary effort—in establishing itself in virtually every country on earth. Within the last century and a half, the Christian Church has occupied more territory and has gained more adherents than in all the preceding centuries of its life. This expansion has been due predominantly to the vitality of the Protestant churches and their missions. In the United States, where both Protestantism and Roman Catholicism have thrived institutionally, the Protestant churches have continued to advance at a rate faster than the increase of the Roman Catholic Church. Both have gained more rapidly than the growth of population. In the period from 1926 to 1950, church membership in the United States increased 59.6 per cent as compared with a gain in population of 28.6 per cent. During this same period the membership of the Protestant churches gained 63.7 per cent as against a Roman Catholic growth of 53.9 per cent.

Derivation and meaning. At least half the significance of "Protestantism" is concealed by the current meaning of the word "protest." As a result of the curious inversion of common usage, the term "to protest"—derived from the Latin *protestari*—has acquired a modern connotation that is largely negative. Until the middle of the eighteenth century—two hundred and fifty years after Luther nailed his ninety-five theses to the church door in Wittenberg—the word meant "to profess" or "to declare openly." Thus in Shakespeare we have: "Do me right or I will protest your cowardice" (*Much Ado about Nothing,* v. i); and "Youths that even now protest their first manhood" (*Macbeth,* v. ii). As late as 1755 Johnson defines "protestation" as "a solemn declaration of resolution, fact, or opinion." The negative significance of the word, meaning "to object," "to protest against," has had only two centuries of currency.

Protestantism as a movement in church history actually incorporates both meanings of the word. It is an organized and continuing objection to some central beliefs and practices of the Roman Catholic Church and it cannot be understood apart from this "protest against." It is also a positive declaration of convictions which are regarded as essential to the Christian faith and message. It is, negatively, a repudiation of certain prominent aspects of Roman Catholicism and at the same time, positively, a recovery and reaffirmation of what Protestants believe to be original truths of the uncorrupted gospel. It therefore comprehends both negative and positive elements—emphases of rejection and of restoration.

Contemporary Protestantism must be viewed in relation to these two accents: first, as a protest against some of the teachings and claims of the Roman Catholic Church; second, as a vigorous and positive affirmation of what Protestants regard as the witness of the Christian message in its distinctiveness and purity. Both Protestantism and Roman Catholicism have this reciprocal significance for each other. Neither is understandable in its contemporary form without awareness of the points at which it is in tension with the other. "Modern Roman Catholicism was radically reorganized in creed, government, and worship in reaction to the Reformation, and is historically incomprehensible save as a protest against Protestantism" (J. H. Nichols, *Primer for Protestants,* 1947, p. 7).

Historical origins. While a number of pre-Reformation Protestants are recognized—most notably Wyclif in England and Hus in Bohemia—Protestantism was given its initial impetus and character by the work of Martin Luther and John Calvin, who together were supremely influential among the Reformers of the sixteenth century, whose thought and writings have remarkable relevance for Christian theology today. When Luther, the Roman Catholic priest, published his ninety-five theses, he had no notion of starting a movement outside the Catholic Church. His statement was a protest against practices associated with the sale of indulgences. It was not even a general condemnation of the theory of indulgences. The Pope, he held, had power to remit penalties which he himself had imposed or which were imposed by the canons of the Church. But the Pope, said Luther, had no power to cancel *guilt*, nor could he exert any effect upon persons in purgatory—an authority which was vociferously claimed for him by the supporters of indulgences.

Luther's protest, which at first seemed directed only at a specific abuse of a single practice of Roman Catholicism, was quickly transformed into a challenge to the whole sacramental-clerical-hierarchical system of the Roman Church. He consciously purposed only the removal of institutional abuses which many Catholics had acknowledged as requiring amendment. His critique of those abuses, however, was so drastic and fundamental that it precipitated the vast movement known as the Reformation.

Principal doctrines. Doubtless the most succinct way of setting forth the central teachings of Protestantism is by contrasting them with Roman Catholic dogma; and in an article as brief as the present essay some reliance will have to be placed in that method. By itself, however, it conveys a distorted impression of the character of Protestant faith and practice.

For one thing, this method of contrast misrepresents the experience of the believer. Devout members of Protestant churches hold the teachings and practices of their churches precious not because of the challenge they present to Catholicism but because of their efficacy in bringing the faithful worshipper into personal relationship with God. They go to their churches not to testify against anyone but to receive anew the assurance of the divine mercy.

Again, the method of exposition by contrast ignores the

great body of conviction which constitutes the common faith of all Christians, Protestant and Roman Catholic alike. Indeed, so massive is this Christian consensus, and so slight are the differences between Catholics and Protestants by comparison with their agreements in the face of the alternative faiths and anti-faiths now contending for the allegiance of men, that thoughtful members of both groups must be moved to penitence as they consider how little progress is being made toward the reconciliation of these two main bodies of Christian believers.

In the case of Protestant and Roman Catholic, each would affirm vastly more of the other's faith than he would deny. Both believe in the one God, the Creator of the World and the Redeemer of men, who has made known His nature and will and ways through the life, death, and resurrection of Jesus Christ. Both assert man's accountability to this God in response to His requirement of a trustful relationship to Him and a responsible and charitable relationship to one's neighbor.

Even in the much-controverted realm of ecclesiology there is an enormous consensus. In the words of the American Theological Committee's report preparatory to the Lund conference on Faith and Order:

Every communion holds that the Church is not a human contrivance, but God's gift for the salvation of the world; that the saving acts of God in Christ brought it into being, that it persists in continuity in history by the presence and power of the Holy Spirit. Every communion likewise believes that the Church has a vocation to worship God in his holiness and to proclaim the Gospel to every creature, and that she is equipped by God with the various gifts of the Spirit for the building up of the Body of Christ. And every communion believes that the Church is composed of forgiven sinners, yet through faith already partakes in the eternal life of the Kingdom of God. These agreements cover the Church's origin, the mystery of the Church's present being, and the Church's goal. They ascribe to the Church both a divine and a human element, both a possession and an anticipation of the age to come. They imply an insistence upon the holiness of the Church without any identification of this with a mere human moralism; an insistence upon the visibility of the Church without obscuring the tension between the Church as it is now and the Church as it is destined to become.

(World Council of Churches: Faith and Order Commission Papers No. 7, *The Church*)

The area of agreement between Protestants and Catholics is very extensive; nevertheless, the distinctive characteristics of Protestantism begin to be sharply delineated when it is distinguished from Roman Catholicism at several crucial points.

Justification by faith is the classical formulation of the central teaching of Protestantism. This is not to be understood as a new article of belief introduced into Christianity by the Reformers. It is rather the recovery of what they insisted had always been pivotal for the Christian believer —that is, the receiving of Christ's self-offering as the sole and sufficient ground of man's acceptability by a righteous God. He is not justified—made acceptable—by any miraculous power imparted by the sacraments of the Church, as Roman Catholicism affirms, but only by the act of faith which confesses that Christ is both Son of God and Savior of men.

An autobiographical passage from Luther himself makes clear the significance of this teaching. Commenting on Romans 1:17, he wrote:

I greatly longed to understand Paul's Epistle to the Romans and nothing stood in the way but that one expression, "the justice of God," because I took it to mean that justice whereby God is just and deals justly in punishing the unjust. My situation was that, although an impeccable monk, I stood before God as a sinner troubled in conscience, and I had no confidence that my merit would assuage him. Therefore I did not love a just and angry God, but rather hated and murmured against him. Yet I clung to the dear Paul and had a great yearning to know what he meant.

Night and day I pondered until I saw the connection

between the justice of God and the statement that "the just shall live by his faith." Then I grasped that the justice of God is that righteousness by which through grace and sheer mercy God justifies us through faith. Thereupon I felt myself to be reborn and to have gone through open doors into paradise. The whole of Scripture took on a new meaning, and whereas before the "justice of God" had filled me with hate, now it became to me inexpressibly sweet in greater love. This passage of Paul became to me a gate of heaven.

Thus the doctrine of justification by faith means the acceptance of Christ's work of reconciliation and redemption with radical and absolute seriousness. It resists any attempt to modify the efficacy of this work by ascribing to man some other source of merit—an intrinsic capacity for good, or credit gained by good works, or virtue conferred by the sacraments of the Church. It asserts that such good works as man is able to perform are as much a gift of God's goodness as is the bestowal of forgiveness through Christ.

"Grace alone" is the correlative of the doctrine of justification by faith. The *sola fide* demands the *sola gratia*, which is the second watchword of the Reformers. Faith is from one standpoint a decision to accept God's mercy in Christ as sufficient for one's justification, but this decision can be made only because God has already acted graciously to make it possible. Grace is not, as for Roman Catholicism, a *quasi*-physical substance, of which the Church is the appointed custodian and which is to be dispensed in accordance with rules of the Church's making. Grace is of the nature of God's own action, who reveals the fullness of His righteousness by being merciful. It is not bound by institutions or rites but is always freely available when men are enabled by faith to receive it.

Concerning *the nature of man*, Protestantism is freed by its utter dependence on divine grace to adopt a view that is characterized by radical realism. Protestantism denies the Roman Catholic teaching that there is a continuity between man and God. Karl Barth puts the Protestant position uncompromisingly: "We do not say

'God' merely by shouting 'Man' in a loud voice." The teaching of Aquinas, which has become normative for Catholic dogma, that the supernatural is in a sense the completion of the natural and that reason and faith are essentially complementary, is unacceptable to Protestants. According to Protestantism, man is always and at the same time both "justified" and a sinner. His life is by nature, in Luther's vivid phrase, "curved in upon itself," seeking to find within itself the meaning of existence. It is man's nature to attempt to provide his own fulfillment of the meaning of his life—in short, to do what only God can do, who is life's meaning and life's goal. Yet God, through the reconciling work of Christ, accepts man as he is. When man by faith acknowledges this acceptance—this "justification"—he is given at least a partial release from his self-obsession and self-idolatry. He is under obligation to perform good works and to live in charity and reconciliation with his neighbor; but these good works are done not to win merit with God but as offerings of gratitude and as expressions of the freedom bestowed by God's forgiveness.

Protestantism is distinguished by the primacy it accords *the Bible*. This biblicism, let it be acknowledged, has sometimes assumed the form of bibliolatry, but this is a grave distortion of Protestant teaching. The principal medium of revelation is not to be confused with the revelation itself. What Protestants assert in the biblicism is that the concrete historical record of Christ's life, death, and resurrection is normative for Christian faith as over against the traditions of men—including the traditions of the Church, which in Roman Catholicism are given parity with and even supremacy over the biblical witness.

When Protestants affirm the centrality of the Word, however, they do not mean the written Word; they mean the Incarnate Word, which is Christ. "What is offered in the preaching of the Word is Christ. What is offered in the living of the Word is Christ. What is offered in the Lord's Supper is Christ." (James H. Nichols, *op. cit.,* p. 123.) It is the commission of the Church to offer Christ to the community of the faithful, and through that community to the world. "Where Christ is, there is His Church." Protestants are convinced, however, that Christ is most personally, most livingly present, not in metaphysical substance as in the Mass, but in life and power as His Word is addressed *personally* to the believer and to the community of believers. In order to make certain that this may occur, the Church must always place itself "under" the instruction of the Word—and this means the biblical Word. Only thus can it maintain its true apostolicity, which is not guaranteed by any continuity of officials but by fidelity to the apostolic message. Only thus can it protect its gospel from encumbrance by churchly traditions, which are ultimately the "traditions of men."

The doctrine of the *universal priesthood of believers* follows from the conviction that God alone is man's justification and that His acceptance is granted freely without regard for desert or any merit or power bestowed by a sacerdotal institution. The universal priesthood does not mean that every man is to be his own priest and therefore has no need of the community of faith. Still less does it mean that there is no place in the Church for diversities of functions—that in dealing with questions of theology one man's opinion is as good as any other's, or that every person is called to conduct public worship and administer the sacraments of the Church. The doctrine of the universal priesthood of believers means that each man is called to be a priest to every other. According to Protestantism there may be divisions of labor within the Christian community, but every man is equally accountable. Every person is set in a place of maximum responsibility as a witness to God's goodness and mercy for the sake of his neighbor. Luther said: "Every man must do his own believing, just as every man will have to do his own dying." He might have said with equal trenchancy, "Every man must do his own witnessing." The command, "Go . . . and teach" is addressed to all Christians. The apostolate cannot be delegated. "The universal priesthood of believers" thus becomes "the mutual ministry of believers"—and out of this mutual ministry emerges a common ministry to the world.

The Church, in Protestant teaching, is a fellowship of believers. As a fellowship, in which every member is a

priest and witness to every other, it is obliged to deny the
hierarchical principle of Roman Catholicism. As a community of believers, not a custodian of miraculous sacramental power, it must place against the Roman claim of
infallibility the confession that all human institutions are
fallible and in continual need of reformation—including
the Protestant churches. In this confession, Protestants
believe, they are not diminishing the authority of the
Church but are perpetually submitting it to the authority of
Christ, with the prayer that He will remake it in accordance
with the form of His own appearing among men—the
form not of master but of the Servant.

Regarding *the Church's service of the world*, it is the
Protestant conviction that as persons accept the reconciliation and forgiveness of God, brought to them through
Christ, they are under obligation to perform a reconciling
ministry to the world. Thus in Protestantism the church
member's most effective service *to* the Church may be
beyond the Church. It has been remarked that in countries
where the Protestant movement is strong Communism has
failed to make significant gains. In these lands the general
health of society has been maintained at a sufficiently high
level so that Communist efforts to organize discontent have
been unsuccessful. This is due, in part at least, to the fact
that the Protestant churches have encouraged their members to render their Christian service in the various em-
ployments of civil life and have not sought to retain all the
most conspicuous gifts and talents for the benefit of the
ecclesiastical establishment.

Finally, concerning *the unity of the Church,* because
Protestantism has insisted upon the personal and unco-
erced character of faith, its influence has seemed to be
individualistic and divisive. Yet the great Reformers, and
the best informed interpreters of Protestantism in subsequent generations, have always proclaimed the essential
one-ness of the Church of Christ. During the last fifty years
Protestantism—more recently in cooperation with Eastern
Orthodoxy—has formed and led the ecumenical movement, which seeks to maintain the diversity without which
human institutions and fellowships cannot live in health,

but at the same time to find ways of overcoming the tendency of diversity to create division. Protestantism affirms that the true hope of eventual reunion lies in the dynamics of reformation—the resubmission of the Church's life to remaking by the Word and Act of God. In the confidence that God will in His time give to us the requisite humility and charity lies the hope of a healing of the great wound in the body of Christendom—the division between the Protestant and Roman Catholic families of Christ's people.

TRUMAN B. DOUGLASS

Bibliography

John Dillenberger and Claude Welch, *Protestant Christianity Interpreted Through Its Development.*
Walter M. Horton, *Christian Theology: an Ecumenical Approach,* Chapter VII.
James H. Nichols, *Primer for Protestants.*
Wilhelm Pauck, *The Heritage of the Reformation.*
J. S. Whale, *The Protestant Tradition.*

REASON

With possibly a few exceptions, reason in the form of an autonomous rationalism does not play a dominant or even a significant role in contemporary Protestant theology. There is little *a priori* rationalistic theological thought today. In this respect reason by itself is not the determining criterion of truth. Of course the rules of consistency and self-contradiction are relevant principles in that they are aids in avoiding flagrant logical errors. But on the whole reason plays a supporting and not the leading role in most theologies. In its more general sense, reason is an important component in the methodologies of many theologians, but it functions in relation to one or more of the following contexts: faith, revelation, and religious and natural experience. In this space I can outline the alternative roles that reason assumes in these various contexts. I will do this by discussing specific American theologians of two general types: philosophical and non-philosophical.

Charles Hartshorne, a philosophical theologian of the Whiteheadian persuasion, is one of the exceptions noted above. He holds that strict logical analysis presents us with seven major possibilities concerning the absoluteness or perfection of God (atheism being one form of one of these possibilities). One of these alternatives must necessarily be true, since the logical classification of possibilities is exhaustive. By means of religious and rational considerations, including a reconstructed statement of the ontological argument, Hartshorne concludes that God is absolutely perfect or unsurpassable even by Himself in some respects and relatively perfect or surpassable only by Himself in other respects. This is natural theology in its clearest form.

Another philosophical theologian who has been influenced by Whitehead is Henry N. Wieman. Wieman, in contrast to Hartshorne, is a rational empiricist who defines God as an empirical reality that is directly perceived and known in the same sense that any other perceptual object is observed. The function of reason is to enable us to distinguish one concrete reality from another in terms of its form or structure. By means of reason we can discern the structure of that creative event (called "God") which transforms all our values and meanings and recreates our world. For Wieman the range of reason's functioning is limited to empirical realities and their possibilities. We can neither talk intelligently about nor relate ourselves in criticizable faith to a God who transcends our experience and rational criteria.

Paul Tillich stands in contrast to both Hartshorne and Wieman. For Tillich, the structure of reason which deals with ends ("ontological reason") is to be contrasted with reasoning processes which are concerned with means ("technical reason"). Ontological reason enables us to know and formulate the structure of our world, the structure of being. This philosophical effort is a necessary prerequisite for theology. Philosophy or reason asks ultimate questions about the meaning of life. But reason cannot give satisfactory answers to its own questions because its resources for answering are limited to the structure of being which, under the conditions of existence, is characterizable in such terms as brokenness and incompleteness. There can be no natural theology. Only revelation can answer these questions adequately. Revelation occurs when a natural or historical object becomes transcendent to its own depth, to being itself in contrast to the structure of being. The ground of being, known in revelation, transcends but does not negate the criteria of reason.

Among the non-philosophical theologians there is also a fairly wide diversity. The fundamentalists limit the function of reason to that of seeking a kind of consistency between the various sections of God-inspired or infallible scripture which is finally self-authoritative.

In the thought of Reinhold Niebuhr, reason enables us to discern the several types of order in the world and to distinguish objects by means of their forms. But reason by itself is not the essence of man. Reason is finally an element of man's freedom, his capacity for "self-transcendence," whereby he can make himself and his world into objects. Because of his freedom man is able to "stand outside" of all his finite relations. This means that man's search for meaning must extend beyond the world of natural and historical existence to a transcendent meaning which, in turn, is a principle of comprehension which lies beyond our comprehension.

For Richard Niebuhr reason is concerned with pattern and intelligibility. But impersonal or abstract reason cannot furnish us with an adequate pattern by which to interpret the meaning of life. Revelation is a rational principle; or rather it is that special event which provides us with an image or a creative meaning by which we can make the rest of our experience intelligible. The special occasion of Jesus Christ provides reason with the impulse and the first principles it requires to do its proper work.

BERNARD M. LOOMER

Bibliography

Charles Hartshorne, *Man's Vision of God.*
H. Richard Niebuhr. *The Meaning of Revelation.*

Reinhold Niebuhr, *The Nature and Destiny of Man.*
Paul Tillich, *Systematic Theology,* Vol. I.
Henry Wieman, *The Source of Human Good.*

REDEMPTION

As with so many basic words in the religious vocabulary, "redemption" has both a precise, concrete meaning and a more general, comprehensive application. In general, the word is synonymous with "salvation," "atonement," "forgiveness," "justification," *"Heilsgeschichte,"* etc. But originally "redemption" in biblical usage has behind it the particular and definite act of paying a sum of money, or its equivalent, for the restoration of property which has been lost or stolen. Thus "redemption" is related to buying back, setting free, paying a ransom price, deliverance (cf. Exod. 21:30; Lev. 25-27; Job 33:24; Mark, 10:45; I Cor. 6:20; 7:23; I Peter 1:18-19). The suggestion of a financial transaction is still retained in our secular vocabulary when we speak, for example, of the "redemption" of a corporation bond.

The spiritual and religious notion of redemption which is the central theme of biblical history and theology grows out of this concrete situation and action. Thus the God who redeems, ransoms, and delivers Israel out of her bondage is the God who, in Christ, pays the price which restores sinful mankind to freedom and new life. In this act of redemption two interrelated theological emphases are dominant: God's *love* by which He takes the initiative in redemption, and man's *sin* which occasions the situation from which God redeems him

In the history of Christian theology, three definitive theories have emerged to interpret the act of redemption. 1) The "ransom" theory (Origen, Irenaeus, Luther), while retaining the original meaning of the word, emphasizes the costliness of redemption by God in Christ's death on the cross. 2) The "satisfaction" theory (Anslem, Calvin, Brunner), while emphasizing God's redemptive act in Christ, is especially concerned to relate this to the radical character of man's sin which prevents him from saving himself. 3) The "moral influence" theory (Abelard, Schleiermacher, Bushnell), while presupposing both God's initiative and man's sin, seeks to explain how God's redemption becomes available and meaningful for us (see further, essay on "Atonement" by J. Haroutunian).

In all this, however, there is in Christian theology a common conviction: namely, that redemption is effected by God in Christ and that it issues in newness of life. There are, as it were, three *tenses* to this: the *past*—or what God has done for sinful mankind in the life, death, and resurrection of Christ; the *present*—or the new life which is lived because of what God in Christ has done; and the *future*—or what God in Christ will yet do to consummate His redemptive purpose. All three have received attention in contemporary theology; neo-orthodoxy (Barth) has in our day afforded fresh insight into what God in Christ has done; Christian existentialism (Bultmann) has sought to relate "redemption" to life here and now; the second assembly of the World Council of Churches, Evanston, 1954, examined the implications of eschatology under the theme "Christ the Hope of the World."

While there is virtual unanimity among theologians that redemption involves God's gracious saving love in Christ for sinful mankind, there is difference of opinion as to how this is effected and what it means. On the threshold of the modern period, Schleiermacher wrote: "Christianity is a monotheistic faith, belonging to the teleological type of religion, and is essentially distinguished from other such faiths by the fact that in it everything is related to the redemption accomplished by Jesus of Nazareth." This definition puts redemption and the Redeemer at the center of the Christian faith, and this is the classic Christian position. But Schleiermacher himself and others in the nineteenth century frequently suggested that the *principle* of redemption revealed by Christ was of more concern than the *Person* of the Redeemer. Thus Jesus was regarded as an historical exemplar of a universal and eternal truth. "The metaphysical only, and not the historical, can give us blessedness" (Fichte). Hence a popular distinction was made between the religion *of* Jesus and the religion *about* Jesus. "The Gospel, as Jesus proclaimed it, has to do with the Father only and not with the Son" (Harnak). Consequently redemption is interpreted as moral regeneration, the development and realization of man's innate divinity, as illustrated in the God-man, Jesus Christ.

Against this "liberalism," contemporary biblical scholarship and the neo-orthodox school of theology have reacted strongly, reversing the distinction by emphasizing the *Person* of the Redeemer rather than the *principle* of redemption. "This is the stumbling block in Christianity: that revelation, the divine manifestation—that is, eternal truth and everlasting salvation—has to be connected with a fact which took place once for all, or—it amounts to the same thing—that we can never approach God directly but only through the Mediator" (Brunner).

Beyond this, contemporary theologians are struggling with the *meaning* for faith of the redemption accomplished by Jesus Christ. Three examples may be cited. 1) Bultmann's "demythologizing" stops short of what he calls "the event of redemption," Christ's death on the cross. "In its redemptive aspect the cross of Christ is no mere mythical event. . . . The preaching of the cross as the event of redemption challenges all who hear it to appropriate this significance for themselves, to be willing to be crucified with Christ." 2) Reinhold Niebuhr's "dialectic" thinking warns against a pretentious or perfectionist view. "Redemption does not guarantee elimination of the sinful corruptions, which are in fact increased whenever the redeemed claim to be completely emancipated from them." 3) Tillich's "existentialism" translates the religious vocabulary into psychoanalytic terms, so that sin becomes "separation" and grace becomes "acceptance." So "redemption" means—"You are accepted, accepted by that which is greater than you, and the name of which you do not know. Do not ask for the name now; perhaps you will find it later. Do not try to do anything now; perhaps later you will do much. . . . Simply accept the fact that you are accepted."

However conceived, redemption is at the heart of the

Christian faith, for it has to do both with man's separation from God and with God's acceptance of man in spite of his sin.

HUGH T. KERR

Bibliography

Gustaf Aulén, *Christus Victor.*
Emil Brunner, *Christian Doctrine of Creation and Redemption.*

REFORMATION

The Protestant Reformation began on October 31, 1517, when Martin Luther, a professor of biblical theology in the University of Wittenberg, published ninety-five theses on the validity of indulgences. In doing this he did not plan to inaugurate a movement. He merely intended to bring about a proper understanding of the sacrament of penance and particularly of the importance of the Christian's release from temporal penalties, namely indulgences. He hoped that his theses would become the subject of academic discussions and that from such debates changes in the Church's teachings and practices would result. The actual response he received was different from what he had anticipated. In the course of a few months, many hailed his theses as a call to the reformation of the Church. Others criticized him for having attacked the papacy, by whose authority the sale of indulgences had become a common practice. When Luther defended himself against these criticisms, at the same time explaining the reasons that had caused him to speak up, his words made him quickly the head of a popular movement. What he stood for was now connected with that "reformation" which, throughout the Middle Ages, had been advocated off and on by individuals and groups demanding a reform of the Church "in head and members." They protested against the secularization of the Church and the abuses of power and privilege that had become general, especially among the clergy from the popes to the secular priests.

In the course of time, the Reformation allied itself with

these medieval tendencies but it did not spring from them. Its *origins* lay primarily in the religion of Luther. In connection with his religious development, he had been led to rediscover the gospel of the salvation by faith in the strict terms of the New Testament, especially the Pauline Epistles. At the beginning of his career as a professor of biblical theology, probably in the period between November 1512 and July 1513, he found, in connection with his efforts to develop an adequate method of biblical exegesis, what he regarded as the true content of the Christian gospel; namely, the disclosure of God's freely forgiving love in Christ, that must be apprehended in trusting faith and repentance. Henceforth the meaning of the Christian gospel was for him identical with the Pauline teaching on justification by faith and not by works. He was convinced that his religion was in agreement with the whole Bible and that it accorded with the doctrines of the leading Church Fathers, especially Augustine, and those of some of the medieval thinkers, particularly Bernard of Clairvaux and the German mystic, Johann Tauler. As he became more and more persuaded of the truth of his discovery, he turned sharply against the theology of the scholastics. He judged Aristotelian metaphysics to be irreconcilable with the tenets of the Christian gospel, and he rejected also the scholastic coordination of grace and merit. All the while, he was sure that he was dealing with the true faith of the universal Church. Indeed, he continued to be loyal to the hierarchical-sacramental order of the Roman Church and to the requirements of membership in a cloister of the Augustinian friars.

However, when in connection with the debate he had aroused by his ninety-five theses, spokesmen of the papacy accused him of heresy and the papal curia commenced ecclesiastical proceedings against him, he refused to recant any of his views unless he was shown by clear proof that they were irreconcilable with the Bible. Believing that he was speaking on the basis of the Word of God, he chose to pit the authority of the Bible against that of the papacy. In 1520, he produced the famous writings that since then have been considered to contain the principles of the Prot-

estant Reformation: "The Manifesto to the German No-
bility on the Improvement of the Christian Estate," the
tract "On the Babylonian Captivity of the Church," and
the treatise on "The Freedom of a Christian Man." In
these works, he displayed a remarkable originality in interpreting the biblical faith as a religion that relies, in the
name of Christ, on the overflowing mercy and graciousness
of God. Moreover, with regard to the proposals for a
reform of the Church (which, in the meantime, he had
come to regard as inevitable), they reveal him to be a
keen observer of the trends of his time who, with discriminating judgment, had come to appropriate as his
own many of the demands for reform that were current in
his day. He won the support of an ever-increasing following from the ranks of princes and patricians; churchmen
and monks; noblemen, townspeople, and peasants; humanists and patriots. His cause thus quickly became that
of a religious movement, spreading rapidly throughout
Germany and soon all over Europe.

He was filled with a sense of mission, that he had been
called to make room in the world for the free gospel of
Christ so that it might run an unhindered course among
men. He believed himself to be an evangelist to the Ger-
mans and as such he refused to become a social and political reformer; although he recognized that the liberation of
Christianity from the priestly, monastic and sacramental
forms of Roman Catholicism inevitably would have wide
political and social consequences.

Luther and his followers availed themselves of the new
means of communication made possible by Gutenberg's
recent invention of the printing press. Their books and
pamphlets, eagerly sought after by printers all over Europe,
spread the cause of the Reformers everywhere. In Sep-
tember 1522, Luther's German translation of the New
Testament was published. Henceforth the Bible, now
readily accessible to everyone, became the core of the
whole movement. With the assistance of friends and
helpers, Luther completed the translation of the whole
Bible in 1534, but revisions kept him occupied until the

end of his life. Wherever the Reformation movement took a foothold, the Bible, speaking to people in their own languages, proved to be the source of its power.

The Reformers also turned the methods and results of humanistic scholarship to their own ends. The philological interpretation of the Bible and the historical criticism of the Christian tradition that the Christian humanists had introduced and that had found the most splendid expression in the work of Erasmus, were taken over by them and applied not only to the criticism of Roman Catholic teachings and practices but also to the constructive interpretation of the Christian faith. In the course of time, they also became aware of the teachings of the so-called pre-reformers, especially John Wyclif, Hus, and the Brethren of the Common Life, and referred to them in support of their own views. Moreover, they made use, but most unconsciously and unintentionally, of the sentiments of a nascent nationalism and the consciousness of living in a new age of civilization that had come to be felt all over the European world since the beginnings of the Renaissance. They themselves tremendously furthered new cultural trends when, under the leadership of Luther, they broke with the medieval principle of the domination of the state by the Church, rejected asceticism as the basis of the Christian ethic and invalidated the distinction between the "religious" and the "secular." Of greatest practical significance was Luther's teaching on the universal priesthood of believers. Eminently social in its implication, because it affirmed the responsibility of each Christian for the spiritual welfare of his fellow believers, it led to the destruction of the age-old separation between the clergy and the laity. In accordance with these convictions, the Reformers accepted the protection that Christian princes and magistrates extended to them. They even held them responsible for the actual introduction of the Reformation. They argued that because of the refusal or the inability of the Roman bishops to effect a change in the Church, Christian magistrates, acting as "emergency-bishops," had to establish the Church on the foundation of the Word of God for the sake of the spiritual welfare of their subjects.

The *development* of the Reformation was determined mainly by the spiritual power that inhered in the new interpretation of Christianity offered by Luther and his followers. Luther's theological mind proved to be an ever-new source of strength. His profound conception of the gospel overshadowed and formed the views of all the Protestant Reformers, even those who differed with him. Ultimate reliance on the scripture alone and the affirmation that man is saved by grace through faith alone were the foundations of the Reformation movement.

But the development of the Reformation was made possible also by the inability of its enemies to oppose it effectively. On January 3, 1521, the papacy placed a ban upon Luther and his cause, and, on May 25, 1521, the Diet of Worms outlawed him on imperial authority. But neither the so-called "Edict of Worms" nor the papal bull of excommunication were ever executed, because the political as well as the ecclesiastical authorities, i.e., the Holy Roman Emperor and the Pope, lacked the power to carry out their judgments upon the Reformation. This weakness was due to the political conditions prevailing in Germany and in Europe as a whole. Germany was divided into numerous large and small territorial principalities. For a long time they had not been unified under a strong central authority, though together they constituted, as the Holy Roman Empire, the largest European State. Under the leadership of the Elector of Saxony, Luther's Prince, and the Landgrave of Hesse, the Reformation was, since 1526, actualized in several of these territories by the introduction of new evangelical church orders. But no higher political or ecclesiastical authority proved able to prevent such an action, nor was anyone able to prevent the introduction of new church orders in many of the politically autonomous cities, especially of Southern Germany.

The Emperor Charles V, who had been elected in 1519, was a declared enemy of the Reformation. As the head of the House of Hapsburg, he was ruler not only of Germany, but also of Spain, and her newly won American colonies, and of the Netherlands. He also had claims upon

Northern and Southern Italy. Moreover, his dynasty was involved in the affairs of practically every other European state except France. Shortly after his assumption of the German imperial throne, the issue of the control of Italy caused him to be drawn into a war with France. This same conflict kept him occupied throughout almost his entire reign. When the defense of Italy against France did not keep him politically engaged, the affairs of the Spanish kingdom and the necessity to protect Europe against the rapidly expanding imperialism of the Turks demanded his attention. Thus, his political involvements forced him to be absent from Germany for long periods of time. After he had condemned Luther at the first diet of his reign (at Worms, 1521) he left the Empire and did not return until nine years later. By then, Lutheranism had become consolidated in new churches. At the diet of Augsburg they presented a statement of their faith, the so-called Augsburg Confession (June 25, 1530). It was not accepted, to be sure, but despite the great political prestige the Emperor then enjoyed, he was unable to stop the further growth of the Reformation. In the following year, its adherents entered into a defensive alliance with one another. Under this League of Smalcald the Reformation spread rapidly throughout Germany and beyond, being assured, if necessary, of military defense against its foes, particularly the Emperor. When, after many time-saving compromises with the Lutherans, the Emperor was finally ready to launch a war against the "heretics," he succeeded in defeating them, chiefly with the help of Spanish and papal troops (1547), but he was unable to crush them or reap the fruits of his victory. Leaving the religious controversy in Germany unsettled, he abdicated. His son Philip became the heir of his Dutch and Spanish dominions and his brother Ferdinand, the King of Austria, succeeded him as the Holy Roman Emperor. It was he who presided at the diet of Augsburg (1555) at the conclusion of which the German estates ratified the treaty of peace in connection with which the established Lutheran churches were legally recognized in Germany.

In view of the fact that one of the goals of Charles' policies was the control of Italy (because without it he did not believe himself to be able to realize the main objective of his dynastic policies: the establishment of the universal monarchy of the House of Hapsburg), the popes were politically suspicious of him and sometimes even went so far as to align themselves with his chief opponent, the King of France. They hoped thereby to protect their own rule over the papal state and, at the same time, to preserve a balance of power in the European system of states. These papal policies prevented Charles from acting decisively against the "Protestants." *

Thus the popes themselves made the expansion of the Reformation possible. The Emperor believed that a church council could put an end to the religious controversy and he, therefore, repeatedly urged the popes to convene one. But they hesitated to act at his bidding. When, finally, in December 1546, the Council of Trent was opened, its original purpose could not be realized. The Protestants refused to submit to papal jurisdiction and stayed away. The Council of Trent (it met intermittently and did not finally adjourn until 1563) became a purely Roman Catholic enterprise. Under the undisputed leadership of the popes it succeeded in bringing about a consolidation of the Roman Church by setting it in irreconcilable opposition to the Reformation.

The *effects* of the Reformation must be seen primarily in the formation of the Protestant churches. In Germany and the Scandinavian countries *Lutheranism* came to prevail. Its territorial and national churches over which the political rulers exercised the external government were marked chiefly by the concern for pure doctrine defined according to the Augsburg Confession and other characteristically Lutheran creeds, including Luther's catechisms.

* This name was applied to the German Lutherans in 1529 when they submitted to the Diet of Spires a "Protestation," in which they rejected a majority vote of the diet designed to repeal the limited right granted them in 1526 to proceed with a reformation of the Church in their own territories.

The doctrine of the justification by faith shaped their preaching and teaching. From the beginning, their outlook was determined by the person of Martin Luther. This fact made itself felt especially in the conception and practices of the Lord's Supper. The Lutherans adopted Luther's views of the real presence of Christ in the sacrament. They kept themselves apart from all who did not share the belief in Christ's presence "in, with, and under" the elements of bread and wine.

This teaching had first been developed in a controversy between Luther and Ulrich Zwingli, the Reformer of Zurich in Switzerland. He was much more radical than Luther in abolishing Roman Catholic traditions of worship and, in his view, the Lord's Supper was a congregational celebration of the memory of Christ. The church he built in Zurich, a society of disciplined Christians organized in a church-state, was the first of "Reformed" Protestantism. In the course of time, it had to yield leadership to Geneva. There John Calvin molded a Christian commonwealth and developed a form of Protestantism that spread to France, Holland, Scotland, Poland and Hungary. *Calvinism* differed markedly from Lutheranism. Its theocentrism was marked by an emphasis upon the sovereignty rather than the mercy of God, with the consequence that the doctrine of predestination was stressed next to that of justification and the Bible was read as the rule of God, the supreme legislator and sovereign. Calvin was sure that God had prescribed for the Church a definite polity around the four ministerial officers of preachers, teachers, elders and deacons. Under their leadership, the Church was to manifest its life in teaching and preaching, the observance of the sacraments and the administration of Christian discipline. In this form, believed to be divinely enjoined, Calvinism was established in Geneva and wherever else it gained a foothold. Through the Church and the connections of its individual members, the elect, the Calvinists tried to mold society along the lines of biblical morality. Because of the fact that Calvinism arose in the commercial setting of the city-republic of Geneva and that it became the religion of Frenchmen,

Dutchmen and Scots who found themselves compelled to defend their faith against oppressive rulers, its spirit assumed a dynamism and an alertness with respect to public issues, especially politics. Here, too, it differed from Lutheranism whose churches, set in the largely rural territories of patriarchal rulers, did not need to fight for their freedom and therefore developed a conservative political outlook.

The formation of Lutheran and Reformed churches signified the break-up of the age-old unity of Roman Catholicism; but it was characteristic of the Reformers that they continued to adhere to the conception of the *corpus Christianum,* according to which the Christian religion was regarded as the basic unifying force in society. Therefore, they also held the conviction that religious uniformity was the only guarantee of public peace and political unity. Accordingly, the Protestant churches became uniform within the limits of their territorial establishment. Every person had to conform to the requirements and creeds of the established churches. Whosoever was unable to do so had to emigrate. Here lie the roots of the exclusivism and the intolerance that was to mark the relations of the Protestant churches with one another. Though the Reformers themselves, and especially Calvin, worked for ecumenical unity, they could not prevent the conformist practices of their churches leading to general intolerance. Also in Protestantism, Christian and ecclesiastical diversity thus became division.

The main victims of this spirit were the *sectarians,* who dared to set themselves apart from the established churches and formed conventicles. The most influential group among them were the so-called *Anabaptists.* They first arose in Zurich, where some of Zwingli's most ardently evangelical followers objected to his program to realize the Reformation by means of a close cooperation between church and state. They advocated instead the idea that a church, truly reformed according to the New Testament, could not be anything else but a community of the regenerates who were resolved to follow Christ and to practice a life of uncompromising discipleship, declining to rely on political power for the maintenance of religion and refusing to bear arms, to use coercion of any sort, to appeal to the courts or to swear oaths. They objected to infant baptism and observed believers' baptism; hence they were dubbed Anabaptists, i.e., rebaptizers. Since 1525, they expanded throughout Switzerland and Germany. Their nonconformist ideas and practices were interpreted as a defiance of public order and authority. They were ruthlessly persecuted by Protestants and Roman Catholics alike. Thousands became martyrs to their faith. There was no common order among them until, in 1536, the Dutchman, Meno Simons, organized them as a peaceful sect. The Mennonite communities thus became the heirs of the Anabaptist faith. Other sectarians devoted to spiritualist, mystical, and apocalyptic ideals, who had flourished for a time, gradually disappeared. If they survived, they continued their existence in esoteric ways in connection with the activities of individuals who exercised personal influence, but did not succeed in organizing corporate movements.

The "radical" Reformation held no important place in the life of early Protestantism, but it proved to be influential nevertheless. Today many see a kinship between the spirit of the radical Reformation and that of modern liberal Protestantism, especially in the form it has taken in some of the leading American denominations. This surprising fact is due, to a certain extent, to the influence the Reformation sects exercised upon the religious life of England during the sixteenth and seventeenth centuries. The Church of England came under the sway of the Reformation during the reign of Edward VI (1547-1553) and it was definitely aligned with Protestantism by the action of Queen Elizabeth (1558-1603) and her government. Henry VIII had separated the English church from the papacy for dynastic-political reasons (1534); but he was no friend of the Reformation and his exercise of the "supreme headship" over the Church of England did not further the cause of Protestantism. But once death had removed him from the scene, the Continental Reformation began to shape the faith and order of the *Anglican*

Church. While episcopacy was preserved and the continuity with the historic Church maintained, its doctrine, as defined in the Thirty-Nine Articles, became thoroughly Protestant and its liturgy, though preserving ancient forms, was given a Protestant character in the order of the Book of Common Prayer. The constitution of the Anglican Church was an indigenous expression of the spirit of English Christianity, even though it was shaped by the influence of the Continental Reformation, especially Zwinglianism and Calvinism, Lutheranism making itself felt only at the beginning. When, under Elizabeth, Anglicanism became definitely established, many Englishmen protested against the halfway Reformation thus effected. They came to be called *"Puritans"* because they demanded a pure reform according to the rule of God's Word. Their thinking was inspired chiefly by Calvinism and its principles of ecclesiastical polity and discipline, but it was also affected by the notions of the radical Reformers. Puritanism was vigorously suppressed by the Crown in the interest of religious uniformity, which was believed to be the chief bulwark of national unity. Nevertheless, it produced ways of faith, liturgy, polity, ethics and church-practice that reflected, in a genuinely English setting and particularly in opposition to Anglicanism, ideas and ideals that had first flourished in the Continental Reformation in the Reformed churches as well as among the radical Reformers.

What all these diverse Protestant churches and groups had in common was their opposition to Roman Catholicism. They all regarded the Bible as the ultimate norm of Christianity, and they understood the Christian gospel as the proclamation of salvation by grace alone. On this common basis of the Reformation faith, they all recognized the common life and its natural orders as the scene where Christian obedience to God must be actualized. They all abandoned monasticism and asceticism as the conditions of true Christianity and enjoined their members to practice religion in the natural pursuits of home and school, church and state, business and profession. The observance of this innerworldly piety and the abandonment of otherworldly religiousness probably constitutes the most telling effect of the Reformation upon the common life of European civilization.

WILHELM PAUCK

Bibliography

Heinrich Boehmer, *Martin Luther: The Road to Reformation.*
Wilhelm Pauck, *The Heritage of the Reformation,* rev. ed.

RELIGION: NATURAL AND REVEALED

Definition. In Christian theology "revelation" signifies divine self-disclosure in significant communication. Since this disclosure is unique and original, and its contents are unknown apart from the disclosure, it cannot be equated with human discovery. In contemporary theology there is consensus that revelation is embodied in and therefore inseparable from specific historic events, centrally those of the birth, ministry, death and resurrection of Jesus Christ. Moreover, there is agreement that revelation as divine self-disclosure in history embodies a content that may become intelligibly significant for its human recipients. Also there is agreement that, despite its indissoluble ties to a specific past event, revelation must come to present recipients as a present event.

"Natural" religion is in a sense a far more complex term than revelation. But for the fact that, in the parlance of Western culture, it is derived from a specific controversy, it would be necessary to admit under this heading every definition that claims to understand religion as an observable manifestation. Natural religion would then be understood as a general human activity which may be intelligibly analyzed by philosophy, psychology, sociology or a special science of religion. However, in its historical context, natural religion is a normative rather than merely descriptive term. It has come to signify an apprehension of God, not wholly or not at all dependent upon a divine self-disclosure. Natural religion lays claim to a certain valid type of activity or experience, usually involving a being other than self or universe. Even when it does not, natural religion claims that one may validly speak of a total sensitization of the human being, mind, will and psyche in the presence of the totality of the universe, impinging upon him from without and within. Such a sensitization may be heightened or even occasioned by a special event in time, but it cannot intrinsically depend upon it for existence and meaning. Natural religion is at least potentially present with the fact that one is born into humanity.

The concepts "natural" and "revealed" religion are dependent upon each other because both claim normative validity. It is no accident that in Western intellectual history they have existed only in contact or conflict with one another. The area of their contact or conflict is a grave theological problem, because neither term can be substituted for the other, nor has reflection found a common and agreed area from which to view both as aspects of one genus.

History. Since the second century, Christian thinkers have endeavored to bring into systematic relation the confession of Jesus Christ and the diversity of other religious experiences. The immediate background of contemporary questions, however, lies in the impact of seventeenth-century mechanical and mathematical genius upon the cultural and religious thought of the eighteenth century. The success of mathematics and experiment in measuring the movement of objects in space gave rise to a popular intellectual outlook that applied "mechanics" or "natural philosophy" unequivocally to religious questions. A uniformly regulated physical universe in which absolute, objective space and time are evenly distributed called for a God who also governed the moral universe through objective and absolute moral laws. The natures and relations of God and man remain constant. The general claim of a natural religion, therefore, was that in their contents natural and revealed religion must be similar. More radical adherents of this position, the Deists, claimed that the two were identical in substance and that revelation was only a specific outward form or republication of original, natural religion, if indeed revealed religion was not rank superstition.

The adherents of revealed religion took the Bible as its source, and supposed it to contain full-blown all the doctrines that formed the content of revelation: the predestination of the elect, the unity of mankind in original sin, justification of the sinner by faith in the atoning death of Jesus Christ as the promised and incarnate God-man, the inerrancy of scriptural claims being such as to include the literal occurrence of miracles. The response of faith to revelation included acknowledgment of and assent to these given, objective, non-physical facts—facts of an incomparably higher order than the order of nature, but in their factuality analogous to it. By acknowledging the analogy, revealed religion admitted the right of natural religion to be the court to which it must present evidence of its credibility. Obviously this was difficult in the face of a "natural" creed which denied miracles, and recognized only a supreme Being and Purposer whose ways are manifest in a causal law of merit and reward. Natural religion held that the ways of God could be ascertained equally and without impediment by all generations of men through the light of the unaided intellect and earnest moral purpose.

The impasse between natural and revealed religion was broken by technical philosophers—Hume and, to a lesser degree, Kant. They wrought havoc on both by a vigorous theoretical examination of the two questions that "natural philosophy" had left untouched: the nature of substance (or the objective reality that underlies and unifies observable manifestations) and the nature and limitations of the knowing mind. At the beginning of the nineteenth century it was valid to ask if the human mind were more than a grab-bag of sense data and purely abstract forms that have nothing to do with objective reality. The comfortable, if uninspired, theory of a substantial, factual God, to be grasped by the rational mind through its theoretical functions, had dissolved and both natural and revealed religion were left without their most fundamental concept.

Nineteenth-century Protestant theology achieved a surprising degree of agreement in its endeavor to avoid the destruction of religion. Schleiermacher and most theologians after him were determined that Christian theology must once again confess Jesus Christ as the unique source of revelation of God. This confession, however, must not pit Christian faith, as one body of doctrine, over against a distinctly different one called "religion." Nor was Christian faith simply one species within the genus "religion." Christian faith had in common with "religion" the fact that both involved a unique type of awareness wholly different from the abstractly objective assent to dogmatic or rational propositions that characterized natural and revealed religion in the eighteenth century. Religion must involve the living and direct conviction of faith, a special form of awareness which most observers took to be wholly distinct from theoretical (scientific or metaphysical) understanding. However, there was no religion *in general,* for religion, without a specific historic content, was merely an empty form. Thus Christian faith involved neither compromise nor argument with an abstract "natural" religion; for Christian faith had no other content than the historic event, Jesus Christ.

It was acknowledged that insofar as this historic event was subject to a general, theoretical and scientific understanding of history it involved in principle nothing unique. Uniqueness was found only when the historical event and the special religious awareness (or the direct presence of God) are fully united at some point in human experience. This point of "indifference," as it was sometimes called, could not be an assent simply to a theoretical proposition about an external fact. On the other hand, it must not be purely subjective. Nineteenth-century theologians were never able to agree about *the point* at which objective event and concrete subjectivity (or living faith) became one. They did agree, however, that there is such a relation and that it means a basic unity between Jesus Christ and present Christian faith or religion; between objective, historical, concrete divine presence and the subjective spontaneity of response.

The normative element in Christian faith lies in this relation. It is at once revelation and religion. Because it is totally a matter of practical awareness, this relation cannot be directly expressed in conceptual terms. A radical hiatus exists, therefore, between religion and theology. The content of dogma—conceptualization—becomes secondary, an unauthoritative pointer to the religious relationship; that is, a purely temporary expression of a constant fact. A radical break in this constant relation in which revelation and religion are one was inconceivable to nineteenth-century theologians.

Kierkegaard was one of the few thinkers of the nineteenth century to deny not only direct relation between God and the immediacy of awareness, but between such awareness and the past event, Jesus Christ, that determines one's present faith. He and a few like-minded theologians remained isolated voices in their time but have spoken poignantly to the twentieth century.

Contemporary discussion. Present-day theologians are in no mood to return to the eighteenth-century discussion. There is agreement today that the uniqueness of revelation lies not in a dogmatic proposition nor in subjective spiritual certainty but in its character as unique historical event. It is impossible, therefore, to speak of "revealed religion," or to reduce revelation to an instance of a general "religious" type. Revelation and religion are now sharply distinguished. The contemporary discussion over their relation (rather than that of revealed and natural religion) is largely taking place within the confines of a theology of revelation. In seeking to relate the Christian faith to general human experience, theologians are turning largely to the consideration of three types of relationship: theology and philosophy, revelation and history, Christian faith and human culture.

1) The distinction between theology and philosophy (in more popular terms: "faith" and "reason," "revelation"

and "natural" theology or "special" and "general revelation) is in part an inheritance from the nineteenth-century distinction between revelation (or religion) and theology. Many contemporary theologians still insist upon a sharp distinction between theoretical, propositional knowledge and the manner in which one apprehends unique historical events. Revelation involves the confrontation of persons of totally differing dimensions—God and man. This type of thought relies heavily not only on Kierkegaard, but on the distinction Martin Buber has drawn between I-Thou encounter and I-It relationships. Revelation is *the* I-Thou encounter *par excellence,* whereas theoretical reasoning considers the person as an object or an "it." Emil Brunner, Karl Heim, John Baillie, H. H. Farmer, H. Richard Niebuhr and Hendrik Kraemer are among the many theologians who share this view: revelation is for them the unique subject matter of theology and yet may also be pointed to in terms of "existential," personal understanding and cultural experience. The ultimate structure with which the self is here in contact is personal. Religion is a Subject-subject encounter.

Some theologians reject this manner of relating philosophy and theology by complete separation. Not only contemporary Neo-Thomists, but thinkers as diverse as Karl Barth, Paul Tillich and Austin Farrer, have claimed that one cannot separate philosophy and theology by making God's grasp upon us subject to a unique religious or existential apprehension. Rather, the reverse is true, i.e., that the act of God, identical with His being, is the ground and possibility of all our knowledge of God, and therefore the divine act or being (and not unique religious knowledge) is the starting point for a contact between philosophy and theology. In other words, the interpretation of theology in terms other than the purely confessional terms of scripture can be accomplished only by the use of what philosophers have traditionally called metaphysics or ontology. All these men reject the direct attribution of a "personal" dimension to God, asserted by the existentialist theologians. Again, in contrast to the antimetaphysical tendencies of the latter, Barth and Farrer in particular rely heavily on a concept of analogy, i.e., correspondence within dissimilarity, between the divine and created agency.

But within this area of agreement there is ample room for disagreement. Farrer, for example, conceives of two harmonious but quite distinct phases of divine action, natural and supernatural, to which two distinct but generically connected types of thought correspond; metaphysics, natural or rational theology on the one hand, and on the other supernatural, historical or revelational understanding of God. Both Barth and Tillich reject this position. In contrast to Farrer's metaphysical realism, they are deeply indebted to German idealism with its tendency to understand fundamental reality as the concrete self-embodiment of spiritual activity. For Tillich philosophy and theology are distinct rational modes of apprehending the ground of being that underlies all thought and all objects. Theology deals with the universal ground made concrete in historical particularity and impinging upon us so as to form our ultimate concern. Its grasp is upon the truth as concretely embodied and must be symbolic in expression. The intent of philosophy is an abstract, formal and, therefore, ultimately literal understanding of the structure of being. Theology and philosophy are dialectically related or "correlated." Though they are basically the same type of reasoning activity, their apprehensions must be interpreted through each other, the abstract through the concrete and vice versa. They must never be merged into one. Philosophy provides not only the questions but the symbols in terms of which revelation must formulate its concrete answers to the human situation.

Karl Barth occupies a position at once midway between and yet more radical than either Tillich or Farrer. Farrer, in the fashion of the realist, regards God as absolute Substance, and Tillich regards God as pure Subject (beyond objective knowledge), absolutely prior to the objective "thereness" of substance. Barth insists that our only knowledge of God is due to the fact that as abiding Subject, Agent or Spirit, God nevertheless has made

Himself a unique object for human understanding in the incarnation of Jesus Christ—and this miraculously without relinquishing His freedom as absolute, untrammeled Agent over created agency and human reasoning. The abiding ground in the incarnation of this subject-object unity is the eternal unity of subjective agency and objective *thereness* in that specific actuality which is God, and in which He is self-identical in eternity and in His revelation. The concrete act which is the object of theological knowledge is God Himself as Father, Son and Holy Spirit. What now of the relation between philosophy and theology? In its language and manner of conception theology is nothing but philosophy. But the object of such knowledge is wholly unique, the God of freedom and grace who condescends to come to us in Jesus Christ. Thus when philosophy makes this unique object the subject matter of a proper and *concrete* "metaphysical" judgment (which may be done only through the prevenient grace of God) it becomes theology. There is for Barth no dialectic between philosophy and theology, nor are they neatly distinguished yet generically connected activities of thought. Rather, theology is to him the abiding mystery of God's appropriation of common and created human thought (philosophy) to his revelation in Jesus Christ. In a debate with Barth, Emil Brunner charged that for Barth there is no "point of contact" between revelation and natural human thought. The contrary is true. Barth is supremely confident of such a point of contact, but it takes place in the mystery of God's freedom as He provides His own "point of contact" and it need not be "existential" despair over the possibility of achieving genuine, responsible human existence, as Brunner has insisted.

2) The chief inheritance bequeathed by nineteenth-century theology to the present discussion is that revelation does not stand over against some hypothetical "natural" religion, but that the Christian faith arose and developed in a genuinely historical matrix. Thus the issue of relating revelation and natural thought, in addition to its philosophical implications, is that of relating faith and history

Nineteenth-century theology discovered that Christianity is not a ready-made eternal constant but a genuine product of historical change, and that therefore the truth of Christianity cannot be separated from its history. The revolutionary view to which our century has fallen heir is that man is through and through a historical being and that his world is not a metaphysical but an historical world. Faith therefore must be concerned with historical events and not with trans-historical or metaphysical constants.

The latest and most extreme exposition of this point of view comes from Rudolf Bultmann and his colleagues (e.g. Friedrich Gogarten). To them the uniqueness of Jesus Christ lies not in the original "mythological" or at least metaphysical picture of Him, but in our translation of its meaning into the terms of the contemporary, living "existential" history of free selves. Genuinely historical faith arises when the New Testament's witness to Christ becomes as witness an effective Word to contemporary existence. In an extreme fashion this represents the endeavor, now prevalent, to separate living, experienced, existential or salvitic history from purely objective history with its data and its accurate description of past events.

Faith, it is claimed, can operate only in "living" history. But as a result the event as recorded datum of the past recedes into insignificance. Some nineteenth-century thinkers had undertaken to demonstrate that Christianity is the spiritual apex of the religious idea working its way through history, continuous with all other manifestations of that same idea which constitute as it were the stepping stones for Christianity. Other historians claimed that, like every cultural phenomenon, Christianity is but an eclectic sampling of its changing historical environment. Both points of view denied the absolute uniqueness of revelation. Over against them many theologians held that revelation, as unique act, becomes embodied in unique historical events. But in that case revelation seems to strike into history as a foreign element, much as revealed religion appeared as a foreign body to eighteenth-century natural religion. In this situation there may be promise in the endeavor to find a middle road between unrevelational history and unhistorical revelation, by stipulating two types of history, be they called secular and sacred or objective and existential. In any case, the problem of relating revelation and faith with history remains vexed. Bultmann's attempt to find revelation in existential history is only one extreme alternative among many others to relate faith and history by distinguishing two types of history.

3) We can only give summary attention to what may well be the crucial discussion within the broad context of our topic in the immediate future. The historical understanding of faith encouraged in the latter part of the nineteenth century the emergence of the study of the history of religions and, on English-speaking soil, of "comparative religion." As such, these studies have for the present lost their theological excitement. In the meantime, however, the growth of the ecumenical movement and the rising tide of independence among the "younger" churches beyond Western culture have contributed to the urgent necessity for a theological understanding of the cultural, including the religious, matrix of civilizations, both those of the West and of the East. We may add two further facts. In the first place, as Arnold Toynbee has taught us, we are now beginning for the first time to live in a genuinely universal period. The various living civilizations of the world are beginning to encounter each other directly. This fact is largely due to the cultural aggressiveness of the West, many of whose cultural forms have now been willingly accepted by other cultures in the very endeavor to fight back in behalf of their own cultural autonomy and the revitalization of their own ancient traditions. Secondly, the renewed insistence of contemporary theology on the complete uniqueness of revelation in Jesus Christ has made for a revival of theological interpretation of missionary activity. This radical claim for the uniqueness of revelation is bound to see all the cultures and religions of the world in a fairly relativistic light. From this judgment the Christian religion itself is not to be excepted, inasmuch as it is the religious form of

a culture that is not absolute, but relative and finite like all the rest. Ours is perhaps the first time when this fact has been fully and widely accepted as a theological doctrine. Absolute authority may be claimed for Jesus Christ but not for the Christian religion. One must add here the growing conviction among theologians that the culture of the West is in large degree secular (using this term as a factual and not evaluating description) and is therefore, in its own way, fresh missionary territory.

In this situation few theologians would attempt a direct evaluating comparison between revelation as seen in Christian faith and the religions of human cultures. H. H. Farmer, among theologians, and Arnold Toynbee have attempted it, the latter in a manner reminiscent of the eighteenth-century search for a universal natural religion. But neither endeavor seems destined to gain a wide following. Most theologians would avoid two extreme positions. The first is the assertion that all cultural religions are pure unbelief in the face of revelation; the second is the opposite tendency, the acceptance of every religion as having a truth by virtue of which it naturally tends toward completion in the gospel and for which it is a proper and direct preparation. It is between these two extremes that the present theological discussion has tried to wind its way, from Nathan Söderblom, its greatest precursor in the West in our century, to Hendrik Kraemer, the outstanding pioneer of the present discussion in the ecumenical movement. But the time may be at hand when the main focus of this particular discussion (including the troublesome problem of the place of the Old Testament in its relation to the acceptance of the gospel by non-Western peoples) will rightly pass from the West to the churches and theologians of the East. (See articles on "Revelation" and "Thomism".)

HANS W. FREI

Bibliography

John Baillie, *The Idea of Revelation in Recent Thought.*
Austin Farrer, *The Glass of Vision.*
Hendrik Kraemer, *Religion and the Christian Faith.*

H. R. Mackintosh, *Types of Modern Theology.*
H. Richard Niebuhr, *Christ and Culture.*
Paul Tillich, *Biblical Religion and the Search for Ultimate Reality.*

REPENTANCE

Repentance has two basic meanings: a turning to God (*shuv*) and regretting a wrong done. The former meaning is found in the Old Testament especially in prophetic writings where Israel is summoned to turn away from idolatry and uprighteousness to the worship of the Lord and obedience to His Law and will (Amos 4:6; Hosea 2:7; 7:10,16; 14:1; Is. 44:2; 55:7; Jer. 3:12,22; 5:3; 15:1; Mal. 3:7 f). Repentance here is a turning to the God of Abraham, Isaac and Jacob; to the Lord who has delivered His people from bondage in Egypt and settled them in the land promised to their fathers. This God is contradistinguished from other gods or idols in that He has entered into covenant with His people, by whose terms they are to be merciful and just one toward another. Repentance is to turn away from inhumanity and oppression, and to exercise compassion and decent regard for the well-being of those in need: the poor, the fatherless, the stranger, the widow (Deut. 16:11, 14:24, 17:19; Job 31:17 f).

Secondly, repentance is *nacham,* which has the basic meaning of regret, of acknowledgment that one has done wrong, and sorrow or contrition over it. In this sense God Himself is said to have repeatedly repented (Gen. 6:6-7; Ex. 32:14; Judges 2:18; I Sam. 15:11; Jer. 26:3). This involves also a change of mind, and decision to do otherwise (Ps. 110:14; Jer. 4:28; Amos 7:3,6; Jonah 2:9, 3:10). The classic expression of such repentance is Ps. 51, which indicates that contrition was connected especially with religious observances and sacrifices.

In the New Testament these two motifs are combined, although the prophetic predominates. Repentance here is to turn away from sin and wickedness, and to God and righteousness. This was basic to the teachings of both

John the Baptist and Jesus. Jesus, however, regarded sin in essence as alienation from God and the misery of the lack of trust in God's goodness and power. Therefore, repentance was a putting away of doubt in God, and the anxiety and lostness which follow from it; and a return to God in the confidence and joy of a trusting son (Mark 1:15; Luke 15; 17:3,4; Matthew 3:2). *Metanoō* in the New Testament is the turning of the sinful man to God. It is the unitary act of a man as a unitary being, involving his mind, will, affections. Therefore, Paul was quite right in interpreting repentance as total change, a dying and rising, a renewal, a new creation (Rom. 12:2, 6:5-12; II Cor. 5:16-19; Eph. 2:1-10). It should be added that central to Christian repentance is faith in Jesus as the Christ (Acts 2:38; 3:18-21). To repent is to accept Jesus as "the way, the truth and the life," and to live and act accordingly.

It is no wonder that an adequate discussion of repentance extends to the doctrines of grace, faith, justification, conversion, etc. It is easy to think of it primarily in terms of regret for wrongdoing and willingness to make amends (as in the Catholic doctrine of penance). It is easy to emphasize the emotional elements in it, and to think of it in terms of "godly sorrow" as was done by puritan and pietist. It is no harder to conceive of it in moral terms as an act of the will against sundry shortcomings. Thus in the history of Christian thought the doctrine of repentance has varied with the several conceptions of the meaning of salvation which have been entertained in different churches and elaborated by different theologians. Various ways of understanding man, in terms of mind, will, emotion, have contributed to the endless discussions of the subject. But it seems to the writer that much confusion and peripheral discussion would be avoided if one kept in mind that "man's business is with God"; that God's business with man, according to scripture, is concerned primarily with the justice which is essentially humanity, as described by the Law of God; that the Law is the Law of Moses as interpreted by the prophets and fulfilled in Jesus Christ. Repentance is a returning to God and, in that very act, man's returning to himself and to his neighbor, to that freedom which expresses itself in love or justice, and the practical consequences of this in man's relations with man.

When repentance is thought of in terms of a radical reorientation of human life, the question arises as to whether it is an act of God or an act of man. The question is deep and difficult. Clearly repentance is a human act, but its possibility is created by God Himself through His dealings with His people, as consummated by Jesus Christ and extended, by the Spirit of God, in the Church (Jer. 31:31 f; Ez. 36:22 f; Ps. 51; Acts 11:15-18; John 3:1-8; Rom. 8:1-11).

JOSEPH HAROUTUNIAN

Bibliography

William Douglas Chamberlain, *The Meaning of Repentance.*
Hugh Ross Mackintosh, *The Christian Experience of Forgiveness.*
Vincent Taylor, *Forgiveness and Reconciliation, a Study in New Testament Theology.*

RESURRECTION

"If Christ has not been raised, then our preaching is in vain and your faith is in vain" (I Cor. 15:14).

Paul's warning to the Corinthians is probably the most concise expression of the self-admonitory mood in which modern Protestant theologians reflect on resurrection. Moreover, the logic that Paul sets forth in I Corinthians appears to be still decisive for our thinking, insofar as the quest of modern faith to understand the biblical tradition concerning resurrection compels us to face two fundamental Pauline assumptions. The first is the conviction that the gospel cannot be abstracted from the proclamation that Christ *is* risen. The second is the complementary affirmation that the "image of the man of dust" has been transmuted in us into the "image of the man of heaven" by the appearance among us of Jesus Christ. There is, as a consequence, a fundamental involvement of all men with one another, so that whether we speak of Man as such (Adam) or Jesus Christ, each must suffer for the other's sake and share in the other's destiny, and this representative manhood, in whose image we are stamped, is more determinative of our being than any external laws or powers.

The resurrection of Jesus Christ. The renewed theological effort to grapple with the biblical tradition concerning the resurrection of Christ is attributable in large part to the deepened understanding of the mind of the primitive Church afforded us by New Testament criticism. We can no longer think of Jesus' purported rising from the dead as a simple instance of miracle, because the whole gospel appears to be rooted in that very tradition. In its present form, the organization of the Gospels reflects, at virtually every critical juncture, the luminous memory in the mind of the earliest Church of the apostolic resurrection encounters. D. F. Strauss (*Life of Jesus,* 1836) pointed out this fact in his criticism of Schleiermacher's rationalistic rejection of the resurrection narratives. The significance of this feature of the New Testament's structure is that it leaves even the critic no possibility of making a hard and fast distinction between the so-called historical Jesus and the risen Christ, unless he is prepared to do violence to the historical consciousness of the New Testament itself. Admittedly, it is difficult to acknowledge consistently the full implications of the fact that we have no access to some Jesus of history who, comparable to a "thing in itself," can be known independently of the resurrection-consciousness of the primitive Church. But the price of such a hypothetical immediate knowledge would entail our discounting the earliest Church and its gospel and contenting ourselves with a private and nameless "Jesus" of our own. Albert Schweitzer's classic, *The Quest of the Historical Jesus,* draws a picture of precisely such an anonymous Jesus.

To the extent that theology recognizes the resurrection

tradition as the integument of the gospel, it confronts the task of interpreting the sense in which the resurrection-gospel can be understood as historical. The continuing virtual hegemony of the methods of eighteenth-century natural science in biblical historical study has persuaded a great many theologians of the advantages of philosophical idealism in presenting the meaning of Christ's resurrection. For, though idealism has not challenged the idea of nature as a deteriorating closed system, it has ostensibly surmounted it. Emil Brunner, C. H. Dodd, and F. C. Grant have all adopted a broad and often vague Platonism in picturing the resurrection of Christ as a wholly transcendent occurrence, though the boldest statement of this type remains that of Karl Barth in his commentary on Romans (2nd edition) in which the resurrection of Christ appears as the annihilation of history. However, this divorce of the resurrection of Christ from ordinary historical experience logically implies a further question: How could such a transcendent event be known? 1) The "Hegelians" treat the resurrection as a piece of imagery that was projected by the myth-making faculty of the primitive mind in an effort to express the internally apprehended meaning of the crucifixion (D. F. Strauss, Rudolf Bultmann); 2) The "sacred history" school includes the resurrection in a stream of exclusively God-determined events that is visible only to the God-created eye of faith (the Barth of *Church Dogmatics*). Satisfactory as these interpretations may be, with respect to their philosophical consistency, they are incapable of showing that Christ's rising from the dead reveals anything new in principle about the nature of history in general and about our own historicity in particular. Instead, they use the resurrection of Christ as a symbol for the negation of history, not its transformation. In the main, then, it would appear that the treatment of resurrection merely shows that both philosophy and science have convinced most theologians that only in a superficial sense is actual history illuminated by the rising of Christ; essentially history remains the realm of becoming and hence of death

The resurrection of "those who are Christ's." The crux of the problem in the biblical "resurrection" tradition is the form of the relationship between Christ and other men. Traditional Chalcedonian Christology has obscured, by fastening attention on the relation of the divine and human natures in Christ, the more important question about the change wrought in human nature as such by the Christ who represents man before God. Nevertheless, the Pauline notion of the representative manhood of Christ, insofar as it has found continued expression in such men as Irenaeus and, more ambiguously, in Schleiermacher, Tillich and Barth, is more than a negligible relic of gnosticism. To be sure, modern economics, politics, and existentialism indicate the depth of our inability to comprehend human relatedness either within or without Christ, and even the New Testament cannot conceal the profound doubt occasioned in the Church by the "falling asleep" of some before the end-time. Be that as it may, however, the biblical picture of Jesus Christ as the representative man, the man from heaven, the second Adam, implies that the resurrection was not the mere vindication of Him who was Son of God by nature, but the triumph of the Son of Man in grace; that death originated not outside but inside our nature, upon which it feeds; that our salvation is a consequence, not of the intrusion into our humanity of an alien and scarcely supportable metaphysical principle, but of the manifestation of that true humanity whose image we all shall bear. The view of human nature and divine grace adumbrated by the resurrection faith of Christianity differs from all others in that it gives ultimate validity to the order of historical experience. Resurrection is the confirmation of the order of creation and the preservation of that which otherwise would be lost in either God or death.

RICHARD R. NIEBUHR

Bibliography

John Baillie, *And the Life Everlasting.*
A. M. Ramsey, *The Resurrection of Christ.*

REVELATION

"Revelation" (Latin *revelatio*, Greek *apokalypsis*) literally implies an "unveiling" of a hidden mystery. In scholastic thought, both Catholic and Protestant, "revealed theology" is regularly contrasted with "natural theology" as an authoritative unveiling of truths about God inaccessible to reason, and nowhere clearly written upon the face of nature. St. Thomas Aquinas defines revelation as "divine truth which exceeds the human intellect, yet not as demonstrated to our sight but as a communication delivered for our belief." (*Summa Contra Gentiles*, IV, chap. i.) Calvin, it is true, declares that in Holy Scripture God opens "his own holy mouth"; but he would certainly agree that what is thus disclosed does not dispel all mystery. Revelation does not imply that there are no clouds and no thunders on Sinai when the Lord speaks there, but only that some clear meaning comes through from God to man.

In recent Protestant theology, the old scholastic distinction between natural and revealed theology is generally questioned, and a new conception of revelation has appeared, based upon a less rationalistic theory of religious knowledge. According to this view, religious revelation does not consist of the communication of propositions about God to be believed; it consists of the confrontation of God and man through actual historical events, such as the Flight from Egypt, the Babylonian Captivity, and the Life of Christ. What is disclosed in such events is "not truth concerning God, but the living God Himself" (Temple, *Nature, Men and God*, p. 322). He guides the events providentially; He inspires prophetic interpreters to appreciate the meaning of the events and others to record them in such a way as to bring out this meaning; finally, He opens the eyes of the hearers or readers to His presence in these events, and their inward ears to His word for them. While all events in the whole world process are potentially pregnant with divine meaning ("general revelation"), certain key events in human history, above all in the history of Israel ("special revelation") have the quality of bringing out the meaning in all events, and so focusing the main Purpose of God that to confront these events is to be called to serve that Purpose. This is supremely and uniquely true of the events of the life of Christ, in whom the divine act and the prophetic interpretation of the meaning of the act coincide completely, so that here we meet "the Word made flesh."

Every conception of revelation involves a conception of inspiration. The scholastic conception of revelation has generally been accompanied by a theory of the plenary, verbal inspiration of the Bible. Since God speaks propositionally in the Bible, and God is omniscient, every word of the Bible must be infallibly true. The theory of God-acting-in-events has other implications. Since God confronts us through the meaning of events, any report or comment which powerfully conveys that meaning may be divinely inspired, whether or not it is factually inerrant. The Bible can thus convey a true revelation of God, and its writers can be God's inspired interpreters, while at the same time they are thoroughly human and fallible.

Non-Christian revelations of God are not excluded necessarily, in this view. Most religions have no such sense of the presence of God in history as the Jewish and Christian faiths; but if God is truly present in history, He must be present in all history, acting in events whose meaning may be only dimly discerned. It is one possible consequence of the view above described that it can see these dim intimations as *preparatory revelations* leading up to the definitive revelation in Christ, or *secondary revelations* permitting this primary revelation to be differently applied and interpreted in different cultural environments.

WALTER M. HORTON

Bibliography

J. Baillie and H. Martin (editors), *Revelation*.
J. Baillie, *The Idea of Revelation in Recent Thought*.
H. R. Niebuhr, *The Meaning of Revelation*.

RIGHTEOUSNESS

Righteousness is defined as uprightness, conformity to the norm. Biblical usage of the term differs from current usage in two important ways: the range of the term's meaning, and the standard by which righteousness is measured. In modern usage righteousness is restricted to an ethical quality, conformity to the ethical norm, and the norm is relative, depending upon the standards of the community or group.

In biblical usage, however, the norm is consistently the righteousness of God, not the standards of the community, and there is a much wider spectrum of meaning, due to the dynamic character of Hebrew language. Thus righteousness may mean: 1) a quality, conformity to the norm, the modern use of the term; 2) an activity, the doing of righteousness (In this sense righteousness is equivalent to an act of mercy, as in Matthew 6:1.); 3) the result of this activity, the state of things brought about by the doing of righteousness.

Because biblical thought is not relativistic but dominated by its theocentric norm, we can only understand the concept of righteousness if we begin with the righteousness of God. It is first a quality in God, His uprightness and holiness. In contrast to the deities of surrounding nations, the God of Israel is not arbitrary or capricious, does not make unfair demands or act vengefully, but is fair in His dealings. He also requires righteous conduct of His people and will judge them by His law. Human righteousness is thus assessed by the most strenuous standards and is driven to its highest ethical peak.

Secondly, God's righteousness is His activity, the way He establishes righteousness in His world. The prophets develop the notion that God will vindicate His people and establish righteousness for them. To the ethical meaning of righteousness is thus added the soteriological meaning, the deliverance or salvation that God will accomplish for His people.

Thirdly, God's righteousness is the state of things resulting from His activity, the accomplishment of His purpose. This aspect underlines the eschatological character of the term and forms part of the Messianic hope of Israel, the yearning for a world "in which righteousness dwells."

It is this dynamic character of the term that enables St. Paul to view the gospel as the revelation of the righteousness of God. The coming of Jesus Christ as the Messiah of Israel is the righteous activity of God by which He accomplishes salvation for His people. This does not indicate a relaxation of ethical requirements; the coming of Christ means rather a sharpening of ethical sensitivity, as the Sermon on the Mount shows. It is a vision of the way the tremendous requirements of God's righteousness are to be met. Man in his self-centeredness is unable to achieve the true worship and service of God required of him. He is burdened by the guilt of unfulfilled demands, alienated from God who is the source of his life, and frustrated by his inability to break out of egocentricity. Achievement of God's righteousness is possible only if God does something to make it possible. This He does by offering righteousness in the person of Jesus Christ. He who responds in faith to Jesus Christ is accounted righteous.

Righteousness is thus primarily the righteousness of God, that which He requires of man in conformity to His holiness, that which He bestows through faith in Christ, and the result of this activity, the life in Christ which works out this righteousness in love to neighbor.

WARREN A. QUANBECK

Bibliography

J. R. Coates (editor), *Bible Key Words.*
Anders Nygren, *Commentary on Romans.*

SACRAMENTS

A classic definition of sacraments, contained in the catechism of the Anglican Book of Common Prayer, states that they are "an outward and visible sign of an inward and spiritual grace." This definition aptly summarizes the teaching of the early Fathers of the Church, notably St. Augustine, and the medieval scholastic theologians. It would be acceptable to most Christian theologians today, with the following amendments: a sacrament is distinguished from other sacred signs by its express institution, whether by word or by exemplary action, of Christ Himself. A sacrament is efficacious only when it is performed in and by the Church acting through recognized ministers or by agents who intend to act for the Church.

The latter point needs to be stressed. Apart from the context of corporate church life, a sacrament is meaningless, if not, more extremely, a superstitious piece of magic. To be a Christian involves more than a personal faith in the redeeming act of God in Christ. It demands an incorporation into the community where the effects of Christ's redemption in reconciliation and charity may be actualized and nurtured. A sacrament cannot be performed by an individual for himself alone; it requires at least another party. Thus a sacrament is more than a visible token of God's free favor and grace offered to one who accepts His redeeming love in faith and devotion. It is an instrument whereby the individual is made a member of a covenant-community and ordered by its disciplines and responsibilities. To say that any particular sacrament is necessary to salvation does not mean that God is tied and bound to bestow His grace only by this means, but to affirm that in all normal circumstances an individual is made a partaker of Christ's redemption by being related to others who share the same benefits. In the sacraments, therefore, both the personal and the social relationships of Christian salvation are publicly ratified, accepted, and communicated.

In the Reformation era Catholics and Protestants differed in their emphases upon the way in which sacraments conveyed divine grace. Catholics stressed the objective efficacy of sacraments when duly performed with sincere intention by authorized ministers using the proper form (words) and matter (elements or actions) of a sacrament. Protestants tended to emphasize the subjective conditions of penitence and faith in the recipients of sacraments as a condition of receiving beneficially the promise of grace proclaimed by the Word of Christ and offered with the sacramental signs. There is, however, no necessary contradiction in these approaches. The Catholic did not affirm that grace operated apart from faith, though he believed that faith itself was a gift of grace. The Protestant was equally insistent that the sacraments be duly performed, as the Church had received them from the Lord, with the proper form and matter.

The bitterest controversy between the two parties centered in their definitions of the manner in which the divine grace inhered in or was conveyed by the sacramental signs, particularly in the case of the Lord's Supper (also called Holy Communion, Eucharist, Mass). All of the Protestant Reformers were unanimous in rejecting the medieval dogma of Transubstantiation: that the substance of bread and wine were miraculously changed by consecration into the substance of Christ's Body and Blood, the accidents of the elements only remaining. But the Reformers differed widely among themselves in their interpretations of how the Body and Blood of Christ were conveyed in or with the blessed elements, whether substantially, spiritually, or virtually. Their differences were as much the result of varying philosophical presuppositions as of divergent interpretations of the words of Christ at the Last Supper. None of the Reformers, however, opposed an objective, effectual presence of Christ in the Supper offered to those who would receive Him by faith. Today, though the different over Transubstantiation still divides Catholic and Protestant believers, the issue of the Real Presence of Christ is no longer controverted with such energy and feeling.

Another occasion of controversy at the time of the Reformation concerned the sacrificial interpretation of the

Lord's Supper. Again, the Protestant Reformers were unanimous in rejecting the medieval doctrine that in the Mass Christ was offered anew, albeit mystically, for the remission of sins of the living and the dead, as a derogation of the once-for-all character of Christ's sacrifice for sin upon the Cross. But both sides of the controversy tended to think of sacrifice overmuch in terms of expiation and propitiation. Recent studies in the history of sacrifice have shown that propitiatory conceptions are neither original nor necessary to an understanding of sacrifice, and have stressed its meaning in terms of gifts offered to the deity for the enhancement of life and of divine-human communion. The notion that the Lord's Supper is, in any sense, a repetition or re-enactment of Christ's sacrifice, to appease an angry God, is not held by any reputable theologian, Catholic or Protestant. Rather the total act of its celebration, in offering, consecration, and communion, is a realization in the here and now of the reconciliation of men to God and to one another, wrought by the redeeming presence of Christ in the midst of His own people.

One other difference between Catholics and Protestants concerned the number of the sacraments. The former, following Peter Lombard and Thomas Aquinas, claimed there were seven sacraments, although the early Fathers of the Church had settled upon no determined number. Most Protestants accepted only two sacraments as instituted by Christ and therefore generally necessary to salvation: Baptism and the Lord's Supper. Lutherans, however, were inclined to receive also the sacrament of Penance. In recent times, many Anglicans have also acknowledged not only Penance to be a sacrament, but also the other four of medieval definition: Confirmation, Matrimony, Unction, and Holy Orders. That is, they would agree that these five rites are more than mere sacred signs, but they would not place them in the same rank as the gospel sacraments of Baptism and Lord's Supper.

The issue concerning the number of sacraments has been considerably tempered of late, however, by the recognition of the artificial value placed by the medievalists upon the number seven. It is now commonly admitted, for example, that in the early Church no clear distinction was drawn between Baptism and Confirmation, since both rites were part of a single complex of initiatory ceremonies that included also the celebration of the Eucharist. Twice a year, at Easter and at Pentecost, the Church observed the full sacramental mystery of participation in the death and resurrection of its Lord. This mystery conveyed the fullness of grace: the forgiveness of sin, rebirth as the adopted children of God, the gift of the Holy Spirit, incorporation into the Body of Christ, and the earnest of eternal life in the age to come.

The initiatory aspects of this "Easter mystery" were, of course, only performed once for each individual Christian believer. But the Eucharistic banquet was repeated, for the continual renewal of the Church's life in Christ, on Sundays and other major holy days that commemorated the Easter experience. Moreover, the reconciliation of penitents was usually associated with the Easter ceremonies, as a restoration of lapsed Christians to full communicant privilege, to repair them, so to speak, in the status that was theirs after their prime initiation. Thus Penance was a kind of substitute for a second Baptism and Confirmation. Unction and Holy Orders were always administered in association with the Eucharist; and for centuries the only marriage rites performed by the Church were nuptial celebrations of the Lord's Supper. The early Church did not think so much in terms of a specified number of distinct sacramental actions, as of varied sacramental applications of the one redemptive act of Christ for the edifying and ordering of His Church.

Sacramental theology today, both among Catholics and Protestants, is undergoing not only a great enrichment, but in some ways a fundamental re-orientation of perspective through the revival of biblical theology, the notable increase of interest in the writings of the early Church Fathers, and the exchange of viewpoints and experiences provided by the ecumenical movement toward Christian reunion. In the sacraments, the wholeness of the gospel of Jesus Christ is proclaimed and offered. The mighty acts of God in Christ, done once-for-all, in the life, death, resurrection, and exaltation of Christ for man's redemption, are made presently operative and effectual in the Body of Christ's members. The Kingdom of God, which Christ came to bring among men—the realm in which Christ is obeyed as Lord and whose citizens are obedient to His law of love—is actualized. And at the same time this experience of redemption in Christ and subjection to the demand of His sovereign rule is a real and present foretaste and earnest of the glorious consummation of God's purpose that shall be revealed in the last times. The sacraments are therefore mysteries in which the limitations of time are transcended. The historic, saving events and the future fulfillment that these events promise are appropriated here and now in the mystery presence of Christ and in the incorporation of His faithful ones as members one of another in Him. This mystery is accomplished by the Holy Spirit. The manifestation of the Spirit in the Church, by His operation in Word and Sacrament, is the assurance of Christ's continuing, universal presence in power to His Church in history and of the final transformation of the world in a new creation, of which the risen Christ is the first-fruits.

The understanding and appreciation of sacraments in the Church have been further enriched by modern studies in fields other than Bible and theology. Psychologists, for example, have pointed out the significance of sacramental worship as an engagement of the whole man, through actions that bring into play the bodily senses no less than the inner workings of mind and spirit. Many of the basic actions of sacraments, such as washing, eating, and drinking, correspond to deep-seated, unconscious desires in man for sustaining and intensifying the forces of life. The sacraments give direction to these fundamental drives in creative ways, beneficial both to the individual and society.

It is perhaps too early to assess what may be the full impact upon Christian sacramental theology of the newer currents in philosophy in the study of man's unique capacity of symbolization, whether through verbal signs or by dramatic actions. These new directions of inquiry touch inevitably upon myth and ritual, component elements in any sacramental rite; and they promise to teach us much about the importance of the Church's sacraments as instruments whereby men communicate with one another at the deepest levels of meaning, and seek to bring into a rational unity of understanding their total relationships with God and with one another in nature and in history.

MASSEY H. SHEPHERD, JR.

Bibliography

Neville Clark, *An Approach to the Theology of the Sacraments.*
F. W. Dillistone, *Christianity and Symbolism.*

SALVATION

"Salvation" has decisive importance in the vocabulary of theology because it points to an experience that is utterly central to faith itself. This experience may be characterized briefly as the gracious act of God whereby man is delivered from his sinful selfhood into newness and fullness of life. That is, salvation is something done in and for man by the will and work of God. To the Christian, this takes place "through Jesus Christ our Lord," since in Him God takes our conditions upon Himself, moves to bridge the gap which our own sin has caused, and empowers us to become what He intends us to be.

Thus the term salvation moves between certain polarities of meaning, rather than signifying a simple or static situation. The first of these concerns its negative and positive aspects. Salvation always signalizes a liberation or release; and this in turn implies a threat or danger to man from which he needs to be delivered. To be a man at all is to be involved in pain, loss, and estrangement—in short, to lead a precarious and even perilous existence. It means that one's very self is constantly menaced both from without and within by dark, destructive forces which are indicated by such words as sin, guilt, or death. Not only what the world can do to man, but what man can do to himself, is here in view. "The misery of man without God," to use Pascal's phrase, is therefore presupposed in every Christian rendering of salvation. There is that in man's own condition against which he needs to be guarded, from which he needs to be preserved or freed, and of which he must be made aware, however painfully or reluctantly.

And yet salvation ought not to be conceived as mere escapism. The possible deliverance from these evils which the Christian faith proclaims must be more strenuously understood. It is not that man is removed to a safe place in existence where danger cannot overtake him, but rather that he finds an unexpected—and undeserved—power to stand fast and not be shaken in the midst of danger. The security and integrity vouchsafed by God's saving act are ultimate and spiritual, not immediate and circumstantial. Thus the biblical writings generally insist on both the dubious and vulnerable character of human existence and the genuine possibility of liberation and preservation offered in the midst of and indeed in spite of all the perils that hedge man about.

The main stress in the Christian understanding of salvation is therefore upon the positive nature of the saved life. The word itself means health or wholeness of human being; more than safety alone, it has in mind essential soundness or completeness—the fullest and truest realization of a man's own powers and values. For the saved life means the human life dynamically transformed from within; this happens when man experiences in himself the same drive toward wholeness which moves throughout all levels of creation, and recognizes in this experience the forgiving, restoring, reconciling work of the Creator.

So we come to the second polarity embraced by the term salvation, that between the human and the divine factors to which the saving of man is jointly attributed. If human wholeness, as has been said, comes by way of divine enabling this does not mean that man contributes nothing to his own salvation. Neither does it mean that man is translated, so to speak, out of his finitude and creatureliness. It is when human life is founded upon openness to God, and only then, that salvation can occur. Such openness, or trust, or faith, may be described again and again in terms of receptivity or captivity, since this is actually the feel of the experience itself; but clearly it represents an arrival by means of man's own freedom at a situation where God can address him and act on his behalf. Paradoxical language is probably inescapable at this point; in affirming God man also affirms his true selfhood, but this is nonetheless a genuine self-affirmation rather than a self-negation.

Again, the saved life is the fully human life, spacious and unhindered, free for God. Yet its very freedom, in the sense of spontaneity and authenticity, can only be seen as the gift of God because it is also the desire and decision of man. In order for salvation to be God's real work in human life it cannot be exclusively God's work, utterly apart from all man's latent resources and existent capacities. It must represent instead their utilization and transformation. God must accept us if we are to accept Him, and this is not so much an external necessity placed upon God as it is the inner logic of the situation in which we stand before God. Here the theme of God's forgiveness comes surely to the fore, or what has been called the divine initiative, which does not contradict the place of human freedom in the plan of salvation but rather assumes it, addresses itself to it, and builds upon it. Yet one's last word, of course, must be that man's real freedom to be himself comes only by the surrender of all claims to isolated independence or self-mastery. Precisely this is what man contributes to his own salvation, which he must "work out by fear and trembling" for the very reason that "salvation belongs to God."

It is in Jesus Christ that God makes plain the ultimate conjunction between divine forgiveness and human fulfillment. To call Christ the way, the truth, and the life is to express this fact which is lived and known by those to whom this supreme disclosure has come. Whatever doctrine of the atonement we adopt, it points to the faith-fact that God in Christ was reconciling the world to Himself. We become aware that this is so insofar as we make ourselves accessible to the power of God which Christ makes available to us. Hence salvation is "by faith alone," which means to put one's life at God's disposal by holding oneself open and ready before His healing and forgiving grace. Still more concretely, it means accepting God's healing and forgiving grace. Still more concretely, it means accepting God's acceptance of us in Christ, since only love can rightly answer love. This truth, moreover, is not a matter of our knowing until it becomes a matter of our doing. God not only requires this of us, He enables us to fulfill it, through Jesus Christ who, in the words of Irenaeus, "became what we are that he might make us what he himself is."

ROGER HAZELTON

Bibliography

Donald M. Baillie, *God Was in Christ,* pp. 157-202.
David E. Roberts, *Psychotherapy and a Christian View of Man,* pp. 114-143.

SECULARISM

Secularism is a comparatively new concept in Christian theology. There is no evidence of its use as a specific concept before the nineteenth century, and it did not become widely used until the twentieth century. Not only is it a recent addition to theological discussion, it is also an ill-defined and ambiguous concept. Secularism has been used to define almost any spirit of opposition to Christianity regardless of the source of content of that opposition. Such a definition is so broad that it is useless; nevertheless, it is often encountered in contemporary theological polemic.

The ancient Roman Church distinguished between the sacred and the secular on the basis of the Church and the world. All that which was in and of the Church shared in the nature of the sacred. All which was of the world and that outside the Church was secular. Even the priests not in religious orders and serving in the parishes of the world were called "seculars" instead of "regulars."

Secular is derived from the Latin *saeculum* which means the age or the world. Rome had a complex yet simple theory of the relation between the secular and the sacred. The secular had its own proper base and function, but it only fulfilled its proper function insofar as it was completed by and under the direction of the sacred. The secular was to serve and be transformed by the sacred. The Church was to control the "world."

The Renaissance, in the name of human nature, and the Reformation, in the name of the gospel, destroyed the old pattern of the relation between the sacred and the secular. Both protested against the Church's domination and control over the world. Nevertheless, they moved in different directions. The Renaissance combined with a series of complex historical factors to produce a spirit of autonomy in society and culture. Autonomy is the basis of what has come to be called secularism.

Autonomy asserts the essential non-religiousness of all structures of life. The age or the world is to be understood completely on its own basis. Man and the world are the measure of all things. Nothing unconditional is encountered through culture or through human reason. If religion emerges, it is only the glorification of one of the facets of this life—of reason, of the vitalities, of aesthetics, or of the state. Thus, secularism centers on the world and seeks to make life meaningful completely apart from God, from the source of life, or from anything unconditional.

As a consequence, a culture and society developed that had all the external marks of Christian influence and insight but lacked genuine Christian foundations. It was, in fact, a post-Christian or a genuinely secular culture. The Church remained, ethics and mores still appeared to be Christian, but the religious substance that produced them was dissipated. This was especially true in those nations where the churches retained establishment and special privileges. Neither religious liberty nor church establishment prevented the growth of a secular culture.

A more drastic consequence was the eruption of demonic forces that smashed even the remaining Christian forms of ethics and mores. Both Fascism and Communism represented an extreme consequence of a strictly secularist point of view. One found ultimate meaning in the vitalities of blood and race. The other located the meaningfulness of life in a dialectic of history that would produce the triumph of the proletariat. Secularism removed all concern with the ultimate and sought fulfillment only in this age, this world, this life. But it was not enough. Life was not endurable without divinizing some structure or facet of life itself. So infinite pretensions were made in behalf of finite reality.

Protestantism stands in a peculiar relationship to secularism. On the one hand, it helped to produce secularism. By its very nature Protestantism affirms the rights, privileges, and relative autonomy of various facets of life. It broke the control of the medieval Roman Church over art, literature, politics, and society. Protestantism asserted the absolute necessity of a secular reality. Human reason and aesthetic capacities had rights of their own that could not be controlled or fulfilled by the Church. Furthermore, these centers in culture were often sources of necessary judgment against the pretensions and perversions of the Church. To suppress or to control secular culture, Protestantism argued, was to destroy and pervert a creation of God in the name of God.

To be sure, Protestantism had no clear, unambiguous understanding of the relation between the sacred and the secular. It was positive about only two points. Protestantism was committed to defending the relative autonomy of the secular world, yet it was equally committed to affirming that all areas of life were responsible to God. This ambiguity has placed Protestantism in an exceedingly difficult position. History reflects the working of its peculiar relation to the secular.

A variety of ways were developed by Protestantism to assure that all facets of life reflected a divine source. Yet, in doing this it often destroyed the relative autonomy of so-called secular life. Puritanism in New England sought and maintained a rigid control over the total culture. However, the very nature of Protestantism broke through this structure. Though convinced that God had revealed His nature and will preeminently in the creation of the new community, the Church, Protestantism was equally convinced that service to God was also to be found in the faithful pursuit of the diverse activities of life.

The problem of Rome has always been the devaluation of the secular in order to enhance the role of the Church. But even where the Church has succeeded in maintaining control, the culture has often succumbed to the secular. Protestantism is caught in a different situation. It is difficult to assert simultaneously the relative autonomy of the secular order and the primacy of the Christian vision of life. Because Protestantism has accepted the relative autonomy of the secular and now lives in an age when the secular asserts complete autonomy, it is constantly tempted to blame all evils on the triumph of secularism. This it can never do.

There is a concerted effort in contemporary Christian theology to discover, while rejecting secularism, new means of nurturing and appreciating the secular. It is an attempt both to discover how the secular points beyond itself and to educate the secular to acknowledge within itself an unconditional element. Such an attempt rejects all efforts to make the secular self-sufficient. In this way the relative autonomy of the secular order and the primacy of the Christian vision of life are both maintained.

JERALD C. BRAUER

Bibliography

E. E. Aubrey, *Secularism a Myth.*
Paul Tillich, *The Protestant Era.*

THE SELF

The concept of the self has been current in popular usage for ages but it has not, until recently, been a respectable scientific or philosophical concept. In philosophy, the self was divided into body and mind in the thought of Plato and Aristotle; and Western thought, whether idealistic or naturalistic, followed this way of looking at the self. Kant spoke of the "self of transcendental apperception," but he meant the analytical and logical tools which the human mind used in organizing experience. Hume was dubious about whether there was an experience of self-identity. He reasoned that when one experienced the self one always experienced the self engaged in the act of perception, and therefore one did not have a pure experience of selfhood. Idealistic philosophers, such as Bosanquet, regarded individual selfhood as a defect from which a purer rationality must extricate the mind. The mystic tradition since Plotinus, although clear that there was a particular self when viewed as an object, called attention nevertheless to the mystery of the indeterminately receding self when viewed as subject. It could, however, in the view of Plotinus, be finally separated by a process of introversion from particular selfhood and become identical with universal consciousness. In this conviction Western mysticism agreed with the mysticism of the Orient in which the final redemption of the particular self issued in a state of identity between the human and the divine self. "Brahman and Atman are one." Freudian psychology speaks of the "ego" or the coherent self and of its complicated relation with the lower "id" or the sum of man's instinctual drives and impulses. But it denies any capacity of self-transcendence and defines the "super-ego" as the force of the social disciplines of the community upon the self. The more objective psychologists are uncertain whether it is possible to speak of the self, except in language of poetry, as distinct from its organism or its mind. This is to say that psychological scientists are as prone as were classical and modern philosophers to separate the self into two parts, mind and body. In the process it becomes unclear whether there is such an identity as the self, though the language of common sense persists in speaking of "myself" and "yourself"; and the poets and the dramatists have never doubted that they were dealing with integral entities in picturing the *Dramatis Personae* of their tales and stories.

The most obvious reason for the different approach to the self by common sense and art on the one hand, and the more speculative disciplines on the other hand, is given in the incongruity of the character of human selfhood. The human personality is involved in the flux of nature, dependent upon its necessities and limited by its ends. It is also capable of transcending the natural flux, both by its rational and analytical faculties, which enable it to make itself, as well as the world, the object of its thought and by a further capacity to transcend its own rational faculties and, as a perennially particular subject, to make its own organism and rational faculty the object of its contemplation.

Augustine was the first great thinker of the West to emphasize the reality of the transcendent self. He insisted that it was the self, or the "I," which operated in all of its faculties. "It is I who remember in my memory, and understand in my understanding, and will in my will," he declared. The Augustinian emphasis upon the self is the fountain source of what has become known as the "existentialist" philosophy, of which the Danish philosopher and theologian, Sören Kierkegaard, was the most noted nineteenth-century exponent. He set the term, the "existing individual," against the idealistic system of the philosophers, more particularly Hegel, and insisted that no conception of "essence" could do justice to the freedom and finiteness of the existing individual. The incongruity of individual existence must be apprehended by "passionate inwardness" or "passionate subjectivity"; that is to say, not by the study of essences and structures, but by a subjective awareness of the incongruity.

Kierkegaard's existentialism has influenced many philosophers who have not shared his Christian faith. Heidegger has elaborated existentialism into a prescription for "authentic" as contrasted with "unauthentic" existence. The contrast is between individual existence which drifts into anonymity and complacency and one which asserts the unique freedom of the human spirit in defiance of the threat of death.

Karl Jaspers has been influenced by both Kierkegaard and Nietzsche to examine the limits of rational analysis and scientific objectivity in exploring the depth and height of selfhood and the corresponding mystery of what he defines as "transcendence"—an undogmatic reference to the mystery of existence, which, like the mystery of human selfhood, exceeds the limits of rational comprehension.

The French existentialist, Sartre, has gone one step further in emphasizing the unique and radical freedom of the self transcending self. He denies that freedom is conditioned by any essential nature. "There is no human nature," declares Sartre, "since there is no God to have a conception of it. Man simply is. . . . Man is nothing else but that which he makes of himself." Thus, in the emphasis upon pure freedom, including the freedom to make of himself what man desires and decides, the pendulum has swung to the opposite extreme from Aristotle's conception of man's essential nature. In time a more sober consideration of the paradox of human freedom and finiteness will undoubtedly prevail. There is an incongruity in the heart of human existence, because man is both a creature of nature and a free spirit, capable of rising indeterminately in his creativity above both natural limits and conditions. Kierkegaard thought that this incongruity could be grasped only by passionate inwardness, but it is subject to analysis if the observer is aware of the incongruity and does not obscure one or the other aspect of it by trying to fit human nature into some simple system of rational or natural coherence.

REINHOLD NIEBUHR

SERMON

One of the Christian's continuing problems has been God's problem from the beginning: communicating, getting through, saying what has to be said in the way most apt to be heard. The Old Testament, seen so, is the record of God's ancient effort to make His will known, to speak not only to a nation but to the world through a nation. The Christian claim is that the decisive breakthrough, the ultimate address is in Jesus Christ. What we know of God in Jesus Christ becomes the measure by which we identify and interpret other communications.

Christ is the distinctly pronounced Word in whom we find the sense of all the rest of God's communications which otherwise hang like troubling hints in the world's memory.

To the Church falls the task of repeating, extending, italicizing God's communication with the world. Before ever it improves manners or reforms morals or binds up wounds or feeds the hungry, the Church has news to proclaim. This proclamation is the first reason for the Church's existence. The Church is the sign of God's successful communication; the Church lives to keep that word sounding, to amplify that word in the world. The urgency of God's communication is now the urgency of believers' proclamation.

This proclamation, of course, does not have to be all verbal, any more than God's communication in Christ was all verbal. Protestant Christians especially have to remind themselves of this obvious fact. For Protestants have been tempted too often to make their service of the Word all wordy.

Again, both Catholic and Protestant Christianity have missed too often what is probably the prime proclaimer: the Christian life. It was in a particular life and death that God finally broke through. And it is by lives and deaths reflecting that one that the world's attention still can be directed to the news which quite literally makes all the difference in the world. Christian proclamation is not all cerebral and oral; it is vital, whole. The lives and works of people still speak for God, turning others to the prime life and work in which God spoke decisively, determinatively.

But when the proclamation has been well celebrated, painted, sung, lived, there is still need for thoughtful, verbal explication of the good news of God. There is also need for spoken invitation, for specific bidding to company with the Christ who is God's Word. This part of the proclamation can be impromptu or contrived, conversational or literary, public or private. It can come from anybody, anywhere, any time. But one of the com-

ponents in the rites of Christian worship, the sermon, is
the usual means for this articulated, logical witness.

The sermon is reasoned address about God's address
to men. Though it is sometimes done with virtuosity it
is not a showpiece. Though it is reflective it is not a
lecture. Though it may be written down and published
it is not essentially literary. It is person to person, face
to face correspondence; a hearer, telling; one who has
met a Person, presenting Him.

A sermon is a man speaking and men hearing, in the
context of worship, about a God who has spoken and a
Church that has heard. As such, the sermon is not the
main point of our worship; the sermon is at the service
of our worship, the part of worship which shows the
whole point of our worship. But where a sermon obtrudes,
tries to take over, is not content to systemize and state
the whole sense of the whole worship, there a sermon
fails and devotion is flawed.

So does a sermon fail when it is interpreted as a
preacher's performance, a pulpiteer's production, an ora-
tion to be listened to. A true sermon is none of these
things. It is a communication, it is a straight telling which
must be heard or there is no communication. So congregations are as involved in sermons as are preachers. A
sermon is not just something said, but something heard,
too. All Christians within hearing are a part of a sermon.
Only one man may talk, but the sermon is as much the
reaction and response in the pew as it is the utterance
in the pulpit. Congregations are not audiences; they are
participants, taking into themselves what is spoken, determining by what the words do to them and what they
do to the words what the sermon finally is.

No sermon is a preacher's free creation. The communication he will point to in his address is God's very own.
The whole point of all the preacher's saying will be what
God has already said. And the congregation's apprehension of what the preacher says will operate too in deciding
what the sermon turns out to be. The preacher's part,
between the Beginner and the finishers of all sermons,

is to order his thoughts, relating them both to God's answer and to man's questions, invoking God's blessing on the attempt and his hearers' cooperation in the endeavor. A sermon is an ordered event within worship in which words spoken and words thought are put at the immediate service of the Word.

THEODORE A. GILL

Bibliography

Emil Brunner, *The Divine-Human Encounter.*

SIN

The original scriptural definition of sin is "missing the mark," but that definition does not exhaust the connotations which the concept has achieved; moreover, some of its current connotations, particularly those which identify sin with sexual irregularities, are certainly too conventional to comprehend what is meant by sin in classical Christian thought.

Since Augustine it has been the consistent view of Christian orthodoxy that the basic sin of man was his pride. In this view Christian thought agreed with the conception of the Greek tragedies, which regarded *hybris* as man's most flagrant fault and one which was invariably followed by punishment or *nemesis*. The basic sin of pride does not mean some conscious bit of exaggerated self-esteem, but the general inclination of all men to overestimate their virtues, powers, and achievements. Augustine defined sin as the "perverse desire of height," or as man's regarding himself as his own end, instead of realizing that he is but a part of a total scheme of means and ends.

The traditional view is that sin began with the "Fall of Adam." Those who hold more optimistic views of human nature believe that the doctrine of the Fall is an unwarranted pessimism. Such critics contend that the assessment of excessive self-regard as a universal human weakness is derived from a dogma which is in turn derived from a primitive myth. Actually the view that men are "sinful" is one of the best attested and empirically verified facts of human existence. It has been obscured by those philosophies having their rise in the Enlightenment. Such philosophies either derived the evils of human history from specific causes (as for instance the Marxists, who derived it from the institution of property) or regarded social evil as due to the inertia of ignorance or natural passion or social institutions. The implication of such views was that the release of human reason from the bondage of such inertia would gradually overcome the prejudices, passion and parochial loyalties of ignorant human beings.

The answer to the question as to whether the concept of sin is still meaningful in modern life depends upon the power of the rational faculty to master the power of interest and passion. If the self can be mastered by reason, sin is an outmoded concept. But if the self is able to continue to use its rational faculties as instruments of its own interests, the concept remains meaningful. The two non-religious thinkers of modern times whose estimates of human nature correspond to those of religious pessimism were Hobbes and Freud. Hobbes held the view that reason was invariably the tool of the self's interest. "Rational" men distinguished themselves from brutes, not in achieving some end which transcended their interests, but in giving their interests a range which brutes could not achieve. Hobbes therefore approached a view of man which has sometimes been defined as that of "total depravity." He failed to recognize that the freedom of man over natural impulse was the source of both creativity and destructiveness in men, of both the inclination to justice and the inclination to take advantage of other men.

Freud's pessimism derived from the fact that he regarded the "ego," or the rational and coherent self, as an uneasy broker between the pleasure-seeking "id" and the "super-ego" which was the sum total of the social disciplines in which the self was involved. Freud was therefore pessimistic about the course of civilization because he felt that the increasingly complex disciplines of a cultured community would repress the id-ego more and more, and that these repressions would result in aggressive tendencies. Both forms of pessimism are probably too pronounced because neither fully comprehends the paradox of human freedom and the creative and destructive capacities which arise from man's transcendence over the immediate ends and desires of nature.

The concept of "original sin" is even more offensive to most modern men than the concept of sin. Its original meaning was "inherited sin" or *"erbsuende,"* and Christian orthodoxy explained it as a taint which all men inherited from the fallen Adam. The concept had no place in Jewish thought. This gives rise to some interpretations which contrast the so-called optimism of Judaism with the pessimism of Christianity. Actually the Jewish doctrine of the "evil inclination" (*yetzer ha-ro*) which every man has inherited is almost identical with the Christian doctrine of original sin. In fact, Jesus knew nothing of the Pauline doctrine of an inherited sin, but spoke only in terms of the rabbinic doctrine of the evil inclination.

Whatever may be the traditional doctrine, the real issue is the universality of the corruption which results from undue self-regard. Certainly no one would regard a traditional doctrine of a transmission of evil from generation to generation as meaningful. But the idea of a universal inclination in the human heart or self is not only meaningful but is empirically verifiable. It means merely that the capacity and inclination of the self to give its interests undue regard can arise on every level of culture and of moral attainment. The taints of vanity in the lives of the saints would attest to the inclination as well as the power lusts of a Napoleon or Hitler. The universality of the taint does not preclude the possibility of mitigating or aggravating egotism by education, social engineering, cultural disciplines, or any other method of channeling or transfiguring man's basic and inordinate self-regard. Nor would it preclude the relation of this self-regard to all forms of creativity. Actually all creative impulses are probably inextricably related to the self-regarding ones, but not in such a way that the latter are absolute prerequisites of the former. It is significant that political science usually presupposes some version of the doctrine of original sin despite the unpopularity of the concept in modern culture since the Enlightenment.

REINHOLD NIEBUHR

SOCIETY

The problem of society for Christian thought takes at least four forms. 1) The Church is a society; it needs to be understood sociologically as well as theologically. 2) The relation of the Church to its social context is a perennial problem both for normative theories of the Church and for programs of evangelism and moral action. 3) Implicit if not explicit conceptions of the nature of social existence are involved at many points in theology and ethics. 4) There is a concern for the "good" society.

The metaphors used to understand the Church are similar in many instances to those used to understand other social groups. E.g., the idea of the "Body" of Christ is an organismic analogy that also occurs in secular social thought. The Church is both an "institution" and a "community." For sectarian theories institutional forms are secondary and in some instances considered to be only necessary evils; the true Church is a spiritual fellowship, e.g., Emil Brunner's idea of the Church. In Catholic theories institutional forms are of the very being of the Church, or at least necessary for its well-being.

The relations of the Church and Christ to culture have been delineated in two important typologies in modern Protestantism. First, Ernst Troeltsch characterized "sect-type" religious bodies in part in terms of their rejection of culture and secular society. This was done to create morally and religiously pure communities. "Church-type" bodies seek to make the Church co-extensive with the society in which it exists; there is an open attitude toward the culture. Underlying these differences are two types of factors: a) theological differences, e.g., Christ as judging Lord for the sects, and Christ as redeemer and sanctifier of life for the churches; and b) social differences, e.g., the sects tend to thrive among the socially disinherited; churches tend to flourish among those who have achieved an important level of social and cultural status. In North America the "denomination" is a phenomenon located on the continuum between sect and church; it seeks to have an impact on society and culture without either dominating or absorbing them.

Second, H. Richard Niebuhr, in *Christ and Culture*, has delineated five theological positions pertaining to the relation of Christ to culture and society. "Christ against culture" characterizes the sectarian position. Christ is sole authority over the Christian; the culture's claim to loyalty is resolutely rejected. The "Christ of culture" position characterizes those who feel no tension between world and Church, social behavior and gospel. "Christ above culture" positions are grounded in the idea that a synthesis between Christ and society is possible in which both are affirmed without complete separation and without full identification of the two. A radical dualism is involved in the "Christ and culture in paradox" position. The depravity of man and society makes an easy imposition of Christ on society impossible, yet society is one realm in which the Christian must live. Finally, many understand Christ to be "the transformer of culture"; i.e., while taking seriously human corruption (as do the dualists) they affirm that culture is under God's rule, and Christians must undertake social responsibility in obedience to God. These types of relation occur throughout history.

c) Notions of the nature and function of society are involved in Christian thought at many points, but particularly in theological method and in ethics. In the former there has been a trend since the nineteenth century which sees the Christian community (the Church) as the social source of our Christian knowledge of God. In Ritschl and H. R. Niebuhr there is a strong sense of the significance of "the sociology of religious knowledge," i.e., the manner in which the meanings of religious ideas are closely bound to the society in which they emerged and continue to be expounded. Religious ideas are not simply social projections; they are revelatory of God's being; but the social dimension of our apprehension and understanding of the revelation is seriously considered.

In ethics, social understanding moves toward the two poles noted in the *Gemeinschaft-Gesellschaft* distinction of German sociology, i.e., society as essentially a personal community in which important unity exists without formal structures, and society as associations in which there are concentrations of purpose and power in formal organizations. The ethics of the communal, interpersonal understanding stress the importance of the Church as a community of believers out of which Christian moral action occurs, as in F. D. Maurice, Horace Bushnell, and in contemporary writing, Paul Lehmann and Alexander Miller. The ethics of an institutional understanding stress the need for countervailing powers to achieve relative justice in the depersonalized structures of international relations or the domestic economy, as in Reinhold Niebuhr. These two poles obviously are not mutually exclusive.

d) Various Christian groups have held conceptions of the "good society," Roman Catholic and Anglican ethics shape their visions around exposition of natural moral principles and Christology. Thus in Roman Catholic ethics, e.g., Maritain's or those of the papal social encyclicals, a new humanistic synthesis analogous to that of medieval society is constructed. It calls, for example, for the representation of the interests of labor and consumers in industrial management. The Christendom Group of the Church of England (Dement, Reckitt, et al.) developed comparable proposals in the light of the English situation. Protestants, with a minimum of the positive content given in the natural law tradition, and relying heavily on the Bible for authority, have tended to identify the good Christian society more readily with particular phases of Western social development. Thus Walter Rauschenbusch saw the Christian society in terms of a democratic socialism similar to that of the liberal reform movements of 1890-1920. Other contemporary popular writers seek to identify the Christian society with Herbert Spencer's *laissez-faire* order of life. Recent Protestant Christian social ethics have been averse to the development of blueprints of the good society. They begin with a recognition of the temptation to absolutize highly relative historical movements, and accept a state of relative good and evil in human history. The fulfillment of life in God's Kingdom will come in the end of time. Yet within the morally ambiguous structures we can act as Christians; principles for the illumination of our situation and for guidance in action come from our Christian heritage and from many other sources. E.g., see the ethics of the Niebuhrs, Brunner, Bonhoeffer, and others.

JAMES GUSTAFSON

Bibliography

H. R. Niebuhr, *Christ and Culture.*
Reinhold Niebuhr, *Moral Man and Immoral Society.*

SOUL (BODY)

The very juxtaposition of the words "soul (body)" indicates the problems involved in defining either word. For Christian thought, standing as the inheritor of both Greek and Hebraic traditions, has lived for centuries with an ambiguity resulting from the fact that, broadly speaking, in Greek thought "soul" is defined in dualistic opposition to "body," while in Hebraic thought no such dualism can be discovered and the ideas which the two words convey cannot clearly be distinguished from one another. In lieu of an exhaustive linguistic analysis, which is not possible here, only the conclusions of contemporary thinking can be suggested; detailed treatment is given in the bibliographical suggestions.

In Greek thought, particularly as it comes from Orphism and as it is expressed in the earlier Platonic dialogues, there is a marked dualism between the soul and the body. The soul belongs to a divine, eternal realm, and is the undying, indestructible part of man, which is unfortunately confined to the body during life on earth. The body is nothing but a hindrance to the soul. Salvation thus involves the extrication of the soul from the body, the immortal part of man ultimately finding release from the confines of the finite, mortal body. An old Greek proverb sums up the belief: "The body is the prison-house of the soul."

This way of thinking is so deeply imbedded in Western culture that it is often difficult to see how sharply differentiated from it is the biblical assessment. The word "soul" in particular, has a very different meaning for the biblical writers, than the understanding which modern Christians have usually assigned to it. The Old Testament word *nephesh* basically means "breath," and the term is often used simply to designate "a living being" (not always a human, sometimes an animal), and the word, along with the New Testament equivalent, *psyche,* can mean "life," and even "person" or "self." Thus it is clear that the term is much broader in biblical usage than is commonly supposed. It can be taken to stand for the *unity* of personality, as Hebraic thought conceived of man as a unity rather than as a duality of body and soul.

The meaning can be further clarified by noting its relationship to the word "body." In Pauline thought, for example, the body (*soma*) is an inclusive word for the psycho-physical unity of the flesh (*sarx*) and soul (*psyche*). No hard and fast distinction between the two can be established. The body is the whole man, and not a detachable part of man which is distinguished in dualistic fashion from the soul. J. A. T. Robinson, summarizing a discussion of the matter, says: "Man does not have a body; he is a body . . . He is flesh-animated-by-soul, the whole conceived as a psychophysical unity" (*The Body*).

That this is not just a Pauline idiosyncrasy, is made clear by the results of Old Testament scholarship as well. H. Wheeler Robinson makes clear that the same idea of unity pervades the Old Testament. "The idea of human nature [in the Old Testament] implies a unity, not a dualism. There is no contrast between the body and the soul, such as the terms instinctively suggest to us" (*Religious Ideas of the Old Testament,* p. 83). Again, "The Hebrew idea of personality is an animated body and not an incarnated soul." J. Pedersen (in *Israel,* p. 171) goes so far as to say, "The body is the soul in its outward form." There is, in fact, no distinctive word for "body" in Hebrew; such a word is not needed because there is no separate part of man, distinct from his "soul," which needs to be so distinguished. It is interesting to note that this very ancient sense of the interrelatedness and unity of the human personality is being substantiated by modern research in psychosomatic medicine, the very name of which (*psyche-soma,* or "soulbody") shows the impossibility of a cleavage between the body and the soul.

The Hebraic view, then, makes necessary a different assessment of the human personality than is supplied by the familiar distinction between body and soul, and indicates that the underlying fact is unity rather than duality. D. R. G. Owen concludes a long survey of the New Testament materials with the comment: "There is little trace of body-soul dualism; instead, man is regarded as a unity. This personal unity that is man can be called, as a whole, either *soma* (body) or *psyche* (soul) or *sarx* (flesh) or *pneuma* (spirit), depending on the point of view from which man is being considered, but the point is that none of these terms refers to a part of man; they all refer to the whole" (*Body and Soul,* p. 196).

ROBERT MCAFEE BROWN

Bibliography

D. R. G. Owen, *Body and Soul.*
H. W. Robinson, *The Christian Doctrine of Man, The Religious Ideas of the Old Testament,* Ch. IV.
J. A. T. Robinson, *In the End, God.*
J. A. T. Robinson, *The Body.*

SPIRIT

The notion of "spirit" has too often been treated integrally with "the Holy Spirit"; for, while the two are necessarily related and very possibly are implicates of each other, "spirit" has to do with the human and "Holy Spirit" refers primarily to the divine. The "tripartite" nature of man, recognized by Christian tradition from Irenaeus to Erasmus, has regarded man as a complex of body, soul, and spirit. When the term "spirit" has been elided from this definition, as in Boethius, the temptation toward intellectualism sets in. If man is an "individual substance of a rational nature," as Boethius held, the self is tempted to divinize itself by virtue of its rational part. On the other hand, if "spirit" is stressed too much, as by Erasmus, the self may be tempted to deify itself by virtue of spirit. "The spirit makes us gods; the flesh makes us beasts; the soul makes us men," was Erasmus' view. No doubt he was seeking in the "soul" a proper mean between the other two; but man's proneness to overreach himself makes the formula dangerous. "If there were gods how could I bear not to be one," said Nietzsche. It would appear that Irenaeus' formula is best: the perfect man, said he,

"Consists of these three, flesh, soul, and spirit. One of these saves and fashions—that is, the Spirit. Another is united and formed—that is, the flesh; while that which lies between the two is the soul, which sometimes follows the Spirit and is raised by it, but at other times sympathizes with the flesh and is drawn by it into earthly passions." (*Ad. Haer.* V. ix. 1)

We are today a bit restive, however, with those views of human nature which divide man into "parts," however defined, and tend thereby either to scorn the "flesh" and deny its proper claims or to neglect the wholeness of the self and its dynamisms. We are suspicious equally of the angelic escape into an otherworldliness of the "spirit" and of the demonic escape into some obsessive assertiveness of the ego-centered "self." In times when the self is thrust back upon itself the term "spirit" functions descriptively as the central or core concept of the inner psyche or ground of being of the authentic "self."

Kierkegaard was seeking such a view when, in response to the question "what is man?" he replied, "Man is spirit. But what is spirit? Spirit is the self. But what is the self? The self is a relation which relates itself to its own self . . ." by virtue of a third term, the term of its relation to the ground of being. In Kierkegaard's words, "by relating itself to its own self and by willing to be itself the self is grounded transparently in the Power which posited it" (*The Sickness Unto Death,* tr. by Walter Lowrie, pp. 17, 19). Theologically this implies its grounding in being understood as the sustaining power of the Holy Spirit; psychologically, it means that "synthesizing" of all the terms of its conscious and unconscious conflicts by bringing its energies into productive accord with its real and authentic "spirit" or being.

Clearly Saint Paul had a similar view in mind when he distinguished (in the *Epistle to the Romans*) between the "carnal" self and the "spiritual" self. In so far as the self was not faithfully related to God it became carnally minded. (This is not the partitioned "flesh" of Irenaeus and Erasmus, an Hellenic view; but is the non-Godly, and therefore anti-Godly, orientation of the self *as a whole*.) In so far as the self is related to God in faith it is spiritually minded. Thus Barth is justified in commenting that "he who has encountered the Spirit existentially has encountered his own existential existence in God." (*The Epistle to the Romans,* 6th ed., tr. by Edwyn C. Hoskins, p. 237.) It is this "mind of the Spirit," which Saint Paul identifies with "the Spirit of Christ" (Rom. 8:9) which is life and peace.

STANLEY ROMAINE HOPPER

Bibliography

Nicolas Berdyaev, *Freedom and the Spirit.*
Sören Kierkegaard, *The Sickness unto Death.*
Anders Nygren, *Commentary on Romans.*

SYMBOL

Symbol (from the Greek *symballein,* which means "to throw together") is a pattern or object which points to an invisible metaphysical reality and participates in it. In this participation symbols differ from myths, for the latter tell about the metaphysical *beyond* but do not represent it. Symbols are conceived by vision or intuition, not by means of rational thinking (in the Bible: the visions of Ezekiel or the Revelation of John; or in the Middle Ages: the visions of Hildegard of Bingen). While allegory and typology may be considered methods of interpretation, the symbol is itself an ontological category. In modern usage the terms symbol and symbolism do not—as it was formerly often understood—mean something which is opposed to reality, but, on the contrary, they embrace reality.

Symbols are not rigidly fixed, but are flexible, comprising a complexity of connotations (fish is both the symbol of death and life). To the extent that the symbol hints at the divine it forms a link between the human and the superhuman. Symbolism, as that language of the mind which expresses what is beyond rational recognition, serves to distinguish the human from the animal world. Animals react to signals, not symbols. The signal belongs only to the physical world and is therefore clearly separated from the symbol. Only man has formed "a symbolic universe of which language, myth, art, religion are part" (Cassirer). Not only modern philosophy, but certain schools of psychology and art-philosophy as well have rediscovered the importance of symbolism, cf. C. G. Jung's contention that the symbolic world of dreams often exposes ancient archetypes.

Symbolism in the past and present. The rich tradition of pagan religious symbolism (the circle and swastika of prehistoric times; the sacred King, Father, Mother, etc.; the nature-symbolism of Northern Europe) supplies the fundament of symbolic tradition on which Christianity draws. Christian belief, based on the complex unity of Christ's death and resurrection, requires symbols in order to express the unity of truth in which it believes and for which it hopes.

The New Testament uses symbols freely. *Christian art,* adopting pagan symbols, has filled them with new meaning (the fish, for example, combines pre-Christian values with the Christian hope of eternal life). There is a widespread symbolism of *animals* (phoenix, lamb, dove, eagle, etc.), *plants* (vine, tree of life, laurel, etc.), *geometric signs* (cross, triangle, star, etc.), *objects* (crown, wheel), and many other similar groups or clusters of symbolic usage. All these symbols are not isolated phenomena, but parts forming the powerful symbolic realm in which the life and death of the early and medieval Christian took place.

The task of the modern scholar is: a) to explain the meaning of the symbols of early Christianity on the basis of contemporary categories of understanding, and b) to discriminate between genuine symbolism (the baptismal rite, for example) and the *post hoc* symbolic interpretation which later writers have given to things which originally possessed no symbolic relevance.

Symbolism is not restricted to visible images, but is also at home with the *spoken word* (cf. the pagan mystery cults and the importance of the "holy word"). The outstanding example of this usage in Christianity is the Apostle's Creed, the *"symbolum apostolicum."* Spoken at baptism the creed presented a true symbol, a sacramental key and password opening "the entrance into life everlasting," an "ever-present guard," giving "great protection" (Ambrose). Besides this creed, all of the official creeds of the universal church are called "symbols."

The creed originated in connection with the baptismal rite, i.e., with the sacramental core of Christian worship. The earliest and major sacraments of the Christian Church, baptism and the eucharist, are essentially symbolic in the sense previously defined, since they embrace death and resurrection. Their elements are parts of the ritual initiate's participation in the body of Christ. Herein lie the roots of the symbolic character of Christian *liturgy*, with its objects, language, gestures, colors, vestments.

The task of reinterpretation. While for the Middle Ages the symbolic realm was meaningful, the modern secularized world has lost touch with it. The symbols of the past are to a great extent dead. Yet symbols need life and interpretation in order to be true. The question as to how much of the New Testament can speak to us today depends on our ability to reinterpret adequately its symbolic imagery and language. It is the task of our time to "rediscover the questions to which the Christian symbols are the answers in a way which is understandable to our time" (Paul Tillich). This task lies not only with theology. Poetry and the arts (especially abstract art), which have opened our mind and eye to the understanding of symbolic forms, also have an important task to perform.

ERIKA DINKLER-VON SCHUBERT

Bibliography

Ernst Cassirer, *The Philosophy of Symbolic Forms; Language and Myth.*
Herbert Read, *Icon and Idea.*
Max Schlesinger, *Geschichte des Symbols.*
Paul Tillich, *Systematic Theology I.*

THOMISM

Thomism is the embracing term by which the philosophical and theological teachings of St. Thomas Aquinas (1225-1274) and his followers are expressed. Recommended for special consideration by Pope Leo XIII in the encyclical *Aeterni Patris* (1879), these teachings, variously interpreted, are followed to a greater or lesser extent by most Roman Catholic thinkers, as well as by certain other philosophers and theologians.

Thomism synthesizes divergent viewpoints and so presents a remarkably comprehensive description of reality and experience. In philosophy, it is partially Aristotelian. Thus its theory of knowledge is empiricist, for it insists on the sense origin of all knowledge, rejects Platonic, Augustinian (q.v.) and idealist views of cognition, and employs cosmological, rather than ontological, arguments for the existence of God. It combines this empirical orientation with an intellectualist account of the power of reason and its superiority to will, unites this with a pluralistic metaphysics of separate individual substances, and by means of its doctrine of the soul as the "substantial form of the body," maintains a naturalistic emphasis on the psycho-

physical unity of man. These Aristotelian views are reconciled with a modified Platonic doctrine of the immortality
of the soul, as well as with a somewhat monistic Neo-
Platonic metaphysics which maintains both divine immanence and transcendence and declares that there is an
"analogy of being" between God and creatures, for these
latter exist only by participating in God's being. Yet
pantheism and determinism are avoided, and the Christian
doctrines of creation and of the radical otherness and
freedom of God are preserved, by means of the view that
creatures are fundamentally dynamic acts of existence,
limited by their essences, while God alone is pure act in
whom essence and existence are identical. In ethics, Thomism is naturalistic in that it holds that a consideration of
nature leads to the discovery of natural moral laws. However, rational reflection also shows that nature needs to be
perfected by supernatural revelation and grace, for man's
desires are essentially, though implicitly, directed toward
infinite goodness and happiness and so can be satisfied only
by an eternal vision of God which man cannot by his own
strength attain.

Thus Thomism combines great confidence in the power
of reason with an emphasis on the need for faith. It holds
that philosophy is, in principle, independent of faith in
revelation; yet they complement each other, for that part
of philosophy which deals with God—natural theology—
prepares the way for faith. Faith, in turn, provides
guidance to the Christian Thomist. Assured that the truths
of reason and revelation cannot contradict each other, as
God is the source of both, he undertakes to show the
irrationality of views which oppose faith.

In revealed theology, Thomism largely follows traditional teachings, especially those of St. Augustine. Its
originality lies in its greater use of reason to systematize
and defend such doctrines as the Trinity, incarnation,
predestination, grace and sacraments. These cannot be
proved to be true and so must be accepted by faith rather
than reason; yet reason can show that they are not irrational and that belief in them is not unreasonable.

From the Thomist point of view, other theological approaches are narrow and therefore irrationalist. Augustinians imperil reason and philosophy by not clearly distinguishing them from theology and faith. Much liberal theology concentrates on individual religious experience at the expense of reason and the Church.

Theologians of the Reformation tradition (e.g., Karl Barth) so over-emphasize sin, on the one hand, and revelation, on the other, as to lose sight of the analogy of being between the divine and the human. They therefore err by denying that some goodness remains in sinful man, and that genuine natural knowledge of God is possible. Existentialists, and those who describe revelation and faith as an "I-Thou encounter between God and man," forget that revealed truth also has genuinely objective aspects. Thomists try to show that each of these approaches is true in what it asserts but false in what it denies. Each is one-sided, and so fails to satisfy that need for the systematic and inclusive understanding of reality which Thomism seeks to supply.

GEORGE LINDBECK

Bibliography

Etienne Gilson, *The Christian Philosophy of St. Thomas Aquinas* (trans. I. T. Eschmann).

E. L. Mascall, *He Who Is; Existence and Analogy; Christ, the Christian and the Church.* These present a non-Roman Catholic version of Thomistic theology and philosophy.

TRANSCENDENCE

The term "transcendence" indicates the view that God stands above or beyond the world. Such views may be regarded as elaborations of the spatial image—certainly one of the most ancient and persistent images in man's history —of God as above man and man's world. This metaphor is clear from the etymology of the word: *trans* meaning across, and *scandare* meaning to climb. The terms transcendence and immanence may be taken as polar words, like "up" and "down," "high" and "low." While the former holds God to be above man and his world, the latter holds that God or the divine is within human experience or within the world.

In the prehistory of religion, man's first gods seem clearly to have been holy powers of the nature and society upon both of which he was so obviously dependent. As such, these gods were immanent rather than transcendent. In some developed cultural traditions, the view of divine immanence persisted. Thus in ancient Greece and Rome the gods were personified aspects of nature and society. Similar attitudes occur in the classical tradition of China.

Many religious teachers and traditions have, on the other hand, understood deity as transcendent, or, to employ the spatial metaphor, as being above or beyond man and man's world. In Indian religion, the Upanishads teach a transcendent One who is beyond the particular things and activities of the world, but who may be sought within the human heart. A similar view may be seen in China in the *Tao Teh Ching*. In Greco-Roman culture, Plato's idea of the Good and Absolute Beauty expresses such a principle. The teachings of Plotinus systematically describe such a transcendent One with whom a human being may be united in mystical rapture. Many other Western mystics have followed Plotinus in this understanding of deity. A consequence of such views is that the world of everyday experience is reduced to the status of appearance or illusion. Often it is regarded not only as unreal but as essentially evil as well.

Among the various faiths and philosophies of mankind the Judaeo-Christian Bible is unique in its paradoxical assertion that God is both above the world and in the world, i.e., both immanent and transcendent. This assertion may be taken conversely as the paradox of biblical faith with which theology since Kierkegaard has been so concerned. The God of the Bible stands above the world as its sovereign lord, its creator and its savior; but He appears in the world to set men tasks to do, speaking to men in demand, in promise, in healing and fulfillment.

The consequences of this biblical view of God may be observed in the doctrine of creation as expressed in

Genesis. The teaching of Genesis is that creation or the world is real, but not the supreme reality; that it is good, but not supreme goodness. The world and all things in it are good, but are not God. As Reinhold Niebuhr has observed, this view avoids both the idolatry of immanence views and the nihilism of solely transcendent views of God. The Genesis writer remarks: "God saw what he had made and behold it was very good." (Gen. 1:31.) Biblical religion is enabled by this transcendent-immanent understanding of deity to be world-affirming without becoming idolatrous. Idolatry means worshipping some aspect of the created world as God.

Historically, Judaism has been more consistently world-affirming than Christianity. In the early centuries of Christianity many of the church fathers came perilously close to world-negation. But it is significant to observe that whenever Christianity was presented with a system of belief involving world-denial, as in Gnosticism or Manichaeanism, such systems were rejected as heretical in the name of the Lord of all creation, i.e., the transcendent-immanent God.

The central dogma of Christianity, the incarnation of God in Jesus Christ, may also be taken as an illustration of the transcendent-immanent God. Here, the God who is above all creation comes decisively into the world for man's salvation in the figure of Jesus of Nazareth. Conversely, the affirmation of the figure of Christ as a unique and decisive disclosure of the transcendent God is the feature common to all forms of Christian faith and distinctive to Christianity among the religions of the world.

In every age and in every tradition of Christianity the two aspects of deity, transcendence and immanence, have found varying expression. In the recent past and present, Protestant liberalism, while not altogether surrendering the transcendence of God, has emphasized the divine immanence. God is a reality disclosed within nature, history and man. This emphasis has accorded with the desire of liberal theology to harmonize religion with science, with modern thought and with human spirit.

The type of religion and theology sometimes labeled neo-orthodoxy has vigorously, and even violently, opposed liberal theology at precisely this point. Beginning with Karl Barth, and continuing in such thinkers as Emil Brunner, Richard and Reinhold Niebuhr, and many others, neo-orthodoxy, or, better, neo-protestant theology, has taught a view of God who stands above man's world in transcendent sovereignty and judgment. This view of God marks a return both to the teaching of the Protestant Reformers and to the Bible. Only after a man stands thus under the judgment of the Holy One is he able to experience God's grace and redemption. This grace may be understood as the desire of the transcendent God to draw near to man in love. God's love or grace is appropriated by man in the attitude of faith. The transcendent God thus becomes immanent in the faith of men who apprehend and receive His grace.

JOHN A. HUTCHISON

Bibliography

Karl Barth, *Dogmatics in Outline.*
John Calvin, *Institutes of the Christian Religion.*

TRINITY

The doctrine of the Trinity (or triunity of God) refers to the one being of God as Father, Son and Holy Spirit. Since the early centuries of the Church it has been considered the primary and distinctive aspect of the Christian conception of God, and even as the central "mystery" of Christian faith, both as enshrining the deepest truth of Christianity, the root of all others, and as being the most difficult to state adequately.

The concept as such is nowhere explicitly expressed in the scriptures, though such passages as Matthew 28:19 and II Corinthians 13:14 are suggestive. The doctrine itself was thus formulated in the Church, as the community sought to explicate the meaning of the revelation in Jesus Christ. The terminology which became standard in the West (God is *una substantia,* one being or nature, *et tres personae,* three "persons") goes back to Tertullian, at the beginning of the third century. The crucial steps in establishing the doctrine as official teaching of the Church were taken at the first two general councils (at Nicaea in 325 and Constantinople in 381), as a result of the conflict with Arianism. It was affirmed that both Jesus Christ as Son of God and the Holy Spirit are unqualifiedly of the same being as God the Father, i.e., fully God, yet without dividing God. Further elaborations in both East and West built on this foundation.

Though the doctrine has from time to time been attacked as "unscriptural" or "irrational," and in nineteenth-century Protestantism was much neglected as not important, recent years have seen a renewed discussion and appreciation of its meaning. The present discussion is generally less concerned with traditional points of debate (e.g., the acceptance in the West of the *filioque,* affirming that the Spirit proceeds from the Son as well as from the Father, which became an ostensible reason for the division of the Eastern and Western churches) than with the basic intention and import of the doctrine.

The concept of Trinity is thus seen as an attempt to describe the fullness of God as revealed in Christ. That revelation involves a fundamental three-foldness, signified by the terms Father, Son and Holy Spirit. God confronts man in Jesus Christ, i.e., He is truly present as the Son or eternal Word. But He is also apprehended as the Father, who "sends" the Son. And He is known as the Holy Spirit, opening the hearts and minds of men in faith. Yet it is the same God who is present throughout. The words Father, Son and Holy Spirit refer to one and the same God, but the Christian cannot say who God is without pointing to the distinct form and content of His self-giving in Christ and of the illumination of the Holy Spirit. The doctrine of the Trinity is thus a summing up of the gospel.

It is sometimes suggested that this means simply a three-fold viewing of God, that He is seen by the believer under three aspects, or that the doctrine refers to the activity of God as Creator, as Redeemer and as Sanctifier.

But, it may be replied, if Christian faith speaks of a real disclosure or revelation of God, then "Father, Son and Holy Spirit" must refer not simply to human viewing, but to God Himself, not only to ways in which God is related to the world, but to His "ways of being God." He is in Himself Father, Son and Spirit, one God.

Any attempt to speak of the nature of God's inner life can be made only in recognition of the essential mystery of His being. Most recent efforts to express meaningfully the idea of the three-in-oneness of God recognize that the traditional terminology is often misleading to the modern man. This is particularly true of the translation of the Latin *persona* as "person." The Latin word did not mean what the English "person" means in common parlance. The latter would suggest three personal divine beings in God, hence tritheism. In contrast to this, the doctrine of the Trinity is intended to affirm, not deny, the oneness of God. It refers to an inner richness or complexity, not dividing God into parts, but describing the nature of His oneness as a living and full unity.

Further explication leads currently in two directions. Some writers suggest that our word "person" or "personality" is better used in relation to the oneness of God. The believer confronts one Thou, one personal being. Father, Son and Holy Spirit are His "ways of being" the one divine person. God is thus to be understood primarily by analogy with the individual person, though embracing within Himself movement and self-giving, which is the ground of His communion with men. Others insist that the phrase "three Persons" expresses an indispensable truth, the reality of communion or fellowship within the divine life. God is better conceived after the analogy of social existence, though with an intensive unity far exceeding all we know in human life.

Neither of these two analogies, however, is held to the complete exclusion of the other. Whether one side or the other is emphasized, it is recognized that the analogy only imperfectly reflects the mystery of the divine life.

CLAUDE WELCH

Bibliography
D. M. Baillie, *God Was in Christ.*
Claude Welch, *In This Name, the Doctrine of the Trinity in Contemporary Theology.*

THE VIRGIN BIRTH

It is a mistake to suppose that stories of virgin births are frequently found in the mythologies of non-Christian religions. Supernatural births are found both in the Bible and elsewhere, but they are hardly ever, perhaps never, virgin births. Usually the mother bears a child either long after the age of child-bearing, or despite the fact that she is well known to be barren. Biblical examples are the mothers of Isaac, Samuel, and John the Baptist. In each of these cases the father is as much a channel of the supernatural action of God as is the mother. In Greek mythology and Mahayana Buddhism we find no instance of true virginal conception (which is perhaps a better term than virgin birth). There was certainly no expectation among the Hebrews that the Messiah would be born of a virgin. Indeed in patriarchal societies—from which all these examples are derived—there would certainly have been great resistance to any such idea of short-circuiting the father's role. The reference to Isaiah 7:14 by early Christian apologists was almost certainly due to an exegetical mistake.

The Virginal Conception does not mean that the Holy Spirit fertilized the ovum of the Virgin Mary. On the contrary, it means that the Holy Spirit brought it about that the Virgin miraculously conceived without fertilization. Parthenogenesis certainly occurs among some insects and crustacea, and there is one well-documented case of a rabbit conceiving without fertilization. Some experts hold that the possibility of parthenogenesis among humans can certainly not be ruled out. However, examples of this kind are quite irrelevant to any understanding of the New Testament miracle.

The New Testament evidence is not as strong in the case of the Virgin Birth as it is in that of the Resurrection. There is, however, no evidence at all for any other alternative, and those who accept the complete doctrine of the Incarnation would probably contend that the Virgin Birth accords perfectly with their belief that the Eternal Son of God entered the realm of nature and history by assuming human nature unto himself without emerging as a consequence of natural processes.

Those who deny the Virgin Birth usually tend toward some kind of adoptionism or nestorianism in Christology—what is often called a "reduced Christology"—and toward some kind of naturalism in philosophy.

The early Church Fathers (e.g., Irenaeus) connect the history of the Virgin Birth particularly with baptismal regeneration and the idea of the renewing of all things in Christ. For them, He is the "second Adam," a new creation who is related to the new humanity that shall be in the Kingdom of God, precisely as Adam was supposed to be related to the fallen humanity which is now on earth. Properly understood, the Virgin Birth does not in any sense imply that there is a sinful or unclean element in normal sexual relations. It is concerned solely to explain how the pre-existent Son of God entered into our world of nature and history, despite the fact that He eternally transcends it. Whether or not we accept the Gospel narrative depends primarily on the Christological and philosophical presuppositions with which we approach it. From one point of view it may seem impossible, while from the other it appears to be the most natural thing in the world. The Koran, incidentally, accepts the Virgin Birth while denying the Incarnation, and the whole tradition of the Church—which of course includes the Reformers as well as the great Catholic fathers—distinguishes carefully between the assertion of the virginal conception and the doctrine of the Incarnation. The latter is indeed the ground of the former.

J. V. LANGMEAD CASSERLEY

Bibliography

Mascall, *Christian Theology and Natural Science,* pp. 307-311.
Vincent Taylor, *The Virgin Birth.*

VOCATION

Vocation is one of many biblical words which has undergone a mutation in recent centuries. A vestige of its
original meaning is preserved in the use of the term
"vocation" to designate the work of those persons who
have an ecclesiastical function. Popular employment of
the word to cover any person's occupation represents,
however, the complete emptying of its original content.

That popular usage associates vocation with one's business or profession is historically understandable, for vocation *is* related to one's work. The two, however, are not
identical. It is very urgent that the biblical understanding
of the relationship of work and vocation be recovered.
Only by such a recovery may the bearing of faith upon the
common life, and the rootage of all work in man's relationship to God, become apparent.

The fundamental source of the biblical understanding of
vocation, as of all else, is God. Vocation is from God. It
is God who calls. In the literal sense God calls both by
giving names to persons and to things and by summoning.
These acts suggest the way in which God claims His own
for Himself and sets men's destiny for them. The initiative
lies not with the creature but with the Creator.

Although God designates names for things, it is primarily with His call to men that scripture is concerned.
Created free, men are at liberty to pursue other ends, other
images of manhood, than those for which they were
fashioned by God. It is to rescue men, to return them to
that life of wholeness in relationship to Himself, that God
extends His call of judgment and mercy. To have a vocation is to be re-called into living relationship with God and
into the community of His people.

To have a vocation from God is to know oneself called

to be a saint, not in the sense of having superior moral or mystical capabilities, but as one who has gained a new relationship to the world. In scripture there is but one vocation, common to all Christians: to become the children of God and to live as such. Called to believe the mighty acts of God, men must also—since they have not been removed from the world—live in responsible obedience to God wherever they may be.

It is at this point that vocation has ramifications for men's work. It is not by their work that men are saved. The gifts of grace and of faith are from God. Nor are these gifts given in varying degrees. All those who receive, receive equally. The Reformation denies all hierarchies of spiritual status. There is a universal priesthood of all believers.

This means that there is no God-preferred work. The clergy have not entered upon labors which assure their superiority to the commonalty. Nor, on the other hand, is the clergyman any more accountable to serve God responsibly in his work than is any Christian in his.

Work is of the order of God. It is not a punishment for sin, for Adam was instructed to labor before the Fall (cf. Gen. 1:28; 2:15). Work is inherent to the humanity for which men were created. Yet, by the Fall, work itself was blighted. Work became an order from God. It is only with the sense of Christian vocation—the call to repentance and to faith—that men may overcome work as a curse in the new freedom to serve God and man by one's work. The work itself is not the vocation, although it is for most men the most significant opportunity in which they may with hand and mind give evidence of the calling which has been granted to them.

DAVID J. MAITLAND

Bibliography

W. R. Forrester, *Christian Vocation.*
J. H. Oldham, *Life Is Commitment; Work in Modern Society.*

NOTES ON THE CONTRIBUTORS

JAMES LUTHER ADAMS, formerly Professor of Religious Ethics on the Federated Theological Faculty of the University of Chicago, is presently Professor of Christian Ethics at the Harvard Divinity School. Dr. Adams translated the essays that appeared in Paul Tillich's *The Protestant Era*. A contributor to numerous volumes, he is also the author of *The Changing Reputation of Human Nature* and *Taking Time Seriously*.

PAUL ALTHAUS, Emeritus Professor of Systematic Theology at the University of Erlangen, has been, since 1927 President of the *Luther-Gesellschaft*. He is the author of many books, including *Grundriss der Ethik* (1953) and *Die Letzten Dinge* (1922; 6th edition, 1956).

THOMAS J. J. ALTIZER, Professor of Bible and Religion at Emory University, is the author of *Mircea Eliade and the Dialectic of the Sacred* (1964) and other books.

BERNHARD W. ANDERSON, Professor of Biblical Theology at Drew Theological Seminary since 1954, is the author of *Rediscovering the Bible* (1951) and *The Unfolding Drama of the Bible* (1953).

CONRAD BERGENDOFF, former President of Augustana College, is the author of the following works: *The Making and Meaning of the Augsburg Confession, Christ as Authority, The One Holy Catholic Apostolic Church*, and *The Doctrine of the Church in American Lutheranism*.

JERALD C. BRAUER, Dean of the Divinity School of the University of Chicago, is the author of *Protestantism in America*.

ROBERT McAFEE BROWN, presently Professor of Religion and Theology at Stanford University, is author of *P. T. Forsyth: Prophet for Today, The Significance of the Church*, and *The Spirit of Protestantism*.

DAVID CAIRNS is Professor of Practical Theology at Christ's College, Aberdeen, and Lecturer in Systematic Theology at the University of Aberdeen. He is the author of *Gospel Without Myth?*

EDWARD JOHN CARNELL, former President and Professor of Apologetics of Fuller Theological Seminary, is the author of *An Introduction to Christian Apologetics* and *The Theology of Reinhold Niebuhr.*

J. V. LANGMEAD CASSERLEY is presently Professor of Apologetics at Seabury Western Theological Seminary. Among his books are *Toward a Theology of History* and *The Church Today and Tomorrow.*

E. LaB. CHERBONNIER, Professor of Religion and Head of the Department of Religion at Trinity College, Hartford, is the author of *Hardness of Heart* (1955).

H. F. LOVELL COCKS, formerly Principal of Western (Congregational) College in Bristol, England, is the author of *The Nonconformist Conscience* and *By Faith Alone.*

ARTHUR A. COHEN is the author of *Martin Buber* (1958) and *The Natural and the Supernatural Jew* (1963).

FRED DENBEAUX, Professor of Bible History at Wellesley College, is the author of *Understanding the Bible* and *The Art of Christian Doubt.*

JOHN W. DESCHNER, who has taught theology at Perkins School of Theology in Dallas, did his doctoral work at the University of Basel.

JOHN DILLENBERGER, Professor of the History of Theology and Dean at the Graduate Theological Union, is the author of *God Hidden and Revealed* (1953) and co-author, with Claude Welch, of *Protestant Christianity: Interpreted through its Development.*

ERICH DINKLER, formerly Professor of New Testament and Early Christianity at Yale University and since 1956 Professor at the University of Bonn, is, with Rudolf Bultmann, editor of *Theologische Rundschau* and one of the editors of the encyclopedia *Religion in Geschichte und Gegenwart.*

ERIKA DINKLER-VON SCHUBERT is a former lecturer on Christian art at the Yale Divinity School and member of the editorial board of the encyclopedia *Religion in Geschichte und Gegenwart*.

TRUMAN B. DOUGLASS, Executive Vice-President of the United Church Board for Homeland Ministries, is the author of *Preaching and the New Reformation* (1956) and co-author, with Constantinos A. Doxiades, of *The New World of Urban Man* (1965).

EDWARD DOWEY, Professor at the Princeton Theological Seminary, is author of *The Knowledge of God in Calvin's Theology* (1952).

ROBERT NEWTON FLEW, who held the Chair of Systematic Theology in Wesley House (1937-1955) and was President of the Methodist Conference in England for 1946-47, is the author of *The Idea of Perfection in Christian Theology* (1934), *Jesus and His Church* (1938), and editor of and contributor to *The Catholicity of Protestantism* (1950).

HANS W. FREI, formerly Professor of Theology at the Episcopal Theological Seminary of the Southwest and presently Associate Professor of Religion at Yale University, is a contributor to *Faith and Ethics* (edited by Paul Ramsey).

MAURICE S. FRIEDMAN, Professor of Philosophy at Sarah Lawrence College, is the translator and editor of numerous works of Martin Buber and author of *Martin Buber: The Life of Dialogue* and *Problematic Rebel: An Image of Modern Man*.

LANGDON B. GILKEY is Professor of Theology at the Divinity School of Vanderbilt University, and author of *Maker of Heaven and Earth* (1959) and *How the Church Can Minister to the World Without Losing Itself* (1964).

THEODORE A. GILL was educated at Princeton Theological Seminary, Union Theological Seminary, and the University of Zurich, where he received his doctorate. He is presently managing editor of *The Christian Century*.

JAMES M. GUSTAFSON received his doctorate in Christian Ethics from the Yale Divinity School and is presently Associate Professor of Religion at St. Andrews Presbyterian College.

ROBERT T. HANDY, presently Professor of Church History at Union Theological Seminary, is author of *We Witness Together*.

JOSEPH HAROUTUNIAN, Professor at the Divinity School, University of Chicago, is the author of *Wisdom and Folly in Religion* (1940) and *Lust for Power* (1949).

JULIAN N. HARTT, Porter Professor of Philosophical Theology at the Divinity School of Yale University, is the author of *Toward a Theology of Evangelism* and *The Lost Image of Man*.

ROGER HAZELTON, Professor of Theology and Dean, Graduate School of Theology, Oberlin College, is the author of numerous works, among which are *God's Way With Man* (1956), *New Accents in Contemporary Theology* (1960), and *The New Testament Heritage* (1962).

STANLEY ROMAINE HOPPER, Dean of the Graduate School at Drew University and Professor of Christian Philosophy and Letters, is the author of *The Crisis of Faith* and editor of *Spiritual Problems in Contemporary Literature*.

DOUGLAS HORTON, Emeritus O'Brian Professor of Divinity, Harvard University, is the author of *The Meaning of Worship* (1959).

WALTER M. HORTON, Emeritus Professor, Graduate School of Theology, Oberlin College, is the author of *Christian Theology, an Ecumenical Approach*.

JOHN A. HUTCHISON, Professor of Philosophy and Religion, Claremont Graduate School, is the author of *Ways of Faith, Christian Faith and Social Action,* and *Language and Faith*.

HANS JONAS Professor of Philosophy on the Graduate Faculty of the New School for Social Research, is the author of *Zwischen Nichts und Ewigkeit* (1963) and *The Gnostic Religion* (1963).

HUGH THOMSON KERR, JR., Professor of Theology at Princeton Theological Seminary, is the editor of *Theology Today* and the author of *Positive Protestantism* (1950). He has edited *A Compendium of Calvin's Institutes* and *A Compendium of Luther's Theology*.

PAUL LEHMANN, Auburn Professor of Systematic Theology, Union Theological Seminary, is the author of *Forgiveness* (1940) and *Ethics in a Christian Context* (1963).

GEORGE LINDBECK, Professor in the Department of Philosophy and at the Divinity School of Yale University, is author of *Dialogue on the Way* and co-author of *The Papal Council and the Gospel*.

BERNARD M. LOOMER, former Dean of the Federated Theological Faculty of the University of Chicago, is presently Professor of Philosophical Theology in the University's Divinity School.

DAVID J. MAITLAND is Chaplain and Associate Professor of Religion at Carleton College.

JOHN MARSH, since 1953 Principal of Mansfield College, Oxford, was a Member of the Commission on Faith and Order and delegate to the Amsterdam and Evanston Assemblies of the World Council of Churches.

CARL MICHALSON, Professor of Systematic Theology at Drew University, is author of *The Hinge of History* (1959) and *The Rationality of Faith* (1963).

ALEXANDER MILLER, formerly of the Department of Religion at Stanford University, is the author of *Biblical Politics* (1943), *The Christian Significance of Karl Marx* (1946), and *The Renewal of Man* (1955).

ALLEN O. MILLER, Professor of Systematic Theology at Eden Seminary, a delegate to the 3rd World Conference on Faith and Order (1952), is the author of *Invitation to Theology* and co-author of *The Heidelberg Catechism*.

A. T. MOLLEGEN, Professor of New Testament Language and Literature at the Protestant Episcopal Theological Seminary in Virginia, is author of *Christianity and Modern Man* and co-author of *Preaching the Christian Year*.

JAMES MUILENBURG is Gray Professor of the Old Testament at the Graduate Theological Union, San Francisco Theological Seminary, and author of the commentary on Second Isaiah in the *Interpreter's Bible* and of *The Way of Israel*.

J. ROBERT NELSON, former Secretary of the Commission on Faith and Order of the World Council of Churches, was Dean of the Divinity School of Vanderbilt University. He is author of *The Realm of Redemption* and *Criterion for the Church*.

REINHOLD NIEBUHR, Graduate Professor of Ethics and Theology at the Union Theological Seminary, is the author of numerous books, the most recent being *Man's Nature and His Communities*. In addition to *Leaves from the Notebooks of a Tamed Cynic*, Living Age Books has published his *Essays in Applied Christianity*, edited and selected by D. B. Robertson.

RICHARD R. NIEBUHR, Professor of Theology at the Harvard Divinity School, is author of *Schleiermacher on Christ and Religion* (1964).

ANDERS NYGREN, the Bishop of Lund, Sweden, is the author of the monumental *Eros and Agape*.

SCHUBERT M. OGDEN is Associate Professor at Perkins School of Theology and author of *Christ Without Myth* (1961).

WILHELM PAUCK, Professor of Church History at Union Theological Seminary, is the author of *The Heritage of the Reformation* and *The Church Against the World*.

JAROSLAV PELIKAN, Professor in the Divinity School of Yale University, is the author of *From Luther to Kierkegaard* (1950), *Obedient Rebels* (1964), *Religion and the University* (1964), and editor of Volumes 12, 13, and 21 of Luther's *Works*.

OTTO A. PIPER, Emeritus Manson Professor at Princeton Theological Seminary, has written, among other books, *The Church Meets Judaism* and *Protestantism in an Ecumenical Age*.

W. NORMAN PITTENGER, Professor of Christian Apologetics at the General Theological Seminary (New York), is the author of numerous works, the most recent being *Proclaiming Christ Today* (1962) and *The Christian Understanding of Human Nature* (1964).

WARREN A. QUANBECK is Professor of Systematic Theology at Luther Theological Seminary (St. Paul), and editor of *God and Caesar* (1959).

ALEXANDER SCHMEMANN is Dean of St. Vladimir Seminary (New York City) and editor of *Ultimate Questions: An Anthology of Modern Russian Religious Thought* (1965).

MASSEY H. SHEPHERD, JR., Professor of Liturgics at the Church Divinity School of the Pacific (Berkeley), is the author of *The Worshop of the Church, At All Times and in All Places,* and *The Reform of Liturgical Worship.*

ROGER LINCOLN SHINN, Dodge Professor of Applied Christianity at Union Theological Seminary, is the author of *Christianity and the Problem of History, The Sermon on the Mount, Life, Death, and Destiny,* and *The Tangled World.*

JOHN E. SMITH, Professor of Philosophy at Yale University, is the author of *Reason and God* and *The Spirit of American Philosophy.*

DOUGLAS V. STEERE, Thomas Wistar Brown Professor of Philosophy at Haverford College, is the author of many books, including *On Listening to Another* (1948), *Work and Contemplation* (1957), and *Dimensions of Prayer* (1963).

SAMUEL ENOCH STUMPF, Professor of Philosophy and Chairman of the Department of Philosophy at Vanderbilt University, is the author of *A Democratic Manifesto* (1954).

PAUL TILLICH was Nuveen Professor of Theology at the University of Chicago. He died in 1965. He was the author of *The Religious Situation, The Protestant Era, The Courage to Be,* and a *Systematic Theology* (in three volumes).

LEONARD J. TRINTERUD, Professor of Church History at San Francisco Theological Seminary, is the author of *The Forming of an American Tradition, The Origins of Puritanism,* and *A Reappraisal of Tyndale's Debt to Luther.*

HENRY P. VAN DUSEN was until his retirement President of Union Theological Seminary. He is the author of *Spirit, Son and Father, One Great Ground of Hope,* and *A Vindication of Liberal Theology.*

W. A. VISSER 'T HOOFT is General Secretary of the World Council of Churches. His *Rembrandt and the Bible* is a Living Age Book. Among his numerous publications are *The Meaning of Ecumenical* (1953), *The Renewal of the Church* (1956), *The Pressure of Our Common Calling* (1959), and *No Other Name* (1963).

CLAUDE WELCH, Berg Professor of Religious Thought and Chairman of the Department, University of Pennsylvania, is the author of *In This Name: The Doctrine of the Trinity in Contemporary Theology* (1952), *The Reality of the Church* (1958), and co-author, with John Dillenberger, of *Protestant Christianity: Interpreted through its Development.*

HENRY NELSON WIEMAN was, at the time of his retirement, Professor of Religion at the University of Chicago; he then went to teach at the University of Southern Illinois. He is the author of *Religious Experience and Scientific Method* (1952), *The Source of Human Good* (1947), and *Man's Ultimate Commitment* (1963). He is co-author, with R. W. Bretall, of *The Empirical Theology of Henry Nelson Wieman* (1963).

DANIEL D. WILLIAMS, Professor of Systematic Theology at Union Theological Seminary, is the author of *God's Grace and Man's Hope* (1949), *What Present Day Theologians Are Thinking* (1952), and *The Minister and the Care of Souls* (1962).

WILLIAM J. WOLF, Howard Chandler Robbins Professor of Theology at the Episcopal Theological School (Cambridge, Mass.), is the author of *Man's Knowledge of God* (1955), *No Cross, No Crown: A Study of the Atonement* (1957), and *The Religion of Abraham Lincoln* (1963).

H. A. WOLFSON, Emeritus Nathan Littauer Professor of Hebrew Literature and Philosophy at Harvard University, is the author of *The Philosophy of Spinoza* (1934), *Philo* (1947), *The Philosophy of the Church Fathers, I* (1956), and *Religious Philosophy* (1961).